Indonesia
Philippines
Burma
Malaysia

M000118582

Opposing Suharto

- mobilizational opposition
- semioppositional
- alegal (dissidents)
- civil society

structural weaknesses of opposition

3 factors:

1) Opposition dynamics
2) socio-economic change
3) elite fractures.

EAST-WEST CENTER
SERIES ON

CONTEMPORARY ISSUES IN ASIA AND THE PACIFIC

Muthiah Alagappa, Series Editor

Timothy Pachirat

Opposing Suharto

COMPROMISE, RESISTANCE, AND
REGIME CHANGE IN INDONESIA

Edward Aspinall

STANFORD UNIVERSITY PRESS
STANFORD, CALIFORNIA
2005

Stanford University Press
Stanford, California
www.sup.org

Library of Congress Cataloging-in-Publication Data

Aspinall, Edward.
Opposing Suharto : compromise, resistance, and regime change in Indonesia / Edward Aspinall.
    p.   cm.—(Contemporary issues in Asia and the Pacific)
Includes bibliographical references and index.
ISBN 0-8047-4844-6 (alk. paper)—ISBN 0-8047-4845-4 (pbk : alk. paper)
    1. Indonesia—Politics and government—1966–1998. 2. Soeharto, 1921–   3. Opposition (Political science)—Indonesia—History—20th century.   I. Title.   II. Series.
DS644.4.A85 2005
320.9598'09'049—dc22   2004008168

Printed in the United States of America on acid-free, archival-quality paper.

Original printing 2005

Last figure below indicates year of this printing:
14   13   12   11   10   09   08   07   06   05

Designed and typeset at Stanford University Press in 10/12 Sabon.

*A Series from Stanford University Press
and the East-West Center*

CONTEMPORARY ISSUES IN ASIA
AND THE PACIFIC

Muthiah Alagappa, Series Editor

A collaborative effort by Stanford University Press and the East-West Center, this series addresses contemporary issues of policy and scholarly concern in Asia and the Pacific. The series focuses on political, social, economic, cultural, demographic, environmental, and technological change and the problems related to such change. A select group of East-West Center senior fellows—representing the fields of political science, economic development, population, and environmental studies—serves as the advisory board for the series. The decision to publish is made by Stanford.

Preference is given to comparative or regional studies that are conceptual in orientation and emphasize underlying processes and to work on a single country that addresses issues in a comparative or regional context. Although concerned with policy-relevant issues and written to be accessible to a relatively broad audience, books in the series are scholarly in character. We are pleased to offer here the latest book in the series.

The East-West Center, headquartered in Honolulu, is a public, non-profit educational and research institution established by the U.S. Congress in 1960 to foster understanding and cooperation among the governments and peoples of the Asia-Pacific region, including the United States.

EAST-WEST CENTER SERIES ON CONTEMPORARY ISSUES IN ASIA AND THE PACIFIC

Contents

Acknowledgments

Many people assisted with the preparation of this book and the Ph.D. dissertation upon which it is based. In Indonesia, I owe a debt of gratitude to many individuals and groups who generously shared their time, insights, and experiences with me, allowed me to access their archives, and invited me to witness or participate in seminars, meetings, and other activities. Without their support, this study would not have been possible.

Laksamana Sukardi gave me time and office space and helped to arrange interviews with many PDI leaders and others. Bondan Gunawan was a source of much insight into nationalist politics and introduced me to many useful contacts. Among NGOs, I spent much time at the YLBHI office in Jakarta, and many of the then directors and staff there were most generous. Among those to whom I owe particular thanks are Adnan Buyung Nasution, Mulyana W. Kusumah, Hendardi, Rambun Tjajo, Teten Masduki, and Tedjabayu.

I spent much of my time with activists who were either students or recent graduates from student politics. They not only informed me about the student activist scene but also provided many of the crucial building blocks of knowledge about Indonesian politics on which this study is based. Among those to whom I am most grateful are Harry Wibowo, (the late) Harry Pribadi, Item, Daniel Indrakusumah, Standarkiaa, I. Gusti Anom Astika, Djatih Waluyo, Wilson, and Mahmud. Members of Yayasan Geni, DMPY, Yayasan Arek, the *Ganesha* group at ITB, and various branches of the PRD were not only generous with their experiences and archives but also let me stay at their offices or homes, sometimes for weeks at a time.

In Jakarta, I was lucky to share a house with Colin Rundle and James Balowski, who provided many interesting discussions and a pleasant home environment. Kirsty Sword shared her home with me during an eventful two months in late 1995.

In Canberra, the Department of Political and Social Change in the Research School of Pacific and Asian Studies at the Australian National University not only supported me during my years of postgraduate study but also provided me with a research fellowship during which I completed most of the revisions to this manuscript. In the department, I owe thanks to Beverley Fraser and Claire Smith for their support. Allison Ley provided much help in editing the manuscript. David Reeve and other colleagues in the Department of Indonesian and Chinese Studies at the University of New South Wales were also very patient as I struggled to complete my Ph.D. while learning the ropes of university teaching. More recently, colleagues at the University of Sydney have also been very generous. Kathy Ragless put me up during many visits to Canberra, proofread the manuscript, and has been a great friend.

My supervisor, Harold Crouch, shared with me his wide-ranging and detailed knowledge of Indonesian politics and contributed greatly to the design of this study. R. William Liddle, Ben Kerkvliet, Marcus Mietzner, and Ken Ward also read the Ph.D. or book manuscript in whole or in part, as did the two anonymous reviewers for Stanford University Press. They provided me with many valuable comments and saved me from many errors (any remaining ones are my own responsibility). Meredith Weiss, Kit Collier, and Kyaw Yin Hlaing provided helpful comments on Chapter 9 at very short notice. Muthiah Alagappa of the East-West Center supported the publication of the manuscript and offered invaluable advice. Siobhan Campbell, Elisabeth Jackson, and Sally White provided editorial and research assistance. Tony Hicks at Stanford University Press carefully saw the book through to publication.

I also thank Glenn Flanagan, who has been a constant source of support and inspiration. Finally, my parents, Donald and Anita Aspinall, introduced me to Indonesia and provided much encouragement and assistance through my years of study. I dedicate this book to the memory of my father, whose life was a model of scholarly integrity.

Sections of this book draw on previously published material. Parts of Chapter 5 draw on "Students and the Military: Regime Friction and Civilian Dissent in the Late Suharto Period," *Indonesia* 59 (April) 1995: 21–44. Passages in Chapter 8 use material from "Opposition and Elite Conflict in the Fall of Soeharto," in *The Fall of Soeharto*, ed. Geoff Forrester and R. J. May (Bathurst, New South Wales: Crawford House Publishing, 1998), 130–53; and "The Indonesian Student Uprising of 1998," in *Reformasi: Crisis and Change in Indonesia*, ed. Arief Budiman, Barbara Hatley, and Damien Kingsbury (Clayton, Victoria: Monash Asia Institute, 1999), 212–38. Many of the ideas expressed in this book were first explored in "The Broadening Base of Political Opposition in Indonesia," in *Political Oppositions in Industrialising Asia*, ed. Garry Rodan (London and New York: Routledge, 1996), 215–40.

Preface

> In Pancasila Democracy there is no place for Western style opposition (oposisi ala Barat). In the world of Pancasila democracy we have deliberation (musyawarah) to achieve consensus (mufakat) of the people. Here we do not have opposition like that in the West. Opposition for the sake of opposing, for the sake of being different, is unknown here. (Dwipayana and Ramadhan 1989, 346)

This statement, from President Suharto's 1989 autobiography, makes it clear that in his "New Order" government the very concept of opposition was an official anathema. Suharto and other regime leaders expounded a "Pancasila ideology" which extolled "traditional" and "authentic" Indonesian values of mutual assistance (*gotong royong*), deliberation (*musyawarah*), and consensus (*mufakat*).[1] They insisted on the fundamental unity of state and society and routinely portrayed individuals and groups which challenged them as selfishly placing their own narrow interests before those of society as a whole. Such opponents, they argued, forfeited their rights to participate in the consensual life of the body politic. An all-pervasive and often brutally effective coercive apparatus was always ready to be deployed against such people. Even leaders of the permitted political parties thus routinely denied that their parties were "oppositions." When liberal intellectuals such as Muslim scholar Nurcholish Madjid advocated the need for a "loyal opposition" within the New Order framework (see, e.g., Madjid 1994), they were rounded upon by government spokespeople.

And yet opposition was ubiquitous, at least in the late Suharto years. During my first research trip to Jakarta in early 1993, I informed a new acquaintance that my research topic was "opposition." "Who do you mean by the opposition?" he asked. "These days, everybody in Indonesia is in the opposition." This was at the height of a period known as *keterbukaan* ("openness"), when officials from the president down announced that the government would be more tolerant of differences of opinion and modify its old "security approach." Newspapers were full of reports quoting academics, party politicians, and retired officials making sometimes fundamental criticisms of the regime. (Indeed, newspaper reports often did not even bother to report any particular event but were simply cobbled-together collections of the views of noted critics on this or that issue.) Almost every day there were reports of protests by students, workers, or Islamic youth groups. Neighbors, taxi drivers, and other casual acquaintances often complained about the depredations of the president's children or the exactions imposed on them by low-level bureaucrats. During my months in the capital, I attended a seemingly endless series of functions on the Jakarta seminar circuit, where topics like democratization, human rights, and openness were dissected in minute detail.

Yet the mood was almost universally pessimistic. Suharto had been in power since 1966, he had seen off challenges in the past, and his control of government and society remained formidable. It was difficult to imagine political change. Except for a small minority of radical activists, even the most outspoken critics of the regime were reluctant to believe that anything more than cosmetic reform would occur in the foreseeable future.

At first, the pessimism seemed to be justified. Beginning with the ban of three of Indonesia's highest-circulation and most widely respected current affairs magazines in June 1994, the government began to wind back *keterbukaan*. It arrested some of the most outspoken critics and expelled others from the formal political system (the most famous example being the removal of Megawati Soekarnoputri as head of the Indonesian Democracy Party [PDI] in 1996).

Eventually, Suharto's regime did come to a spectacular end. In the early months of 1998, the Asian financial crisis wreaked a devastating impact on the Indonesian economy. There was a growing barrage of public criticism directed at the president by academics, Islamic leaders, human rights activists, journalists, and other public figures. A wave of student protest swept the country, stretching the capacities of the military. Violent rioting occurred on the streets of Jakarta, causing over one thousand deaths. This dramatic escalation of unrest precipitated a fracturing of the ruling elite. Some of the president's most loyal lieutenants deserted him. Finally, on the morning of May 21, 1998, Suharto resigned.

Even during the mass unrest that led to Suharto's downfall, however, opposition remained poorly organized. There was certainly no central coordinating body for opposition, as in some struggles against authoritarian rule. To be sure, certain leaders of formal organizations did play an important role in criticizing the government, such as Amien Rais, the head of the large Islamic organization Muhammadiyah. But he played this role primarily as an individual; Muhammadiyah had too many assets at stake to project itself as a unifying vehicle of democratic struggle, and it represented only one part of Indonesia's population, the "modernist" Islamic community. Instead, a proliferation of groups, ranging from small student committees and nongovernmental organizations (NGOs) through to established and government-recognized organizations like Muhammadiyah contributed in varying ways to the rising tide of public opposition. The groups that played the most important role in breaking the political impasse were precisely those that were most able to mobilize with a minimum of organization. Students were concentrated together in their campuses near the city centers and were well placed to establish an array of mostly ad hoc and temporary protest organizations. The urban crowds which took to the streets of Jakarta on May 13–14, attacking shops, security forces, symbols of authority, and (in many cases) the property and persons of the ethnic Chinese were the antithesis of an organized and disciplined opposition movement.

This apparent paradox—the organizational weakness of opposition, contrasted with the ubiquity of the oppositional mood during the late Suharto years, and its eventual capacity to force through political change—is a major focus of this study. Coming to grips with this paradox will also help to explain the durability of the Suharto regime, as well as the manner by which it came to an end.

Opposing Suharto

1

Regime and Opposition

In Indonesia today there are only two real choices: to be a "critical partner" or to be an underground subversive . . . most people choose the former.

Panda Nababan (interview, November 27, 1995)

This senior Indonesian journalist's comment neatly sums up the dilemma facing Indonesians who wanted democratization during the Suharto years. At least for middle-class critics in the big cities, the choice was never a stark one between total submission to the government and conspirational preparation for its overthrow. Instead, many options existed for those who believed that they could pursue change by gradualist and nonconfrontational means and voice criticism of the regime in indirect or careful ways.

This book presents a study of the development of opposition to Suharto's rule and the ways by which opposition undermined the legitimacy of his government, raised the costs of governing, and eventually forced Suharto from office. It is, in other words, a study of the methods used by opponents of Suharto to create political space, test his regime's limits of tolerance, and confront and challenge that regime. As the reader might expect, it is thus in many ways a study of bravery and audacity in the face of intimidation and brutality. Yet, as Panda Nababan's comment above suggests, it is also a study of ambiguity, ambivalence, and compromise.

The argument advanced in this book starts from the proposition that

the mixture of repression and toleration, of coercion and co-optation that
the regime used to control dissent had a profound impact on the forms
that opposition took. The combination produced an opposition that was
eventually very effective at performing some of the tasks necessary to
achieve democratization, such as|undermining the legitimacy |of authori-
tarian rule. But it was less well-suited to performing others, such as formulating an alternative to the regime's ideology or organizing an alternative to its leadership. The nature of the opposition so produced helps us
to understand the sudden and tumultuous way by which Suharto's rule finally ended in 1998, as well as the fact that when Suharto did resign, opposition forces were unable to take control of the government.

Many existing studies of Suharto's "New Order" regime have drawn
attention to its reliance on violence. Various authors have emphasized the
centrality of the security forces in the structure of the regime, the hegemonic power of the regime's authoritarian ideology, the various techniques of repression it used, and the military's propagation of a culture of
violence (see, e.g., Crouch 1988a; Heryanto 1993; Anderson 2001). The
brutal effectiveness of the repressive apparatus was an important reason
why the Suharto regime survived so long. The use of coercion against opponents, and the tactics which opponents developed to avoid such coercion, receive much attention in this book. Coercion, however, was only
half of the regime's winning political formula. It was not repression
alone, but rather the|combination of repression with toleration for con-
strained forms of political action that made Suharto's New Order one of
the most durable and successful third world authoritarian regimes.|

The combination of repression and toleration is a common feature of
resilient authoritarian regimes. Regimes that rely on little else but repression to maintain themselves often end up radicalizing society and creating powerful revolutionary oppositions. This is especially the case with
"sultanistic" regimes, which are characterized by unrestrained and arbitrary personal rule by the dictator. Such regimes lack significant pockets
of pluralism in official structures and do not tolerate even the most tem-
perate of detractors. In such circumstances, even otherwise moderate critics often view regime overthrow as the only realistic strategy (Cuba's
Batista and Nicaragua's Somoza are classic examples; see Chehabi and
Linz 1998a, 1998b; Snyder 1998; Thompson 1995). For most of its existence, Suharto's was not such a regime. Individuals who held views somewhat at variance with the dominant group in the government were able
to fill numerous niches in officially recognized or tolerated institutions,
including political parties, religious bodies, student groups, and nongovernmental organizations (NGOs), so long as they did not threaten the
|regime's fundamentals.| From such institutions, political actors could

make constrained criticisms of the authorities, promote the interests of their constituencies, and try to bring about political change.

Many years ago, Juan Linz argued that such "limited pluralism" could be very debilitating for opposition in authoritarian regimes. He gave as an example Franco's Spain in the late 1960s, where there was a "widespread tone and mentality of opposition" yet a "simultaneous failure of structural or principled opposition" (Linz 1973, 176). He explained: "The semifreedom under such regimes imposes on their opponents certain costs that are quite different from those of persecution of illegal oppositions and that explain their frustration, disintegration and sometimes readiness to co-optation, which contribute to the persistence of such regimes as much as does their repressive capacity" (Linz 1973, 273).

Semifreedom of this sort contributed greatly to the Suharto regime's longevity and effectiveness. The provision of rewards, including material ones, for those who participated in official regime structures, combined with the fear of sanctions applied to those who stepped outside them, produced a great deal of qualified, ambivalent, and hesitant participation-opposition. This was especially so for the middle-class and elite groups who benefited materially from the regime's economic development policies. This combination of rewards and sanctions stifled the emergence of a unified opposition movement possessing a coherent counterideology, common platform, and organized mass base. Whenever there were signs that such an opposition—what I call mobilizational opposition—might emerge, the state swiftly repressed it and oppositional impulses were redirected back toward more ambivalent forms. As a result, division, mutual suspicion, and ideological incoherence predominated. Critics of the regime were scattered through a wide range of institutions. Even the institutionalization of civil society—in the form of NGOs, for example—contributed to the domestication of opposition by providing opponents with strong material and other interests for avoiding confrontation with the state.

Individuals who aspired to bring about the democratic transformation of the political system thus had to make a complex political calculus. They had to balance the very real risks of repression, which they would run if they opposed the regime openly, against the dangers of ineffectiveness, co-optation, and capture if they became ensnared in officially controlled institutions or kept their activities within the limits of tolerated political behavior. As a result, the struggle for political change was marked as much by caution and compromise as it was by confrontation, risk taking, and repression. It was not played out merely between an increasingly assertive and courageous civil society and a coercive state (as some comparative literature in the "civil society versus the state" vein would have us assume). Instead, a large part of the struggle for political reform was carried on from a "gray area" located between state and society. Some of the most dramatic political conflicts of Suharto's final decade in office were played out for control *within* societal and state institutions. A multiplicity of ties connected actors who were ostensibly in the societal arena with groups, individuals, and factions in the state apparatus.

Despite the weaknesses of principled opposition, the Suharto regime did eventually come to an end. This end occurred by way of a society-initiated transition, involving mass protests and riots, substantial violence and destruction, splits in the army, and the splintering of the upper echelons of the government. Moreover, in the decade preceding the collapse there was an uneven but dramatic increase in societal unrest and opposition, described in this book. Three main processes which contributed to the growth of opposition are examined in this study: (1) changes in Indonesia's social structure brought about by decades of economic growth; (2) disunity within the governing elite; and (3) the ways by which the various opposition groups tested the boundaries of political tolerance, built new alliances, experimented with new strategies, and gradually expanded the political space available to them.

The tumultuous manner of Suharto's final fall was dictated, however, not only by the strengthening of opposition that had occurred in the preceding decade, nor even only by the devastating intervention of the Asian financial crisis. It was also a result of a process of change taking place within the regime itself. By the mid-1990s, Suharto's regime was undergoing a process of late-term "sultanization," in which the dominance of the president, and that of his family and inner circle, became more and more pronounced, more venal and all-pervasive, precisely as tensions related to presidential succession were increasing. From the early 1970s, Suharto had been a dominant force in the regime. By the end of his reign, the regime was more and more resembling a personalist dictatorship. Suharto reduced the scope for factional competition within the ruling elite and, in response to the spread of opposition, closed off some long-standing avenues for semi-independent political action. The gray area between state and society narrowed markedly, setting the scene for a more dramatic struggle between state and society in 1998.

The fact that Indonesia's New Order was becoming more sultanistic when it came to an end, as we shall see, had important implications for the mode of its collapse and subsequent democratization. Opposition in Indonesia in 1998 remained poorly institutionalized, deeply divided, and largely ideologically incoherent, typical of opposition under the "semi-freedom" of classic authoritarian regimes. Yet opposition was forced to the forefront of a turbulent and society-led regime transition in a manner similar to political transitions in sultanistic or similar regimes where the hard-line element is strong. The result was that when Suharto's government collapsed, principled opposition remained weak, allowing for a rapid reconsolidation of the ruling coalition which had underpinned the New Order, the subsequent blurring of the division between "reformist" and "status quo" forces, and numerous obstructions to democratic transition and consolidation.

Varieties of Opposition in Suharto's New Order

In his classic 1975 study of nondemocratic regime types, Juan Linz argued that authoritarian regimes were to be distinguished from totalitarian ones largely on the basis of their "limited pluralism." While totalitarian systems were dominated by "monistic centers of power," some space always existed in authoritarian regimes for independent political action, so that, as he argued in a slightly earlier article, "there remain groups not created by nor dependent on the state which influence the political process one way or another" (Linz 1970, 255–56). Suharto's New Order was such a regime. Although it had the military, or ABRI, at its core, from the outset the New Order was never narrowly based on the military alone. The chief power centers instead sought to co-opt and incorporate most other social and political forces in subordinate positions.

In contrast, however, to the more or less unconstrained pluralism of liberal democracies, Linz stressed that participation in authoritarian regimes was always fettered by coercion, or the threat of it. There was no place in such a regime for a legally sanctioned opposition that openly competed for political power. This was the case in Suharto's Indonesia. However, there were gradations of coercion. Repression tended to be greater once critics moved beyond simply making criticisms to mobilizing their supporters against the regime. It was harsher against lower-class than against middle-class groups, harshest of all against groups that rejected the regime's ideology. The chief target was the political left. The regime's primary claim to historical legitimacy was that it had "saved" the nation from communist treachery in 1965. It came to power amid one of the late twentieth century's greatest massacres, when an estimated five hundred thousand supporters of the PKI (Indonesian Communist Party) were killed. Tens of thousands of PKI prisoners remained in detention until the late 1970s. Anticommunism, expressed by repetitive warnings of the *bahaya laten PKI* (latent danger of the PKI) and *ekstrim kiri* (extreme left), remained central to regime discourse until the very end. The regime also repressed horrifically secessionist movements and their supporters in East Timor, Papua, and Aceh. From the mid-1970s, tough policies were also applied against activists whom the regime accused of desiring to establish an Islamic state. Typical of authoritarian regimes (Linz 1973, 211), however, under Suharto the boundaries of legality were fluid and unpredictable. Political activities which one day or at one place might be tolerated would at another time or place attract severe repression. The very unpredictability of repression inclined critics of the government toward caution, greatly contributing to its efficacy.

Defining and categorizing opposition behavior in a nondemocratic regime presents many difficulties. One way to begin is suggested by Detlev Peukert (1991) in an article on working-class resistance under the Third Reich. Peukert proposes a scale, sliding from "non-conformist behavior," through "refusal," "protest," to "resistance." Criteria for locating particular behaviors on the scale are the extent to which they involve *public* and *intentional* challenge to the authorities. Peukert's scale is useful for reminding us that while one end of the opposition spectrum is represented by organized, collective, and public action, the other dissolves into a range of more individual, private, and equivocal acts. These might range through satire and jokes, refusal to participate in regime programs, and other forms of passive resistance and nonconformity. This study is primarily concerned with the more "public" and "intentional" end of the spectrum, obviously a much larger space in a regime like Suharto's than under the Third Reich. It is important to remember, however, that publicly articulated opposition always overlies a wellspring of more private resentments and insubordination.

Building on Linz's own typology of organized opposition under authoritarian regimes, this study identifies four main responses to the mixture of repression and tolerance under New Order authoritarianism. It must be stressed that these are ideal-types and, as with any typology, there is always much overlap between the various categories.

First, there was *mobilizational opposition*, namely those groups that explicitly expressed a desire to replace the regime with another system and which tried to organize and mobilize a support base to achieve this aim. Such opposition was by its nature illegal and repressed. Under normal conditions it could exist only in underground form, emerging into the open during abnormal conditions, such as the relatively liberal atmosphere of *keterbukaan* (openness). Chapter 5 looks at the emergence of the mobilizational trend among student activists.

Semiopposition, by contrast, was defined by Linz (1973, 191) as comprising "those groups that are not dominant or represented in the governing group but that are willing to participate in power without fundamentally challenging the regime." In Indonesia, this form of political activity was characterized by participation in the formal structures of the regime—legislatures, parties, and the like—and was associated with "work-from-within" strategies of political reform, as well as compromise, partial and often unclear goals, and the utilization of regime language and ideological formulas to argue for political change.

Semiopposition was by far the most common of our four categories. This was largely because it became the primary political expression of the three major mass-based *aliran* (political streams) which (along with the communist left) had dominated Indonesian political life between 1945 and 1965. These three *aliran*—modernist Islam, traditionalist Islam,[1] and Sukarnoist nationalism—were not eliminated by the New Order regime, unlike the communist left. Instead, the regime tried to circumscribe and control them. It channeled their chief political expressions into the two surviving parties, the PDI (Indonesian Democracy Party—the subject of a case study in Chapter 6), which became the chief political vehicle for Sukarnoists, and the PPP (Development Unity Party), which incorporated both modernist and traditionalist Islamic interests. These parties were subject to many explicit constraints (e.g., they had to formally pledge their allegiance to the regime's guiding Pancasila ideology and accept its "Broad Outlines of State Policy"). Most important, however, the government constantly intervened in their internal affairs, especially in the selection of leaders. There were also many *ormas* (societal organizations)—religious organizations, student groups, and the like—which traced their origins to the pre–New Order *aliran* and which maintained varying degrees of independence. However, the regime tried to confine these organizations to a strictly defined "social" sphere, separate from the world of *politik praktis* (practical politics). Some such organizations, especially those representing lower-class groups like peasants and workers, were forced to merge into state-controlled corporatist bodies like the Federation of Labor Unions and enjoyed little autonomy.

The rewards for those willing to cooperate with official programs and offer the government political support could be substantial. Prominent party or *ormas* leaders could gain access to patronage in the form of contracts, company directorships, or more straightforward kickbacks. Other rewards for participation were direct subsidies and other concessions for the organizations concerned, their social programs, and their constituencies. For example, the major Islamic organizations such as the modernist Muhammadiyah and the traditionalist Nahdlatul Ulama (NU) ran networks of *pesantren* (Islamic boarding schools) and other institutions that received substantial government largesse. Even so, from time to time, vehicles of semiopposition could become sources of open challenge to the regime.

Falling between the two extremes of semi- and mobilizational opposition is *alegal opposition*. In Linz's (1973, 191 n35) terms, this refers to "opponents whose activities, without being strictly illegal, have no legal sanction and run counter to the spirit if not the text of the Constitution and laws of the regime. They are outside the law: alegal."

"Alegal" opponents tended to make more fundamental criticisms of the regime than did semiopponents. They generally evaded severe persecution by refraining from mobilizing or organizing a mass base against it. In New Order Indonesia, as in many other nondemocratic regimes, alegal opposition was frequently associated with bold and outspoken "exemplary individuals," especially artists, intellectuals, student activists, religious leaders, and the like. The most characteristic form of alegal opposition, especially in the early stages of opposition activity, is *dissidence*.[2] Dissidents are frequently disillusioned supporters of or participants in the regime or the coalition that established it. Accordingly, dissidence is characterized, first, by professions of loyalty to foundational regime ideology and, often, calls to "return" to the regime's original laudable aims. Dissidents can frequently secure a measure of protection from repression on the basis of a history of personal involvement in the regime or ideological affinity with it. Second, and most characteristically, dissidents rely on moral suasion; they tend to address those in authority and appeal to them to initiate reform rather than calling on society to take action or organizing their supporters behind a reform platform. The major Indonesian dissident groups discussed in this book (the Petition of Fifty and Forum Demokrasi) were frequently highly condemnatory of the regime. Security forces monitored their activities and curbed them by selective police action. But they were not driven to extinction by persecution, partly because of the prominence of many of the individuals involved, partly because they did not endeavor to mobilize a mass base.

A fourth category was *civil society organizations*, or what I label *proto-opposition*. Since the 1980s, there has been tremendous academic interest in the concept of civil society, and it has emerged as a central and ubiquitous analytical tool in the literature on democratic transitions. In some literature, it appears as a synonym for "society" and is pictured as an undifferentiated force engaged in a heroic zero-sum conflict against the state. Other definitions are cast at a higher level of abstraction, such as those that emphasize rule setting and legitimation functions (e.g., Harbeson 1994, 4). For present purposes, it is sufficient to note that most contemporary usage of the term centers around phrases like a "sphere of autonomy," "independent public space," or "free public sphere," located between private or family life and the state, where citizens are free to pursue their joint interests. A key feature of this dominant liberal-pluralist definition is that civil society organizations pursue limited goals. They do not aim to acquire political office, but instead they "seek from the state concessions, benefits, policy changes, relief, redress or accountability" (Diamond 1994, 6).

Civil society organizations are thus to be contrasted to alegal and mobilizational opposition by their pursuit of strictly limited and partial aims, while they may be distinguished from semiopposition by their relative independence from state structures. As noted above, in New Order Indonesia many interest groups, especially "sectoral" organizations representing lower-class groups, were incorporated into state-controlled corporatist bodies. But there were also a variety of bodies that maintained a degree of independence from state interference. As the New Order regime consolidated through the 1970s and 1980s (and as in many other authoritarian regimes in Southeast Asia), there was a startling proliferation of nongovernmental organizations (NGOs). NGOs, which constitute the focus of Chapter 4, endeavored with varying success to maintain autonomy from state interference while promoting particularistic policy reform rather than total regime change. The civil society model of opposition to authoritarianism, in Indonesia as elsewhere, was thus characterized by incrementalism rather than confrontation. Even so, despite their partial aims, civil society organizations can become a refuge for many and varied oppositional impulses during repressive conditions (Bratton 1994, 57). They can harbor individuals who aim to transform, even overthrow, the authoritarian regime. During more liberal political conditions such aims could, and in Indonesia in the 1990s did, become explicit—hence the term *proto-opposition.*[3]

Despite the emphasis in some democratic transitions literature on the struggle between civil society and the state, the preceding observations suggest that in nondemocratic systems like Indonesia's New Order there could often be a fluid boundary between semioppositional participation within the system and more fundamental opposition from the outside. This accords with observations made by other observers of democratic movements. X. L. Ding, for example, challenges the state-civil society framework for understanding the political crises experienced by many communist governments in the late 1980s, including the emergence of mass protest movements. He argues that much opposition to Dengist rule in China was initiated by a "counterelite" operating from within official or semiofficial academic institutions, rather than from an autonomous zone outside the state (Ding 1994a, 1994b). He labels this phenomenon "institutional parasitism" or "institutional amphibiousness." The discussion of Indonesian opposition in the following pages similarly suggests that significant challenges to authoritarian rule may originate from institutions located in the blurred "gray area" between state and society. Opposition groups that appear at first sight to be located in the societal domain may likewise maintain a range of ambiguous ties within the state. The vague boundaries between state and society in New Order Indonesia also meant that the growth of opposition frequently took the form of battles for control *inside* organizations endeavoring to shrug off state control (the discussion of the PDI in Chapter 6 particularly illustrates this point).

Another recurring theme in the following chapters is that the New Order's combination of repression with toleration for limited forms of political action had debilitating effects for all manner of opposition. Challenging the regime openly, in the mobilizational pattern, ran a great risk of repression. It was made even less attractive by the possibility of pursuing alternate avenues of more constrained opposition. In contrast, trying to manipulate the regime's rules of the political game and working within official and state-controlled structures like the parties could be unproductive, frustrating, and demoralizing. It also exposed many semiopponents to accusations that they had been co-opted or bought off (and such accusations were often quite true). Meanwhile, the leaders of civil society organizations like NGOs, in order to safeguard their institutions and constituencies, quickly recognized the boundaries of tolerated political behavior and engaged in various forms of self-censorship and self-limitation to avoid suppression. Alegal opponents over time came to inhabit a kind of "dissident niche" from where they could criticize the regime, but they lacked access to a wider constituency.

Accounting for the structural weaknesses of opposition might help to explain why a regime such as the New Order can last so long. It tells us little, however, about how oppositions can grow and mount a sustained challenge to the regime. For this to occur, opponents need to recalculate their possible success, take novel risks, and experiment with new forms of political action. This is what happened during the final decade of Suharto's rule. New forms of mobilization emerged, previously passive social groups (such as labor) began to mobilize, even semiopponents like the PDI, which had previously been derided by political observers as thoroughly compromised, managed to challenge the regime. Eventually, albeit after a catastrophic economic collapse, opposition became so great that Suharto was forced to resign.

The growth and escalation of opposition was an enormously complex process and no single study can attempt to encompass the full range of factors that contributed to it. To cite just one example, this study pays little attention to the influence of global changes, such as how critics of the

Suharto regime drew inspiration and learned lessons from other "third wave" democratizations (in part this omission is because studies by Anders Uhlin [1993, 1995, 1997] deal with this theme). Instead, this book focuses on three main processes.

The first process was internal to opposition itself. Much of this book is dedicated to studying the diverse strategies and techniques used by various opposition groups to bring about political change. The sum product of all these activities was a multifronted battle along the boundaries of permissible political action, in which critics and opponents of the regime constantly tried to probe regime weaknesses, exploit divisions, and expand the political space available to them. In this process, opposition groups would learn from, and compete with, one another (the more radical and risk-taking groups, such as students, played a particularly important pioneering role). Indeed, the spread of opposition was as much a competitive enterprise as it was a cooperative one; time and again groups were motivated to take political action by the fear that they were losing ground to their ideological rivals. The processes by which opposition grew, learned lessons, competed with one another, experimented with new tactics, and forced open new political space are very much the bread and butter of this study, especially the case studies in Chapters 3 to 6. By the steady accumulation of experience, the slow and arduous building of networks, and the compounding of minor victories, opposition could grow.

The second and third processes look beyond developments internal to opposition to broader factors. Among the massive political science literature on democratization, two main theses account for the growth of opposition to authoritarian rule. The first is that oppositions grow, and regimes are transformed, in response to socioeconomic change. The second is that splits within ruling elites provide the crucial impetus.

Opposition, Social Change, and the Middle Class

There is, of course, a long tradition in political science literature of seeking the origins of democratic impulses in economic and social changes. After all, a large body of quantitative, cross-national studies reveals a positive relationship between higher levels of socioeconomic development and liberal democracy (Rueschemeyer, Stephens, and Stephens 1992, 26ff). Economic growth, in this view, is the chief motor of political change, producing or strengthening social classes that demand greater representation, and eventually transforming the political structures created during an earlier stage of development. In particular, many writers in both liberal-modernization and Marxist-derived structuralist traditions have long identified the middle classes as being chief agents of democratization.[4]

Middle classes are typically ascribed a democratizing function because they are attributed with interests in democratization (including interests in limiting capricious state interference in their own affairs and encouraging social stability) as well as greater resources for achieving their aims (for one thing, as Tun-jen Cheng [1990, 10–11] notes, middle-class protestors are less likely to be shot at than are the lower orders). This view retains considerable currency in recent democratization literature. According to Samuel Huntington (1991, 67), for example, "Third wave movements for democratization were not led by landlords, peasants, or (apart from Poland) industrial workers. In virtually every country the most active supporters of democratization came from the urban middle class."

This study is primarily concerned with various forms of middle-class opposition (although it will become apparent that I do not subscribe to a simple version of the "middle-class-as-agents-of-democratization" thesis). The groups studied in the following chapters—NGOs, student activist organizations, dissident groups, and political parties—were mostly led by those who, by dint of relatively privileged social and educational backgrounds, had the resources and the capacity to devote themselves to the grand political project of democratization.

When Suharto came to power in the 1960s, Indonesia was an overwhelmingly agrarian society. The urban middle classes formed a tiny and fragile social layer, squeezed economically by the hyperinflation of the final years of Sukarno's rule and threatened politically by the rising tide of communism. In this context, a good part of the nation's most prosperous urban groups allied with the military in 1965–66. By the mid-1990s, Indonesia's social landscape had been transformed after three decades of sustained economic growth under the New Order. Real per capita gross domestic product had tripled between 1965 and 1990 (Hill 1994, 56). The proportion of the workforce employed in agriculture had dipped below 50 percent. The middle class, however measured, had become a much larger, more amorphous and confident entity than it had been three decades earlier.

Change in political structures did not match the transformation of society. Once the basic outlines of the regime were established in the early 1970s, they were not altered. President Suharto remained firmly in control and grew increasingly inflexible with age. The contradiction between an increasingly vigorous and assertive society and a rigid political structure provoked much of the social and political unrest of the 1990s.

The "middle-class-as-agent-of-democratization" thesis has been much criticized in comparative literature. It is obvious that in many actual historical cases middle-class groups have supported, or have been ambivalent about, authoritarian rule. Dietrich Rueschemeyer, Evelyne Stephens, and John Stephens, in their major comparative historical study of democratization, have this to say on the role of Latin American middle classes:

> The middle classes played an ambiguous role in the installation and consolidation of democracy. They pushed for their own inclusion but their attitude towards inclusion of the lower classes depended on the need and possibilities for an alliance with the working class. The middle classes were most in favor of full democracy where they were confronted with intransigent dominant classes and had the option of allying with a sizeable working class. However, if they started feeling threatened by popular pressures under a democratic regime, they turned to support the imposition of an authoritarian alternative. (Rueschemeyer, Stephens, and Stephens 1992, 8)

Thus, middle classes were important in the coalitions that founded authoritarian regimes, including Indonesia's New Order. In many developing countries, such as Singapore, they have long coexisted comfortably with nondemocratic rule. During the late New Order many authors argued that significant sectors of the Indonesian middle classes, such as state bureaucrats and businesspeople dependent on patrimonial links to the state, continued to support the regime (Robison 1990; Chalmers 1993). During the 1990s, feature writers in the Indonesian press often derided the middle classes as either politically apathetic pleasure-seekers obsessed by consumerism or conservative supporters of the political status quo.

Middle-class support for democratization is often conditional and hesitant, and most often forthcoming for only limited democracy. In countries recently undergoing democratization, middle classes have frequently supported political reform and then pulled back at the threat of lower-class unrest.[5] Initial democratic breakthroughs have often combined electoral democracy with continued restrictions on political, social, and economic claims by subordinate groups. By extension, I suggest in this book that the hesitant and often ambivalent nature of much middle-class semi-, alegal, and proto-opposition in authoritarian regimes may reflect structural weaknesses and ambivalent middle-class attitudes about political change. Time and again, desire for political reform combined with deep insecurities about potential unrest from below and the risks of losing the continued benefits of New Order economic growth to produce many erratic and irresolute forms of opposition.

It is necessary to carefully assess middle-class relations with other social groups and the state. The middle class cannot be viewed in isolation
from the wider historical, political, and class context. Even setting aside
the tremendous social and political heterogeneity of the middle class,[6] the
middle class cannot be reified as a consistently democratic force, nor as a
consistently illiberal one. This is the core of the argument made by
Rueschemeyer, Stephens, and Stephens: the political weight and attitudes
of the different classes are themselves historically structured by a particular country's path to industrialization and by an array of other factors.
It is particularly important to examine "the *structure of class coalitions*
as well as the *relative power of different classes*" in each historical case
(Rueschemeyer, Stephens, and Stephens 1992, 6; italics in original).
Changing middle-class relations with the lower classes (are these seen as
a threat or a possible ally?) and with the ruling elite (oppressor or pro-
tector?) are especially crucial for understanding middle-class attitudes toward democracy.

In Indonesia, it was not only the middle classes that became more politically restless during the 1990s. Parts of the rural population also mobilized, especially in conflicts over land. In the new factories on the outskirts of major cities, an industrial working class emerged and flexed its
muscles with an unprecedented strike wave early in the decade. There
were also many signs of discontent in the *kampung* that housed the
amorphous mass of the urban poor, who had flooded into cities like
Jakarta throughout the New Order period. Detailed studies of political
action in these social sectors are already being written (see, e.g., Hadiz
1997; Kammen 1997; Lucas 1992, 1997; Ford 2003). The present study
will not reproduce this literature. It will, however, pay attention to how
middle-class political leaders and activists oriented and reacted to signs of
political unrest in these other groups. What emerges is that much of the
impetus for the revitalization of middle-class opposition through the late
1980s and 1990s derived from rather lower down the social hierarchy,
both indirectly and via putative cross-sectoral alliances pioneered by
NGO and student activists, as well as by the reinvigoration of older vehicles for populist alliances, such as the PDI.

Opposition and Regime Disunity

Much of the literature on democratic transitions produced in and since
the 1980s is marked by a deliberate turn away from class and structural
explanations, toward an emphasis on the unstructured and indeterminate
nature of transitions and the crucial role played in them by the choices

made by state and opposition elites. One recurrent theme in this "contingent choice theory," as it has been called (Zhang 1994, 110), is the importance of divisions inside the ruling bloc. Such divisions are viewed as being especially important for the first phase in the democratization sequence, namely "liberalization," when the authoritarian government tolerates previously suppressed forms of political expression. In Guillermo O'Donnell and Philippe Schmitter's (1986, 19) oft-quoted formulation, "there is no transition whose beginning is not the consequence—direct or indirect—of important divisions within the authoritarian regime itself, *** principally along the fluctuating cleavage between hard-liners and soft-liners." Similarly, Adam Przeworski (1986, 56) suggests,

> Where some perspectives of an "opening" (*apertura*, "thaw") have appeared, they have always involved some ruling groups that sought political support amongst forces until that moment excluded from politics by the authoritarian regime. This is not to say that once liberalization is initiated, only such chosen partners are politically mobilized: once the signal is given, a wave of popular mobilization often ensues. But it seems to me that the first critical threshold in the transition to democracy is precisely the move by some group within the ruling bloc to obtain support from sources external to it.

The emphasis on regime soft-liners partly derives from the view that successful democratization necessitates, at least, acquiescence by sections of the old regime: "No transition can be forced purely by opponents against a regime which maintains the cohesion, capacity and disposition *** *Burma* to apply repression" (O'Donnell and Schmitter 1986, 21). As the above passage from Przeworski shows, divisions in the government are also considered crucial because they may open new space for initiative by nonstate actors. One or more of the competing elite factions may decide it is advantageous to seek support from the broad political public, or from particular constituencies, by making concessions in the form of greater toleration for public dissent or particular policy reforms. Alfred Stepan describes this process as the "courtship of civil society" or the "*downward reach* for new allies in civil society" (Stepan 1988, 7; italics in original).

Many writers note that after the original gesture toward political liberalization, the process may quickly escalate. Often, a snowballing of opposition and protest occurs. During this period, all varieties of political opposition may endeavor to transform themselves from the debilitated forms they represented under consolidated authoritarianism. Elite factions are then forced to adjust to the new realities, and the process may proceed far beyond what its initiators contemplated (O'Donnell and Schmitter 1986, 26–8, 48–56; Mainwaring 1989, 196–97). Conversely, depending on the shifting balance of forces within the regime and elite threat perceptions, escalated opposition can trigger a retreat to repression.

In Indonesia, analysts have long drawn attention to the interaction of regime disunity and opposition activity. In the early 1970s, for instance, the upsurge of student and intellectual protest that culminated with the Malari riots of January 1974 coincided with considerable tension within both army and cabinet. Over subsequent decades, observers of Indonesian politics, including the New Order's domestic critics, spent much time trying to identify hairline cracks in the regime. Whenever outbursts of opposition occurred, it was a common practice to search for the *dalang* (the puppet master of the Javanese *wayang* shadow theater) in the political elite whose hand was behind it. By the late 1980s, however, would-be democratizers had long confronted a relatively unified state apparatus. This changed in the late 1980s, and the initiation of *keterbukaan* was preceded and accompanied by significant friction between elements in the army on the one hand and President Suharto and his closest followers on the other. Amid numerous signs of growing dissatisfaction in ABRI, the president and his supporters took the unprecedented step of cultivating a new Islamic support base, a move marked by the formation of ICMI (Indonesian Muslim Intellectuals' Association) in 1990. As the discussion in Chapter 2 indicates, many analysts of Indonesian politics argued that it was this tension inside the regime that motivated the tentative steps taken toward liberalization from the late 1980s and the attendant energization of opposition.

There are reasons, however, to question the way in which regime disunity is treated as a key determinant of political change. Michael Bratton, for example, argues that African case studies suggest that the logic frequently operates in the opposite direction to that suggested by O'Donnell and Schmitter:

This formulation depicts the relations of civil society to the state as being far too passive and reactive. Undoubtedly, opposition actors in society stand ready to exploit any divisions that emerge in the state elite and to expand any political opening provided by official concessions. But civic action, especially in the form of mass political protest, commonly comes first, precipitating splits within the ruling group and causing the government to concede reforms. (Bratton 1994, 63; see also Adler and Webster 1995; Collier 1999)

In the first instance, Bratton's comment suggests that it is important to look at how opposition can affect the calculations made by regime actors. Just as regime disunity can prompt energization of opposition, greater opposition can deepen dissension within a ruling bloc and induce some regime leaders to initiate liberalization. Even if we accept, however, that internal regime friction may trigger liberalization and energize opposition, it is still not enough to focus exclusively on the "courtship of civil society" by regime elements. The courtship metaphor suggests that societal actors submissively wait to be wooed. It is just as important to explain how opposition actors respond to such overtures, as well as to more vague hints of discord within a regime. The present study aims to do this by looking at the complex and active processes by which Indonesian opposition actors made "readings" of regime-level conflict, analyzed the opportunities so presented them, and tried to make use of them.

In Indonesia from the late 1980s there was a vigorous debate among civilian groups which had long been excluded from power about how to respond to the new cracks in the regime. One response was simply to increase mobilization, hoping to raise the costs of governance, exacerbate internal tensions, and pave the way for the regime's overthrow. More moderate critics of the government used more persuasive methods, relying on lobbying, moral appeals, and force of argument to try to build links with, and stiffen the resolve of, regime soft-liners. Others (remembering the frequency of semiopposition and "institutional amphibiousness") tried to build alliances with patrons in the state who they viewed as supportive of their agendas and to penetrate sites within the state apparatus itself.

These debates were complicated and intensified because they became entangled with long-standing conflicts about the role of Islam in political and social life. The Suharto group's attempt to cultivate a more Islamic image prompted many previously critical Muslim activists to join ICMI. They sought to achieve some long-standing Islamic political and social goals by closer cooperation with government. Some critics of the government attacked this not only as an instance of co-optation, but also as a dangerous attempt to mix religion and politics and promote Islamization of the regime.

The dilemma of cooperation versus confrontation faces opposition groups in any authoritarian regime. The relative weight of moderate versus confrontational approaches will largely be shaped by the regime's history, structure, and internal cohesion. The greater the element of pluralism and semiopposition, the greater the willingness for compromise and negotiation. In such circumstances, many critics of the government will be used to dealing with regime officials. They will not believe in an unbridgeable divide between state and society. Where at least semiopposition is relatively institutionalized, societal leaders will also be more able to enforce restraint on their followers (Zhang 1994, 112). The opposite situation will obtain in regimes where the reactionary "standpatter" element is strong (Huntington 1991, 144–5; O'Donnell and Schmitter 1986, 34–5). This is especially so in sultanistic regimes, where personalistic dominance by the ruler and widespread use of terror preclude the emergence of reformers within the regime or moderate opposition outside it. Here, as noted above, even groups instinctively inclined toward moderation will often believe that they have little choice but confrontation.

Indonesia is an instructive case study on this score because it combines elements of both patterns. When the first signs of internal conflict within the regime became apparent in the late 1980s, the legacy of previous decades of semipluralism meant that regime critics were well versed in moderate and gradualist approaches. Many prodemocracy activists viewed the tentative signals of support for reform within the ruling elite with great hope. They tried to build links with potential reformers within the state and hoped for a gradual and negotiated process of political transition. However, as we shall see in later chapters, a process of "sultanization" in the later years of Suharto's rule imparted elements of the confrontational pattern to the Indonesian transition. By the mid-1990s, the regime was deep in the midst of a transition toward an increasingly personalized form of rule. Suharto was taking action to reimpose his authority in the ruling elite and to reinstate hard-line policies against opposition. Ultimately, Suharto's dominance of the ruling elite impelled Indonesia on the path toward a sudden, society-initiated process of regime change.

Structure of the Book

Chapter 2 presents background material on the origins of the New Order regime and opposition to it. It also provides an overview of the transformation of the regime by the late 1980s, the initiation of its *keterbukaan* policy, and political dynamics during the first part of the 1990s. The core of the study comes with Chapters 3 through 6, which present detailed case studies of the various forms of opposition introduced in this chapter. They are dissident groups (alegal opposition), nongovernmental organizations (proto-opposition), student dissent (mobilizational opposition), and the PDI (semiopposition). Chapter 7 returns to a wider focus and comprises an analysis of the political crisis triggered by the government's removal of Megawati Soekarnoputri as leader of the PDI in 1996. Chapter 8 analyzes the dramatic upsurge of opposition that led to Suharto's resignation in 1998. Chapters 9 and 10 conclude by revisiting the general questions raised in this chapter.

This book is the product of about ten years' research, being a revised version of my doctoral dissertation that was completed at the Australian National University in 2000. Beginning with a sixteen-month visit to Indonesia in 1993–94, I made one-to-two-month return visits to the country in each succeeding year. During that period, I had the privilege to meet many members and leaders of the groups whose activities are discussed in the following pages. As well as gaining much material from publicly available sources, I obtained access to the archives of papers, pamphlets, magazines, and other ephemera held by many groups and individuals. I conducted over 150 interviews with critics and opponents of the Suharto government, as well as a smaller number with government officials. Most important, I was granted the opportunity to participate in and observe many meetings, workshops, and other activities and to learn from countless informal and private conversations with political activists. Without the great generosity of the participants in Indonesia's struggle for democracy this book would not have been possible.

Some disclaimers are in order. Some will object to my choice of case studies. The choice does not imply that I necessarily found the groups I focus on to be the most important political actors in late Suharto Indonesia. Rather, they represent a cross-section of oppositional responses to New Order authoritarianism. For reasons of space alone, I was obliged to be ruthless. As explained above, my interest is primarily in middle-class forms of political action and in those groups which called for democratization of the regime's political structures. We shall see, however, that debates about strategies for democratization inevitably became intertwined with other debates, notably on how to respond to social inequality and on the proper place for Islam in the political order. I have deliberately excluded secessionist movements (most prominently in our period, those in East Timor, Papua, and Aceh), which sought not merely to reorganize the Indonesian nation-state but to break away from it. These movements proceeded on the basis of very different political logics than did the groups which constitute the focus of this book. Similarly, I have not devoted a separate chapter to "Islamic" forms of opposition. In part, this was for practical reasons; balanced treatment of Islamic politics in our period would have required a separate book-length study, and accounts are already available (e.g., Hefner 2000; Porter 2002). In part, however, this was because the Suharto government pursued a policy of rapprochement with political Islam from the late 1980s. This meant that questions about the proper role of Islam infused all opposition debates. These debates are considered in following chapters.

2

Suharto's New Order

ORIGINS AND OPENING

If input from society, the people's aspirations are not accommodated within the system, the result is that many people become frustrated, and aggressiveness can spread. . . . What I proposed was to strengthen the system, not to destroy it.

Former legislator, Colonel Roekmini Koesoemo
Astoeti, referring to the initiation of "openness"
in 1989 (*Editor*, September 18, 1993, 42–43)

Much of the literature on transitions from authoritarian rule describes the turning point in the democratization process as the *abetura* (opening) or liberalization phase, when the state begins to show greater toleration for dissent. Although the opening is typically linked to conflicts within the governing elite, it frequently allows the "resurrection of civil society" and expansion of political actions and demands (O'Donnell and Schmitter 1986, 26, 48–56). Indonesia after 1988 followed this pattern. Although there were signs of increased activity among groups like students as early as 1986–87, the watershed was the initiation of *keterbukaan* (openness) by military representatives in Indonesia's national legislature, the People's Representative Council (DPR) in 1989. Although liberalization was always hesitant and partial, for several years after 1989 there was more toleration of dissent, gradual loosening of press controls, and steady escalation of opposition activity. Eventually, the government opted for renewed repression, and by mid-1994 a retreat from openness was discernible.

The Origins of the New Order and
Its Opposition, 1965–1988

The "openness" policies of the late 1980s contrasted dramatically with the tenor of Indonesian politics in the preceding decade. In the mid-1980s, the New Order was, to borrow from R. William Liddle (1988), at the "height of its powers." The political climate was highly repressive, there was little overt opposition, and the government and military appeared unified.

It is important to remember, however, that this had not always been the case. In the 1970s, there were two episodes of significant mass unrest (in 1973–74 and 1977–78), serious divisions in the military, and rising Islamic opposition. Many observers of Indonesian politics in the late 1970s were far from sanguine about the regime's long-term prospects.

The instability of the New Order in the 1970s largely resulted from the breakup of the coalition that had put the regime in place. Unlike in some military-based regimes, the New Order did not come to power as the result of a coup against civilian politics in general. Instead, it arose as a result of a military-civilian coalition (albeit a coalition in which the military was dominant). In the mid-1960s, Indonesia was on a leftward course. Under President Sukarno's Guided Democracy (1959–66), the country had experienced considerable economic, social, and political turbulence. Sukarno had tried to unite the major warring factions by means of ideological formulas which stressed national unity. In fact, he had presided over a political system undergoing dramatic polarization. The two major contenders for power were the Indonesian Communist Party (PKI) and the army. The army had extended its power by suppressing regional rebellions and by taking control of many nationalized foreign firms. The PKI had become the third-largest communist party in the world, and Sukarno was increasingly dependent on it for mass support. The party's civilian opponents, meanwhile, were on the defensive and were cultivating allies within the army; their chief organizations were either banned (Indonesian Socialist Party [PSI] and the modernist Islamic party, Masyumi), under threat of banning (Islamic Students Association, HMI), or being wrested away from them by the left (Indonesian National Party, PNI).

The "September 30 Movement" affair of 1965, when leftist soldiers kidnapped and killed six senior army officers, triggered the formation of a broad coalition against the PKI and, subsequently, the Sukarno government. Although the army was the key player, important civilian groups

cooperated with it. Members of Islamic mass organizations, especially
Nahdlatul Ulama, played a major role in killing PKI supporters in the
countryside. University students, in close cooperation with military officers, held noisy demonstrations which turned the initially anti-PKI mood
against Sukarno and his "Old Order." Many journalists, legal professionals, intellectuals, economists, and others also rallied to the anticommunist and anti-Sukarno cause, organizing seminars, establishing newspapers, and in other ways trying to give the military a policy framework
for the new government; some of the most capable of such people became
technocrat ministers in Suharto's early cabinets.

However, the removal of the PKI and Sukarno from the political scene
left little effective counterweight to the army. From the late 1960s, the
government restructured the political system in a way that generated discontent among some of its civilian allies. The New Order regime has been
well described elsewhere (see, e.g., Crouch 1988a; Liddle 1999b), so it is
possible to be brief here. In general terms, the New Order relied on three
pillars of control.

First, the New Order extended, formalized, and consolidated|military
control over political life.|The *dwifungsi* (dual function) doctrine legiti-
mated a sociopolitical function for ABRI, as well as a defense and security role. ABRI officers were appointed to posts in the legislature and bureaucracy; a formidable intelligence apparatus was developed, as was the
military's "territorial structure," which shadowed civilian government
structures all the way down to the village level.

Second, the government restructured the chief institutions of political
and civil society. The inherited infrastructure of parties, legislatures, and
elections survived, but it was transformed by a combination of intervention, manipulation, and blunt coercion. The regime refashioned Golkar
(*Golongan Karya*, Functional Groups) as its electoral vehicle. Enforce-
ment of "monoloyalty," by which civil servants were expected to sever
their links with the political parties, massive mobilization of state resources, and widespread intimidation delivered Golkar 62.8 percent of
the vote in the 1971 elections, and similar victories in later ones. A "floating mass" policy aimed to insulate the rural population from politics by
limiting the operation of political parties below the level of district capitals.[1] In 1973, the surviving parties were forced to fuse into two unstable
agglomerations (the secular nationalist PDI and the Muslim PPP), which
were subject to constant state supervision and intervention in their internal affairs. The government also attempted to control the furthest reaches
of associational life. In particular, organizations of subordinate classes,
like workers and peasants, were either eliminated or corralled into corporatist "sole organizations."

Third, the government sought to construct a comprehensive ideological justification for authoritarian rule. Government agencies fashioned a revivified "Pancasila ideology," which stressed social harmony and the organic unity between state and society. According to the "family principle" (*asas kekeluargaan*), individuals and groups were expected to subordinate their own interests to those of the society as a whole. All forms of division, and political opposition in particular, were labeled inimical to the Indonesian national character.

In a pattern similar to many authoritarian regimes, opposition in the first two decades of the New Order was largely produced by the splintering of its founding coalition. People who had been victims of that coalition were mostly not in a position to mount effective resistance. In particular, the massacres of 1965–66 and subsequent repression denuded the political landscape on the left. Most former supporters of the PKI and other radical groups had been killed or imprisoned or were terrified of persecution.

Former allies of the military, by contrast, had a limited license to criticize the authorities, especially initially. In the late 1960s, Islamic leaders were among the first to become openly disillusioned. Many of them were shocked by clumsy army intervention in their organizations and by government policies that they saw as hostile to the interests of the Muslim community. Liberal intellectuals and former student activists, as well as many Muslim leaders, were also frustrated by the failure to legislate to uphold judicial independence and the rule of law. Many of them criticized the failure to overcome corruption, single-mindedly pursue economic modernization, and defend bureaucratic rationality. As early as 1967, students demonstrated against high prices for public transport, foodstuffs, and other basic commodities. From the late 1960s, journalists from several New Order newspapers—*Indonesia Raya, Harian Kami, Nusantara,* and *Mahasiswa Indonesia*—campaigned vigorously against corruption. In 1970 and 1971–72, students organized street protests on the same issue and against Mrs. Tien Suharto's pet project, the Taman Mini "Beautiful Indonesia in Miniature" park, which they viewed as a repeat of the wasteful prestige projects of the Sukarno years.

Initially, the tone of criticisms was reserved and respectful. In the late 1960s, when the first seeds of doubt began to germinate in the minds of supporters of the New Order, such people generally remained emotionally committed to the new government and shared its belief in development and stability. Many of the intellectuals, journalists, and former students who were most critical on issues like corruption and the rule of law believed that mass politics and ideological conflict had contributed to Indonesia's problems and that strong government was needed to bring about economic and social modernization. In any case, they could see no realistic alternative to the new government.

In the late 1960s and early 1970s, such supporters-turned-critics thus tended to avoid attacking the government and its political and economic programs per se. Instead, they aimed to "save" them from mismanagement and corruption. Some students and intellectuals, for example, initially believed that President Suharto was sympathetic to modernizing ideals but was surrounded by a clique of corrupt generals. They thought their duty was to awaken him to the truth about corruption and other government failings.[2]

Many such individuals also sought to formulate a new role that combined a critical posture with continued adherence to the New Order "partnership." For example, there was much discussion of the concept of "social control," which envisaged that sympathetic civilians would monitor the exercise of power and offer constructive criticism when it was abused, thus contributing to the effective running of the state.

There was also a strongly moral tone to early criticisms. For instance, when a group of former student activists including Arief Budiman, Asmara Nababan, and Marsillam Simanjuntak criticized the government's handling of the 1971 election campaign and called for an election boycott, they labeled themselves *golput* (*golongan putih*, or white group, indicating that voters should pierce the blank part of the ballot slip rather than any of the party symbols), implying moral cleanliness and withdrawal from the dirty and corrupting world of politics. They called for the population to withdraw passively and be a "good audience" (Sanit 1992, 48), rather than advocating mobilization against the government.

As time passed, disillusionment among some former allies of the military mounted. Corruption was worsening, and there were signs that Suharto, his family, and associates were involved in some of the worst cases. ABRI was becoming more entrenched in power and hostile to criticism, while government economic programs seemed to be creating social dislocation and providing few benefits to the poor. Criticisms on such themes by students, journalists, and sundry political leaders reached a crescendo in the months prior to Malari (the January 15 Calamity) in 1974, when student protests against a visit by Japanese prime minister Tanaka were quickly overtaken by riots elsewhere in Jakarta. The government stamped down hard on dissent. It banned eleven newspapers and one magazine and detained over seven hundred persons from a wide variety of groups, some for two years.

The space for political dissent, even by former allies of the military, narrowed dramatically. Even so, in the approach to the 1977 elections and the 1978 MPR (People's Consultative Assembly) session, there was a further round of student protest, accompanied by open expressions of defiance by intellectuals, artists, Muslim leaders, party legislators, and retired officials. This time, opposition had a stronger antigovernment and anti-Suharto tone, with student councils calling for an "extraordinary session" of the MPR to hold Suharto to account for "deviations from the 1945 Constitution and Pancasila."

This renewed outburst of political discontent led Benedict Anderson (1978, 2) to suggest that "the coalition which has kept Suharto in power since 1966 is breaking up." In retrospect, however, the dissent of the 1970s seems like a dying spasm of the old New Order coalition. The government was able to control it with relative ease. In January 1978, troops occupied campuses. The government again arrested many students and other dissidents and suspended six newspapers. An era of increased authoritarianism began, and the political space for opposition, even by former coalition partners, narrowed further.

The start of the 1980s saw tight political control. Press restrictions were enforced, and a "Normalization of Campus Life" policy saw the permanent abolition of student councils. Even respected national figures who had criticized the government, like the "father of the army," General (retired) Abdul Haris Nasution, suffered political and economic ostracism.

As open and organized opposition became more difficult, oppositional impulses were sometimes expressed by sudden outbursts of violent confrontation. The more characteristic response, however, was a retreat of opposition into civil society, a turn toward forms of action that avoided direct confrontation with the state. NGOs multiplied, most of them gaining some legitimacy in the eyes of the state by pursuing developmentalist aims. Many Sukarnoists, modernist Muslims, and others established a range of ostensibly apolitical "cultural" or "educational" groups as a means to perpetuate their old political affiliations.[3] Even Nahdlatul Ulama disassociated itself from PPP and the formal political arena.

How did the Suharto government manage to pull back from the precipice to which loss of civilian support brought it in the 1970s? Two factors were key. The first was the government's economic gains. The crisis of 1965–66 had occurred amid economic breakdown, including hyperinflation of around 500 percent. Even at the time of the Malari affair, there was considerable economic disruption; for example, an influx of mostly Japanese investment in the textile industry had destroyed much of the indigenous batik industry. However, a sharp increase in world oil prices during the early 1970s brought a revenue windfall. Between 1971 and 1981, Indonesia's real gross domestic product expanded at an annual rate of 7.7 percent (Hill 1996, 16). Economic growth dampened political discontent by delivering rising living standards to many groups, as well as furnishing the government with funds with which to buy social peace. After Malari, the government was able to make various neopopulist adjustments to economic policy, providing small and medium indigenous businesses with special programs and increasing expenditure on poverty alleviation and basic infrastructure in rural areas.

Economic growth was particularly important for securing middle-class support, or at least acquiescence. Although the 1970s saw considerable discontent among groups with independent incomes and professional interests in a free public sphere (notably private lawyers and journalists), overall the middle class remained small, insecure, and worried about unrest. The state was economically dominant, and many middle-class people remained dependent on it, either as civil servants or via patrimonial business ties. Despite pockets of discontent and more widespread cynicism, there was no wholesale desertion of the middle class, or even the intelligentsia, from the New Order. Most saw little point in openly challenging the state when its supremacy was so clear and while it was delivering economic growth.

The second factor that ensured the New Order's ascendancy was Suharto's success in imposing unity within the ruling elite, especially the army. Many observers of Indonesia in the 1980s drew attention to Suharto's tremendous political skills, especially his ability to control subordinates by distributing patronage and manipulating conflict between them (Jenkins 1984, 145–56; Liddle 1985, 1991; Crouch 1988b).

In the early 1970s, a multiplicity of intimate ties had connected the dissident milieu with government and had provided sustenance to opposition. During the struggle against Sukarno in 1965–66, many intellectuals, students, and other critics developed personal links with ABRI officers and others who later became senior government figures. As disillusionment with Suharto grew, middle-class critics continued to place great hopes in whatever general or faction they viewed as being most sympathetic to their own aims.

The resulting enmeshment of dissidence and regime factionalism was clearest in the months leading to Malari, when escalating societal criticism coincided with growing tension within the regime between "military professionals" around Kopkamtib (Command for the Restoration of Security and Order) commander general Soemitro and the freewheeling "political" and "financial" generals Ali Moertopo and Soedjono Hoemardani. This conflict partly overlapped with another schism on economic policy, pitting the second group against the civilian technocrats (Crouch 1988a, 306–17; Robison 1986, 131–75). During these months, many civilians sought government or army backers, while the feuding groups within the regime tried to find civilian proxies. In particular, many in liberal middle-class circles viewed the technocrats sympathetically and looked to General Soemitro, who had been promoting himself as a reformer, as a potential ally. Drawing on their experiences from 1966, some calculated that protests could create conditions that would enable Soemitro, if not to move directly against Suharto, at least to force him to remove Moertopo and his coterie. This proved to be a misreading of Soemitro's intentions and underestimated both Moertopo's and Suharto's capacities to retaliate.[4] The subsequent post-Malari crackdown on civilian dissent was accompanied by a parallel tightening of Suharto's control within ABRI. Soemitro and many of his followers were sidelined, while Moertopo's own influence declined soon thereafter.

This consolidation of Suharto's control narrowed the scope for cross-fertilization between opposition and factionalism within the ruling elite. In the late 1970s, a few important officials were prepared to be openly sympathetic to critics of the government, such as Jakarta governor (1966–77) Ali Sadikin or foreign minister and later vice president Adam Malik. But such individuals mostly did not keep their posts for long. In the late 1970s, some student activists and others had hopes for various generals, including Soerono, Widodo, and Mohammad Yusuf, especially when the latter two signaled unease about overextension of the military's political role (Jenkins 1984). But once again, these officers proved unwilling to confront Suharto.

Suharto's personal skills played more than a small part in the greatly increased internal unity and stability of the regime between 1974 and the late 1980s. But the economic boom of these years was also crucial. Suharto positioned himself at the apex of a pyramid for distributing the resources generated by the oil boom economy (Robison 1993, 49; Crouch 1986). He used timber concessions, easy lines of credit, contracts in the petroleum industry, and similar perquisites to tie prominent officials to him personally. This pattern was reproduced at all levels of the state, and distribution of patronage became the chief means for securing the cohesion and loyalty of the bureaucracy. Similar methods were used to buy the compliance of retired bureaucrats, party chiefs, and community leaders who might otherwise have been inclined to oppose Suharto.

The Transformed Social Landscape

Loss of civilian support had threatened the Suharto government in the 1970s. By the late 1980s conditions were changed dramatically. A seemingly omnipotent state loomed above a weakened and mostly quiescent society. Ironically, however, the very factors that accounted for the New Order's triumph—rapid economic growth and Suharto's predominance—also contained the seeds of its eventual downfall.

Economic growth generated a tremendous increase in wealth at the apex of the economy, reflected in the dramatic expansion of family-owned conglomerates with interests in many sectors of the economy. As in the past, most conglomerates were owned by ethnic Chinese business-people who had prospered through personal links with powerful officials. In a country where ethnic Chinese were a small minority of the population (approximately 3 to 4 percent) and still the target of popular resentment, this section of the new capitalist class was unable to stake a direct claim on political power.[5] However, by the late 1980s an important "indigenous" group of new capitalists had emerged. Twenty years of access to the levers of economic decision making had generated spectacular cases of capital accumulation, especially by the families of Suharto and other senior officials. Even during economic liberalization from the mid-1980s, the commanding heights of the economy were dominated by crony capitalists. As a result, big business was politically conservative. The fate of the major groups was tied closely to the regime, and they had little interest in economic regularization, let alone political democracy (Crouch 1994, 116–17; Hadiz 1997, 176–81). During *keterbukaan* no significant element of big capital provided even ambivalent support to democratic opposition.

By the late 1980s, the middle class was also a larger, more amorphous, and confident social entity than the tiny and besieged group which had supported the army in 1965. A brash and exuberant consumer culture was plainly visible in the shopping malls, fast-food outlets, nightclubs, golf courses, business schools, and housing estates that mushroomed in and around the big cities. Consumption indexes grew spectacularly; for example, sales of sedans increased from 159,700 to 263,300 between 1987 and 1991 alone (UN Industrial Development Organisation / Economist Intelligence Unit 1993, 169, 173). The new enthusiasm was not limited to a few top beneficiaries of economic growth; alongside luxurious shopping centers like Jakarta's Pondok Indah Mall and Plaza Indonesia, there were many less ostentatious supermarkets which catered to the more modest tastes of the growing lower-middle-class market. The growth of a new *santri* (pious Islamic) middle class was especially obvious, and not only in the traditional petty entrepreneurial sectors but also among professionals and civil servants.

Following the modernization thesis, it could be expected that the stronger middle class would support democratization. The case studies in later chapters do indeed provide examples of increased political assertiveness by some middle-class groups. However, many of the factors that had tied the middle class to the regime in the 1970s continued to operate.[6] Many middle-class people remained dependent on the state for their prosperity because they were civil servants or had business links with state officials or larger crony capitalists. Above all, despite growth, the middle class still represented a small and largely insecure fraction of the overall population, and many of them had little interest in jeopardizing their steadily increasing prosperity for the sake of an uncertain project of regime change.

Economic growth also caused change and dislocation among the poor. Declining oil prices early in the 1980s had prompted a shift toward economic liberalization and export-oriented consumer goods industrialization. By the early 1990s, the manufacturing share of the gross domestic product was 21 percent, compared to 8 percent in the mid-1960s (Hill 1996, 5). Along with the rapid growth of labor-intensive light consumer industry on the outskirts of Jakarta and other cities, a large industrial working class had come into existence. Its members received low wages and experienced poor working and living conditions, owing to the large supply of new workers flooding into the cities, as well as the New Order's antiunion policies. Even so, during the 1990s there was a major strike wave (Hadiz 1997). In rural areas, meanwhile, agribusiness, real estate, infrastructure, and similar projects run by private companies and the state were forcing peasants off their land. Already in the 1980s, there were signs of acute conflicts over land use and ownership. Another politically significant, but undertheorized, group was the urban poor.[7] Because population growth and urbanization continued to outstrip demand for wage labor, a large proportion of city dwellers continued to eke out an existence in the informal sector. The poor *kampung* of Jakarta and other big cities were by the late 1980s better hidden from casual visitors than in the past, but their inhabitants—marginal traders, unemployed youth, petty criminals, newly arrived villagers—still constituted a majority of the urban population. In later years they became a significant political force, albeit often a destructive one.

During the early 1990s, economic growth continued to be important for the regime's survival; absolute poverty continued to decline, ample patronage funds remained available, and the social contract with the middle classes largely held. Nevertheless, growth and the resulting social changes did have negative consequences for political stability. It was not simply that economic growth strengthened groups with interests in reform, like independent professionals and the urban working class. More particularly, tensions arose because economic growth and social change were taking place within a political framework that was essentially unchanged since the early 1970s. Conflict between the old patrimonial framework and new pressures of economic globalization, for example, led to tensions between politico-bureaucrats and technocrats over liberalization policies (Schwarz 1999, 49–97). The increasingly blatant privileges granted to well-connected capitalists, especially Suharto family members, caused resentment among economic players ranging from foreign investors frustrated at policy unpredictability and caprice, through to smaller businesspeople in the regions who lacked privileged access to officialdom. From the early 1990s, readers of the middle-class press lapped up increasingly salacious stories about corruption scandals or the greed of the Suharto children, often disguised as straight business reporting. The terms *kolusi, korupsi,* and *nepotisme* (collusion, corruption, and nepotism) began to recur in the press from the same time. There was also renewed concern about social inequality, as continuing mass poverty contrasted strongly with the signs of great affluence in the cities and what was known about high-level corruption. Phrases like *kesenjangan sosial* (the social gap) and *kecemburuan sosial* (social jealousy) entered the country's political vocabulary. News magazines like *Tempo* regularly featured cover stories on labor conflict, rural poverty, land disenfranchisement, and so forth. As we shall see in later chapters, such concerns fueled opposition to the regime.

Tension in the Regime: Suharto and the Military

By the late 1980s, Suharto had long been the dominant power in the New Order. He was the supreme political authority and final arbiter in all major policy decisions and appointments. Time and again he had proved his ability to see off potential challengers. Even so, the New Order eventually had to face the problem of leadership succession. Suharto was sixty-six years old when he was elected for his fifth presidential term in 1988. Yet, by making the presidency such a powerful institution (Robison 1993, 47–9; Liddle 1985, 1991), he had raised the stakes for all players in the ruling elite who were looking to the future. The presidency was a glittering prize beyond all others; whoever controlled it would presumably control the post-Suharto order. From the late 1980s, as Suharto's inevitable departure drew closer, key individuals and cliques in the regime engaged in complicated maneuvers to secure positions which might influence succession. The vice presidency was the most important, because its incumbent was constitutionally empowered to succeed in case of the president's death or incapacity.

At this point, a clear link can be identified between presidential succession, political liberalization, and the growth of opposition. Because power was so concentrated in Suharto's hands, it seemed that a new president would necessarily be weaker and obliged to seek new sources of legitimacy. Logically, it would be to the advantage of elite players vying for the presidency to cultivate present and future societal support. In this way, tensions surrounding succession could be expected, borrowing from Harold Crouch (1994, 121), to "spill over" into the societal realm and contribute to pressures for political liberalization. As we shall see, elements of this scenario, consistent with what might be expected from democratization literature, were indeed played out in Indonesia from the late 1980s.

Suharto's advancing age and increasing isolation from his subordinates, however, exacerbated the government's inflexibility in responding to pressures for political change. In the early New Order, the military and government were led by Suharto's contemporaries from the "1945 generation" of those who had participated in the independence struggle against the Dutch. Officers like Moertopo, Hoemardani, Widodo, and Yusuf had been Suharto's comrades-in-arms since the independence struggle and had helped him to establish the New Order. Civilians like the technocrats Soemitro Djojohadikoesoemo and Widjojo Nitisastro also had substantial personal authority, and the president relied greatly on them for economic policy and advice. Although Suharto had long been the New Order's supreme power, pushing aside his 1945-generation colleagues when necessary, at least he considered them his peers, consulted with them, and valued their opinions.

During the 1980s, a significant gap developed between the president and his subordinates because of generational change. Officers trained at the military academy in Magelang in the 1960s took control of the military. Their civilian contemporaries (including some who had been student activists in the late 1960s and early 1970s) assumed greater cabinet responsibility. They were less likely to challenge Suharto, and it is safe to assume that he trusted and valued their views less. By the early 1990s, it was widely understood that there was poor communication between Suharto and most cabinet members, who were rumored to be more likely to lobby him via trusted intermediaries (such as his children) rather than speak openly in his presence. This situation contributed to tension and a lack of coordination among senior officials and to the prominence of presidential adjutants, relatives, and their protégés in promotions to key military and civilian posts.[8] Suharto's growing isolation also undermined his political judgment and gave the regime an increasingly inflexible and irrational stamp, equipping it poorly to respond to increasing opposition. It is argued in Chapter 8 that this process of "sultanization" largely ex-

plains the tumultuous way in which Suharto's presidency eventually
ended in 1998.

The greatest challenge to Suharto from within the regime came from
elements in the military. From the late 1980s, there were many signs of
often bitter disaffection within ABRI directed at President Suharto and
his allies. This disaffection was generated by a range of disparate issues,
including sudden or "unfair" promotions and transfers, "scapegoating"
for human rights violations, and interference by nonmilitary politicians
in equipment purchases. Such grumbles were partly linked to the generational change mentioned above, with the president's increasing isolation
from his subordinates and his reliance on handpicked loyalists generating
much resentment among officers who felt sidelined. Two structural factors generated further tension.

First, there was a secular decline in the role played by the military in
the government's policy-making core (Lane 1991, 4–16; Crouch 1994,
120–23). Whereas in the late 1960s and early 1970s the military more or
less constituted government, from the 1980s a growing gap became apparent. As the New Order became increasingly institutionalized, civilian
agencies like the presidency and the state secretariat advanced in policy-
making power, while the civilian bureaucracy, Golkar and other civilian
bodies, including from the early 1990s ICMI (the Indonesian Muslim Intellectuals Association), became increasingly important for recruitment
into senior government ranks. There was a concomitant decline in ABRI's
penetration of the civilian bureaucracy.[9]

Growing military marginalization also reflected the expanding power
of the families of Suharto and other senior bureaucrats, whose increasing
control over large parts of the economy speeded the displacement of mil-
itary-controlled foundations and state enterprises (Robison 1993, 50).
Elite families also began to play a more active political role, evidenced by
the 1993 appointment of two of Suharto's children to the Golkar Central
Executive Board. Such developments added to discontent within ABRI. In
elite circles stories (whether accurate or not) abounded of senior military
officers who worked up the courage to appeal directly to the president
about the favors bestowed on his children, only to be angrily denied further personal contact.[10]

Of course, the military remained influential and retained important
veto power, but its institutional interests influenced policy formulation
less and less, while the government was increasingly legitimated by civilian mechanisms. This was only partially masked by ABRI's continuing
prominence in security maintenance functions. As Max Lane (1991, 7)
argued, "ABRI has become increasingly an instrument carrying out general policies which it has no real say in formulating." As we shall see in

Chapter 3, this situation generated considerable resentment in parts of ABRI. Disgruntled officers complained that ABRI was reduced to a "fire brigade," charged with responding to social unrest generated by decisions into which it had little input.

A second important factor was the role of General L. B. ("Benny") Moerdani and his network, which from the late 1980s served as the principal conduit for military frustrations. During the 1970s, Moerdani (a Catholic) attained a position of extraordinary power by dominating and expanding the military intelligence network. He was a chief architect of the regime's repressive policies against Islamic and other forms of opposition. His authority was strongest during 1983–88 when he was concurrently ABRI commander and minister of defense and security. Informal networks had always permeated ABRI, but that built by Moerdani was particularly pervasive. By the 1980s it constituted a powerful network of political operatives through the military and civilian bureaucracy. Although Moerdani owed his position to his close personal ties with Suharto dating back to the 1960s, by the late 1980s the extent of his power (increasingly being used against his chief rival and fellow Suharto favorite, Sudharmono) represented a threat to the president himself. Suharto thus abruptly dismissed Moerdani as ABRI commander in 1988, although Moerdani continued to wield considerable influence until 1993, both as defense and security minister and through informal channels.

If Moerdani emerged as the focal point of military discontent in the late 1980s, two men were the primary targets of military resentment, chiefly because they most embodied the trend toward civilianization. The first was Suharto protégé Sudharmono. Although he had a military background, as state secretary and general chairperson of Golkar (1983–88), he had attempted to consolidate the independence and power of the bureaucracy (including Golkar's independence from, and even willingness to criticize, ABRI). Conflict between Moerdani and Sudharmono became particularly obvious in early 1988, when ABRI elements campaigned to prevent Sudharmono from being appointed vice president at the March MPR session (Crouch 1988b, 162–65). Tensions peaked when Suharto sacked Moerdani as ABRI commander in February. During the MPR session, there were many signs of military discontent, most obviously a noisy "interruption" of the vote by a previously little-known officer, Brigadier General Ibrahim Saleh. Nevertheless, Sudharmono was unanimously endorsed as vice president, after which military elements launched a bizarre whispering campaign about his alleged past left-wing affiliations. There was also a concerted attempt to restore military dominance in Golkar, resulting in Sudharmono's replacement as chairperson by Wahono, a retired general and governor of East Java.

From 1993, the focus of most open military discontent was the research and technology minister, Bacharuddin Jusuf Habibie. He had a long-standing personal relationship with Suharto, dating back to his childhood in 1950, when he was virtually adopted into the house of the then lieutenant colonel in Ujung Pandang. Suharto wrote affectionately of his protégé in his autobiography that "he regards me as his own parent" (Dwipayana and Ramadhan 1989, 457). From the 1970s, Suharto had entrusted Habibie with the task of leading the state's push into high-technology industry. Military unhappiness with Habibie was prompted by many factors, including the transfer to his jurisdiction of ABRI enterprises, his interference in equipment purchases, and the part he played for Suharto in building a Muslim support base, discussed below.

In certain respects, the tensions of the late 1980s and early 1990s thus continued the pattern of second-level factional competition that had existed in the 1970s. Much apparent military discontent in the 1990s could be attributed to rearguard actions mounted by Moerdani supporters. A new element, however, was that dissatisfaction was now substantially directed at Suharto and his palace group, rather than merely at rival officers. The view that ABRI's institutional interests were threatened was also more pervasive. Moerdani's followers attempted to play upon these concerns, but unease was not limited to them.

It is important, however, to stress the ambivalence of much military discontent and the fluidity of political alignments in ABRI. Not only did Suharto loyalists permeate the military, but ABRI's deeply ingrained doctrine of loyalty and discipline militated against action by those who were unhappy with the president. Many discontented officers were ambivalent about Suharto, feeling that it was time for him to step aside but retaining tremendous residual respect for him.

Such ambivalence also reflected a structural contradiction. Although Suharto's dominance in the regime generated substantial elite conflict about succession, the same dominance prevented such conflict from being expressed openly. The president indicated no clear preference for a successor, established no formal mechanisms to decide on such a person, and gave conflicting indications of when he would vacate his post. He also retained the ability to sideline potential rivals or reformers. In consequence, elite conflict could not mature. The president prevented vying factions from offering concessions to the public that would seriously threaten the established political framework. Intraelite tension thus substantially remained a competition between feuding but loyal lieutenants.

In the 1990s, there were thus manifest contradictions in the behavior of members of the ruling political elite. Senior officials often simultaneously stressed their loyalty to the president, harbored private misgivings about him, sought to present a reformist public face, but also took action to suppress regime critics. Intraregime friction contributed substantially to political uncertainty and provided many opportunities to opposition. But while Suharto remained dominant, there could be no decisive initiative for reform from within the regime.

The Initiation of Openness

Many analysts have portrayed the beginning of "openness" policies in 1989 as being primarily a product of conflict between sections of ABRI and supporters of Suharto (e.g., Budiman 1992; Crouch 1994, 121). While there is much to be said for this view, it is also necessary to place the policy's beginnings in a broader societal context. Elements within the regime, albeit relatively marginal ones, were influenced by early signs of pressures for change from outside the political system and saw preemptive limited political reform as an appropriate response. Reform policies then gathered momentum because they were influenced by both conflict within the regime *and* increasing societal pressure.

Early signs of political unrest, even if they were very faint, preceded liberalization policies. There was a sudden increase in student protest from late 1988 (see Chapter 5). Numerous intellectuals, retired military officers, and other commentators argued in the media that such protests were a sign that official institutions had become too inflexible to adequately reflect popular aspirations. In the late 1980s, the press had also been becoming gradually bolder and provided increasing coverage of the views of many such people, notably General (retired) Soemitro, who reemerged from relative obscurity to argue that it was time to consider political reform and prepare for presidential succession (see Soemitro 1992a, 1992b; Lane 1991, 30–41). Then, in late May 1989, the departing U.S. ambassador, Paul Wolfowitz, called for greater political openness to complement economic liberalization. This call sparked much debate, and from this point *keterbukaan* (openness—the term deliberately echoed the Soviet *glasnost*) became a new catchword in public political discourse.

Although there had been tentative calls for relaxation of political controls from within Golkar and ABRI from as early as 1987, it was not until shortly after Ambassador Wolfowitz's speech that the first serious break in favor of reform opened in government ranks. The initiators were members of the Fraksi-ABRI, the military representatives in the national legislature, or DPR. They included officers with distinguished records, like Majors General Samsuddin (head of Komisi II, the DPR Commission on Social and Political Affairs), Saiful Sulun, and Raja Kami Sembiring Meliala, and Police Colonel Roekmini Koesoemo Astoeti.

On June 21, 1989, the *keterbukaan* era definitively began when Samsuddin and the other Komisi II leaders invited Soemitro to address a public hearing. Soemitro used the opportunity to promote several reform proposals, including presidential succession by an MPR vote between multiple candidates, ministerial responsibility to the DPR, and Golkar independence from the bureaucracy (*Tempo*, July 8, 1989, 22–25). Next, the minister for the state secretariat, Moerdiono, appeared before the commission, where Colonel Roekmini rebuked him, saying that political communication was "blocked." These hearings were widely covered in the press as signaling a dramatic departure from the previously repressive political atmosphere.

In following months and years, these ABRI legislators continued to speak in favor of openness. They exhorted the media to greater boldness in covering controversial issues; at one point Roekmini suggested that censorship had transformed newspapers into "government bulletins" (*Tempo*, July 8, 1989, 23). More public hearings with controversial figures also occurred, including a sensational visit by members of the Petition of Fifty dissident group in July 1991.

The vocal ABRI legislators were part of the military camp most disillusioned with Suharto. Jacques Bertrand (1996, 326) notes that some Fraksi-ABRI members suggested (at least to the foreign press) that it might be time for Suharto to step down. However, according to those involved, promotion of *keterbukaan* was entirely an initiative of the *fraksi* members and was not directly linked to wider machinations against the president. Instead, they said they were motivated by what they viewed as steadily increasing public criticism of the government. Since at least 1987, *fraksi* members had been carefully analyzing press reports of social and political unrest, especially public criticisms of the toothlessness of the legislature. From this they concluded the government needed to find a new, more tolerant approach to handling societal criticisms. Without this, they feared that political alienation and disorder would grow. In the words of Colonel Roekmini, "[We decided] that if we wanted to safeguard the system, we had to be accommodative" (interview, November 29, 1995). Major General Sembiring Meliala likewise suggested that without openness and "the accommodation of aspirations from below," *fraksi* members had concluded "there would eventually be explosions."[11] In short, a genuine "soft-line" liberalizing urge did partly account for the openness initiative.

The role of relatively marginal soft-liners is confirmed by the part played by a group of Golkar DPR members, including Marzuki Darusman, Oka Mahendra, and Bambang Warih Koesoemo. They were part of a reform current which had emerged in the 1980s under the tutelage of Sudharmono and General Secretaries Sarwono Kusumaatmadja (1983–88) and Rachmat Witoelar (1988–93) and which could not be seen as part of the Moerdani camp. This group had long hoped to make Golkar slowly more independent of ABRI and the bureaucracy, strengthen the legislature, and ultimately oversee a gradual loosening of the political system (Vatikiotis 1994; Liddle 1994). From 1989, these Golkar legislators enthusiastically supported Fraksi-ABRI's openness initiative, with Marzuki Darusman telling one foreign journalist, "We are trying to build the semblance of a political system using the DPR" (*Far Eastern Economic Review*, April 20, 1989, 27).

Even so, the "openness" initiative rapidly did become linked to high-level elite conflict. Moerdani and his supporters offered crucial protection to Fraksi-ABRI members against moves to discipline them.[12] ABRI commander Try Sutrisno publicly reprimanded the ABRI legislators when they first demanded *keterbukaan*, but according to Colonel Roekmini, he did this at Suharto's behest and was privately supportive. In 1989 and 1990 Moerdani, army chief of staff General Edi Sudradjat, and other senior officers also spoke publicly on the need to adopt a more open leadership style, abandon "feudal" attitudes, and protect the weak in society (Vatikiotis 1993, 88; Robison 1993, 52–3). By doing so, they made *keterbukaan* official policy of the ABRI leadership.

Suharto's Response: Endorsement of Openness and Rapprochement with Islam

The president responded in two ways to these moves from ABRI. First, he made veiled threats. In September 1989 he said he would "clobber" anyone who attempted to challenge him unconstitutionally, a warning many believed was directed at Moerdani. Second, he attempted to control the openness debate by endorsing it. In his independence day speech in August 1989, Suharto made what Minister for the State Secretariat Moerdiono described as the president's "reply" to public discussions about openness and succession (*Editor*, August 26, 1989, 25). He stressed that Pancasila was an "open ideology" and raised the possibility of a review of the electoral system. His confidante, Admiral Sudomo, announced a loosening of controls on the press (Bertrand 1996, 326). In his 1990 independence day speech, Suharto went further, saying that differences of opinion were to be welcomed as a dynamic force in social life. He also emphasized that ABRI's role in society should be *tut wuri handayani* (leading from behind), which many observers interpreted as implying weakening ABRI's political role (Honna 1999, 90).

The most important response made by President Suharto and his supporters to the increased criticism in ABRI, however, was a series of initiatives aimed at winning Islamic support. This resulted in a dramatic change in relations between the state and the Islamic community, the magnitude—and effects on opposition—of which can hardly be understated.

During the 1970s and 1980s, when officers like Ali Moertopo and Benny Moerdani had dominated, the military had played up the threat from the Islamic "extreme right." The authorities arrested clerics and activists they accused of aiming to establish an Islamic state. As with the targeting of the left, there was considerable spillover of repression against all manner of Islamic activists. Suppression had begun as early as 1967, when Suharto vetoed the resurrection of Masyumi and its leaders, after which the military clumsily but effectively intervened in its successor organization, Parmusi. It reached a new peak when military intelligence manipulated a Komando Jihad terrorist scare before the 1977 election. Security forces monitored sermons at mosques and harassed and arrested outspoken preachers. The final blow came in the early 1980s, when Islamic societal organizations were obliged to accept Pancasila as their "sole base" (*asas tunggal*). This provocative move led to a new bout of tension which peaked with a riot and a massacre by the military in Jakarta's Tanjung Priok port district in September 1984.

Moves against political Islam from the late 1960s were in part simply an element of the wider emasculation of civilian politics. After the elimination of the PKI, Islamic organizations had the greatest potential to challenge the military because they retained an organized mass base, strong institutions, and a resilient counterideology. However, Islam's political marginalization also derived from the cultural gulf that separated the Islamic community, or *umat*, from the new ruling elite. Most senior military officers in the early New Order were suspicious of political Islam. They usually had non-*santri* origins, some being Christians (like Benny Moerdani), while most had Javanese syncretist backgrounds (such as Ali Moertopo or Suharto himself). Some of the civilians in the regime, meanwhile, feared Islamic aspirations and supported the military because they saw it as the only realistic alternative to Islamic dominance. This was especially the case for the Catholic intellectuals associated with Ali Moertopo's Opsus (Special Operations) group, and the think tank he sponsored, the Centre for Strategic and International Studies (CSIS).[13] Much of the bitterest Islamic resentment arose from the cultural gap between the leaders of the *umat* and the new ruling elite and centered on government social policies which those leaders interpreted as attempts to legitimate secular and Javanist norms (such as the proposed introduction of uniform marriage and divorce laws in 1973).[14]

Developing a deep sense of grievance, the Muslim activists, affected by the politics of exclusion, spoke of the military's "Islam-phobia." Former Masyumi leader Mohammad Natsir famously charged in 1972 that the regime treated Muslims like "cats with ringworm" (Hassan 1980, 125; McVey 1983, 199). With such deep resentment among Muslim activists, many observers in the late 1970s and early 1980s believed that political Islam constituted the most significant threat to the regime. There was much evidence to support this view, such as a vigorous PPP election campaign in 1977, a 1978 walkout from the MPR by PPP legislators (over official recognition for syncretist Javanese beliefs), even the social protest *dakwah* (proselytizing) music of singers like Rhoma Irama. Many Islamic activists angrily rejected adoption of Pancasila as "sole basis," and some groups (like HMI) split over the issue. In the early 1980s there was also growth of small militant cells, even sporadic bombing campaigns (although military agents provocateurs may have played some role in these).

For all this, political Islam never had the pariah status of the left. The government preferred to split the Islamic community, fostering purely "religious" activities and accommodationist leaders on the one hand, while suppressing Islamist political aspirations on the other. The state provided significant support to the propagation of Islamic piety, including by funding a massive mosque construction program (Hefner 2000, 79–85, 120–21).

As a result, even the most determined conspirational groups were unable to organize on a sustained basis. Political Islam was most characterized, not by revolutionary politics, but by semiopposition. This was certainly the case with Muhammadiyah and Nahdlatul Ulama (NU), the chief vehicles of modernist and traditionalist Islam respectively, both of which claimed in excess of 20 million followers by the mid-1990s. While maintaining relative independence in the selection of their leaders, they came to a semioppositional accommodation with the government. Particularly outspoken leaders sometimes criticized policies they considered damaging to their constituencies. Overall, however, they accepted the legitimacy of the regime and, in exchange for de facto or explicit endorsement of it, received official toleration as well as financial support for educational activities, *pesantren* development programs, and the like.

At the end of the 1980s, there was a qualitative shift in the government's approach toward the Islamic community, marked by a string of new concessions in social and cultural policy. From 1989, there was new recognition of Islamic courts, provision for religious education in state schools, and tolerance for the wearing of the *jilbab*, head scarf, in schools. In late 1990, the government banned the magazine *Monitor* and jailed its editor when he published an article that many Muslims considered insulting to the prophet Muhammad. Suharto made a well-publicized hajj pilgrimage in 1990, and he and his family adopted a publicly more pious image. Other initiatives included the establishment of a Muslim bank, government sponsorship for Islamic arts festivals, lessening of harassment of Muslim preachers, and the promotion of *santri* officers to senior posts in ABRI. Taken together, these moves constituted a partial Islamization of the public face of the regime.

The centerpiece of the new accommodation was the establishment of ICMI in late 1990. Suharto opened ICMI's founding conference and ordered his trusted lieutenant Habibie to become its chairperson. With such powerful endorsement, ICMI grew rapidly, claiming forty-two thousand members by the mid-1990s (Liddle 1996a, 64). It attracted members of the Islamic middle class, especially state employees (over the preceding two decades many Muslims, such as alumni of the main modernist student organization HMI, had been recruited into the bureaucracy and gradually transformed its social composition from within) and businesspeople linked to the state. In this respect it differed from Masyumi, which was based more on independent entrepreneurs. Like the older organization, however, ICMI attracted urban, educated, modernist Muslims, including many with Muhammadiyah and HMI affiliations. For them, ICMI represented a significant breakthrough, a means to gain access to decision making in the state, and advance the political, economic, and social interests of the Islamic community after decades of exclusion.

The new policy partly represented an attempt by Suharto to cultivate a new support base at a time when he was concerned about his declining support in ABRI. In this sense, ICMI represented an outgrowth of conflict within the regime, and it has been portrayed as such by several scholars (see Crouch 1994; Liddle 1992, 62; Schwarz 1994, 38). But it was also a response to changing sociopolitical realities. As the regime aged and society became more complex, it was apparent that new bases of societal support had to be incorporated into the regime to shore up its legitimacy. The growing urban (mostly modernist) Muslim middle class was a natural candidate for co-optation, not only because it was large, but also because its members had clear interests in continued political stability and growth (for a discussion of ICMI from this perspective, see Hefner 1993). In this sense, the formation of ICMI was the most visible sign hitherto of the New Order's civilianization.

The formation of ICMI substantially transformed the nature of political opposition. Many modernist Islamic regime critics reassessed their positions and joined ICMI (see Chapter 3). Partial neutralization of many kinds of Islamic opposition followed. For example, PPP became increasingly listless. Unlike the secular nationalist PDI, it largely failed to invigorate itself under *keterbukaan*. (For example, in the 1992 elections it publicly reendorsed Suharto's reelection before even Golkar did so.) The large student organization HMI showed similar lethargy (see Chapter 5), and even the Petition of Fifty dissident group was affected (see Chapter 3).

Of course, this process should not be exaggerated. Regime leaders still sometimes warned of threats from the Islamic "extreme right," and Islamic opposition remained substantial. Indeed the new policy did not amount to an overall rapprochement with "Islam," but rather with its modernist wing. NU leader Abdurrahman Wahid was a vocal critic of the government's new use of Islamic appeals (see Chapter 3). Even some modernist leaders remained skeptical, while the role of activists won over to ICMI was far from clear-cut. As we shall see, many of them brought their own political agendas to the organization.

Nevertheless, there was a clear shift in the place of Islam for both regime and opposition. In the 1970s, minority and secular fears of Islam had been used to construct a constituency for authoritarian rule. Those who favored a more prominent role for Islam in the political order became a major engine of opposition, sometimes dragging liberals and nationalists in their wake. From the early 1990s, as we shall see in later chapters, the situation was largely reversed and some opposition to the government was driven by suspicion of Islamic political and social claims. The government concurrently used Islamic appeals to bolster support and undercut opposition. The policy switch involved, and its ramifications, were profound. But one basic element remained: the use of the Islamic-secular divide (and the divide between traditionalist and modernist Muslims) to split opposition.

The new policy exacerbated tension in the ruling elite. It especially alienated Moerdani's supporters in ABRI, who considered that vigilance against political Islam was central to security policy. As Douglas Ramage (1995, 138–44) has illustrated, many ABRI officers and other secular nationalists in the regime feared that ICMI signaled a turn toward "sectarianism" and "exclusivism," which threatened the essentially secular compromise embodied in Pancasila. Such ideological concerns were inevitably intertwined with more traditional competition for position. ICMI functioned partly as a new center of politico-bureaucratic power within the government, essentially as a tool for Habibie and his clientele, and through them, the president. This became clear in 1993 when individuals associated with ICMI secured many positions in the MPR, cabinet, and Golkar. Lower down, in the regional bureaucracy, Golkar, or on campuses, it also became advantageous for ambitious Muslims to be ICMI members. Inevitably, all this generated resentment among secular-oriented officials who were pushed aside.

The Spread of Openness: 1989–1994

The preceding survey suggests that *keterbukaan* was not purely a product of elite conflict, although such conflict encouraged groups in the ruling elite to promote it. As Bertrand (1996, 322) argues, societal pressure was still too weak to "force" the regime to open. However, liberalization was at least partly a response to early signs of societal discontent (why loosen controls in the absence of a potentially receptive societal audience whose sympathies it would be advantageous to win?).[15] This became even more obvious during the early 1990s, when a kind of limited bidding war for public opinion developed. Discontented ABRI officers continued to endorse (limited) liberalization and adopted a soft posture toward some political discontent. The president and his camp continued to reach out to the Islamic community and promote their own reforms. Societal agency also became more important; opponents of the government responded to signs of elite conflict and official talk of openness by testing the boundaries of tolerance. This resulted in a "cycle of mobilization" similar to that experienced by many authoritarian regimes when they experience internal conflict or begin to liberalize (O'Donnell and Schmitter 1986, 26–28).

One of the earliest signs of the new climate was a more vocal press. While the electronic media (the main news source for the majority of the population) remained tightly controlled, from 1989 many major national newspapers and magazines published increasingly lively coverage of controversial issues. Some turning points stand out, like the break in the embargo on reports about the Petition of Fifty dissident group from mid-1991, or the bold *Jakarta-Jakarta* coverage of the 1991 Santa Cruz massacre in East Timor. But overall, the process was slow and tentative. In part it flowed from a noticeable decline in state intervention; in part it involved editors and journalists publishing articles on controversial topics, waiting for a response, and, if there was none, pushing further. A driving force was the hunger of middle-class readers for provocative news, indicated by the rapid expansion of courageous journals like *DëTik*, which burst from nowhere to achieve circulation of almost a hundred thousand by August 1993.

Students and farmers began to hold demonstrations against government policies in 1988–89. Some government officials indicated their disapproval, but most such actions were not violently suppressed. The attendant publicity created a ripple effect, and mass protest rapidly resumed its historic status as a common form of Indonesian political expression. Overall, there was a high level of mass mobilization in the New Order's final decade. Muslim groups organized some large protests over the *Monitor* magazine blasphemy case in 1990, the Gulf War in 1991, and a state lottery in 1991 and 1993. Mass action was also the preferred tactic among lower-class groups, with escalating protests by disenfranchised landholders from 1989, the wave of industrial strikes from 1990, and various other protests (such as huge demonstrations by public transport workers in August 1992 against increased penalties in new traffic laws [*Progres* 1 (3) 1993, 40–45]). Eventually, the mood of defiance spread to historically compliant bodies, such as the PDI, located inside the formal political system.

The twinned themes of *hak asasi manusia* (human rights) and *demokratisasi* became the public themes par excellence of the *keterbukaan* period. Their new prominence partly flowed from a focus by human rights activists and journalists on gross violations, such as killings of civilians by troops in Lampung (1989), Dili (December 1991), and Nipah (1993). There was also growing focus on civil and political rights, partly in response to government promises of greater tolerance. When expectant societal actors established organizations, mobilized supporters, and expressed their views, the state often reacted in a hostile manner. Campaigns for civil and political rights were thus typically reactive or defensive in character; for example, from 1989 there was great press and NGO attention to bannings of political meetings and theatrical productions.

From the early to mid-1990s, the question of wider-ranging democratization of politics moved to the center of the public agenda. A lot of retired generals, intellectuals, legislators, and other elite actors promoted cautious and specific reforms which aimed at reinvigorating the legislative, executive, and judicial branches of government (see Chapter 4). Student groups and some NGOs began to advocate democratization more aggressively.

All this had a cumulative impact on government discourse. Through the early 1990s, senior officials frequently endorsed greater "openness," "communication," and a reduction in the "security approach," although usually in a very abstract way. The government also began to grant concessions. For example, for the first time tribunals investigated certain cases of gross abuses, such as the 1991 Dili massacre, and punished (albeit lightly) some of the soldiers involved. However, there were few substantive reforms. No repressive laws were repealed. Each small step toward liberalization was accompanied by continuing grassroots repression; every official endorsement of reform was balanced by an arrest, a banning, or a trial. There were new attempts to control NGOs and renewed emphasis on reactionary "integralist" ideology, which negated the conceptual boundary between state and society (Bourchier 1997). In sum, the new atmosphere of toleration was entirely contingent and arbitrary, and *keterbukaan* never entailed full liberalization, merely movement in that direction (Uhlin 1993, 519; 1997, 157–59).

The Retreat from Openness:
June 1994 to Early 1996

Conflict within the regime peaked in 1993. The first marker of this was an audacious military fait accompli on the vice presidency. Three weeks before the March MPR session, the ABRI chief of staff for social and political affairs, Lieutenant General Harsudiono Hartas, a Moerdani associate, announced that ABRI commander general Try Sutrisno was the military's candidate for the vice presidency. It was widely suspected that Suharto favored either Sudharmono or Habibie for the post. This was the first time that ABRI had promoted a candidate without first consulting Suharto. Many civilian critics eagerly noted this sign of how deep discord in the governing ranks had become.

Suharto also saw Try's elevation as a sign that he was vulnerable. Since dismissing Moerdani as ABRI commander in 1988, the president had acted where he could to sideline the general's camp followers. From 1992, he had intervened to remove Fraksi-ABRI members who had initiated *keterbukaan*. He also blocked the renomination of Golkar candidates who had supported them. After Try's nomination, Suharto moved quickly to shore up his base. Hartas himself, for example, was moved to the National Advisory Board, a prestigious but powerless body. When Suharto announced his new cabinet in March 1993, only a few ministers had senior military backgrounds, notably Edi Sudradjat, who replaced Moerdani as defense and security minister. Edi, who was concurrently ABRI commander, replacing Try Sutrisno, was a secular nationalist army officer with an impeccable infantry pedigree and long-standing links with Moerdani. He represented those officers who were uneasy about both the president and ICMI. However, he was more or less a lone voice in the new cabinet, which included more Suharto loyalists and associates of Habibie.

In the approach to the Golkar congress in October 1993, Edi Sudradjat openly stated that the organization's next leader should come from the "big ABRI family." Presumably partly as a result, Suharto sacked Edi as

ABRI commander, after only three months in the position. His replacement, Feisal Tanjung, dutifully insisted that the military had no candidate for the Golkar leadership. At the congress, the president's nominee, Information Minister Harmoko, was smoothly appointed to replace Wahono as general chairperson. Other Golkar leaders seen as sympathetic to military interests were also sidelined. The new board contained two of Suharto's own children and several individuals linked to Habibie and ICMI.

These changes reconsolidated Suharto's control over key levers of power, but they also deepened resentment in the military and political elite. After the Golkar congress, there were clear signals of military disgruntlement. Edi's ally, chief of staff for social and political affairs Lieutenant General Hariyoto P. S., publicly stated that Golkar should reduce its dependence on Suharto (*Editor*, October 28, 1993, 21); soon after, he lost his post. In October, "vocal" ABRI legislator Major General Sembiring Meliala made an extraordinary public outburst, telling *DëTik* that Habibie and Harmoko had attained their positions only because Suharto sponsored them (shortly afterward he too lost his post): "If there was no Pak Harto . . . they wouldn't have any role would they? . . . In the map of political forces in the future, if Pak Harto wasn't around anymore, they also wouldn't be around anymore. . . . If Golkar is controlled by other people it would be better if we [ABRI] left it. It must be remembered that up to now, it's been ABRI which backs up Golkar, hasn't it? For example, if in the 1997 election we backed the PDI, the PDI would win" (*DëTik*, October 27–November 2, 1993, 12).

As conflict within the ruling elite continued, Suharto made more concessions to public opinion. These included the release of Islamic political prisoners arrested after the Tanjung Priok massacre and subsequent bombings a decade earlier and an attempt to win over the Petition of Fifty group (see Chapter 3). The most significant reform was the formation in June 1993 of a National Human Rights Commission.

Against this backdrop, 1993 marked the height of "openness." After the March MPR session, major newspapers and, especially, weeklies like *DëTik* and *Editor* pushed the bounds of independent journalism to hitherto unimaginable limits, with detailed coverage of conflict within the government and other controversial issues. Opposition activity also accelerated, with more student protest and Megawati Soekarnoputri dramatically attaining the PDI leadership. Later chapters address the exact relationship between such phenomena and conflict inside the regime. For the present, it is enough to note that the accumulating pressures for change from outside the system now demanded a response from the government, either in the form of unambiguous reform or a return to repression. From mid-1994 it became apparent that Suharto was opting for the second course. He was assisted in doing so by his success in reimposing control over the upper levels of the regime, especially ABRI.

In early 1993, it had briefly appeared that Edi Sudradjat might take Moerdani's place as the de facto leader of disgruntled officers. He certainly promoted many of his followers during his three-month tenure as ABRI commander. However, after he was stripped of this post, he lacked the resources to organize a factional base. Moreover, Edi's sudden replacement was only the most dramatic incident in a broad and accelerating change in the ABRI leadership that through 1993–94 saw many important "discontented" ABRI officers being moved from senior posts.

By mid-1994, a new breed of younger officers without links to Moerdani and his group moved into the key command positions. Many were former adjutants of, or otherwise closely associated with, the president (*Indonesia* 1994, 84). Some, including ABRI commander Feisal Tanjung, the new chief of staff for social and political affairs, Hartono, and head of the ABRI Information Center, Syarwan Hamid, were quickly labeled by the press as "green," or Islamic, officers. Certainly, Hartono was a devout Madurese Muslim, although there were claims that Feisal Tanjung's devoutness was a recent phenomenon (Liddle 1996b, 629n13). These officers harbored their own resentments against Moerdani and his camp, believing that they been locked out of promotions. Whether because of their pious *santri* family backgrounds or for reasons of factional advantage, they were willing to sympathize publicly with Habibie and with ICMI's aim of promoting the interests of the Islamic community. The president's son-in-law Prabowo Subianto was in a class of his own. He had attained a reputation for ruthlessness in counterinsurgency postings in East Timor and Aceh and, in November 1995, was appointed chief of the Kopassus Special Forces, becoming the youngest officer to attain the rank of major general. Prabowo, the son of former trade minister (and Socialist Party leader) Soemitro Djojohadikoesoemo, according to Marcus Mietzner (1999, 230 n14), "lacked a credible Muslim background." Even so, from the mid-1990s he began quietly to cultivate links with fringe Islamist groups.

The rise of these new officers made Suharto more confident of ABRI loyalty and thus set the scene for greater repression. It also made it increasingly difficult to talk of a political elite divided between "palace" and "military" camps, because the military itself was now split. By early 1994 the Indonesian press openly speculated about division between "ABRI *merah putih*" (red and white—the colors of the Indonesian flag— secular nationalist officers) and "ABRI *ijo royo-royo*" (green, or Islamic, officers). To further complicate matters, some of the up-and-coming younger "red and white" officers, like the president's former adjutant, Wiranto, were very loyal to Suharto even while they viewed some of the "green" officers as their rivals. At the same time, there was also mounting discontent in Golkar and among secular ministers disturbed by the rise of Habibie and his supporters (see Chapter 3).

The event which most marked the return to repression was the banning of three news magazines, *DëTik*, *Editor*, and *Tempo*, on June 21, 1994. These had been among the most enthusiastic supporters of the new press openness. *DëTik*, a cheap tabloid, had achieved spectacular sales by its pioneering investigative reporting, while *Tempo* had long been Indonesia's most respected newsweekly.[16]

After the bannings, the return to coercion accelerated. The security forces arrested and tried several prominent dissidents, such as outspoken former PPP legislator Sri Bintang Pamungkas, who was charged in 1995 for allegedly insulting the president in a speech he had made to Indonesian students in Germany. The military response to street protests became increasingly unpredictable; some protests were still tolerated but many others were violently dispersed (although lethal force remained rare). There was more harassment of prodemocracy activists, including leaders of previously mostly inviolate organizations like LBH (the Legal Aid Institute). Street toughs (*preman*) were increasingly used to terrorize opponents. There was also a return to bellicose language, including emphasis on the danger of resurgent communism. This reached an early crescendo in late 1995, when a campaign initiated by the president alleged that the PKI was behind almost all opposition to the government through *organisasi tanpa bentuk* (organizations without form; Honna 1999, 96–103).

However, repression never became entirely unconstrained or indiscriminate, nor did the atmosphere of openness entirely dissipate. Instead, coercion was focused on the most overt challenges and aimed to limit societal mobilization and criticism rather than smash it entirely (which, by now, would have required great repression). Indeed, military and government officials sometimes argued that repression was a necessary adjunct to openness, a means to ensure that reform did not give rise to "excesses" or "radicalization," which would threaten the controlled and gradual democratization they claimed was under way. There was still acknowledgment of the importance of human rights, as well as some symbolic reform gestures (e.g., in 1995 ABRI representation in the legislature was reduced from one hundred to seventy-five seats).

The Limits of Coercion

Coercion thus masked an important shift in regime discourse. From the mid-1990s, regime leaders routinely acknowledged that *demokratisasi* was unavoidable. Even at times of great repression, and often coexisting uneasily with continued statements about the "finality" of Pancasila democracy, government and military leaders regularly insisted that democratization was proceeding, albeit slowly, in pace with economic development and in keeping with Indonesia's national character and ideology. In the words of ABRI Commander Feisal Tanjung in late 1997, greater transparency and democracy were not something that could be "bargained over" anymore (*Kompas*, September 2, 1997). Such admissions, even if designed primarily to disarm government critics, represented a significant change from a decade earlier, when senior ABRI officers' repertoire when speaking of democracy had been limited to endless reiterations that Indonesia already practiced its own unique form of "Pancasila democracy." In short, societal forces had already succeeded in winning a major battle of political ideas with the regime. There was a faltering of confidence within the regime, and some of its leaders now conceded that political reform was inevitable, even if they took no steps to bring it about.

Increased repression was also no longer able to contain opposition entirely, nor force Indonesian politics back to its pre-*keterbukaan* mold. Instead, coercion and threats sometimes galvanized resistance. This was evident from the time of the 1994 press bannings. In the past, moves against the press had mostly been met with fearful acquiescence. This time, there were large and angry demonstrations in many cities. Previously cautious intellectuals, artists, and others condemned the banning. An activist coalition formed to oppose it, uniting the broadest range of nonformal opposition yet to coalesce against a government policy (Heryanto 1996, 245–53). The government's campaign against alleged communist "organizations without form" similarly failed to effectively intimidate those it targeted. In the 1970s, even the allegation of communist links was a devastating means of enforcing silence. Now, many intellectuals regarded the accusations with open derision, and those accused defended themselves in the press and even threatened to sue (*Jakarta Post*, October 18, 1995).[17]

The emphasis on conflict within the ruling political elite in this chapter has thus not been intended to depict opposition groups as passive onlookers in the *keterbukaan* process. Instead, they played an active role in pushing forward liberalization. We are now in a position to look in more detail at how they did this.

3

Regime Friction and Elite Dissidence

We accept, we will not become an opposition and will not become an institution.
. . . It seems that the government sees a tiger but what really exists is a pussycat.
The attitude towards a cat should not be the same as that towards a tiger. Because
we are just a cat, well, there's no problem.

Abdurrahman Wahid, referring to Forum Demokrasi
(*Suara Merdeka*, April 10, 1991).

During the 1970s, regime spokespeople began to speak disparagingly
about the *barisan sakit hati* (ranks of the resentful). They used this term
to denigrate many prominent Indonesians who were beginning to criticize
the government, especially those who had supported the New Order in its
early years. Such people included former student activists and intellectuals disillusioned by the resurgence of corruption, leaders of the anticommunist political parties pushed aside since the late 1960s, and even some
military and civilian officials who had held high office in the government's early years but who had clashed with Suharto and his inner circle.
By calling them a *barisan sakit hati*, regime leaders tried to suggest that
such critics were not motivated by desire to serve the public good, but
rather by personal frustration.

The *barisan sakit hati* label was unfair, but it does draw attention to
the thin line that separated the government from some of its staunchest
critics. During the 1970s, many people who had been closely associated
with the regime in its early years had to come to terms with political mar-

ginalization. Over time, many individuals who found no place in the new system, or were disillusioned by what they saw, eventually made their peace with the regime or faded into political obscurity. Among those who continued to criticize the government, the characteristic style of opposition was dissidence. As noted in Chapter 1, dissidence is a form of opposition marked by a moral tone and a petitionary style, and it is common in regimes which proscribe more organized forms of opposition and mobilization.

Dissidents in Suharto's New Order tended to call for a return to the regime's own foundational ideals and for the "proper" implementation of its ideology. As former supporters of the New Order, their criticisms often had a backward-looking, even nostalgic tone, and they relied on moral suasion, appealing to the power holders to change their ways. They preferred lengthy petitions and memoranda to demonstrations or underground methods. In turn, even when they condemned the regime, dissidents were rarely hunted down by the security forces, although they might be harried and harassed.

This chapter provides studies of three dissident groups in the New Order's final decade. The first, the "Petition of Fifty," was Indonesia's best-known such group. It was formed in 1980 when a group of fifty prominent retired generals, politicians, and others put their names to a letter criticizing President Suharto. By this time, the group's signatories were already mostly isolated from the levers of power. Using their moral authority to make public criticisms of the government was one of the few political options remaining open to them. Forum Demokrasi (Democracy Forum) and Yayasan Kerukunan Persaudaraan Kebangsaan (Foundation for National Harmony and Brotherhood, or YKPK), in contrast, were both formed in the looser political conditions of the 1990s. Forum Demokrasi was made up mostly of intellectuals and NGO and religious leaders who had never held high political office, while YKPK resembled the Petition of Fifty insofar as it included retired military officers and Golkar politicians.

The Petition of Fifty arose as a by-product of Suharto's consolidation of power and the narrowing of representation within his regime during the 1970s. By the time Forum Demokrasi and YKPK were established, political conditions were very different. In the early 1990s, disunity within the regime again became an important political factor. The line between dissident activity outside the state and factionalism within it once more became blurred. Put crudely, dissidents who favored a negotiated path to reform were faced with a choice between the apparently reformist bloc within ABRI or the Islamic reformers of ICMI, behind whom stood

Minister Habibie and Suharto himself. The renewal of regime conflict had a great impact on the politics of dissidence, eventually driving a wedge into the Petition of Fifty group and influencing in fundamental ways the two new groups established in the 1990s. This chapter thus looks not only at the pattern of dissident opposition activity itself, but also at the emergence of reform tendencies, however stunted, *within* the regime.

Elite Discussion of Reform During *Keterbukaan*

From the late 1980s, many ideas that a decade earlier had made the signatories of the Petition of Fifty objects of the regime's ire became common topics of public debate. Themes such as greater communication between government and society, toleration of political differences, and presidential succession were promoted publicly and regularly, not only by marginal groups but also by individuals with close or ambiguous relationships with the government. Retired generals, Golkar and ABRI legislators, intellectuals acting from institutions formally part of the state apparatus (like LIPI, the Indonesian Institute of Sciences) or close to it (like CSIS, the Centre for Strategic and International Studies), and—from the mid-1990s—cabinet ministers all spoke out on the need for change.

Many such people advocated change in the government's tone or style rather than proposing detailed institutional reforms. For example, from 1990 CSIS intellectuals produced publications calling for a reformulation of Pancasila ideology to allow for greater openness. They argued that existing constitutional arrangements were sufficient but that the party system and legislature should be invigorated and strengthened (see, e.g., Silalahi 1990, 1991). (CSIS was Lieutenant General Moertopo's old think tank and had in earlier years done much to formulate a justification for authoritarian rule; its leaders had moved closer to Benny Moerdani from the late 1970s.) General Soemitro reverted to his role as military reformer from pre-Malari days. From retirement he wrote voluminously in the media promoting greater press freedom, presidential succession, reduced appointments to the legislature and MPR, the end of "floating mass" policies, and other reforms.

The reform proposals made by Soemitro and figures like him tended to share two features. First was a *fin de régime* tone of praising the New Order for past achievements while arguing that it was now necessary to adapt to changing social, economic, and global realities. Researcher Mochtar Pabottingi, in a 1995 LIPI publication entitled "Reexamining the New Order Political Format," argued that reform was necessary in order to adapt to social changes. He evoked the image of the bridge across a deep ravine in Kafka's "The Bridge" to make his point:

We are all now on top of the New Order bridge. From its beginning in 1966 to the fiftieth anniversary of our republic [1995] we could still feel an intensity of passion, almost ecstasy, in viewing the horizon and broad possibilities before us. It cannot be denied, that this regime has indeed recorded great achievements. However, on the other hand—especially in the last ten years—we have also felt our bridge beginning to wobble. There are signs that both sides of the ravine, the resting place of both ends of the New Order bridge, are beginning to crumble— the side that supported us in the past, and the side where we have hung our hopes for the future. (Pabottingi 1995, xi)

This tone of trepidation about the future viability of the political system was due not simply to the age of the New Order, but more particularly to that of its helmsman. Suharto's dominance in the New Order, plus the lack of preparation for succession, contributed to an uneasy mixture of anxiety about potential unrest and hope for political reform when many people looked to the future.

Second, precisely because change was considered necessary to safeguard stability and other New Order achievements, mainstream proponents of reform argued that it should be carefully planned and managed. General Soemitro, for example, was insistent on this point:

Change and reform should be implemented in an *orderly* manner, on the basis of clear concepts, and in stages. We do not desire drastic changes, because each change tends to bring with it instability, vacuum, confusion and even chaos. . . . The Indonesian nation does not wish to experience a situation like that in the Philippines, we do not wish there to be victims like there were in the Tiananmen incident, and we also do not want a vacuum and confusion like there is in Eastern Europe and Russia. (Soemitro 1992b, 170–71)[1]

Despite their guarded tone, the frequency with which such suggestions arose in public discussion during *keterbukaan* underlined the collapsing political certainties of the time and the regime's faltering legitimacy. They also dovetailed with signs of tensions within the government itself. These tensions gave new hope to reformers. Indeed, while many proposals for reform were presented as disinterested calls for change, unrelated to considerations of realpolitik, others reflected greater awareness of the practicalities of reform. Even General Soemitro, for example, argued that his proposals were aimed at convincing Suharto himself that changes were needed. His "only hope" was that Suharto would see the need to step down and hand over to an anointed successor before a political crisis occurred.[2]

In the early 1990s, other reform proposals became linked even more closely to factional politics. This was because the state now contained two important focal points for moderate reformist hopes: ABRI and ICMI.

Military Factionalism and Support for Reform

As noted in the preceding chapter, an important political development in the late 1980s and early 1990s was the beginning of public advocacy of reform from within the armed forces. It is crucial to put this development in its proper perspective. Officers who were most deeply disillusioned with the president and most likely to speak out on the need for a new political approach had previously been committed to authoritarian rule and military dominance. No one personified this better than Moerdani himself, who had elevated the role of the intelligence apparatus, overseen the military's brutal invasion of East Timor, and was held personally responsible by many of the regime's critics for some of its more barbarous acts, such as the Tanjung Priok killings of 1984. Other outspoken "red and white" officers, including the most vocal members of the Fraksi-ABRI, to say nothing of more senior commanders like defense and security minister (1993–98) General Edi Sudradjat, were also officers of the old school who deeply believed that ABRI's role in the 1945–49 national revolution imparted to it a rightful, even "sacred" role in political affairs.

Identifying anything approaching a common position on political reform within ABRI was thus impossible, and not only because Suharto prevented the consolidation of a faction opposed to him. Disillusionment in ABRI was largely driven by causes not related to the question of political reform per se. Instead, disillusionment was motivated by factors like the perceived marginalization of ABRI, tensions surrounding presidential succession, and hostility toward Sudharmono, Habibie, ICMI, and the "politicization" of Islam. Even Moerdani supporters and other "red and white" officers who were most discontented with Suharto (and it should be stressed that not all red and white officers *were* critical of Suharto) were never interested in developing a comprehensive reform vision. Instead, the crux was always struggle for position within the regime.[3]

As a result, most antipalace officers were caught in a contradictory political logic. On the one hand, they aimed to ensure a continued political role for the military. On the other hand, their political marginalization made them look critically on the regime. Most such officers expressed their primary concern as being the decline of ABRI's political weight, its transformation into a "tool" of government. In the words of the most radically reformist officer of the 1988–92 DPR, Roekmini Koesoemo Astoeti,

ABRI is no longer dominant; it is no longer even involved in decision making. It is only Suharto who makes the decisions. ABRI is simply the implementer of what the government decides. And yet, the politics of ABRI should be the politics of the state, not the politics of the government. If not, then ABRI will be just like the armed forces in other countries. ABRI should be able to correct the government. Now it can do nothing, and ABRI recognizes it is no more than the fire brigade. We hope that ABRI can be more independent in the future. (interview, November 29, 1995)

Other military officers (albeit mostly recently retired ones) interviewed for this study had similar views. They frequently said that the erosion of ABRI's leadership role meant *dwifungsi* was "losing its true meaning." Such language partly expressed the frustration produced by political marginalization. At least at the philosophical level, however, it also reflected a quintessentially militarist outlook: these officers were concerned by the military's supposed subjugation by the government (i.e., Suharto) and wanted to defend its independent role. The officers most active against the palace and ICMI were thus often doctrinally inflexible. Even vocal ABRI legislators frequently condemned "liberalism" and opposition and defended ABRI's sociopolitical role. There was thus no simple division between military "soft-liners" and palace "hard-liners." In many respects, the officers most alienated from Suharto retained highly authoritarian views.

However, because discontented officers found themselves (and, as they saw it, the military as an institution) in an increasingly marginal position, they had both the opportunity and motive to look at the regime with a more critical gaze. This even applied to some of those who had been most implicated in the regime's repressive policies. As Michael Vatikiotis (1993, 144) suggests, "Moerdani's ejection from the Suharto inner circle apparently convinced him of the need to encourage political openness and look for new leaders." Like-minded officers noted the growing mood of restlessness in society and that ABRI was often blamed for harsh policies for which, as a mere "fire brigade," they believed it was not truly responsible. Believing that the long-term legitimacy of the New Order and ABRI's political role were endangered, they concluded that adjustments were necessary. As they retired, or were sidelined, their views hardened, and they began to seek civilian allies.

Although it is not possible to point to an open and comprehensive ABRI reform position during *keterbukaan*, it is feasible to describe several key ideas about reform which circulated among discontented officers.[4] Above all, in part because of sensitivity to Suharto's increasingly sultanistic rule, such officers hoped for a government which was cleaner and more efficient but which remained authoritative and able to maintain political stability and economic growth. Rather than concentrating on the institutional reforms that might be needed to bring this about, and similar to military dissidents in many countries (including coup plotters in democracies), they talked in terms of a more "moral" regime and purer application of regime doctrine. As Major General Sembiring Meliala put it, "We agreed that the appropriate Pancasila political system existed, but it needed better implementation" (interview, November 16, 1996). Many dreamed of a semiauthoritarian system like Singapore's, where strong government and probity purportedly existed, without thorough political deregulation.

To the extent that discontented officers (especially those in the DPR) agreed that a change in governmental approach was needed, they focused on greater "openness," involving more press freedom and the like. There was also talk of stronger "control" mechanisms, especially that the DPR should be a more assertive watchdog which could curb abuses by the executive. This was what Fraksi-ABRI members attempted to achieve from 1989. Even retired officers (except, notably, those linked to the Petition of Fifty) rarely took such arguments to their logical end by advocating deregulation of the party system. However, some officers floated various reforms that fell short of this, such as reducing intervention in the parties, delinking Golkar from the bureaucracy or allowing PDI and PPP representation in cabinet.[5] Similarly, there was widespread recognition of the need to limit (future) presidential powers by measures like limiting the number of terms served by a single incumbent.

Even the most ardent military supporters of reform usually insisted that ABRI's sociopolitical role was inviolate. But they often said that changes in "implementation" were necessary, that the "security approach" should make way for a "communicative approach," and that ABRI should be truly neutral ("above all groups") in settling political conflicts. Only a tiny minority of serving officers contemplated more decisive withdrawal from politics.

A final caveat is necessary. As we know, as *keterbukaan* ended, many command positions passed to officers who Suharto felt were more loyal, including a group of allegedly "green" officers like Feisal Tanjung, Hartono, Syarwan Hamid, and Prabowo. Whatever their personal piety, this group viewed ICMI and related Muslim groups as potential allies in the struggle against Moerdani and his supporters. They were also affected by pressure for political reform, assuming control precisely as the inevitability of democratization became a common theme in national po-

litical discourse. Many of them publicly acknowledged the need for reform. Taking their cue from the president, they said that ABRI should
deepen its *tut wuri handayani* (leading from behind) approach, by which
they meant ABRI should maintain a political role, though not always in
a prominent manner. On the role of civilians in government, they often
adopted a softer line than those associated with the old Moerdani group,
even if this was principally because it accorded with presidential wishes
(as when Feisal Tanjung agreed to the appointment of Information Minister Harmoko as Golkar leader in 1993). Because Feisal, Hartono, and
other "green" officers were willing to cooperate with Habibie and ICMI,
many ICMI activists argued that they were in fact the "real ABRI democrats."

However, because such officers owed primary loyalty to the president,
in practice they tended to adopt reactionary attitudes toward political opposition, especially when it seemed directed against the president or the
government's reconciliation with Islam. They thus became chief architects
of the retreat from *keterbukaan* policies in the mid-1990s.

ICMI and the Revival of "Reform from Within"

In ABRI, support for reform was linked to growing political marginalization. Movement in ICMI was in the opposite direction. Suharto sponsored the organization to attract wider support in the face of deteriorating relations with ABRI. ICMI's vigor thus largely resulted from the entry
into it of political actors previously excluded from official politics who
now adopted a "work-from-within" strategy.

Other writers have described in detail the foundation of ICMI, noting
that the organization was based on a coalition of diverse forces (Hefner
1993; Ramage 1995, 90–101; Schwarz 1999, 173–93; Anwar 1993,
1995). Its strength was largely derived from President Suharto's backing,
with Habibie as his chief agent. Government bureaucrats with little apparent previous commitment to Islam or political reform dominated its
leadership. But ICMI also attracted some people who had previously
been outspoken critics of the government. These included intellectuals
such as Imaddudin and Ismail Sunny (both arrested in 1978), NGO activists like Dawam Rahardjo and Adi Sasono, and the prominent
Muhammadiyah leader Amien Rais. Beyond these were much wider circles of (mostly modernist) Islamic leaders and organizations who sympathized with ICMI and all it symbolized.

Islamic social and political activists who joined ICMI argued that they
were pursuing three main goals (see Ramage 1995, 90–101).[6] First was

simply greater respect for Islamic sensitivities and a more prominent role for Muslims within the New Order. They were impressed by government policies from the late 1980s that ceded ground to Islamic social and cultural claims. In the language of Indonesian neomodernism, they argued that ICMI assisted the goal of establishing an "Islamic society" (rather than an "Islamic state") and was an extension of the Islamic renewal which had been visible in society for over a decade. Some took these arguments further and argued that ICMI was a vehicle for the "Islamization" of the government and bureaucracy, a means to achieve "proportionality": representation of Muslims in positions of power proportionate to their share in the population of the country as a whole (i.e., approximately 90 percent). Sometimes this was linked, though rarely openly, to demands for *dekristenisasi* (dechristianization) of the government.

Second, some in ICMI saw the organization as a vehicle to promote neopopulist economic measures involving use of state resources to alleviate poverty and develop small-scale indigenous (Islamic) business. Individuals like Dawam Rahardjo, Adi Sasono, and Umar Juoro had spent years supporting such policies from within community development NGOs. After the formation of ICMI, their chief institutional stronghold was the Center for Information and Development Studies (CIDES), a research institution headed by Adi.

Third, for some, ICMI was a vehicle to promote political democratization. Some of the organization's supporters said it did this simply by overcoming hostility between the government and the Islamic majority. This was vital because if suspicion on one side and fear and resentment on the other continued, democratization would be impossible. The most reformist supporters of ICMI, only a small minority, went further and argued that democratization required "civilianization" of government because military dominance was the main block to democratic reform. Hence, enhancing the role of civilian structures (like ICMI) and promoting civilian leaders (like Habibie) was itself part of democratization. This attitude, of course, reflected the historical enmity between much of the modernist Islamic community and the officer corps, at its worst when officers like Moertopo and Moerdani in the 1970s and 1980s had inflated the Islamic threat to legitimate a continued military role. Antimilitary sentiment was mixed with a sense of historical grievance and desire to punish those officers and their followers (such as in the Catholic-dominated CSIS) considered responsible for past misdeeds.

Reformers attracted to ICMI pursued a typical "work-from-within" strategy. As constitutional expert and former critic of the Suharto regime Ismail Sunny put it, "Don't be an opposition just for the sake of being an opposition. If we can bring about change from the inside, what's wrong with that? The New Order government has heard and taken account of the Islamic *umat*" (*Tempo*, October 3, 1992, 30). The goal was to win important positions in government structures, from where ICMI activists hoped to wield power and achieve their aims.

However, as argued by Adam Schwarz (1994, 176; see also Liddle 1996b, 625), Suharto had "been careful to structure ICMI in a way that constrains the inclinations of its more radical members." Reformist ICMI members were outnumbered in the organization's leadership by bureaucrats and other "New Order Muslims." Working from within also necessitated abandoning frontal criticism. The neomodernist intellectual Nurcholish Madjid, a participant in ICMI (albeit one eventually disillusioned by the experience), argued that those who entered ICMI were required to compromise to achieve a "secure area for freedom [of] action." If they made direct demands for democratization, "from that moment ICMI would lose many things, and would not be able to do much. It could be completely finished" (*Forum Keadilan*, April 8, 1996, 97–98).

Because ICMI depended on backing from Habibie and, ultimately, Suharto, ICMI "radicals" felt obliged to support both of them, especially initially. Before the 1993 MPR session, ICMI activists such as Dawam Rahardjo and Amien Rais championed Habibie's vice presidential candidacy and endorsed Suharto's reelection. To explain what they described as a *"figur tetap, policy berubah"* (same person, change of policy) strategy, they made great play of Suharto's "change of heart" toward Islam (*DëTik*, March 3, 1993, 9; Ramage 1995, 106). Ultimately, such people justified support for the Habibie-Suharto camp as more than mere tactics. Because their aims included "Islamization," ICMI radicals were enthusiastic participants in factional conflicts aimed at removing those they considered unsympathetic to the interests of the *umat*. These included Moerdani and his cohorts and the Christian technocratic ministers Johannes Sumarlin, Radius Prawiro, and Adrianus Mooy, whom ICMI activists blamed for economic policies which benefited Chinese conglomerates and marginalized Muslims. Participation in ICMI's struggle to gain a foothold within government thus became self-justifying, subsuming separate social and political aims.

As factional alignments within the regime changed, ICMI reformers also readjusted their attitudes toward ABRI. This was especially apparent after Feisal Tanjung became ABRI commander in 1993 and Syarwan Hamid, Hartono, and other ICMI sympathizers followed him into senior positions. Talk of "demilitarization" among ICMI supporters gave way to discussion of the need to foster healthy relations between the military and the Islamic community.[7] Such officers also sought support within ICMI ranks; for example, Syarwan Hamid worked closely with CIDES,

often using it as an informal think tank, while Hartono and Prabowo recruited intellectuals (notably Din Syamsuddin and Amir Santoso) from a
different group in ICMI to their own Center for Policy and Development
Studies.

The dilemma, of course, was that the compromises ICMI activists
made often discredited them in the eyes of other activists and the broader
public. Many people viewed ICMI as little more than a doorway into the
halls of power for ambitious Islamic leaders; a common joke was that
ICMI stood for Ikatan Calon Menteri Islam (Association of Islamic Ministerial Candidates). It is important, however, to stress the ambiguous
character of co-optation, which might not only broaden a regime's support base but also result in institutions being used for purposes at odds
with those intended for them by the regime's core leaders. As CIDES operator and former HMI leader, Eggi Sudjana (interview, November 29,
1995), put it, "We know that there is an attempt to co-opt us. But you
can only be co-opted if you are not aware [of the attempted co-optation].
We are aware, and we try to use that co-optation."

Under Suharto, ICMI reformers succeeded only in establishing themselves on the regime's periphery. Some of them secured important posts in
ICMI itself, notably Adi Sasono, who became secretary general in 1995.
But they never won cabinet posts. Nevertheless, many used their new positions of influence to promote gradual democratization and other reforms. For example, CIDES tried to influence government policy in a
range of areas, employed critical academics and former student activists,
and published material on controversial topics like human rights. It invited outspoken government critics to its seminars, explicitly attempting
to play a brokerage role between government and opposition (e.g., *Republika*, November 22, 1995; November 28, 1995). Eventually, many
ICMI activists argued that the various reforms implemented by the government from the early 1990s vindicated or even resulted from the ICMI
strategy.[8]

If anything indicated the ambiguous character of co-optation it was
the signs from 1993 that some ICMI activists were reevaluating their support for Suharto at a time when the increasingly erratic and nepotistic
character of his rule was becoming obvious. In particular, Muhammadiyah leader Amien Rais campaigned unexpectedly and strongly on
the issue of presidential succession. In a December 1993 Muhammadiyah
meeting, he advanced six "criteria for succession" in 1998 (the next time
the MPR would meet), with a list that strongly pointed toward Habibie.
Although the delegates initially greeted the proposal with acclamation,
they eventually declined to endorse it, fearing the political consequences;
according to the organization's secretary, Ahmad Syafii Ma'arif, delegates

agreed to it "in their hearts" but worried that "local authorities who are only just now getting on well with Muhammadiyah, will become distant once more" (*DëTik*, December 22–28, 1993, 19). At a CIDES seminar in February 1994, Amien presented a paper entitled "Succession 1998: A Must," in which he highlighted problems which had been accumulating under the government, including "the cult of the individual," growth of corruption, and a "blunting of vision and creativity" in leadership. The "national leadership" (note the euphemism) was "exhausted," he argued, and "rotation" was needed for democratization, clean government, and social justice (Rais 1994).[9]

By this time, Amien was becoming an increasingly important figure. He was from an old Muhammadiyah family in Solo and had risen to national prominence in the organization as leader of a group of "modernizers," younger professionals and intellectuals who were pushing aside the conservative *ulama* who had led it since the beginning of the New Order. Amien, who lectured in international relations at Gajdah Mada University in Yogyakarta, was widely admired for his knowledge of Islam and his Arabic language skills. He was also American-educated (he wrote his Ph.D. at the University of Chicago on the topic of the Muslim Brotherhood in Egypt). He was respected in modernist Islamic circles for his skills as an able thinker, tactician, and speaker. His political science training apparently also helped him to clinically identify the political problems which were accumulating in the early 1990s (certainly many of his public statements about the problems the nation would experience if the succession issue was not addressed look prescient in retrospect). On the other hand, Amien's critics in secular nationalist, traditionalist Muslim, and Christian circles feared his narrowness and accused him of anti-Chinese and anti-Christian "sectarianism."[10]

In following years, Amien continued to promote presidential succession and Habibie's prospects. He also became head of the 28-million-strong Muhammadiyah in 1994, when its previous leader died. However, Muhammadiyah was an entrenched institution, which according to Amien ran forty institutions of higher learning, dozens of hospitals, hundreds of clinics, and approximately seventeen thousand schools (*Forum Keadilan*, August 4, 1994, 83). As he became openly critical of the government from the mid-1990s, Amien was thus often pressured by provincial and district leaders of the organization, who feared that his attitude would endanger funding and other relations with the government at the local level.[11] He also faced the threat of being displaced by leadership rivals who openly made a play for government backing by attacking him for being too critical.[12] Although Amien defeated this threat when he was confirmed as Muhammadiyah leader at a congress in 1995 (a congress attended by President Suharto), he had to tread a careful line in later years. He continued to be outspoken on various controversial issues. But he also often stressed in public meetings and in a book he authored on the topic (Rais 1995) that Muhammadiyah's approach was one of "high politics" only; the organization would speak out in order to raise the level of ethics and morality in public life, but it was not interested in the "low politics" of gaining seats in the legislature, attaining executive office, or becoming a pressure group.

Elite Dissidence Par Excellence: The Petition of Fifty

By the time *keterbukaan* began in 1989, the Petition of Fifty group had been Indonesia's best-known dissident group for almost a decade. It came into being in May 1980 in response to two speeches made by Suharto. Fifty prominent individuals signed a petition criticizing the president's speeches in forthright terms. Among those who signed were two former prime ministers from the era of parliamentary democracy, seven former ministers or officials of ministerial rank, and ten senior retired ABRI officers representing all four services, including the "father of the army" and former Armed Forces commander general (retired) A. H. Nasution.[13]

Suharto was angered by this display of dissent. Immediately after the petition was presented to the legislature, intelligence chief Yoga Sugama announced that those who had added their names would be "isolated"; their work permits and business licenses would not be renewed, and credit lines to state banks would be cut off (Jenkins 1984, 169). Many of them were eventually forced from their jobs, and a ban on media coverage was imposed on them. Group members described this treatment as a form of "civil death."

During the early 1980s, partly as result of this ostracism, the group evolved into an archetypal dissident group. A Petition of Fifty "working group" gathered weekly at the opulent central Jakarta home of former Jakarta governor Ali Sadikin. At these meetings, group members discussed recent political developments and drafted letters spelling out detailed reform proposals. They then sent these to the DPR, ministers, or the president.

Among those who attended the weekly meetings in the 1980s were Sadikin himself; a former head of the national police, Hoegeng Imam Santoso; former prime minister and leader of Masyumi, Mohammad Natsir; a former minister of mines during the early New Order, Slamet Bratanata; the Catholic intellectual Chris Siner Key Timu; and A. M. Fatwa, a well-known Islamic preacher who had been harassed for his criticisms of the government since the mid-1970s. The heart of the group was a kind of alliance between senior retired military officers and former modernist Muslim politicians, mostly from Masyumi, along with various former PNI and Christian party leaders.

Despite their impressive credentials, as the 1980s drew to a close, members of the group remained political pariahs; some associated with it were in jail, and the government banned all its members from traveling overseas and maintained the media blackout on their activities. Senior government officials insisted that this would remain the case until those who had signed the Petition in May 1980 had recanted and apologized to the president. So it was a great surprise that, without such apologies being forthcoming, Petition of Fifty members made a dramatic return to public life in mid-1993. For several weeks almost every major national newspaper and magazine featured cover stories about the group and its members' views and activities. This change came about in a way that reveals much about the dynamics of dissidence in the late New Order and its interaction with factionalism within the regime.

The Petition of Fifty came together as a response to the narrowing of the political spectrum represented in the New Order government during its first decade. Government and military leaders accused Petition of Fifty supporters of exhibiting "post-power syndrome." By this they meant they were people who, having once enjoyed the fruits of office, now criticized the government only because they had lost power. Sarwono Kusumaatmadja, then secretary of the Golkar group in the legislature, made this accusation in 1979 when referring to lobbying activities by some of those who later signed the petition (*Kompas*, July 29, 1979, cited in Effendi 1989, 204–5):

They think that it is enough just to hold discussions, seminar discussions, use the newspapers, and then hope that change will take place. Whereas the reality is, if they really hope for change, they also have to play the game (*ikut main*). However, unfortunately, not a single one of them has genuinely made a real political move. . . . They are disappointing, only limited to mobilizing public opinion. Yes . . . that's good, but it clearly will not be effective. Because they have lost one of the main resources necessary to carry out reform, they no longer possess power. . . . Well, it's only after retiring that they have started to wake up and have regrets, and then talk about democracy.

There was some justice in such criticisms. Certainly, many of the retired officers associated with the Petition of Fifty had been important players in Indonesia's slide toward authoritarian rule from the mid-1950s. General A. H. Nasution was the most important army general in the first decade and a half of independence and had led the military's push for an extended political role. His "middle way" doctrine, although denying that the army strove for absolute dominance, legitimated this extension and later became the foundation for the *dwifungsi* doctrine. Retired army lieutenant general H. R. Dharsono (who did not sign the Petition of Fifty but was a regular participant in working group meetings during the 1980s) was one of the New Order's leading "radical" officers who from 1965, in David Jenkins's (1984, 33–34) phrase, "displayed an undisguised disgust for the existing political groupings and who supported immediate use of the army's power to force through rapid modernization." As territorial commander in West Java in 1969, he forced surviving political parties in the province to merge into two groups, an early and ambitious attempt at the sort of political restructuring which became official policy in the 1970s.

In reality, however, a complex mixture of personal and political frustrations accounted for the alienation that these retired officers and officials felt. Many of them had parted ways with Suharto over essentially political matters. General Nasution may have been a military hawk, but he was also an officer cast from a different mold than Suharto. He was a devout Muslim, had long maintained warm relations with modernist Islamic politicians, and disapproved of extensive corrupt activities by military officers. His personal enmity with Suharto dated back at least to 1959, when, as army chief he had transferred the then Colonel Suharto from his post as Central Java military commander, apparently for his involvement in a smuggling racket. After the September 30 affair, Nasution was deftly outmaneuvered by Suharto. Ali Sadikin was a Sukarno appointee as Jakarta governor and was admired by civilian critics of the government for his relatively open attitude (Budiman 1969). He was removed from office two months before his second term was due to expire in 1977, after "allowing" Golkar to suffer an electoral defeat in the capital to PPP. Hoegeng had been removed as national police chief after "tracking down an import racket that led to Madame Suharto" (Jenkins 1984, 292). Slamet Bratanata fell foul of Suharto and was dismissed as minister for mining in 1967 when he attempted to assert some degree of financial accountability over the state oil company Pertamina. Many of the former civilian officials associated with the Petition of Fifty had been prevented altogether from playing a significant political role even during the New Order's early years. Suharto personally vetoed the political rehabilitation of former Masyumi leaders like Mohammad Natsir in 1967–68, while PDI leaders like Manai Sophiaan (formerly of the PNI) and D. Walandouw (formerly of the Protestant party Parkindo) were forced out of the party leadership in the late 1970s.

The late 1970s was not a favorable time for criticism of Suharto or military dominance. In the aftermath of expressions of protest like the 1977–78 student movement and the PPP walkout from the 1978 MPR session, Suharto was rising to unquestioned dominance in the military. The regime was restricting space for societal criticism. The Petition of Fifty was itself a reaction to this political closure; it was triggered by two unscripted speeches Suharto made to army audiences in which he reacted to criticisms being made of his government (Jenkins 1984, 157–58; Sundhaussen 1981, 817–19). In the first speech, Suharto warned his audience of threats to Pancasila and the 1945 constitution, suggesting that prior to the birth of the New Order "our national ideology had been smothered [literally: drowned] by a range of ideologies, whether that be Marxism, Leninism, Communism, Socialism, Marhaenism, Nationalism, and Religion." Referring obviously to the PPP, he called for vigilance against "political parties which as well as Pancasila also add other foundations." He stressed, therefore, that ABRI needed to "always increase our vigilance and choose partners, friends who genuinely defend Pancasila and are not in the slightest degree hesitant about Pancasila." In his second speech, made before the army's special forces, Suharto attacked those who spread gossip that he had a famous movie star as a mistress and that his wife received commissions and determined the allocation of tenders. Such gossip, he said, was "only intended to undermine Pancasila and the 1945 Constitution by first getting rid of me," perhaps because those who propagated it viewed him as their "main political obstacle."

The "Statement of Concern," which later became known as the Petition of Fifty, expressed "the deepest possible disappointment of the people" with the two speeches. It outlined six points of concern, including that the speeches created a false impression of a "polarization" between those who strove to preserve Pancasila and those who sought to replace it; they misinterpreted Pancasila in order that it could be a "means to threaten political opponents," although "Pancasila was intended by the founders of the Republic of Indonesia as a means to unite the Nation"; they invited ABRI to take sides based on the "biased" evaluations of those in power; and they gave the impression that "there are those who consider themselves the personification of Pancasila so that every rumor about themselves is interpreted as [evidence of] anti-Pancasila attitudes."

Given their political backgrounds, it is little surprise that those who signed the petition objected to Suharto's use of Pancasila and military doctrine to attack his critics. People like A. H. Nasution had been Suharto's military and political equals or seniors and viewed him essentially as an upstart. They also believed that they better understood Pancasila and military ideology than did Suharto himself. Their repeated, almost plaintive refrain in the many papers they produced in later years was for the "pure and consistent implementation of Pancasila and the 1945 Constitution" and a return to the original "resolve" (*tekad*) of the New Order.[14] The retired officers associated with the group likewise justified calling for a reduction of the military's political role and its disengagement from Golkar in terms derived from standard military doctrine. Using language which was strikingly similar to that used a decade later by military critics of Suharto, they said that ABRI was becoming a "tool of the government" (or in other formulations, of President Suharto or Golkar).[15] As a historical product of the Indonesian revolution and people, the military had responsibilities and loyalties to the Pancasila and 1945 Constitution which transcended those to the government of the day. In an early and rather extreme formulation, Ali Sadikin argued that the military should be prepared to "clobber" any group that deviated from the basis of the state, including those in government: "as it carries out *dwifungsi*, ABRI should be owned by the whole people, including whoever is in government, whether that is PDI, PPP or Golkar, so long as they govern in accordance with the prevailing politics and rules of the state. 'But if they deviate, then ABRI has its *pentungan* [club, cudgel], doesn't it?'" (*Suara Karya*, October 12, 1979, cited in LKB 1980, 40)[16]

The retired officials associated with the group also consistently emphasized the need for moral regeneration among the authorities. As individuals who had supported or participated in the regime in its early days, they were reluctant to view it as flawed or misconceived from the beginning. Instead, they generally attempted to understand its shortcomings as the product of a process of degeneration, attributable in the first instance to the moral failings and culpability of those in power. Because they had had personal dealings with Suharto and other senior officials, it was also perhaps not surprising that many of them personalized their antipathy, blaming Suharto or other officials (most commonly Lieutenant General Ali Moertopo) for the New Order's sins.[17]

Their exclusion from political office and public life further reduced the signatories' sense of connection with the government and prompted them to look on it even more critically. In the 1980s, Petition of Fifty members thus moved beyond a sense of personal betrayal toward a more systemic explanation of the regime's faults. They concluded that it was the uncontrolled and unregulated character of state power under Suharto that allowed opportunities for corruption and abuse. Lord Acton's famous dictum, "power corrupts . . . absolute power corrupts absolutely," became a recurrent term in the group's statements, as did phrases like "abuse of power," "concentration of power," absence of "control," and the like. The solution they advocated, in addition to moral renewal, was the constraint of power by constitutional and legal order. From the large body of material the group produced (by 1987 collated into a 264-page book), a reasonably clear program of political reform emerged. As David Bourchier (1987, 10) notes, this centered on calls for "freedom of political organization, free elections, an end to unconstitutional bodies (e.g., Kopkamtib), oppressive laws (e.g., the 1963 Subversion Law), corruption, and monopolistic economic practices." By the late 1980s, most of the retired officers associated with the group also argued that the military's political rule should be dramatically wound back and that *dwifungsi* should be expressed, at most, by maintaining a small elected ABRI representation in the MPR. Even this, however, should dwindle away as the 1945 generation passed from the scene.[18]

The Petition of Fifty group was a classic dissident group. It carefully addressed all its appeals for change to the president, other senior officials, or state institutions. As they put it, they did not seek to overthrow the government but were merely providing state officials with "corrections and reminders" (*koreksi dan peringatan;* see, e.g., Sadikin 1986, 12). Although their statements were officially directed to the legislature and other state institutions, they also rapidly circulated through opposition circles. However, because of the continuing media blackout, their broader impact was limited. Only the group's modernist Islamic members retained a link to a readily identifiable mass base. It was no surprise, therefore, that the Petition of Fifty should be affected by the general repression of political Islam that marked the early 1980s. The catalyst was the 1984 killings of Muslim protestors in Tanjung Priok, which took place after residents accused low-ranking soldiers of desecrating a local mosque. After security forces arrested mosque officials, an angry crowd had marched on local police and military headquarters. Before they got there, they were confronted by troops, who shot dead a large number. The petition working group released a "white paper" questioning the official version and suggesting that the source of the unrest was the government's violation of the constitution.[19] The government responded harshly. Among the scores of activists subsequently arrested, three were associated with the petition: A. M. Fatwa, H. M. Sanusi, and Lieutenant General Dharsono, all of whom were sentenced to long prison terms for subversion. This blow deepened the mood of alienation in the group. Members became particularly bitter toward General Moerdani, who they viewed as being responsible for the killings and ensuing crackdown.

Within a few years the political climate in the country had changed. As *keterbukaan* gathered pace from mid-1989, Petition of Fifty members sought a wider airing for their views. True to form, they principally did this by petitioning those in authority, requesting that the restrictions they faced be relaxed, and proposing broader reforms. In 1990, for example, the working group advocated a "national political convention" to establish a framework for a negotiated transition to democratic rule. They stressed that presidential succession was crucial, also that political change should be gradual and constitutional and based on "respect for the institution of the presidency."[20] According to one group member, this was an "attempt to offer Suharto a peaceful way of stepping down" at a time when his own intentions remained unclear (interview, Chris Siner Key Timu, October 30, 1995). At the same time, the group courted the new mood of discontent in ABRI, praising the initiatives of the ABRI legislators, and encouraging ABRI to discuss mechanisms for succession with retired officers.

Although the government had successfully isolated the group, its members retained considerable moral authority and were widely respected in the broader public. In the looser political conditions of *keterbukaan*, any element in the ruling elite that could facilitate the group's reentry into national political life, or win its support, would gain obvious political kudos. An early breakthrough came when Fraksi-ABRI members invited Petition of Fifty members to a public hearing at the DPR in July 1991. Speaking in front of DPR members and journalists, group members had an unprecedented opportunity to recount their experiences and relate their views about political matters. Among the ABRI legislators, Sembiring Meliala told the press that "all of us in the ABRI fraction believe that they are still within the system," while Saiful Sulun called them "people who feel responsible about the life of their nation" (*Tempo*, July 13, 1991, 29, 30). These were remarkable expressions of sympathy by serving ABRI officers for Suharto's most famous public critics.[21]

Eventually, it was Minister Habibie who made the decisive move to reconcile the group with the government. At a chance meeting with him in early 1993, Ali Sadikin questioned Habibie about a management controversy at PT PAL, the state-owned shipbuilding enterprise he managed. Habibie responded by inviting Sadikin to inspect PT PAL's Surabaya plant, later gaining Suharto's approval for this plan. Eventually, on June 3, Habibie took Sadikin and other petition leaders (along with other retired officers like Soemitro) on a guided tour of the plant, during which they avoided political comment, instead praising the enterprise's achievements. This excited much media speculation that the group was preparing to be "embraced" (*dirangkul*) by the government. Some student groups and other critics of the government alleged a betrayal. At this point, senior ABRI officers, notably Commander Feisal Tanjung, apparently acting under Suharto's instructions, quickly ruled out political reconciliation. A month later, petition members accompanied Habibie to the state aeronautics plant in Bandung, where they tried to correct the impression that they had surrendered. Sadikin publicly questioned the punishment experienced by petition signatories, weeping as he contrasted A. H. Nasution's treatment with his record as founder of the army. An angry Suharto ordered Habibie to discontinue contact, and planned visits to other Habibie enterprises never eventuated.

Nevertheless, "reconciliation" continued more selectively. Within days of Sadikin's speech, the elderly and ailing retired ABRI officers associated with the petition—Nasution, Dharsono, and Hoegeng—were given medical treatment at state expense. The most senior military officers in the land, including Feisal Tanjung, paid them highly publicized bedside visits. In July, Suharto invited Nasution to meet him briefly at the presidential palace. By year's end, Nasution had become a frequent guest at important state ceremonies and had been awarded a "veteran's star." These meetings seemed primarily designed to respond to the accusations of inhumane treatment. Contact did not resume with more active—and healthy—petition leaders like Sadikin. Even so, the "reconciliation" was a major news story and marked an important advance in press openness. Media coverage of group members resumed, and there were frequent and lengthy interviews in news magazines like *DëTik* and *Tempo*. The overseas travel ban was ended, and Fatwa and Sanusi, who still had years of their post–Tanjung Priok prison terms to serve, were released.

For Petition of Fifty leaders like Sadikin, the political calculations underlying the "reconciliation" of mid-1993 were simple; they had not chosen marginalization and had always appealed to the authorities for dialog. Sadikin and the others thus struck a conciliatory tone when Habibie initiated contact. Although they refused to apologize to the president, they said that they bore no grudges and wanted to meet him, and they suggested a broader "national dialog." Ali Sadikin, when asked whether he still wanted to meet Suharto, replied, "On our side, we are ready. I've even ordered a couple of safari suits, because my older ones are a little small (laughs). I wish to respect him as a president. From my side, there is no feeling of vengeance. I just feel that what I've been doing for the past years was providing correction, which I view as a responsibility of a comrade in struggle" (*Editor*, June 12, 1993, 21).

The government's motives were less clear. Habibie no doubt partly hoped to boost his own prestige by effecting reconciliation with the government's most prominent critics and drawing them permanently into his orbit. Suharto, in his customary style, allowed Habibie to test the water but called a stop when he considered the process had gone too far. Above all, the episode must be viewed against the background of the shifting dynamics signaled by government sponsorship of ICMI. The Petition of Fifty was a product of the political conditions of the late 1970s and early

1980s, when the government identified Islam as a major security threat. In addition to the modernist Islamic leaders active in it, some of the retired officers associated with the group, notably A. H. Nasution, were unusually pious. Petition members also had a history of deep hostility toward General Moerdani.

From 1993, several Islamic leaders in the group publicly endorsed the changed climate in government-Islamic relations. The most enthusiastic was A. M. Fatwa. According to *Tempo* (July 24, 1993, 34–35), while still in jail he telegrammed Habibie to offer support for ICMI and to apply to join the organization. In numerous press interviews after his release he praised President Suharto's purported change of political and religious heart: "Even though I am criticized for it, I still give thanks that Pak Harto had a new awareness after he went on the *hajj*. . . . I was a critic of Pak Harto's policies in the late seventies and eighties. But I do not want to be imprisoned by my old opinions if someone has really changed. We should give thanks, after seeing that the old realities have really been changed" (*Tiras*, November 9, 1995, 52).

Less outspoken but more important was Anwar Haryono. After the death of Mohammad Natsir in 1993, he was the leader of the Dewan Dakwah Islamiyah Indonesia (Indonesian Council for Islamic Proselytizing) and the most prominent modernist Muslim in the Petition of Fifty. Dewan Dakwah was established in 1967 as a chief vehicle for social and religious activities by former adherents of Masyumi when it became clear that the government would not allow the party to reemerge. In its first twenty-five years, Dewan Dakwah developed a reputation for promoting an austere scripturalist version of modernism, entailing hostility to pluralist interpretations of Islam, as well as visceral hostility to "Christianization" (see Liddle 1996c; Hefner 1997, 2000, 106–13). From the early 1990s, this organization, which had been a political outcast during the 1970s and 1980s, reassessed its view of the government. Haryono met President Suharto several times in delegations of Islamic leaders and from 1993 frequently spoke in favor of ICMI and the government's new sympathetic attitude toward Islam (see *DëTik*, November 17–23, 1993, 22–23). In 1994, Dewan Dakwah explained its qualified support for the new dispensation thus:

Entering the 1990s, we see a change in the political weather [*cuaca politik*, to distinguish from a more fundamental change in *iklim*, climate], although it must be acknowledged that this change has so far affected only the weather and has not yet touched any wider area. The color green [i.e., the color of Islam] is becoming visible in the Indonesian political rainbow, although it is still faint. . . . In this change of weather, it is up to all parties, whether they want to play an active role, or simply be spectators. (*Media Dakwah*, April 1994, 31)

In subsequent years, the changed tenor of government-Islamic relations increasingly affected the Petition of Fifty group. Some prominent members, notably Sadikin, refused to compromise. Others were torn between their old loyalties and their determination to take advantage of the new political context. Haryono and Fatwa were especially reluctant to be associated publicly with the working group's most critical statements, and from early 1994 the group rarely issued statements signed by all members. As we shall see (in Chapter 7), a public split finally occurred.

Reform and Resistance to "Islamization": Forum Demokrasi

If the Petition of Fifty was partly neutralized as some of its members were swept into the Habibie-ICMI orbit, the government's courtship of modernist Islam also generated opposition. Forum Demokrasi was an example. Although, as we shall see, there were important differences between the two groups, there were also similarities. Forum Demokrasi was another coalition of individuals from Indonesia's elite who had widely differing *aliran* backgrounds, but most lacked links to a mass political base (the main exceptions in both groups were Islamic leaders). Both groups also confronted the same dilemma of wishing to promote political reform but lacking the mass followers, constitutional instruments, or strong links to politico-bureaucratic power necessary to bring reform about. They also faced the ever-present threat of repression. In both cases, the outcome was a form of dissidence: statements expressing deeply held moral convictions and desire for reform, but lacking a convincing political strategy.

Forum Demokrasi was launched in April 1991, a time of great political uncertainty. Openness had been proclaimed two years previously, but substantive political reform had not eventuated. Presidential succession remained a possibility at the MPR session two years later. In October 1990, the magazine *Monitor* placed the Prophet Muhammad as its readers' eleventh-most popular figure. Angered Muslims staged large demonstrations against the magazine around the country. Modernist leaders like Nurcholish Madjid and Amien Rais called for the magazine to be banned. Information Minister Harmoko obliged and, for good measure, *Monitor*'s editor was jailed for blasphemy. Shortly thereafter, ICMI was formed, attracting many of those who had been most vociferous against *Monitor*.

Those involved in Forum Demokrasi were younger than the mostly 1945-generation Petition of Fifty signatories and included few former officials. Whereas the older group was formed around a military-Masyumi core, Forum Demokrasi was essentially a gathering of Nahdlatul Ulama (NU) leaders, prominent liberal intellectuals, Catholics, and "post-PNI" nationalists. Prominent Catholics at the founding meeting included pastors Mangunwijaya and Frans Magnis Suseno. Liberal intellectuals and journalists included Rahman Tolleng, Arief Budiman, Marsillam Simanjuntak, Todung Mulya Lubis, Daniel Dhakidae, and Aswab Mahasin. Most of them had been student activists in 1965–66 or shortly thereafter, and all had belonged to the Jakarta liberal dissident milieu in the 1970s (according to Arief Budiman, the group's first meeting was like "a reunion, a piece of nostalgia" [*kangen-kangenan*; *Tempo*, April 13, 1993, 18]).[22] Some of them were closely associated with major NGOs (Lubis was a former director of the Legal Aid Institute, while Dhakidae and Mahasin had long associations with the prominent social research foundation LP3ES and its journal, *Prisma*). The group member most closely identified with the nationalist *aliran* was Bondan Gunawan, a 1970s leader of the Sukarnoist student organization the Indonesian National Student Movement (GMNI). Nahdlatul Ulama was above all represented by Abdurrahman Wahid, the organization's chairperson since 1984. As the leader of an organization claiming some 30 million members and a political player with many contacts in the ruling political elite, he was by far the most prominent Forum Demokrasi member, the one to whom the others looked for leadership.

The creation of Forum Demokrasi excited intense expectations in the press and critical middle-class circles. Many hoped that it might become a coordinating vehicle for a revitalized democratic movement. Its founding document (Forum Demokrasi 1991a) listed four aims which, while couched in general language, fanned such hopes. These aims were (1) "to broaden the participation of public opinion in efforts for the maturation of the nation through the democratization process"; (2) "to increase communication between groups of supporters of the democratization process"; (3) "to build links between a range of efforts in the struggle for democratization, such efforts being presently scattered and very small"; and (4) "to preserve the tradition of the struggle for democratization through all vehicles and publications." Initial plans were ambitious; large public meetings were scheduled, a permanent working group established, and a building hired for a secretariat. Forum Demokrasi "branches" were established in Semarang and Yogyakarta.

The reaction from senior government and military officials was hostile. Interior Minister Rudini (who was considered relatively "open") was typical: "The Forum consists of people with heterogeneous backgrounds. Some of them are even liberal, so if it is not controlled it could become an opposition institution, unknown to the institutions of Pancasila" (*Jawa Pos*, April 9, 1991).

Officials were especially concerned about the group's name, which was reminiscent of organizations that had recently led democratization movements in Eastern Europe. In an attempt to defuse the situation, Abdurrahman and others negotiated directly with senior officials. Soedibyo, the chief of the State Intelligence Coordinating Agency (Bakin), devised a list of "parameters"—including that the group would remain loosely organized, that it would not be "political" or act as an "opposition"— which Abdurrahman and the others accepted in order to prevent Forum Demokrasi's suppression. From the start, Abdurrahman's response was conciliatory, assuring the government that "there is no need to be frightened of us" and that Forum Demokrasi was not "any kind of pressure group" (*Tempo*, April 13, 1991, 20).

These concessions did not prevent further harassment. In early 1992, police twice closed down Forum Demokrasi functions, while senior officials continued to condemn the group. Following these initial blows, the group's vigor and cohesion began to diminish. Its public declarations became increasingly irregular. Eventually, it turned into a small, informal working group, consisting of a handful of dedicated members who met to discuss political developments. In short, it resembled the Petition of Fifty. Its public statements, however, tended to be more minimalist than those produced by the older group. Far from a detailed program for democratic reform, they merely described in general terms the absence of democracy and basic freedoms in the country, sometimes satirically exploring the gap between the ideals of "Pancasila democracy" and the reality. Abdurrahman's phrase *"demokrasi seolah-olah"* (as though democracy) was a recurring motif: "Our society is actually in an 'as though' atmosphere: as though the law is already strong, as though a democratic system already functions, as though the actions of the rulers are always constitutional, as though there is freedom and so on" (Forum Demokrasi 1991b, 3; see also Wahid 1992).

If the Petition of Fifty was greatly influenced by government hostility to political Islam at the time of its formation, Forum Demokrasi was partly a reaction to the government's conciliation of political Islam in the 1990s. In effect, the group became the major public critic of ICMI. The *Monitor* affair was the principal trigger for the group's formation, because it seemed to encapsulate its members' worst fears, combining militantly expressed intolerance, government appeasement of it, and suppression of free expression. Abdurrahman stated,

[Forum Demokrasi] arose from our concern at signs that the tendency to favor one's own group [*mementingkan golongan*] was increasing. At the same time, the spirit of togetherness [*kebersamaan*] and democracy is growing weaker. . . . Isn't [the *Monitor* affair] a case where sectarian feelings defeated the national spirit? People speak more about achieving the aims of their own group than the basic needs of the nation. Quite apart from everything else, this [the banning of *Monitor*] has killed off a vehicle of democracy. If this is allowed to go on, democracy will be trampled on in this country. (*Tempo*, April 13, 1991, 20)

Douglas Ramage (1995, 45–74) has written extensively on the views of Abdurrahman Wahid, especially his long-standing commitment to religious tolerance and the "living political compromise" embodied in Pancasila, whereby Indonesian Muslims accepted that they did not deserve preferential state treatment. Ramage notes that from the start Abdurrahman refused to join ICMI and was openly critical of it, partly because he saw it as manipulation of Islam by Suharto for political ends, mostly because he disagreed with its supporters who promoted "Islamization" of society and government. For him, "Islamization" meant elevating Muslims as a special class of citizen, threatening the consensus that protected minorities and national unity. At the same time, his critics alleged that his hostility toward ICMI was partly a continuation of long-standing competition between traditionalist and modernist Muslims and reflected Abdurrahman's resentment of the modernists' newfound access to political power and state resources. In any case, he certainly pulled few punches in his criticisms, in one interview implausibly comparing ICMI with the Nazis because some members insisted on 80 percent representation for Muslims in formal institutions (*Forum Keadilan*, April 1, 1993, 74). Liberals and nationalists in Forum Demokrasi shared similar views, but none of these individuals were able to articulate their concerns as forcefully as Abdurrahman. As a Muslim leader of unrivalled stature, he had the authority to criticize ICMI in a way that would have exposed others (especially non-Muslims) to accusations of "Islam-phobia."

Forum Demokrasi members' concerns about dangers to national unity from "sectarianism" and "primordialism" resonated with long-standing government security discourse, especially ABRI's preoccupation with threats posed by sentiments based on SARA (Suku, Agama, Ras dan Antar-Golongan, or ethnic, religious, racial, and group identities). Some statements by Forum Demokrasi members certainly echoed old middle-class fears of the mob; at the group's launch, for example, Aswab Mahasin, referring to the *Monitor* case, said the group believed democracy was not simply an "ideal" but also a "problematic," involving the questions of "majority versus minority," and of "politics of the masses, especially that which takes a 'mob' [English in original] form, or is violent" (*Tempo*, April 13, 1991, 19).

In contrast to regime discourse, however, Forum Demokrasi members argued that primordial sentiment could be combated only by democratic methods, indeed that "sectarianism . . . is a symptom which arises because of the lack of freedom and democracy" (Forum Demokrasi 1991b, 1). In a *Tempo* article (Lubis 1991), human rights lawyer and Forum Demokrasi member Todung Mulya Lubis argued that highlighting dangers of sectarianism did not tacitly endorse antidemocratic measures taken in the name of preventing SARA-based conflict. Top-down methods created "pseudo-social harmony, or, even worse, social uniformity," he wrote, while genuine harmony could be guaranteed only by promoting democracy, social diversity, and human rights.

Forum Demokrasi statements tended to elucidate general democratic principles rather than appeal for specific reforms. This was partly because they were addressed to society as much as to the state. Members harbored few illusions that they could pressure the state to reform, but they also wanted to encourage conditions for democratic governance within society, especially a culture of tolerance and civility involving respect for difference and minorities. Their perspective also reflected the gradualist approach adopted by many liberal reformers who became active as part of the 1966 generation, reached political maturity in the early New Order, and accommodated themselves to the slow pace of political change thereafter.

In Abdurrahman's case, the starting point is to remember that in the late 1970s it had appeared that NU was emerging as possibly the country's most serious "opposition" force, precisely at a time when the tenor of politics was becoming increasingly repressive. The organization was the target of government hostility, especially within PPP, where government operators cooperated with other party leaders to sideline NU politicians. When Abdurrahman took over the NU leadership in 1984, he sought to remedy this situation by accepting Pancasila as NU's "sole basis" and withdrawing the organization from PPP and the formal political arena (it will be remembered that the early 1980s was a time when a general "retreat into civil society" was visible in a range of groups). Abdurrahman argued that NU made these shifts to escape from the government suspicion and control it experienced while it remained in PPP. By doing so, NU could develop a "distinctive, independent voice" on development and politics (Ramage 1995, 56). He said that NU should focus on social and economic "catch-up" in NU rural communities by pursuing "community development"–style projects and more conventional business ventures, including the development of a national banking network (van Bruinessen 1991, 196). The new strategy resembled that pursued by many NGOs in its emphasis on long-term grassroots economic, cultural, and social change rather than political confrontation with the state. The similarity with NGO strategies was not coincidental; Abdurrahman had been involved in the social research institute LP3ES and its *pesantren* development program since the 1970s.

The most immediate effect of NU's reorientation was a climate of mutually beneficial accommodation with the government. The government reaped the rewards with a dramatic fall of PPP's vote in 1987 (from 27.8 percent to 16 percent). For NU, relations with the bureaucracy improved at the local level, often resulting in financial assistance for development programs in *pesantren* and other activities. Martin van Bruinessen notes that Abdurrahman campaigned for reelection at the 1989 NU congress by stressing his acceptability to the government. In the NU leader's view, "being oppositional was perhaps more heroic but it did not leave one the freedom to do the things that really matter" (van Bruinessen 1991, 193).

Abdurrahman was also well known to have close ties with ABRI leaders. He developed especially warm personal relations with Moerdani after the Tanjung Priok affair, when the two toured *pesantren* together, aiming to dampen military-Islamic hostility. Abdurrahman later said, "I did this in the interests of NU, so that nothing untoward should happen between NU and the military. My term was like the Gudang Garam [a tobacco company] slogan, 'strive for safety' [*Upayakan Selamat*], ha-ha-ha" (*Forum Keadilan*, April 1, 1993, 76). As Greg Fealy (1994, 90) argues, such attitudes toward the state held by NU leaders must be viewed within the context of Sunni doctrines, especially those associated with the Syafi'i school, which stress "caution, moderation, and flexibility" and enjoin against rebellion against even despotic rulers. These produced a strong tendency toward accommodationism and quietism. Abdurrahman told his biographer that this relationship with Moerdani was one of mutual convenience and that he was "sickened" by Moerdani's "willingness to use violent means" (Barton 2002, 391). Even so, once Moerdani's star began to wane, Abdurrahman continued to defend him publicly. He privately described Moerdani as a man with a lively intellect (the two shared a love for the espionage novels of writers like John Le Carré) who had transformed himself from a narrow military man obsessed with security and stability into a man of wider interests and vision (interview, November 6, 1995).

Although none had a record to match that of Abdurrahman, other Forum Demokrasi members, many of whom had press and NGO backgrounds, were also well schooled in the nonconfrontational methods that had characterized middle-class dissent since the 1970s. Some had cooperated extensively with the military during the 1965–66 campaign against Sukarno, or subsequently. Even if they had been profoundly disappointed with the outcome, they had learned valuable lessons in the politics of strategic and tactical alliances. With this background in mind, it is striking that Forum Demokrasi adopted positions that in some respects dovetailed with those of discontented military elements. First was hostility to President Suharto. Some Forum Demokrasi members openly (but more often privately) argued that achieving democratization required first aiming at the removal of Suharto. There were few open statements of this position, except by the intellectual Marsillam Simanjuntak: "We're saying, Democracy is good, we need freedom to organize. I say that's wrong! I say we must elect a new president. Although it will be difficult, that is where we must begin, so that freedom to organize and democracy can become easier to achieve" (Simanjuntak 1991, 12, cited in Uhlin 1995, 143).

At its simplest, the core of this argument was a belief that Suharto's hold on the presidency represented the single greatest obstacle to democratization. This followed from the personalized and pervasive character of the president's power and his hostility toward reform. As Simanjuntak (1994, 306) put it, "The system has become dependent on a person, or better still, the system and the leader has blended into one body, a sight common only in absolutist regimes." A new president would necessarily be weaker and would have to make reforms to renew governmental legitimacy. It followed that accelerating presidential succession was a strategic priority.

Although Abdurrahman himself never made this argument so clearly, he publicly implied support for succession. In 1993, he resisted pressure for NU to endorse Suharto's reelection (Ramage 1995, 59–62). Forum Demokrasi itself released a statement before the 1992 general election that suggested that only elections which could bring about change, including the "possibility of a change in President," would be meaningful (Forum Demokrasi 1992, 4).

Antagonism toward the Habibie-ICMI group was a second potential point of common interest. This related not only to ICMI's alleged sectarianism (the theme emphasized in public criticisms), but also to tactical alignments, given that ICMI had become part of the president's support base. Abdurrahman publicly and energetically denigrated as an "empty myth" the ICMI reformers' line that democratization required "demilitarization" and "civilianization." He accused Petition of Fifty leaders considering "reconciliation" with Habibie of being captured by this myth (*Forum Keadilan*, July 8, 1993, 95), prompting an angry public exchange with Ali Sadikin and other Petition of Fifty leaders. For Abdurrahman, "the question is actually not only whether [a person] is a civilian or military, but which one will better improve democratic life." A civilian would not necessarily be better than a military officer, but might be "an opportunist who only serves one person" (*Kompas*, May 21, 1993). The attack on Habibie, his loyalty to Suharto, and his presidential ambitions was obvious; indeed, Abdurrahman publicly stated his preference for Try Sutrisno over Habibie as vice president during the 1993 MPR session.

Abdurrahman was also obsessed with the risks of a military backlash against critics, and against his own position. He argued that allying with ICMI and Habibie to promote demilitarization was a risky strategy because it might lead not only to "an undemocratic entrenched civilian bureaucracy" but also to "a cornered military" and hence "fascism" (interview, December 6, 1993). This was really the nub of the issue. For Abdurrahman, as for many others in Forum Demokrasi and broader middle-class opposition circles, successful democratization required military participation, or at least acquiescence. This was not only, or even most importantly, because of the priority placed on presidential succession, but simply because the military remained the country's most powerful political institution. Abdurrahman believed that the military and the Islamic community were the two decisive forces that would determine whether democracy or pluralism survived in Indonesia and that "democratization must be able to accommodate the needs of these two groups" (*Kompas*, September 16, 1991; see also *Tempo*, September 28, 1991, 39). He repeatedly said that dialog with the military was possible, telling a magazine in early 1993, "We are not up against the power of the military [in democratization]. It's not like that. I can easily talk with those generals about democracy. The only thing that the military is worried about is that excesses will occur. So we should sit down with them and discuss how to get rid of these excesses" (*Forum Keadilan*, April 1, 1993, 76).

All this does not necessarily imply that there was a conspirational alliance between Forum Demokrasi and military elements, even if some leftist groups made this accusation (Madjid 1991), as did some ICMI supporters. Forum Demokrasi members like Simanjuntak and Rahman Tolleng had participated as students in the 1965–66 New Order coalition and had been disillusioned by the results. They were well aware of the pitfalls of cooperating with the military. Abdurrahman himself argued that in order for the military to be "brought forward," democrats had first to make clear that they would not yield on principles. He believed that in a "marriage of convenience," however, the military might give strategic concessions (interview, December 6, 1993).[23]

Any possibility of a de facto alliance with the military, however, was prevented by the latter institution's continuing reactionary character. Even the officers most disillusioned with Suharto continued to view advocates of democratic reform with suspicion. Moerdani ally Lieutenant General Harsudiono Hartas, for example, bitterly attacked Forum

Demokrasi in 1992, warning that it contained "new left" and "new right" elements and would be permitted only if it did not aim to "change the existing system" (*Kompas*, April 25, 1992). Within a few months this very man was instrumental in promoting ABRI interests by securing Try Sutrisno's vice presidential nomination against Suharto's wishes.

Forum Demokrasi failed to develop partly because conflict within the ruling elite did not itself develop. While the reformist impulse, especially in ABRI, remained weak, Abdurrahman and other Forum Demokrasi leaders wanted to avoid the Petition of Fifty's fate. They confronted the perpetual dilemma of semiopponents and dissidents who wanted to develop a critical stance while keeping their positions of influence in societal organizations, academia, and the media. Above all, this was Abdurrahman Wahid's dilemma. As the leader of NU, he was both uniquely powerful and vulnerable, simultaneously the greatest strength and weakness of Forum Demokrasi. Although he was reluctant to risk direct confrontation with Suharto, in the early 1990s the president became convinced of a Moerdani-NU-Catholic-Nationalist conspiracy against him. As a result, Abdurrahman's position in NU became insecure. At the NU congress in 1994 he barely survived a massive campaign to unseat him, backed by pro-ICMI palace officers, including then chief of staff for social and political affairs Hartono (Fealy 1996).

Facing such pressures, it is not surprising that Abdurrahman did not wish Forum Demokrasi to risk confrontation. Some other group members (especially the non-Muslims) were perhaps even more cautious. The more outspoken intellectuals like Marsillam Simanjuntak, who had initially hoped that Abdurrahman would become a rallying figure for broader prodemocratic forces, became increasingly disillusioned with his reticence. Yet their own options were limited because among them only Abdurrahman had the stature and mass support to emerge as an alternative national leader.

The Growing Ranks of the Barisan Sakit Hati: The YKPK

As noted in Chapter 2, after his 1993 reappointment, Suharto increasingly moved against those in the military and bureaucracy he viewed as potentially disloyal or threatening to the Habibie-ICMI group.

The disillusioned element inside ABRI remained most important, although by 1994 Suharto loyalists held most key commands. Many of the vocal officers of previous years had been, or were shortly to be, retired or moved aside. This often freed them to speak out more openly, but it also dramatically reduced their institutional strength. From about 1993 there were also growing signs of friction within the civilian bureaucracy and Golkar. A number of overlapping groups were threatened by the ICMI-Habibie ascendancy and were in varying degrees concerned about the slow pace of reform and Suharto's dominance. There were the Golkar "progressives" like Marzuki Darusman and Oka Mahendra who had risen to prominence during the 1980s. Many of them had participated in the *keterbukaan* push in the DPR from 1989 and subsequently lost their positions when Suharto intervened against them.[24] Others in Golkar and the bureaucracy were Christians, or from a looser network of individuals who had a history of personal or family ties to the PNI and its associated *ormas* (societal organizations), "represented" in the cabinet by the minister of transmigration and forest settlement, Siswono Yudohusodo.[25] Such groups in turn could draw on extrabureaucratic constituencies via links to the political parties, academia, media, student organizations, and such like. Add Abdurrahman Wahid's NU supporters and the kind of secular-oriented liberals attracted to Forum Demokrasi, and there was a potentially broad coalition opposed to ICMI and Habibie.

As in previous episodes of heightened elite discontent, many of those who emerged as spokespeople had *already* been pushed from leadership positions. However, a number of senior serving officials were sympathetic to anti-ICMI views. They included cabinet ministers Edi Sudradjat, Siswono Yudohusodo, and Sarwono Kusumaatmadja, as well as DPR Speaker and former Golkar head Wahono. These individuals became increasingly outspoken from about 1993, although they expressed their concerns in elliptical language, mostly speaking to the press about the danger of *disintegrasi bangsa* (national disintegration) posed by unnamed threats of "primordialism" and "sectarianism." This was in part code for criticism of ICMI.[26] Eventually, they spoke out on topics like the rich-poor gap, corruption, government bias in favor of conglomerates, and the need for greater communication between government and society. In a typical statement in late 1995 (*Suara Pembaruan*, November 7, 1995), Siswono said that absence of "channels for the representation of societal aspirations" was leading to "political blockages," social disorder, political hatred, and violence. He urged the country to continue moving toward democratization and to discard old, inflexible concepts.

In 1993, discussions began in middle-ranking Golkar and bureaucratic circles about forming an organization to counter ICMI. Various ideas were canvased; the initial model was an organization for "intellectuals" (like ICMI) but open to all religious denominations. Eventually those involved in these discussions sought supportive patrons. Ministers Sarwono Kusumaatmadja, Siswono Yudohusodo, and Edi Sudradjat were approached and found to be sympathetic. The plans were first hinted at publicly when Sudradjat called for the formation of an organization for intellectuals based on "*kebangsaan*" (nationalism) at a Yogyakarta seminar in March 1994.

The first public attempt to establish such an organization occurred in May 1994, when General (retired) Alamsjah Ratu Perwiranegara, a 1960s confidant of Suharto, flagged the formation of an Association of Nationalist Intellectuals (ICKI). However, he stepped back in the face of Suharto's disapproval. Shortly afterward, former members of the formerly PNI-affiliated student organization GMNI established a "Communication Forum" (FKA-GMNI). This was an attempt to tap the large number of GMNI alumni who since the 1960s had pursued successful business, bureaucratic, and political careers. It also aimed to rival the influential KAHMI, the association of alumni of the modernist Islamic student organization HMI, whose ranks included important officials like finance minister Mar'ie Muhammad and which constituted the organizational backbone of ICMI. About one thousand people attended the launch of FKA-GMNI, with keynote addresses from Edi Sudradjat and Siswono Yudohusodo. Siswono became the first cabinet minister to attack ICMI publicly when, to the applause of the crowd, he stated that although the "concepts" behind ICMI were positive, "as it has developed it has become too involved in politics" (*Forum Keadilan*, June 9, 1994, 93). He told the press that he had received Suharto's blessing for the formation of FKA-GMNI. The directness of his attack on ICMI suggests that he was confident of presidential backing for this too. Confidential sources at the time suggested that at least Siswono and Sarwono had approached Suharto around this time and that he had given them the impression that he shared their concerns about "radicals" inside ICMI. Some of their supporters spoke about the "pendulum" of presidential approval swinging back in their favor.[27] Suharto's proclivity for playing his subordinates against each other by sending conflicting signals was well known. The important point is that many of those who challenged ICMI were not necessarily opposed to, or willing to risk confronting, the president.

In this atmosphere, a number of new organizations were formed in late 1995.[28] The most important for our purposes was YKPK, which was launched on October 23, 1995. Its sixty-eight members included prominent national figures from such a wide range of political backgrounds that it was dubbed a *kelompok pelangi* (rainbow group). Prominent retired military figures associated with it included Lieutenant General Bambang Triantoro (chief of social and political affairs under Moerdani, 1985–87), Lieutenant General Kharis Suhud (MPR and DPR Speaker during the *keterbukaan* initiative, 1988–93), and Major General Samsuddin (the former ABRI legislator who had been central to launching *keterbukaan*). There were also several NU leaders close to Abdurrahman Wahid, such as Matori Abdul Djalil (PPP secretary general, 1989–94) and Abdurrahman's younger brother Hasyim Wahid. Golkar members, most of whom were close to Wahono, included twelve current DPR members and vocal members of the 1988–93 DPR like Marzuki Darusman and Oka Mahendra. Also involved were several prominent Catholics and Protestants, most of whom had Golkar or PDI backgrounds, other prominent PDI leaders, and several GMNI alumni linked to Forum Demokrasi figure Bondan Gunawan.

YKPK was formed after a long process of negotiation that had included Golkar and former Fraksi-ABRI legislators, as well as Forum Demokrasi members (although it was eventually decided that Forum people would not become members). Forum Demokrasi participants insisted that the new group should not seek presidential "blessing" (*restu*). Eventually, senior retired military officers from the anti-ICMI camp, including former chief of staff for social and political affairs Hariyoto P. S., defense and security minister Edi Sudradjat and Speaker of the DPR and MPR Wahono were consulted.

YKPK's spokespeople claimed for their group a wide-ranging brief to promote national unity, prosperity, equality, and democracy. The main emphasis was the by now familiar discourse about dangers to national unity; (unnamed) groups were putting their own interests before those of the nation, undermining "national spirit," and risking national disintegration. The group's founders made standard disavowals of political aims, denied that they intended to oppose ICMI, and stressed that they would only hold seminars and promote discussion about the nation's future. Some of the group's leaders, especially Triantoro, remained deeply conservative; others, like Matori Abdul Djalil, were more outspoken in favor of democratic reform.

The senior officials who had been most outspoken on the issue of "national disintegration," notably Wahono, Edi, Siswono, and Sarwono, immediately endorsed the organization. Edi said it was a "good idea," which had "long been awaited by the broader community"; Siswono praised its aims as being "very noble" (*Tiras*, November 2, 1995, 25; *Kompas*, October 26, 1995). Suharto, however, made his disapproval clear when he told reporters that the new organizations would have to be "evaluated" in accordance with laws that "regulate the freedom of association" (*Kompas*, November 2, 1995).

YKPK, and the government officials who quietly endorsed it, represented a broad coalition that included long-standing advocates of reform from outside ruling circles and individuals from deep within official politics, some of whom had previously evinced minimal support for reform. Its formation marked the first occasion since the 1970s that such a coalition had been distilled in a formal organization. To be sure, the military officers and Golkar officials who joined YKPK had mostly already retired or been removed from their posts (or perhaps feared that this would shortly be their fate). In this respect, YKPK was similar to the Petition of Fifty; it was a collection of *already* marginalized officials, a fact made much of by media outlets sympathetic to ICMI and the palace. But the ABRI officers involved consulted closely with officers who remained senior in government, especially Minister Edi Sudradjat. The Golkar members may have already mostly been pushed out of Golkar leadership bodies, but they maintained some positions of influence, especially in the DPR (although they mostly lost these when the list of candidates for the 1997 election was announced in 1996). They also had links to cabinet ministers like Sarwono and Siswono.

The evolution of YKPK is instructive as to what may happen to groups in an authoritarian regime who lose out in factional competition. In this case, friction within the regime compelled members of the ruling elite to seek societal allies, putting them on the road to supporting political reform. Within weeks of the group's formation, YKPK leaders spoke out more forthrightly in favor of political change. Soon they were advocating "democratization" and "political restructuring," ABRI being "above all groups," clean implementation of the forthcoming general elections, and opposing "corruption and manipulation" (*Kompas*, January 6, 1996; January 10, 1996). Establishment critics of ICMI were undergoing a transformation reminiscent of that experienced in the mid-1970s by the officials who later signed the Petition of Fifty. As they saw their positions of power slip away, they first blamed immediate rivals (Ali Moertopo, Habibie) and then (albeit to varying degrees) Suharto himself. Eventually, they made common cause with civilian critics and advocated significant political reform.

However, YKPK did not signify an absolute break in the ruling elite. Its members and sympathizers were united above all by apprehension about ICMI and what it represented. Some of the ABRI retirees aligned with YKPK were still preoccupied with the competition for power in the regime and intended to use it to promote Try Sutrisno for the presidency in 1998. Many YKPK supporters, especially those who maintained senior positions, were also not prepared to abandon all hope in Suharto. Despite their outspokenness on various political issues in 1995–96, ministers Sarwono and Siswono were at the same time among the first cabinet members to endorse Suharto's reelection publicly (perhaps precisely because their positions were tenuous). While some YKPK members were resigned to an open break with the president, others hoped for a change of heart on his part. In the words of Midian Sirait, one of the Golkar veterans who joined YKPK, "If Suharto sees that the work of YKPK is effective, he might be influenced by it. This organization is partly an attempt to show Suharto that it is not only Islam and ICMI which have power and potential, but so do we. . . . At some time Suharto will probably need to find a new national consensus, and he will probably invite all forces, including us" (interview, Midian Sirait, November 28, 1995).

It is hard to avoid a conclusion that the New Order ruling elite had experienced a serious degeneration since the time of the Petition of Fifty. The individuals who signed the petition in 1980 had mostly been contemporaries or near-contemporaries of Suharto and had been prominent in national politics before 1965. They parted ways with Suharto very early on, as the shape of the New Order became clear. Their backgrounds gave them the moral and ideological conviction necessary to challenge the president openly. The former officials who joined YKPK, and the serving ones who endorsed it, had spent their political lives in the bureaucracy during the New Order's mature years. For most of their careers they had exhibited few misgivings about the regime and had been thoroughly ensconced in its patrimonial structures. They were also used to seeing Suharto as the master political player and ultimate source of political authority and found it difficult to imagine a different kind of politics. Many of them were unable to break with Suharto openly until the last days of his rule, let alone to develop a clear program for political reform.

To appreciate what the YKPK civilian reformers gained from such a group, it is necessary to recall the conviction among some Forum Demokrasi members that democratic change was contingent on Suharto's departure. Some involved in discussions prior to YKPK's formation saw its primary function in this light, as a means to prize open hairline cracks in the regime. In particular, they hoped it might push those in the ruling elite who were hostile to Habibie and having doubts about Suharto further along the road to an open break. Splitting the regime would itself hasten the process of its breakdown and open new spaces for societal initiative. Political leaders like Abdurrahman Wahid also believed that democratic reform would by necessity come about by a gradual and negotiated process. It was thus imperative to seek allies and potential negotiating partners in the ruling elite. As one NGO activist associated with the YKPK put it, the organization was a meeting place for elements from inside and outside the regime, an attempt to pursue regime change not from outside the state, but "on the line separating the state and society" (interview, Syarif Bastaman, November 7, 1995).

Beyond Elite Dissidence

Despite their very different backgrounds, the Petition of Fifty group, Forum Demokrasi, and YKPK fitted a dissident model in two crucial respects. First, they shared an alegal character; the government did not ban them but instead constrained them by harassing them and threatening them with more serious repression. Second, all three groups adopted a strategy essentially based on moral suasion. Their chief public activity consisted of releasing statements advocating reform, which they generally addressed to the regime's leaders (although Forum Demokrasi also directed its appeals to society).

For both the Petition of Fifty group and YKPK, dissidence was a product of marginalization within the ruling elite and an expression of frustration, even hopelessness, on the part of formerly influential leaders now isolated from institutional power. The establishment backgrounds of those involved inclined them toward conservative views; the former officials in YKPK especially so, given the gradual ossification of the New Order elite. Forum Demokrasi was quite different. Its initiators were non-state actors. However, they (especially Abdurrahman Wahid) retained important positions of influence in state-tolerated institutions, and this made them politically cautious. For both Forum Demokrasi and YKPK, attitudes toward political reform were also complicated by concerns generated by the rise of ICMI.

Dissidence is a common form of opposition in nondemocratic regimes. It frequently expresses a mood of political alienation shared by wide sections of the population. But it is often ineffective as a strategy. Michael Bernhard (1993, 312), for example, discussing dissidence in Eastern Europe in the 1970s, writes, "For dissidence as a strategy to have succeeded, ruling elites would have had to heed the suggestions of dissidents. . . . Ultimately, [dissidence] was reduced to the articulation of an agenda for change without any concrete program to implement it, except a hope that those in power would listen."

In the *keterbukaan* years, many radical younger activists derided groups like the Petition of Fifty, with their voluminous output of political statements, as being engaged in no more than a "*revolusi kertas*" (paper revolution). Some members of all three groups told the author that they had no illusions that their organizations could play a decisive role in initiating political change. They often believed, however, that it was morally incumbent upon them to speak out against the government, to put on the record their objections to its venality and authoritarianism. In the words of Ali Sadikin (interview, November 16, 1995), the main function of the

Petition of Fifty was to "say what is right is right and what is wrong is wrong."

In this respect, these groups did play a significant exemplary and symbolic role. Figures like Ali Sadikin and Abdurrahman Wahid were widely respected by the political public for their moral courage (witness how often they appeared on the covers of magazines and newspapers; editors clearly believed that they helped sell their publications). The relative press openness during *keterbukaan* allowed the transmission of their views to a large part of the population. In this way they contributed to the general strengthening of popular democratic sentiment.

Another characteristic of the three groups was their entanglement with regime conflict. During the *keterbukaan* years there was no clear dividing line between calls for reform from "inside" the state and dissent from the "outside." None of the three groups simply issued disinterested moral appeals for reform. They always had an eye on splits within the regime and the opportunities these offered. They believed that reform would be impossible in a unified state dominated by Suharto. Forum Demokrasi thus had at least implicit potential for a coalition with disgruntled army elements. There was also a reverse flow toward the regime, with ICMI attracting sympathy from many Muslim activists and leading to attempts to co-opt the Petition of Fifty. YKPK, in contrast, was essentially a product of the marginalization of ICMI's opponents.

These groups, especially Forum Demokrasi, failed to become rallying points for a broader democratic movement partly because fractures within the ruling elite did not deepen as rapidly as their supporters expected in the early 1990s. Suharto's reimposition of control, especially over the army, prevented any definitive break in favor of reform inside the regime. Dissident groups never found the bargaining partners or allies that they hoped for.

Proto-opposition

NGOS AND THE LEGAL AID INSTITUTE

A mature state and government actually needs LSMs [NGOs] to play a critical role. Basically, the government faces many dilemmas in carrying out develop-ment, for example: the emergence of contradictions between economic growth and modernization on the one hand and environmental pollution, resource dam-age, violation of human rights, marginalization of the weak or the trivialization of culture on the other hand. Here, the government needs LSMs to be like their "opponents in a game of ping-pong," so that they can together improve the qual-ity of development. Sometimes, the LSM role brushes up against politics. That's the risk which must be paid to improve the quality of development.

M. Dawam Rahardjo (LSM, *Tempo*, February 8, 1992, 92)

The most visible cultural expressions of the growth of the Indonesian middle class through the 1970s and 1980s were the upward mobility and confident consumerism apparent in the country's new shopping malls, su-permarkets, and suburban housing estates. Politically, one product of middle-class growth was apathy and widespread alienation from politics, although it also provided Golkar and other corporatist bodies like ICMI with many ambitious recruits. During the decades of middle-class growth, however, a quite different kind of middle-class culture and poli-tics was also being forged in numerous run-down offices around the country. This was the culture of the socially committed NGO activist.

The NGO world was not always in conflict with the statist and con-sumerist aspects of New Order middle-class culture. On the contrary, there was a large overlap between the NGO milieu and other parts of middle-class life, including academia, the press, and the bureaucracy. Many NGO activists made considerable sacrifices in pursuit of what they saw as their social responsibilities. Others were almost as concerned about material and career advancement as their counterparts in the civil service and private enterprises. Many NGO activists were suspicious of the state, but most were convinced that they needed to cooperate with it in order to achieve their aims.

Even so, NGOs (like the civil society realm more broadly) became an important refuge for critical political impulses. Especially during the final two decades of the New Order, NGOs were an important alternative site for social and political activism, one in which middle-class activists viewed their primary responsibility as assisting society's weak and marginalized. NGOs became means for activists to create new linkages across class boundaries. Overall, however, perhaps the most important role played by NGOs was encouraging a new kind of political imagining which, in contrast to the New Order's emphasis on state guidance and control, promoted societal self-reliance and popular participation. This chapter provides an overview of Indonesia's NGO movement. We begin with a historical survey of the growth of NGOs, then analyze the range of strategies that NGOs pursued during *keterbukaan*. The chapter concludes with a case study of Indonesia's best-known human rights NGO, the Legal Aid Institute (LBH).

The NGO Boom

The dissident groups discussed in the previous chapter espoused general and explicit political aims but were institutionally weak, having at most a few dozen members. NGOs, in contrast, often deliberately strove to avoid "politics" but had a significant organizational presence. Following the early 1970s, when NGOs were very few, their numbers increased rapidly. By 1981, the rural development NGO Sekretariat Bina Desa listed some two hundred NGOs; in 1983 the environment group WALHI claimed that three hundred were part of its network (Hadad 1983, 9). By the beginning of the final decade of the New Order, although reliable estimates were difficult to locate, NGOs existed in scores or even hundreds in every province. In 1989, 3,251 NGOs were registered with the government; by 1996, coordinating minister for politics and security Soesilo Soedarman estimated that there were some eight thousand NGOs in Indonesia (Sinaga 1993; *Republika*, November 4, 1996).

A huge variety of organizations were encompassed by the term *NGO* or its Indonesian near-equivalent, *Lembaga Swadaya Masyarakat* (LSM, translated by Philip Eldridge [1995, xvi] as "self-reliant community institution.") Many Indonesian NGOs were tiny, informal groups, operating out of shabby rented buildings or private homes, struggling to cover basic operating costs. A few were large, professional organizations (the BINGOs—Big NGOs) headquartered in multistoried air-conditioned buildings in Jakarta, with staff throughout the country and access to lucrative sources of government or overseas funding.

The range of activities pursued by NGOs was very diverse, but (allowing for great simplification) there were two main categories. The largest group in the late 1980s and 1990s was concerned primarily with "community development." Some such NGOs operated on a small scale, encouraging alternative technology, income-generating, housing, health, or educational projects in poor communities. Others were larger and acted as intermediaries between community groups and sources of commercial, government, or overseas credit for similar projects. Some of Indonesia's longest-established and biggest NGOs, such as Bina Swadaya and Bina Desa, focused on this kind of work. They did soon achieve a very large scale; by 1989, for example, Bina Swadaya claimed links with eighteen thousand small-scale cooperatives and "self-help groups" (Eldridge 1995, 67). The common thread uniting the community development paradigm was a "practical" approach to improving the lot of the poor; as one NGO leader expressed it in the 1970s, "We are looking for people who want to get their hands dirty" (Soedjarwo 1978, 58; see also Eldridge 1995, 57–86, and Hadiwinata 2003, 120–67, for case studies of community development NGOs). Leaders and activists in community development NGOs, although they may have been critical of elements of government policy, mostly did not see themselves as being in opposition to the government; more frequently they viewed the relationship as a partnership.

The second group, although it overlapped with the first, consisted of "rights-oriented" NGOs, representing what Telmo Frantz (1987) has referred to as "institutionalized social movements." These conducted advocacy work on many issues: environmental protection; consumer affairs; workers', farmers', or women's rights; legal aid; defense of indigenous communities; and so on. Some rights-oriented NGOs, such as LBH, were large and had existed since early in the New Order. The major environmental NGO, WALHI (the Indonesia Environment Network), was founded in 1980. Many such NGOs were very small and informal and had been established only since the 1980s by former students or other activists. During the *keterbukaan* years, such rights-oriented NGOs were responsible for NGOs acquiring a new image of political visibility and assertiveness. By the mid-1990s, the term *LSM* had become virtually synonymous with criticism of the government, and senior officials routinely complained about LSM activism.

This new image was ironic because Indonesia's NGO movement had arisen as a way to allow intellectuals and activists to pursue their goals while *avoiding* confrontation with the state. In general terms, NGOs were members of the broader family of civil society organizations; they were located in the civic domain, "between the family and the state," and did not seek political office. Two features distinguished NGOs from other civil society groups. They were "task-oriented," being focused on partial and specific aims (usually one particular aspect of "development"), and they were professionalized organizations of directors, staff, and volunteers rather than mass membership–based bodies. Both factors distinguished NGOs from organizations which were open to entire social categories, like labor unions, professional groups, religious associations, and the like (and which since the early New Order had been subjected to intensive control by the state). In Indonesian terms, the distinction was between and LSMs and *ormas* (*organisasi kemasyarakatan*, societal organizations). The distinction is important; even the largest NGOs often had fewer than a hundred staff and volunteers (though more could be associated with them through networks). *Ormas* could be huge; the NU claimed a total membership of over 30 million.

The origins of Indonesia's modern NGO movement can be traced back to the early 1970s, when many NGOs were established by intellectuals, former student activists, and others who had been politically aligned with the military in 1965–66. NGOs thrived partly because other avenues for independent political participation were narrowing. Most were not, however, initially oppositional in their impetus. Instead, they were expressions of the "ideology of modernization," that loose set of ideas which several scholars have argued came closest to representing the intellectual underpinning of the New Order military-civilian alliance (Liddle 1973; Ward 1973; Raillon 1985). A mélange of ideas was associated with support for "*modernisasi,*" most of which had long been promoted by various anticommunist political forces, especially the Indonesian Socialist Party (PSI). They were given added refinement by the influence of modernization theory, in the 1960s a recent product of American social science, and were promoted vigorously by many anticommunist intellectuals and students after 1965–66. The essence of the outlook was that the New Order represented a historic opportunity to overcome "tradition," "backwardness," "primordialism," and "feudalism" in all spheres. It was now possible to work to replace the agrarian subsistence economy with modern industrialism; traditional cultural values based on superstition and deference with rational problem-solving norms; and the primordial, ideological, mass party system with "pragmatic" "program-oriented" politics.

The founders of most early NGOs thus saw their organizations not as products of disillusionment with the New Order, but as means to participate in its modernization project. Most were charitable or developmentalist in approach and sought to cooperate with government agencies in pursuing their own economic development and poverty alleviation projects. Bina Swadaya (admittedly an extreme case) originated as an anticommunist peasant organization established by Catholic intellectuals in the late 1950s to counter the PKI in rural areas. During the early New Order it made an easy transition to supporting small-scale cooperatives and enterprises among the poor and remained close to Golkar functionaries to the end of the New Order (Bina Swadaya 1995, 1–3; Eldridge 1995, 66–72).

More typical of the broader NGO milieu was the research institute LP3ES (Institute for Economic and Social Research, Education, and Information), which in the 1970s became famous for attracting critically minded young intellectuals like Dawam Rahardjo, Aswab Mahasin, and other former 1966 student activists. LP3ES, too, had New Order links; when it was established in 1970 it was sponsored by several technocrat ministers, including Soemitro Djojohadikusumo, Ali Wardhana, and Emil Salim (Eldridge 1995, 86). As well as continuing research and publication activities, LP3ES went on to run programs in areas like youth unemployment, support for small industry, and *pesantren* development (Eldridge 1995, 88–94).

Given origins of NGOs, and the government's growing hostility toward independent organizations, it is not surprising that through the late 1980s most NGO leaders advocated a partnership role that was strictly "complementary" to that of government.[1] Most NGO leaders went to great lengths to stress that they were not opposed to the government. Even so, the growth of NGOs through the 1970s was also fueled by a gradual shift in the intellectual foundations of middle-class social activism. In the late 1960s and early 1970s, most disillusioned former student and intellectual allies of the military had conceived of the regime's shortcomings in terms of its failure to live up to the promises of *modernisasi*. Through the 1970s, a reorientation took place and many intellectuals became increasingly concerned about the poor and their problems. There was what might be described as a "populist shift" in intellectual trends, and various kinds of neopopulist alternative development thinking began to challenge the elitism of the modernization tradition.

Through the 1970s, through vehicles like the LP3ES journal *Prisma*, a new breed of intellectuals and NGO activists (and some older ones) developed increasingly comprehensive critiques of the government's development program. A common theme was that the government's approach treated equity and poverty eradication merely as elusive long-term goals to be produced by growth in the modern sector. Such critics attacked the government's obsession with "simply increasing the GNP," viewing the poor as mere passive "objects" of development and not paying attention to the possibly deleterious effects of industrialization. Economists like Sarbini Sumawinata and Dorodjatun Kuntjoro-Jakti argued that not only better and cleaner implementation but also changes in economic policy were needed (Robison 1986, 161–62; Sumawinata 1972; Kuntjoro-Jakti 1972). Immediately before Malari, and again in 1977–78, student activists and others combined this critique with attacks on corruption and extravagant living by officials and on foreign investment. Some intellectuals, influenced by the international burgeoning of alternative development thinking, began to promote small-scale rural development, cooperatives, and appropriate technology and argued that equity and rural employment should be the government's immediate policy priorities.[2]

By the late 1970s, partly influenced by international intellectual trends such as dependency theory, a new vogue for "structural" analysis had taken hold, with "structure" virtually displacing "modernization" as the main catchcry of critical intellectuals, students, and NGO activists. In 1979, this trend was reflected in the adoption of the theme of "Structural Poverty" by the Indonesian Association of Social Sciences congress held in Malang (Alfian, Tan, and Soemardjan 1980). Although structural analysis had many variants, the essential theme was that political and social problems were a product of deep inequalities which called for more than mere policy adjustments, but rather fundamental reconstruction of government, society, and the economy (see, e.g., Sasono 1980, 1982; Lubis 1981a, 1981b; Arief and Sasono 1981; also Lane 1982, 122–26).

The rapid growth of NGOs from the 1970s onward was the main practical expression of this evolving critique of New Order development. Although most NGOs still favored partnership with the government, the NGO movement as a whole cultivated a new kind of discourse that depicted the poor as important actors in their own right in the modernization process; "people's participation in development" became a slogan of NGOs from the late 1970s and through the 1980s.

Because NGOs thus stood for the revival of autonomous societal organizing (at least in theory, if not always in practice), they marked an important step in the development of opposition. Dependence on the state was integral to semiopposition and, ultimately, to the dissident model as well. NGOs suggested that society itself, even the poor, should be the main focus of activism (even if that activism was often something as simple as organizing a group of peasants to pool their money so they could buy a chicken coop or some other small business). When this emphasis on self-reliance was combined with the *negara hukum / rechtsstaat* ideal (both terms meaning, essentially, a law-based state, although often translated as "the rule of law") promoted by the smaller number of rights-oriented NGOs like LBH (see below), then it is clear that NGOs nurtured a desire to begin autonomous societal organization, even to defend society from state intervention.

However, it is important not to overromanticize the NGO boom. First, as noted above, most NGOs in fact emphasized a role that was complementary, not in conflict, with the state. Indeed, several NGO leaders introduced and popularized the term *Lembaga Swadaya Masyarakat* (LSM) in the early 1980s precisely because an emphasis on "community self-reliance" avoided the antigovernment connotations of the hitherto popular term *organisasi non-pemerintah* (nongovernment organization; Billah, Busyairi, and Aly 1993, 5).

Second, the flip side of the NGOs' emphasis on societal self-reliance and autonomy was that they thrived as part of a generalized *retreat* of oppositional impulses into civil society. The 1970s and early 1980s was a time when independent vehicles for more explicitly political activities were being repressed (e.g., student councils in 1978) or seeking to abandon the formal political sphere (NU in 1984). NGOs became important for expressing *negara hukum* and neopopulist ideas partly because they were a refuge for activists who lacked avenues for more political expression. Indeed, some NGOs were even coalitions of disenfranchised activists from old political organizations, searching for new means of political expression. For example, in its early years many Catholic, PSI-aligned, and Modernist Muslim intellectuals (typically with HMI backgrounds) were involved in LP3ES. The Consumers Foundation (YLKI) involved many former PNI activists (interview with Permadi, December 2, 1996). Many smaller NGOs from the late 1970s were created by student activists who had been driven off campus and who believed that, given the defeat of their movement in the towns, it was incumbent on them to build links with the rural population.

In sum, NGOs prospered partly because they were tolerated by the state when other forms of organization were suppressed. They survived and grew because of the middle-class and New Order origins of their leaders and their particularistic, partial goals. Even where their leaders harbored far-reaching social and political aims, NGOs did not claim to organize a struggle for political power or to mobilize a mass base.

One feature which assisted the growth of NGOs further illustrates their defensive character. This was the utilization by most NGOs of the *yayasan* (foundation) structure. Under Indonesian law, it was a simple process to establish a *yayasan*; all that was required was an act by a notary. Decision-making power in a *yayasan* was vested in a closed, unelected board of trustees. This meant that apart from board members those involved in an NGO were employees or volunteers rather than members. This helped protect NGOs from the standard methods the security apparatus employed to ensure compliance in membership-based *ormas* or political parties, such as infiltration by progovernment cliques and manipulation of internal disputes (see Chapter 7 for a discussion of this process in the PDI). Government officials were also reluctant to limit *yayasan* by legislation, largely because they themselves used such bodies for the corrupt channeling of "extrabudgetary" funds.

Finally, it should be noted that international influences had a striking impact on Indonesian NGOs. From the 1970s, NGOs grew dramatically not only in Indonesia but also in other parts of Southeast Asia and the developing world. Indeed, these NGOs emerged in tandem with a growing international discourse on alternative development, with all the philosophical, institutional, and financial support that this implied. From the late 1970s, foreign donors became the main source of funding for most Indonesian NGOs. This support in turn helped NGOs to become more independent of, and willing to criticize, the government.[3] Funding allowed NGOs to run projects, hire or purchase buildings, and pay wages to their staff. NGOs became an alternative middle-class career path for those with critical ideas, such as former student activists (Mahasin 1989, 31).[4] Links to foreign agencies also made NGOs ideally suited to play a role as transmitters into Indonesia of new paradigms for thinking about social, economic, and political change. In the 1970s, it was mostly neopopulist alternative development ideas which thus made their way into Indonesia, with concepts like the "basic needs" model (formulated at a 1976 World Employment Conference organized by the International Labour Organization) having a marked influence on the thinking of many Indonesian NGO activists. By the early 1990s, many international agencies were funding projects on themes like gender, civil society development, and even governance reform. This fed directly into the growing political assertiveness of Indonesian NGOs.

NGO Strategies: Engagement, Advocacy, Mobilization

It is not possible here to provide more than an outline sketch of the strategies NGOs used to pursue their social, economic, and political aims (more detailed studies are Eldridge 1995 and Hadiwinata 2003). In general terms, NGOs used three main strategies. The first, "direct engagement with the state," envisaged at most gradual evolution of the political system, and a strong element of survivalism also accounted for it. The second two, advocacy campaigns and mobilization of the poor, partly aimed at winning immediate concessions and reforms, although many NGO activists also believed that they helped prepare for the eventual replacement of authoritarian rule.

Direct engagement with the state and its personnel was above all a strategy associated with community development NGOs. Their aims of improving the living standards of poor communities did not necessarily imply conflict with the government. In fact, many NGOs believed that their goals would be furthered by cooperation. One method was for NGOs to engage government agencies in joint activity on particular development projects, the aims being not only to obtain financial and institutional support for the project concerned but also to convince the officials involved of the efficacy and desirability of community development approaches (hence, LP3ES claimed partial credit for the government's establishment, in 1978 of a directorate-general for small business; interview, M. Dawam Rahardjo, February 1, 1994). Some NGOs also sought to influence policy formulation directly by engaging senior officials in dialog. Many government agencies from the late 1970s became accustomed to cooperating with larger community development NGOs, which they sometimes invited to participate in drafting new regulations and programs. In effect, such NGOs pursued a semioppositional work-from-within strategy, even if their intervention was made from largely autonomous institutions in the civic domain. Dawam Rahardjo of LP3ES spoke in terms of a "friendly tension" between government and NGOs (interview, February 1, 1994). In the words of prominent NGO leader Wardah Hafidz, "If an LSM cooperates with the government, its main task is how to infiltrate and place inside [the government] ideas which are beneficial to society. . . . Our principle should be that although we are faced by a large concrete block, that concrete contains tiny pores which can be scratched open and hollowed out, so that the block breaks open" (Indeco De Unie 1993, 21).

This approach was sometimes depicted as a choice over less palatable alternatives. As Kartjono, the leader of the major rural development NGO Bina Desa put it, it was "the possible among the impossible" or "the best of the worst" (Indeco De Unie 1993, 8). In this view, there was simply little point in challenging the government in a frontal manner. For many in community development NGOs, however, this approach also reflected an essentially benign view of the New Order and the fact that they continued to adhere to a developmentalist paradigm similar to that practiced by the government (as argued by Billah, Busyairi, and Aly 1993; Billah 1994).

There was a clear material foundation for cooperation between community development NGOs and the government. From the mid-1970s the government attempted to address some of the concerns of its populist critics by devising a range of poverty alleviation programs. Even during the 1990s, many key policy makers still supported economic policies that entailed a major role for the state in poverty alleviation. Although the main levers of policy making remained in the hands of liberal technocrats, advocates of neopopulist solutions also found room within government agencies.[5] Just as economic growth shored up government legitimacy among the urban middle class as a whole, government attention to community development approaches provided a zone of cooperation with middle-class activists. Some of the larger community development NGOs, such as Bina Swadaya, kept government links which dated back to the 1960s and early 1970s. The decision by prominent Islamic NGO leaders like Adi Sasono (of LSP, the Institute for Development Studies) and Dawam Rahardjo (of LP3ES) to join ICMI in many ways flowed logically from their long involvement in the intricate process of lobbying and cooperating with government agencies in the development field. CIDES, the ICMI-linked think tank headed by Adi Sasono, became a vehicle to promote within government ranks economic and neopopulist strategies long nurtured in NGO circles. Adi explained that NGOs' aims could not be achieved without access to "power": "My experience based on more than a dozen years involvement in LSMs was that the problems of street vendors [for example], who are frequently relocated, cannot possibly be resolved if we are not involved in decision making on town planning" (Sasono 1995, 45).

Even some rights-oriented or advocacy NGOs maintained links, although usually of a different order, with government officials, inviting them to their public forums, lobbying on particular issues, and sometimes being invited to official consultations (especially by DPR commissions) on draft regulations or laws. From the late 1970s, the Ministry of the Environment and Population (before 1983 the Ministry of Environment and Development Supervision) under Emil Salim was especially amenable to cooperating with NGOs. Indeed, Emil sponsored the formation of WALHI, and the organization was headed for many years by Erna Witoelar, wife of Golkar secretary general Rachmat Witoelar (1988–93). Environmental legislation from 1982 officially recognized the contribution of NGOs, while WALHI and other NGOs participated in drafting environmental impact assessment regulations.

NGO leaders also deliberately sought contact with sympathetic senior government leaders for protection against pressure from the security apparatus. In the 1980s and early 1990s, Emil Salim was even prepared to defend NGOs at moments of high tension, such as after the Santa Cruz massacre in Dili in 1991. After 1993, NGOs had fewer sympathizers in the cabinet, although Salim's successor as environment minister, Sarwono Kusumaatmadja, also promised to protect NGOs.[6]

The political controversy which surrounded NGOs from the late 1980s was largely because many of them adopted or refined a second strategy from the late 1980s, namely *public advocacy campaigns*. This trend became very evident in 1989, when NGOs grouped in INGI (the International NGO Forum on Indonesia) and the SKEPHI-INFIGHT (Indonesian Network for Forest Conservation–Indonesian Front for the Defense of Human Rights) network ran major campaigns against the Kedung Ombo dam development in Central Java, the Scott paper pulp project in Irian Jaya, and the Inti Indorayon pulp mill in North Sumatra. These campaigns involved extensive domestic lobbying, cooperation with student protestors, legal challenges, and other publicity-generating techniques, and even the mobilization of international pressure.

Advocacy campaigns became common in the following years. "Advocacy" (*advokasi*) encompassed a wide range of activities, mostly the basic stuff of pressure group and social movement politics everywhere. Documentation and research, publications, seminars, lobbying, and electronic networking were all part of the repertoire. Press and publicity work were central; NGO activists were adept at using links with sympathetic journalists, especially as *keterbukaan* progressed. Litigation and legal challenges were also important, but these were increasingly viewed as publicity-generating adjuncts to broader campaigns.

The prominence of advocacy partly reflected the adoption of a new campaigning style by some of the larger, long-established NGOs, like WALHI and LBH (see below), whose members increasingly believed that it was impossible to promote reform via formal channels like the legal system.[7] It was also pioneered by new smaller mobilizational NGOs (discussed below). There was increased NGO networking beginning in the 1980s, including numerous regional forums and networks clustered around major bodies like WALHI and LBH (see Hadiwinata 2003, 206–40, for a discussion of one important regional forum in Yogyakarta). The major umbrella body, INGI, was established in 1984–85 as a meeting point for major Indonesian NGOs and their overseas donors and was designed to shadow and pressure the Indonesian government's own donors at annual IGGI (Intergovernmental Group on Indonesia) conferences. INGI, and its successor organization, INFID (International NGO Forum on Indonesian Development), eventually resembled a national, indeed international, peak coordinating body for major NGOs.

After 1989, the best-publicized campaigns organized by NGO coalitions included ones opposing river pollution (1991–92), golf course construction (1993), the killing of the woman labor activist Marsinah (1993–94), and regulations allowing the military to intervene in labor disputes (1993–94). Such campaigns were couched in general human rights language, although from the mid-1990s NGOs also increasingly explicitly framed their demands in terms of "democratization" (e.g., the 1991 INGI conference was the first to include specific recommendations about the need for political democratization [INFID 1993a, 57]).

Many NGO activists argued that advocacy work constituted a long-term and incremental struggle to shift the ground rules of politics and force compounding concessions from the state. In a term that became popular in NGO circles during the early 1990s, this was a "counterhegemonic" struggle (Aditjondro 1990; Tirtosudarmo 1991). The main audience (as distinct from the beneficiaries) of advocacy campaigns were those urban middle-class people who had the education, income, leisure time, and inclination to observe the major public debates of the day and read the quality newspapers in which NGO campaigns were reported. NGOs became, in large part, an instrument for changing middle-class consciousness.

Although the audience for NGO campaigning was primarily middle class, NGOs derived their core legitimacy from working for the poor. The third major NGO strategy was thus *organizing and mobilizing the poor*. However, there were widely varying approaches here. The raison d'être of community development NGOs was practical action to improve living standards. As argued by Eldridge, M. M. Billah, and others, some such NGOs were essentially charitable, some were based on a developmentalist philosophy similar to that of the government, while others argued in neopopulist "alternative development" terminology that they were engaged in long-term "empowerment" (*pemberdayaan*). Mostly such NGOs were based on a self-help philosophy (*swadaya*, meaning self-reliance) and encouraged the formation of small cooperatives in poor communities.

Rights-oriented NGOs, especially larger ones, expressed their commitment to the poor primarily through advocacy work. Although they often stressed the importance of "community organizing," when they campaigned on a land dispute, environmental pollution, or a similar problem, they often had only limited direct contact with the affected community. Typically, NGO workers would visit the site of the dispute and research and document it in detail. Community members might be involved as witnesses or litigants in a court case, but their active participation would often stop there. In short, rights-oriented NGOs (especially the larger and better-established ones) often spoke on behalf of the poor without mobilizing them.

Many NGO activists, however, attempted to pursue a model described as *pendampingan* (literally, accompaniment), *pengorganisasian masyarakat* (community organizing), or, sometimes, *mobilisasi* (mobilization). This was a product of the 1970s "populist shift" in the intellectual underpinnings of NGOs, although it also became more prominent from the late 1980s in tandem with the growing student radicalization discussed in the next chapter. Ideally, such terms meant facilitating the autonomous organization of poor people and their ability to overcome their own social, political, and economic problems. In this model, when a "case" came to the attention of an NGO, activists would enter the affected community, establish contacts, stimulate the formation of small groups, hold training sessions, determine what community members themselves wanted, and organize a public campaign. Such work entailed significant risk of repression and could rarely be carried out openly.

Although members of the larger established NGOs like the LBH were among the first to experiment with the new approach, it really came into its own with a new generation of what Billah (1994) calls "transformative" and Eldridge (1995) calls "mobilisational" NGOs from the mid to late 1980s. As Eldridge (1995, 39–40) notes, the emergence of this new generation was definitively marked by NGO conferences in Bukittinggi (1988) and Baturaden, West Java (1990), which passed resolutions criticizing the "arrogance" of the big NGOs, their "developmentalist" paradigms, and the gulf which separated them from the ordinary people. The essence of such criticisms was that traditional community development approaches could not improve the poor's overall social position because their problems were structural and political in character. Only "empowerment" would lead to change.

Some groups that promoted new mobilizational approaches were designed as more aggressive counterparts to established NGOs. For example, WALHI spawned SKEPHI, which was led by former 1978 student activist Indro Tjahjono. LBH was complemented by numerous smaller legal aid organizations which claimed to be more progressive. Even INGI was mirrored (for a time) by its more radical counterpart, INFIGHT (in which Indro Tjahjono was also prominent). INFIGHT first came to prominence in April 1990, when it organized a meeting between the Dutch minister for development cooperation and chairman of the IGGI, J. P. Pronk, and student activists and peasants, who presented him with a statement about human rights violations and how IGGI aid "has been detrimental to the people." By the early 1990s, there were many small groups, frequently established by former student activists, focused on workers, women, indigenous people, and farmers. Many larger NGOs also took on board "mobilizational" arguments.[8]

An example of a social sector where the new perspectives were practiced particularly intensively from the early 1990s was industrial labor, a risky arena given the government's determination to prevent workers from organizing outside the aegis of its own corporatist labor union.[9] Several NGOs concerned with workers' welfare were established in the late 1970s and early 1980s, but these mostly adopted a purely welfare approach. Some pursued redress through the courts for workers who had been treated illegally or encouraged workers to become active in the state-sponsored union federation. This was the approach adopted by the Jakarta branch of the LBH when it first became active in labor issues in the early 1980s. In this case, a group of LBH activists, led by former University of Indonesia student activist Fauzi Abdullah, was inspired when a number of striking workers approached LBH for legal assistance in 1980. In the years that followed, LBH held training sessions for worker activists recruited in the industrial areas around Jakarta. The initial aim was to train workers about their legal rights (and to this end LBH produced a manual written in a simple question-and-answer format for workers; Saleh 1980). These sessions evolved toward discussion of conditions in participants' workplaces, and from there to discussion of the need to organize. Eventually, by about 1982–83, some workers involved in this program were establishing branches of the official union federation, FBSI, in their workplaces. Some organized strikes and campaigns on wages and conditions (interview, Fauzi Abdullah, November 29, 1995).[10]

Following the accelerated industrialization from the mid-1980s and subsequent increase of industrial disputes, such activities increased greatly. Some NGOs began to promote essentially underground working-class organization. For example, Yasanti was a small women's NGO established in 1982 by former students in Yogyakarta. When it was established, it had adopted a community development approach and encouraged women workers to learn new skills, pool their savings, and establish sewing and similar enterprises (effectively encouraging them to leave wage labor). By the late 1980s, it was organizing training about workers' rights and encouraging small groups and networks of women workers, some of whom were engaging in industrial disputes (interviews, Yasanti activists, March 1994).

Importantly, such NGO labor activism led to attempts to establish labor unions beyond government control. The first, the "Solidarity Free Trade Union," was established in 1990 under the influence of activists

from several NGOs. The more resilient SBSI (Indonesian Prosperous Labor Union) was launched in 1992, drawing on a network of Batak Christian and other NGOs. These initiatives faced great challenges, owing to
both internal divisions and repression; Vedi Hadiz (1997, 136) labels
them "aspiring unions," because they were prevented from operating
within factories and were instead based on informal groups in the *kampung*, or residential areas where workers lived. Middle-class NGO activists still played a crucial role in them. Even so, it was clear that by the
early 1990s NGOs, which were small groups of mostly middle-class activists who worked *for* the poor, were beginning to give birth to new
kinds of mass organization *of* the poor which partly superseded them.

LBH and the *Negara Hukum*

The Indonesian Legal Aid Institute (LBH) was one of the oldest and most
influential of Indonesian NGOs. It was also one of the largest; by 1994 it
claimed ten branch offices and four project bases and employed 129 persons (seventy-four lawyers and fifty-five others; Harman et al. 1995,
205).[11] During the 1990s, LBH represented clients in thousands of court
cases throughout the country, including most of those that involved political controversy, and its leaders appeared in the press virtually daily.
These leaders included some of the best-known public critics of the New
Order. LBH's aims—the establishment of the rule of law and extension of
legal, civil, and political rights—meant that LBH was an archetypal institution of civil society, concerned to defend societal autonomy against the
state. As such, its relations with the New Order government were likely
to be particularly troubled.

The outspoken lawyer Adnan Buyung Nasution established LBH in
1970 as a pilot project of PERADIN, the Indonesian Bar Association.[12]
He designed it as a body to provide pro bono legal aid to the poor, claiming he had been inspired by an earlier visit to Australia in the late 1950s.
From the start, however, LBH defined its mission more broadly and used
the courts to promote the *negara hukum*, or *rechtsstaat*, ideal that the
state should submit to the impartial rule of law and that citizens should
thereby be protected from arbitrary acts.

LBH was unusual, given that most early NGOs were more concerned
with community development. Even so, like most other early NGOs,
LBH presented itself as part of the New Order project. Its founders were
prominent participants in the 1965–66 military-civilian alliance. Adnan
Buyung Nasution himself had been a leader of the anti-Sukarno KASI (Indonesian Graduates' Action Front). He had become increasingly disillusioned from an early date, it is true, by phenomena like growing corrup-

tion and the government's failure to restructure the electoral system. (He says that his last face-to-face discussion with Suharto himself took place in late 1968, when Buyung led a KASI delegation to denounce corruption and abuse of power, prompting Suharto to walk out; interview, Adnan Buyung Nasution, April 13, 1994.) Others involved in LBH had had even more problematic relations with the authorities.[13]

Even so, early LBH documents are peppered with phrases committing the organization to the *perjuangan Orde Baru* (the New Order struggle) and using developmentalist language to describe the organization's mission as one of promoting *modernisasi hukum* (legal modernization) and *pembangunan hukum* (legal development). LBH also received initial sponsorship and financial support from the Jakarta city administration when it was still led by Governor Ali Sadikin. Even President Suharto himself gave his blessing to the establishment of the body, with Lieutenant General Ali Moertopo's mediation (interview, Adnan Buyung Nasution, February 8, 1994). Moertopo himself donated five scooters to it. In its early years, LBH founders remained close to a number of senior military officers and technocrats and shared with them many similarities in political outlook; despite his growing disillusionment with the regime, Adnan Buyung Nasution even campaigned for Golkar in the 1971 election.

Despite such ties, LBH quickly became a source of criticism toward the government on legal issues. Daniel Lev (1978, 38–42) argues that their direct interest in a powerful and autonomous legal system gave many independent lawyers a proclivity for *negara hukum* ideology. Indeed, he argues that "law movements" can arise among broader middle-class groups who look to legal protection against intrusive state action. During the early New Order, many lawyers and other liberals were rapidly losing their initial faith that the government was committed to supremacy of law, and this disillusionment fueled the growth of LBH and its campaigning style.

The kernel of the *negara hukum* argument was that the exercise of state power had to be limited, divided, and controlled if the rights of citizens were to be protected. From the start, LBH lawyers were conversant with the arguments of liberal political theory that in order to protect citizens from state caprice it was necessary to have not only a strong judiciary but also political control mechanisms including civil liberties, separation of powers, and, ultimately, government accountability to the populace via free elections. However, in the early years, like many other New Order intellectuals, they were ambivalent about the government and democratic change. This ambivalence derived partly from liberal intellectuals' own weakness in the formal political arena and their contempt for the old mass-based parties, but it also reflected the continuing influence of the ideology of modernization. Hence, a recurring theme in writings by

LBH leaders in the early 1970s was that weaknesses in the rule of law were partly because of cultural factors, notably the persistence of "feudal" ideas in the general population, which in turn flowed from economic backwardness.[14] A long period would therefore be necessary to create a democratic system (one or two generations, according to Yap Thiam Hien [1973, 29]), and a central motor of this evolution would be cultural and economic change.

LBH leaders in the early 1970s thus most strongly articulated judicial rather than political aspects of the *negara hukum* philosophy. They argued that a strong and independent legal system was a prerequisite for control of state power, and most of their practical activities were centered in courtrooms. Providing free legal aid to clients who could not otherwise afford it was itself an attempt to strengthen the legal system. In this sense, LBH was primarily a service organization; early LBH documents compared its role favorably to that of a free health service for the poor (LBH 1973, 13). However, although LBH provided legal counsel in all kinds of civil and criminal cases, from the start the organization "had no compunction about challenging the government" (Lev 1987, 17). It was involved in political trials and lawsuits in which ordinary citizens were pitted against the state, as when it represented Jakarta *kampung* dwellers forced aside by Ali Sadikin's administration to make way for development projects.

The judicial core of the *negara hukum* philosophy remained a pillar of LBH down the years. Even into the 1990s, the organization was still run mainly by lawyers, including some of the most talented in the country. Its three executive directors during the *keterbukaan* period, Abdul Hakim Garuda Nusantara (1986–93), Adnan Buyung Nasution (1993–96), and Bambang Widjojanto (1996–2001), were all noted courtroom advocates. Representing clients in courts remained LBH's core function, and its lawyers continued to handle most controversial political cases, ranging from subversion trials of East Timorese or Acehnese secessionists, through to appeals against dispossession orders in land disputes.[15] LBH lawyers took their courtroom work very seriously, arguing legal principles strenuously and taking great heart at victories, no matter how small, on points of law. The organization also explored new judicial remedies to state abuses, such as class actions and judicial review of regulations. In short, LBH activists continued to view their role as being that of exemplary promoters of judicial independence, impartiality, and effectiveness. This was despite the great disillusionment caused down the years by the manifest absence of independence in the judicial system; by the early 1990s, no political trial defended by LBH lawyers had resulted in an acquittal.

LBH Campaigning and "Structural Legal Aid"

Despite its early focus on litigation, from the early 1970s LBH openly proclaimed that it aimed to promote "legal reform" and "legal awareness" and to "control" or "correct" government action, playing a role similar to the ombudsman's office in Scandinavian countries (LBH 1973, 12–13). Individuals associated with the organization—including lawyers Adnan Buyung Nasution, Yap Thiam Hien, and Suardi Tasrif, and others like senior journalist and novelist Mochtar Lubis and civil libertarian Johannes Princen—were among the period's most outspoken advocates of civil rights, and many were harassed and detained for their views. However, when it came to their organization, LBH leaders initially disavowed political aims and stressed that there should be no "misunderstandings" with the government (LBH 1973, 15, 16).

As disillusionment with the government increased, LBH lawyers more openly took their *negara hukum* philosophy to broader political conclusions. A turning point was Malari, when several founding members of LBH, including Buyung, were detained or interrogated. The organization survived only by scaling down its activities. In the late 1970s, however, LBH expanded rapidly once more, establishing new branches and relations with overseas donor organizations. In 1980, the Indonesian Legal Aid Foundation (YLBHI) was established and charged with coordinating the different branches. The *yayasan* form was chosen partly to minimize the risks of infiltration by government agents or sympathizers; according to Adnan Buyung Nasution, after Malari, the government had been attempting "to co-opt LBH by putting its own men in LBH or by embracing our men" (interview, December 12, 1995).[16]

From the late 1970s, LBH took on the appearance of a campaigning human rights organization. In 1978, it coordinated a spirited campaign in defense of detained student activists. In 1979, it established a Human Rights Division, and outspoken members of the first post-1966 generation of student activists like Todung Mulya Lubis became prominent in the organization. They organized more vigorous outreach activities: seminars, public meetings, poster and essay competitions, magazines, and, from 1979, an annual Human Rights Report. In the early 1980s, new programs, like training paralegals and "barefoot lawyers," were introduced with the aim of strengthening "community legal resources." There were also early attempts to reach down to poor communities in more direct ways, including rudimentary organizational work among industrial workers in Jakarta.

In the late 1970s and early 1980s, this new campaigning outlook came to be expressed in the concept of *bantuan hukum struktural* (structural legal aid), which was to remain the philosophical underpinning of LBH's approach until the 1990s.[17] Three core propositions were involved. First was that the law itself reflected structural inequalities in society. In the words of a report drafted at a 1980 national legal aid workshop, "Law is a means for the strong to perpetuate their power, while the weak are left far behind with only their weakness."[18] This attitude was part of the populist shift and vogue for structural analysis in critical intellectual circles from the mid-1970s.[19] It also reflected frustration with LBH's previous litigation-based strategy; by the late 1970s, it was manifest that the judiciary was neither autonomous vis-à-vis government nor an effective control over it.

Second, it was suggested that legal aid should aim at fundamental structural change in the legal, social, economic, and political systems. In a 1981 article, Buyung argued, "To build a more just and democratic society, it is necessary *not only* to change the basic outlook of society, which remains essentially feudal [this was the old, modernization philosophy] but also to change exploitative social structures [this was the new element]" (Nasution 1981, 112).

Third, it followed that a new style of legal aid was needed because pro bono assistance for individual cases did not affect underlying nonlegal sources of inequality. The medical metaphor was used once more, this time to criticize pro bono legal aid for being like a "health service which does not take into account social conditions" (Lubis 1981a, 57). Instead, legal aid should aim at the empowerment of the poor; in a formulation by Mulya Lubis (1981a, 58), it should be a "social movement" able to create "power resources" in peripheral social groups. Advocates of the new concept did not suggest that courtroom legal assistance should be abandoned, merely that it should be modified and combined with other measures. Initially, Lev (1987, 21) argues, "structural legal aid" functioned largely to justify the nonlitigational work which LBH already conducted. However, its implications were potentially far-reaching, and as opportunities for political change increased, they proved difficult to reconcile with LBH's litigational orientation.

LBH During *Keterbukaan*: Becoming the Locomotive of Democracy

During the tenure of Abdul Hakim Garuda Nusantara as director (1986–93), LBH further refined its approach. Describing itself as a "public interest legal service" (*Editor*, November 10, 1990, 36–37; February 23, 1991, 41–42), LBH focused legal aid and advocacy on four strategic "structural" areas: civil and political rights, labor, land, and the environment. In each of these areas, conflict between poor citizens and the state was acute, and it was considered that campaigning could most enhance collective rights. LBH was to avoid, so far as possible, involvement in more routine individual civil and criminal cases. Citizens who approached the organization on such matters were mostly directed to alternative legal aid bodies, which had proliferated since the 1970s.

When a case with a "structural dimension" came to the attention of LBH, the organization aimed to move beyond a traditional lawyer-client relationship and instead treat each case, as LBH leaders put it, as the focus for the development of a "social movement." In theory, this required that the LBH involve clients (who were increasingly collective groups) in planning and organizing a broad campaign. During Hakim's tenure, the initial policy was to send legal aid workers directly into the field (e.g., into a village affected by a land dispute) to provide paralegal training and facilitate community organization. It was soon recognized, however, that LBH lacked the resources or flexibility to conduct such work alone. The solution was increased cooperation with smaller NGOs and student activists. Cooperation was often on a case-by-case basis, with a de facto division of tasks. LBH would handle legal aspects, often forming a defense team with lawyers from other NGOs and the Bar Association, coordinate the groups involved, and provide the lion's share of the funding (acting, in effect, as intermediary for the disbursement of funds from overseas donors). The smaller "partner" (*mitra*) groups would spend more time in the field and organize training, demonstrations, and other campaign elements. Such relationships were often tense; the smaller partners often resented LBH's legalism, its control over funds, and its public exposure. Nevertheless, through such ad hoc campaigns, LBH became the center of a broad network of NGOs and student groups.

There was, however, considerable variation between LBH branches. Branches in Bandung, Surabaya, and Yogyakarta, for example, were mostly run by younger individuals, often recruited directly from the student movement. They worked closely with partner groups in advocacy campaigns, sometimes even experimenting with direct organization of poor communities.[20] Some other branches were dominated by lawyers more suspicious of innovation and were inclined to emphasize more traditional litigation-based approaches.

LBH's transformation became clearer after an internal crisis precipitated the return of its founder, Adnan Buyung Nasution, as director in 1993. Buyung was by now Indonesia's most famous lawyer, being well known for his leadership of LBH in previous years, as well as for his flair in the courtroom. In 1986 the justice minister had accused him of contempt of court and suspended him from practicing after he interrupted the judge as he was reading the court's judgment in the subversion trial of Major General (retired) Dharsono. Buyung went to the Netherlands where he wrote a doctoral dissertation on the workings of Indonesia's Constituent Assembly in the 1950s. On his return, he apparently believed the times were propitious for an accelerated campaign for democratization. Mid-1993, it will be recalled, was the high point of *keterbukaan*. In press interviews, Buyung praised the "new attitude" from ABRI officers that was apparent during *keterbukaan* (especially after the Jakarta commander Hendropriyono made a surprise visit to the LBH office in August 1993) and also tried to take advantage of Suharto's own statements in favor of openness: "If President Suharto himself has already talked about change, why should we close off that possibility?" (*Forum Keadilan*, September 16, 1993, 93). He stressed, however, that promises of openness and reform had not yet been put into practice.

Buyung was a fiery orator and a flamboyant and self-confident figure who had no hesitations about promoting himself as a leader of a democratic movement. On his return from Holland, he toured campuses and addressed many seminars and public meetings where he publicized the findings of his own study (in which he argued, counter to New Order interpretations, that the Constituent Assembly had made many achievements and that the 1950s were a high point of constitutional and democratic government). Along with other LBH leaders, he also campaigned publicly and boldly against the ideological underpinnings of the regime, including previously sensitive areas like the sacrosanct (*sakral*) character of the 1945 Constitution and "integralist" ideology. In a series of press articles and speeches, Buyung argued vigorously that such concepts were fundamentally incompatible with aspirations for constitutional democracy.[21]

Buyung also introduced the idea that LBH should be a *lokomotif demokrasi*, the engine of a broad movement for democratization, assisting the development of student groups, human rights bodies, and other civil society groups. He argued that even LBH's previous structural legal aid approach, with its vague emphasis on empowering the disenfranchised, was not enough. Political change was needed if LBH really wanted to achieve its goal of helping the disempowered:

In this decade of the 1990s it is even realized that the structural struggle must be increasingly broadened, in the sense that it is not sufficient just to strive for *empowering* at the *grass root* level, but it instead must also be carried through a political struggle which aims to bring about changes in the direction of democracy. The aim is to restructure the political system and institutions in order that they return to national aspirations for democracy, human rights and law. (Adnan Buyung Nasution in Ibrahim 1995, 24)[22]

Through the 1990s, LBH publications and statements by its leaders stressed the need for thorough political reform. A four-year plan released in 1994 (albeit one not released publicly but produced for overseas donors) stated that the two principal medium-term aims of the organization were the development of "democratic forces in society" and "an increasingly democratic system of government." Various specific benchmarks were proposed by which these goals could be measured, collectively constituting a comprehensive platform for political reform. These benchmarks included greater "limitation of military intervention in social and political life," greater freedom for the press, judicial independence, "development of a more organized national mass movement," and genuinely free elections (YLBHI 1994, 15).

Intertwined with increased promotion of political rights and democratization was the idea of *masyarakat sipil* (later, *madani*)—civil society. This became another constant theme in material produced by LBH (and by many other NGOs and opposition groups) in the 1990s. Although the term was often used loosely, it generally connoted a pluralistic and organized society, guaranteed by respect for civil and political rights. "Civil society" was thus conceived both as a vehicle for achieving democratic reform and as a means to exercise vigilant control over the state, a way of conceptualizing both NGOs themselves and their goals. A paper by NGO activist Billah (1994, 1) which circulated widely in NGO circles was typical: "In a normative sense, NGOs are 'non-governmental organizations' established by the inhabitants of civil society, so that 'ideologically' and 'organizationally' they should be 'independent' from the state. . . . The 'struggle for democracy' is the struggle of civil society against (the uncontrolled power of) the state."

The new civil society discourse partly reflected international intellectual trends, toward which Indonesian NGOs had always been sensitive. In part, it extended the philosophy of "social control" which had been promoted by groups like LBH since early in the New Order. The new terminology made it even clearer, however, that such activists viewed the state as the chief problematic of contemporary political life and as the chief obstacle to democratization. Key documents produced by LBH, and many other NGOs and dissident groupings, primarily conceptualized the struggle as one between the (repressive, authoritarian) state and (an essentially undifferentiated) society.[23] One reflection of this new antistatism was a revival in NGO circles of the old term *ornop*, or *organisasi non-pemerintah* (nongovernmental organization) to replace *LSM* ("self-reliant community institution"), which had initially been introduced in the 1970s precisely because it did not imply opposition to the state.

LBH also intensified its emphasis on the empowerment of lower-class and marginalized groups. It continued to recruit from the student movement, so it was no surprise that the radical, antidevelopmentalist, even anticapitalist populism that characterized student protest groups and many small NGOs permeated LBH ranks.[24] On the other hand, there was sometimes also an extension of antistatist arguments to the economic sphere and an emphasis on the connection between economic and political freedoms. For example, Todung Mulya Lubis, the former LBH director (and board of trustees member in the 1990s) in the early 1990s wrote a series of press articles arguing that economic deregulation should be accompanied by greater legal and political certainty, predictability, and regularization in order to provide a more stable investment climate (see Lubis 1993, 1995).

During the 1990s, as LBH became increasingly assertive and the security apparatus became more concerned about middle-class dissent, senior military officers sometimes labeled LBH "subversive," and security forces occasionally harassed or detained its members or broke up its meetings. Unlike even the early 1980s, when at least Vice President Adam Malik could be called upon, the organization had few protectors in government. However, the government did not ban LBH or take other serious action against it. Its international links and the legitimacy it derived from providing much-needed legal assistance to citizens would have made this a provocative and politically costly act. LBH had a considerable middle-class support base, which Lev (1987, 27–31) argues derived from the most liberal element of the Indonesian middle classes, not only lawyers but also journalists, intellectuals, students, and others. At no time did this appear truer than in the mid-1990s when LBH operated as the de facto center of a broad network of activist organizations, partly justifying the *lokomotif demokrasi* moniker. LBH offices were hubs of activity, meeting places, and press conference venues for many groups. A steady stream of students, NGO activists, lawyers, and others passed through their doors.[25]

Internal Conflicts: The Dilemma of Proto-opposition

From the moment it was adopted, the concept of "structural legal aid" created tensions within LBH. These first peaked in 1984, when a number of lawyers resigned from the organization. They were led by Abdul Rachman Saleh, a former chief of the Jakarta branch, who attacked the concept for relegating litigation to a secondary position. He said this relegation implied loss of faith in the law and set LBH on the path toward organizing an extralegal, even revolutionary movement (Nasution 1984).

During *keterbukaan*, internal disputes again caused major disruption to the organization. In 1993, when LBH had to appoint a successor to Abdul Hakim Garuda Nusantara as director, LBH activists and "partner" organizations held demonstrations in LBH offices. They accused the institute of being undemocratic and ignoring the views of staff and supporters. This dispute was resolved temporarily by several internal reforms and Adnan Buyung Nasution's return as director (Thompson 1993). Conflict flared again in 1995, this time sparked by a leadership dispute in the Yogyakarta branch. In 1996, after Buyung announced he would resign, the dispute over succession became especially bitter. For some months, conflict virtually crippled the organization, eventually resulting in an open split.

These disputes partly reflected the personal enmities and factional fluidity common to most large organizations. But underlying them were two major points of contention. The first concerned participation in decision making. This problem affected all NGOs which used the *yayasan* format that, as indicated above, was adopted by many NGOs both as a matter of convenience and as security against government intervention. Unlike in membership-based *perkumpulan* (associations), whose leaders might be elected, in a *yayasan* ultimate decision-making power was vested in an unelected *Dewan Penyantun* (board of trustees). In the case of the YLBHI, this was dominated by prominent backers of LBH from its early days, like Bar Association lawyers Harjono Tjitrosoebono and Soekardjo Adijojo and New Order dissidents Ali Sadikin and Mochtar Lubis. The board thus tended to reflect the more conservative political outlook which marked dissent in the first decade of the New Order rather than the more radical impulses associated with the younger generations of activists. Some board members indicated that they were uncomfortable with Buyung's *lokomotif demokrasi* idea (see, for instance, Harjono Tjitrosoebono in *Kompas*, November 7, 1993). The board had ultimate power over programmatic, constitutional, and leadership decisions. LBH staffers, volunteers, and branches, not to mention members of "partner organizations," had little formal say on such matters, even if their input into daily operational decisions was substantial. A pivotal issue in the conflicts of 1993 and 1996 was thus the call for greater input in the election of new directors, appointment of branch leaders, program formulation, and so forth.

Intertwined with the organizational conflict, however, was often fundamental discord about the organization's vision. Despite the simplification involved, it is useful to distinguish between a broadly "litigational" pole in the organization, inclined to a more cautious interpretation of LBH's traditions, and a more "political" pole, which favored a more vigorous campaigning style. The contours of this conflict were obscured by the fact that after 1984 LBH lawyers accepted the concept of "structural legal aid," but many of the lawyers in the organization still tended to emphasize that litigation should take precedence and devoted much of their (and hence the organization's) energy accordingly. They also tried to avoid a more political interpretation of the concept. Lawyers in some branches outside Jakarta, where intimidation by the security forces tended to be greater, were among the most cautious.[26] They found natural allies in the board of trustees. Buyung's call for a wider struggle for democracy sparked unease among such individuals, although during the 1996 conflict, Buyung himself ultimately remained loyal to the mainstream tradition in LBH, suggesting that he believed the *lokomotif demokrasi* argument had been overly ambitious (interview, December 10, 1995; Nasution 1995, 25).

The LBH activists and supporters who wanted to take structural legal aid and *lokomotif demokrasi* views in a more frankly political direction were mostly (though not all) nonlawyers. Many former student activists had been recruited to LBH and moved into campaigning and operational posts in the late 1980s. For example, University of Indonesia criminologist Mulyana W. Kusumah became executive director of the foundation in 1993. A group of individuals who had been active on Bandung campuses in the late 1970s and 1980s, including Hendardi, Paskah Irianto, and Rambun Tjajo, were also appointed to executive positions. Such individuals often had close relations with the current and former student activists who cooperated with LBH in advocacy campaigns. Members of "partner" organizations were the bulk of demonstrators in LBH offices in 1993 and 1996. There was thus a loose group of leaders and supporters of LBH who were far more inclined to emphasize campaigning and advocacy work over litigation and who talked about the legal aid movement contributing to a "people's movement," the struggle for democratization, and the organization of subordinate classes.

Although alignments were often complicated, disputes over leadership and internal democracy often intersected with this more fundamental cleavage on philosophy. Many proponents of "internal democracy" argued (at least privately) that their vision of the movement they were building, and the LBH's place in it, differed fundamentally from that of incumbent leaders who remained committed to the professional NGO model. In discussions with me in 1993–94, some described their eventual aim as a "democratically organized mass movement," even some sort of mass political organization or party. Perhaps, they speculated, LBH could be transformed into such a body, or at least help to bring one into being. Conversely, many LBH lawyers and members of the board of trustees believed that an overtly political approach would invite repression. Some of them talked about "outside forces" trying to control the organization and attempts to abandon LBH's principles and disregard its constitution. More bluntly, Adnan Buyung Nasution warned of an unwanted process of "radicalization" occurring in LBH (*Paron*, August 31, 1996, 25).

The conflict in 1996 became particularly inflamed when Buyung's critics raised the question of his ties with government officials and ABRI officers. Buyung had long argued that it was essential to maintain lines of communication with officials in order to obtain information and press for reform. At the height of the furor over the 1994 press bannings, he met with Habibie and ABRI chief of staff for social and political affairs Hartono. Though refusing to divulge the contents of these meetings to fellow LBH members, he presented this contact as a continuation of the approach he had adopted since the start of the New Order:

When I was in LBH [in the past] I always did this; I have had this kind of practice for thirty years. Now, many people in NGOs have an allergy to meeting with people in the government. They believe things should be black and white, there should be no bridge, no discussions, no dialog. I think this is wrong; it has been my practice for thirty years. I would even meet with Ali Moertopo at *lebaran* [celebration ending the Muslim fasting month] events *after Malari*. I went to the marriage of Prabowo. Suharto was there; I even shook hands with him. I was condemned for this by some people, because people hated Suharto so much. But I always believe that although you may be enemies in politics, socially at least you must make a separation. Even in politics, even though you are enemies, you should not cut off communication. (interview, December 5, 1995)[27]

Buyung's attitude was typical of many activists whose experiences of the 1966 civilian-military alliance predisposed them not to adopt a position of outright enmity to the regime and its leaders. Many older NGO leaders like Buyung had backgrounds similar to those of senior officials and moved in the same narrow social circles. Buyung was personally friendly, for instance, with the former minister of justice, Ali Said. From the time he had returned from his studies abroad, he had advocated dialog with ABRI and other regime leaders (see, e.g., *DëTik*, August 18–24, 20). He did this because he believed that there were groups in the ruling elite who might be "vulnerable" to new ideas, and "if the time comes, we might be able to work with them, like we did in 1965" (interview, April 13, 1994).

In contrast, many of the younger LBH staffers and supporters had served their political apprenticeship in the antimilitary student activism of the 1970s and 1980s. (Hendardi, for instance, had been a student leader at the Bandung Institute of Technology in the bleak years of the early 1980s, at the height of the "normalization of campus life" policy when the government was clamping down on student activism.) Such LBH activists feared links with the regime might smack of co-optation. After Buyung's meetings with Habibie and Hartono, therefore, rumors quickly spread in LBH circles that he had made a deal (one rumor was that Habibie had invited Buyung to found a human rights institute under ICMI's sponsorship). Accusations of co-optation by Habibie and ICMI became central to the dispute, with Buyung angrily denying that he was co-opted and defending his long-standing links with former NGO activists in ICMI like Adi Sasono and Dawam Rahardjo. He would not, he said, "sentence" his former friends as traitors to the democratic struggle or draw a black and white distinction between them and prodemocracy groups outside the state (*Forum Keadilan*, October 9, 1995, 95–100). Even so, in the eyes of Buyung's critics, their suspicions were confirmed when immediately after his resignation as YLBHI director in 1996 he took up a lucrative post as legal counsel for IPTN and PAL, the state-owned aircraft and shipping companies run by Habibie. Buyung maintained that this was purely a commercial arrangement.[28]

In any event, Buyung and his supporters, who dominated the board of trustees, eventually won in the conflict of 1996. Buyung's favored candidate, Bambang Widjojanto, a respected lawyer who had headed the organization in Irian Jaya, was appointed as the new director. This resulted in a split. Several LBH leaders, including several prominent nonlawyers, were expelled or left and formed the Indonesian Legal Aid and Human Rights Association (PBHI). Many of LBH's supporters were disillusioned and drifted away or switched their allegiance to the new body, although the organization's basic infrastructure remained intact.[29]

The Limits and Possibilities of Civil Society

During the 1990s, it sometimes appeared that security officials viewed NGOs as a very dangerous source of opposition to the government. True, many developmentalist NGOs still maintained good relations with officials, who thus often differentiated between "constructive" and "destructive" NGOs. Overall, however, the tone of most official pronouncements (especially from ABRI officers) was hostile. At one point, for instance, ABRI commander Try Sutrisno called NGOs which campaigned outside the country "national traitors." Other officers sometimes accused NGOs of harboring "extreme center" elements (equating liberals with more traditional New Order foes of the "extreme left and right"). From the mid-1990s, as advocacy campaigning on behalf of workers, farmers, and other disenfranchised groups increased, some officers began to accuse NGOs of being fronts for communists. There were also various attempts to regulate NGOs and subject them to greater government supervision (see, e.g., Eldridge 1995, 49–50). In the field, many NGO activists, particularly those from newer mobilizational and human rights groups, experienced harassment and surveillance, although such repression tended to fluctuate in response to NGO campaigning (it was high, for instance, immediately after the Kedung Ombo campaign in 1989 and during the election-monitoring initiatives discussed in Chapter 7).

Were these fears justified? The preceding discussion of LBH and the internal conflicts it experienced is revealing of important tensions inherent in the NGO and civil society model of proto-opposition. LBH was the battleground for contradictory urges. On the one hand, there was the weight of LBH's history, its lawyerly and litigation-oriented tradition, and the urge for regulation of the state rather than confrontation with it. There was the pragmatic survivalism embodied in the NGO model, which had enabled organizational integrity despite years of government pressure. Set against these tendencies was the more impatient, even radical tone of newer generations of activists.

The disputes illustrated the contradiction between the NGO form adopted by many middle-class critics in the 1970s and 1980s, and the bolder political aspirations seeking expression during *keterbukaan*. LBH was an institution grounded in civil society, but it became a forum for individuals who wanted it to play an explicitly political role. LBH's attempt to become a *lokomotif demokrasi* ultimately failed to bridge the old format with the new expectations.

NGOs had flourished from the 1970s partly because they represented themselves in a way that did not overtly threaten the state. When political conditions opened up from the late 1980s, the legacy of these origins made it difficult for NGOs to realize the democratizing ideals nurtured by some of their members. The *yayasan* form itself, partly adopted to preserve NGOs during difficult times, was a conservatizing influence. The foreign funding of many NGOs, which had enabled them to survive in the dark years from the late 1970s, also contributed to their domestication. It resulted in a professional stratum with middle-class incomes and lifestyles running the large NGOs. Their leaders feared endangering their institutional resources, their staff, the interests of the communities they served, and their prospects of achieving short-term aims. They generally thus had interests in ensuring that their organizations maintained good standing with the government and did not engage in illegal or otherwise overly risky activity. In the words of Aswab Mahasin, the director of LP3ES between 1986 and 1992, "The larger and stronger an organization is, the greater the political risks to its existence. . . . As a result, it is only the small, the loose and the relatively unorganized who are capable of imagining total change, being very outspoken or taking actions which appear radical" (Mahasin 1995, 7).

Mahasin was skeptical of talk about NGOs being an important force for democratization. He argued that the heterogeneity of NGOs, their organizational characteristics, their methods of working, and the lack of a mass base greatly limited their ability to threaten the government. This was the case even with those that were sharply critical of the government, which coordinated robust campaigns on particular issues and harbored the sharpest democratizing instincts of the middle class. Such NGOs were far from being able to coordinate a mass democratic movement. The most they could do, Mahasin (1995, 8) said, was make "joint statements or protests, which might give rise to irritation, but are not at all dangerous."

In this respect, NGOs were accurate mirrors of middle-class opinion, cautious and ambivalent while trying to influence state action and create an autonomous zone for societal initiative. Given the overall weakness of the Indonesian middle class in the early New Order, in terms of size and degree of financial dependence on the state, it was not surprising that ambivalent forms of political action appeared (remember that even LBH was dependent on state funds in the 1970s). As the middle class expanded and grew more confident, NGOs did too.[30]

In broad terms, the Indonesian experience appears to confirm that where economic growth generates an expanding middle class, an increasingly vigorous civil society may come into being. Although many NGO activists privately harbored dreams of a popular upsurge against authoritarianism, the practical focus of most was achievement of particularistic aims: the improvement of the lot of specific communities, particular reforms in government policy, and so on. NGOs sought to influence, contest, and limit state action at every turn, interacting with, rather than overthrowing, the state.

All this does not mean, of course, that NGOs did not have an important political impact, nor that ABRI officers' concerns about them were entirely unjustified. But NGOs did not represent the kind of revolutionary threat that some officers implied. Instead, most NGOs, as Mulyana W. Kusumah of LBH explained, saw themselves as being engaged in a long-term process: "The NGO strategy is a step-by-step struggle of ideas (*pertarungan ide*). That is what is meant by a counterhegemonic movement. For example, human rights used to be illegitimate; now they're entering [the official discourse], the regime can no longer simply deny that violations take place" (interview, Mulyana W. Kusumah, March 11, 1994).

If present in sufficient numbers, particularistic institutions of civil society like NGOs may contribute to long-term erosion of authoritarian rule. They do this partly by winning immediate concessions, but mostly by challenging authoritarian ideologies and changing underlying assumptions in society about how politics should operate. In short, they may contribute to a new hegemony of democratic ideas and thus lay the groundwork for democratic transformation. NGOs played precisely this role in Indonesia, contributing prominently to what Ian Chalmers (1997, 65) called the "creeping acceptance in Indonesia of notions associated with political liberalism." By the mid-1990s, many issues long articulated by NGOs like LBH had become central to national political debate; the public prominence of human rights was a clear example. Indeed, the chief government concession in this area, the new National Human Rights Commission, was initially widely discussed in the media as an attempt to create an "alternative" to LBH.

NGOs may be important for the long-term delegitimation of authoritarian rule. However, when an intransigent regime fails to respond to changing public discourse and resists pressures for political reform, NGOs are ill suited to become a vehicle to overthrow the regime. Because of the kind of limitations discussed above, they rarely possess the skills, resources, or risk-taking propensity necessary to perform such a function. As authoritarian regimes enter crisis and political space opens, NGOs may thus be superseded politically by bodies which are more openly political in nature, more oriented to mobilization, and more open about wishing to replace the authoritarian incumbents. In short, the locus of struggle may shift from civil to political society (Bratton 1994, 57). This began to take place in Indonesia during the 1990s. Although NGOs still proliferated and remained important in the national political debate, by the mid-1990s the government was becoming more concerned about other political challenges, including mass-based protest movements and the reinvigorated PDI. Our attention now turns to these forms of opposition.

5

Student Activism

FROM MORAL FORCE TO
POPULAR MOBILIZATION

Sixty-one years after the Youth Pledge, has a united spirit aimed at eliminating oppression survived among the youth of today? Have we, the youth of today, forgotten the ideals of unity of the Indonesian youth of sixty-one years ago? Have we, the youth of today, been lulled into only becoming "boys" (like in the film *Catatan Si Boy* [Boy's Journals]), who care about nothing but living a materialistic and hedonistic life, living it up amid our own people who still have to scrape around in the garbage looking for leftover food? . . . NO! We youth must not become a generation of "Boys." We youth must be able to prove that we are not a useless generation, that we are a generation which still cares about the fate of the oppressed people. We must prove that we are able to remove the injustice, oppression, and violations of human rights that still occur in this, our beloved country.

> Statement released by a group of student activists commemorating the "Youth Pledge" of 1928, in Cibodas, October 28–29, 1989

On October 29, 1988, a group of 125 enthusiastic and noisy students from Gadjah Mada University's philosophy faculty made their way down Jalan Malioboro, the main thoroughfare of Yogyakarta. Fifty of them were on bicycles, the rest on foot. As they drew near to the town's provincial legislature, they sang songs and chanted slogans like "Long live campus," "Long live the students," "Long Live ABRI," and "Abolish NKK/ BKK" (by which they meant the government's "Normalization of Campus Life" policy). They had decided to hold the march to commemorate the Sumpah Pemuda, the Youth Pledge of 1928, when young people from around the archipelago came together to pledge themselves to the Indonesian nation, homeland, and language (Foulcher 2000). The students had decided that if they wanted to stay true to the ideals of the Sumpah Pemuda, they had to regain freedom of expression and organization on campuses, or "free and clean" campus democracy, as they put it. They were also aware that in 1988, a full decade after the last major outburst of student protest, street demonstrations were still a rarity in Indonesia. They were at pains to point out that they meant no harm and did not meant to insult the members of the local legislature. As one of the group's leaders put it (*Tempo*, November 12, 1988, 33), "We are not demonstrating, only *sowan* [paying our respects]."

This protest, plus a number of other small demonstrations in favor of "campus autonomy" in Yogyakarta, Bandung, and Jakarta, were at the time seen by many press commentators as marking the long-awaited rebirth of student activism. It was a very modest rebirth. It seems difficult to connect the small group on Yogyakarta's Jalan Malioboro with the images of thousands of students covering the forecourt of the building housing Indonesia's national legislature during the height of the anti-Suharto movement in May 1998. In the intervening decade, however, a variegated but sustained and often radical student activism had come into being. There were long periods of hiatus and major acts of repression, but also moments when students attracted significant national attention. Student activists played an important role in moving new issues onto the political agenda and exploring new forms of political action. In doing so, they laid the ground for the mass student unrest of 1998.

Students have played a prominent role in antigovernment movements in many developing countries. Samuel Huntington (1991, 144) suggests that students constitute "the universal opposition; they oppose whatever regime exists in their society." Comparative political theorists have suggested that students' propensity to protest is due to a range of factors, including their relative autonomy from conservatizing adult responsibilities, their access to learning and new ideas, and their concentration in strategic urban centers (e.g., Lipset and Altbach 1970).

Such factors were reinforced in Indonesia by the place occupied by students in national political discourse, owing to their role in the anticolonial movement and the fall of Sukarno's "Old Order." Despite some official downplaying, the anti-Sukarno student movement of 1966 remained central to the foundational myth of the New Order, reproduced in numerous histories and memoirs, spoken of at countless induction and graduation ceremonies, and commemorated every year by associations of now prosperous 1966 veterans (who included in their ranks prominent

New Order figures like ministers Cosmas Batubara, Akbar Tanjung, and Mar'ie Muhammad). In much wider social circles, there was a widespread assumption that it was natural that students would play a morally motivated "corrective" political role.

The Protests of the 1970s, the Sterile Campus of the 1980s

During the New Order's first decade, students had been a main source of opposition. They were the first to organize protests against the Suharto government, focusing on issues like corruption, the handling of the 1971 election, and the construction of the Taman Mini entertainment park. At this stage, those taking part were few in number and had mostly participated directly in the heady days of the student-military alliance of 1965–66. Their tone was thus one of disillusioned dissidence. During the first years of the 1970s, student leaders like Arief Budiman (a leader of the anticorruption group Mahasiswa Menggugat [Students Accuse]) developed a coherent dissident position, arguing that students constituted a "moral force" seeking to "correct" government rather than a political force seeking to overthrow or replace it (Budiman 1973). The following 1970 statement by Mahasiswa Menggugat conveys the characteristic tone of moral suasion, even aggrieved chastisement from that time:

The aim of these demonstrations is not to overthrow the government, but instead they represent critical support for the government. We see the dangers in the government's action [a price rise], which is destroying the good name of the government in the eyes of the little people. . . . Once again, the government should be truly convinced that the protest actions which we are taking are intended precisely to improve the image of the Suharto government in the eyes of the little people. Because we, the students, also helped to put in place the new order, we feel that we also have responsibility for their good name. (*Sinar Harapan*, January 19, 1970)

In the early 1970s, even as protest intensified, most activists remained reluctant to condemn the New Order in blanket terms. Rather, they emphasized regularization and reform on issues like corruption, development policy, and extraconstitutional institutions, especially Kopkamtib (Komando Operasi Pemulihan Keamanan dan Ketertiban, or Operational Command for the Restoration of Security and Order). However, disillusionment deepened with Suharto and what was seen as the circle of corrupt generals surrounding him. Some student leaders of the protests which preceded the Malari incident of January 1974 calculated that large mobilizations might encourage Kopkamtib commander general Soemitro to move against the president. After the subsequent military crackdown, the next round of large-scale student protests in 1977–78 was even more explicitly antigovernment, antimilitary, and anti-Suharto. It culminated in calls by student councils and senates for an "extraordinary session" of the MPR to remove Suharto from the presidency.

By this time, the student critique of the government was also influenced by the vogue for structural analysis in broader intellectual circles. Combining dependency thinking with the earlier liberal critique of the abuse of power, some students began to focus on the alliance between ethnic Chinese tycoons, government officials, and foreign capital.[1] An undercurrent of antimilitary sentiment which had been evolving since earlier in the decade also surfaced during the trials of student leaders following the 1978 crackdown. A defense speech by Bandung Institute of Technology (ITB) student Indro Tjahjono (1979) entitled "Indonesia Under the Jackboot" was the most explicit student indictment of the military role in politics up to this time. Other students argued in their defense speeches that the most effective way to achieve regularized government was to institutionalize democratic participation by the populace. As ITB student leader Heri Akhmadi (1981, 22) put it, students' "one demand . . . improved administration, can only be achieved through an open presidential election."

Even so, as Max Lane (1991, 3–4) argues, even in 1977–78 most students did not entirely break with the New Order and its political traditions. They continued to argue that the New Order had been an initially sound system which was corrupted by its leaders, and they still expressed loyalty to its core ideological symbols. Thus, one of the defining slogans of 1977–78 was the call for ABRI to "return to the people." The 1966 coalition's aversion to mass politics and paternalistic attitudes toward the common people also remained influential, often being expressed as repudiation of "chaos" or "anarchy." The 1978 ITB *White Book* thus denied that students intended to mobilize the poor: "Students have no intention of creating anarchy. Anarchy will only victimize the little people, who are uninformed and tend to act on their emotions" (*White Book* 1978, 166). The moral force idea remained strong, and most student activists still insisted their role was to provide *koreksi* (correction) and *peringatan* (reminders) to those in power.

Students were such a prominent source of opposition during the 1970s in part because they had a limited license to protest that was not afforded to other groups. This license derived primarily from students' important role in legitimating the military's rise to power in 1966. In the early 1970s, government leaders went to great lengths to appear to accommodate student criticism. Before 1974, technocrat ministers, senior generals, even the president himself felt it necessary to participate in face-to-face meetings with them. Similar meetings occurred in 1977–78, although the student response was by then more hostile, and a planned meeting with the president was aborted. A second factor which set students apart from most other groups, with the exception of the mass Islamic organizations, was that students retained independent organizations which were largely unaffected by the corporatization of associational life. Chief among them were the elected student councils (*dewan mahasiswa*) found on all campuses, which remained fiercely independent. Because their leaders were elected, their legitimacy was strong and they were able to coordinate protest on a national level.

The repression which followed the 1977–78 campus unrest was more thorough and effective than any which had preceded it. Troops occupied campuses, and scores of students were arrested and tried. A package of policies collectively known as NKK/BKK (Normalization of Campus Life / Bodies for the Coordination of Student Affairs) was introduced. These policies extended the reach of depoliticization and corporatist policies to universities. Student councils were permanently "frozen" and replaced by new bodies whose members were appointed by campus administrators and made subject to their veto. A new "Semester Credit System" placed more onerous curricular requirements on students, reducing the time they could spend on political activity. The government banned or suspended many student publications and permanently banned campus political activity. The surviving cross-campus *aliran*-based student organizations like the Islamic Students Association (HMI), a vehicle of modernist Islam, and the National Student Movement of Indonesia (GMNI), in the 1960s affiliated with the Indonesian National Party (PNI), were still allowed to operate, but they were subjected to ever closer government supervision. A press release from the Ministry of Education and Culture made the overall aim clear: "Supposing that there are students who wish to participate in political activity as private individuals, then they should join a political party or Golkar, but they should not bring political problems onto campus" (CSIS 1980, 63).

The government justified all this on the grounds that students' ultimate purpose was to contribute to national development by joining the "technostructure" after they graduated. In the words of education and culture minister Daoed Joesoef, the aim was to ensure that students used their time wisely: "Fill it up with reading, writing, conducting research; don't waste it in the streets."[2]

Overall, the effect of the post-1978 normalization of campus life policies and accompanying repression was to marginalize student activism further. After an initial round of anti–NKK/BKK protests in 1979–80, it became very difficult for students to organize antigovernment activities openly on campus. During the early 1980s, the rare demonstrations which took place resulted in suspensions and other disciplinary action.

In the post-1978 climate, the most critically minded students found refuge in three types of alternative political vehicles. First, they formed study groups in large numbers from around 1982–83 in university towns in Java and, a little later, elsewhere. By 1987 the phenomenon was so widespread that an estimated twenty such groups existed in Yogyakarta alone (*Tempo*, April 22, 1989, 28). These groups varied greatly in size, as well as in political outlook. Mostly they were loosely structured, involving small groups of students who met regularly near campus to discuss social and political theory, recent political developments, local social problems, and the like. Some study groups became better organized and produced regular journals, but most remained informal. Some participants believed that study groups were an entirely new style of student politics which avoided confrontation with government and promoted change by way of reasoned intellectual contributions to public debate (*aksi informasi* [information action], rather than *aksi massa* [mass action]).[3] Others saw them as products of necessity amid repressive political conditions. All used them to deepen their theoretical knowledge; seek new solutions for the country's political, social, and economic problems; and understand the "failure" of previous generations of student activism. This search led some study group participants toward radical literature, including works by Paolo Freire and Franz Fanon, Islamic radicals like Ali Shariati, the Frankfurt school, classical Marxism, liberation theology, and publications of radical groups in South Korea and the Philippines.

The student press became a second important vehicle for activism. In the 1980s, some previously suspended publications were revived, and many new ones were established. Although these were usually published under the aegis of official bodies, like faculty senates, they often attracted the most critically minded students on campus. Student media offices often became informal organizing centers. Activists grouped around publications like *Politika* (Universitas Nasional, Jakarta), *Ganesha* (ITB), and *Arena* (Institut Agama Islam Negeri [IAIN, State Institute for Islamic Studies], Sunan Kalijaga, Yogyakarta) were later important in the reemergence of protest.

Third, NGOs were also important. The banning of political activity on campuses coincided with, and partially accounted for, the NGO boom discussed in Chapter 4. Most NGOs relied on students as volunteers and recruits. Many students became involved in community development NGOs, but the more politically conscious were attracted to those which questioned developmentalism and pursued advocacy work. For example, SKEPHI, the environmental NGO established in 1982 by former 1978 student leader Indro Tjahjono, attracted many student recruits. In Bandung, students visited villages to gather data for LBH legal challenges to land requisition orders. Study groups like Yayasan Geni in Salatiga or Yayasan Studi Masyarakat (Foundation for the Study of Society) in Jakarta also began to take their own first tentative steps at establishing links with poor communities.[4] At the same time that they were studying structuralist and radical theories, some students thus came into direct contact with the poor and their problems, helping to generate the radicalization discussed below.

From about 1985–86, networking activities began among some study group and campus media activists from different cities in Java. These activists began to hold protests on campuses in Java and beyond. Mostly these focused on internal campus issues like increases in tuition fees, corrupt university administrations, and inadequate facilities. Although many students clearly felt strongly about such issues, their prominence was partly a deliberate tactic adopted by activists to avoid confrontation with security forces, giving them some breathing space to learn practical organizing techniques. The potential for more serious, albeit spontaneous, unrest was indicated by major student riots in 1987 in Pontianak and Ujung Pandang. These were sparked by government regulations requiring motorcycle riders to wear helmets. In both cases, many students were arrested, campuses closed temporarily, and in Ujung Pandang, several protestors were shot dead. These protests stimulated numerous "solidarity actions" in major Javanese campuses, consolidating networks between activist groups.

The Rebirth of Student Protest, 1988–1990

The small demonstrations in favor of student political rights in late 1988 marked the beginning of a new and protracted wave of student protest. Through 1989 and 1990, as the issue of "openness" increasingly dominated national political debate, student protests repeatedly grabbed national media attention. Often the demonstrations were very small, but sometimes thousands of students took part. Many new student organizations sprang up, underground pamphlets proliferated, and there was feverish coordinating activity between cities. Demonstrations were initially deferential and polite (often in the form of delegations to the DPR or ministers' offices), but they rapidly became larger and more confrontational and raised more sensitive topics. Although troops often assaulted demonstrators and numerous activists were arrested and put on trial, there was no knockout blow from the security forces.

Two sets of issues dominated the early demonstrations. First, there was a concerted attempt to campaign to extend student political rights and win back space for campus political activities. Many demonstrations called for "campus autonomy," repeal of NKK/BKK, and especially the release of student activists who were on trial. Second, there was great emphasis on problems experienced by poor communities, especially land disputes. Student activists "lived in" in poor rural communities, organized protest campaigns, and mobilized members of the affected communities (discussed below). Activists thus deliberately avoided direct confrontation with the government on what they labeled "elite" issues, such as the presidency, which had predominated in the 1970s. Instead, they chose ostensibly "local" issues which allowed them to express a new populist orientation.

The regional distribution, social background, and organizational form of the new student protest movement was very different from those of previous generations. The 1966, 1973–74, and 1977–78 movements had been centered in Jakarta and Bandung. The new activism was more widely dispersed. In 1989–90, sustained organizing emerged in most of the important university towns in Java: Bogor, Semarang, Yogyakarta, Solo, Salatiga, Surabaya, Malang, Jombang, and Jember, as well as Mataram in Lombok and Denpasar, Bali. Central Java, especially Yogyakarta, was the new focus. Also unlike in the 1960s and 1970s, when students from the elite state universities (especially Universitas Indonesia [UI] and ITB) were the pace-setters, activism now involved more students from smaller and less prestigious private campuses. In Jakarta, the UI was quiescent and students from private campuses like Universitas Nasional, Mustopo, and 17 Agustus were more prominent.

This change reflected the more rigorous application of NKK/BKK on state universities, especially those which had been foci of political activism. But it also reflected the changing shape of tertiary education. Indonesian university students in 1966 were the children of a tiny elite. Economic development and the growth of the middle class eventually created demands for new skills and a larger market for tertiary education. Private universities mushroomed; according to Ministry of Education and Culture figures, their numbers rose from 63 in 1978 to 221 in 1990, with much of the growth in provincial centers. Tertiary education had ceased to be the exclusive preserve of the upper reaches of the narrow cosmopolitan elite of the big cities (many of whom, in any case, now sent their children overseas for study). Instead, it had become more accessible to wider layers, including provincial youths from more humble backgrounds.

Lane (1989) argues that the lower-middle-class origins of many activists contributed directly to the more radical flavor of student activism from the late 1980s. Many militant activists, especially in provincial towns, were certainly the children of teachers, low-ranking civil servants, small-time entrepreneurs, even prosperous farmers. Often personal experiences of family privation accounted for their interest in the problems of the poor. But this was by no means universally so; the most radical activists also included children of upper-middle-class professionals and even relatively senior officials. Budiman Sudjatmiko, for example, who went on to lead the most radical student-based organization, the People's Democratic Union (later "Party"; PRD), was the son of a manager in a Goodyear plant in West Java. (But even Budiman's background typifies the fluidity of the class backgrounds of many activists; he spent his childhood living with his grandparents in a village near Cilacap, and by his own account, the deep sympathy for the poor that this life engendered was what later motivated him to become a political activist [Gunawan 1999, 25–33]). Some activists, such as Yeni Rosa Damayanti, one of the best-known women student activists, who was tried in 1994, were children of ABRI officers, unsurprising given the military's place in the nation's social elite.

In the 1970s, most student protest was organized by the officially sanctioned student councils. This avenue was closed by NKK/BKK. In the late 1980s, the public face of student protest was largely represented by transient and ad hoc action committees (*komite aksi*), which coalesced for particular campaigns and then disbanded. Such committees were themselves alliances of less publicly visible campus-based groups centered on study groups or campus newspapers, which acted as organizing and recruiting centers. Open citywide organizations also began to appear. The prototype was the Yogyakarta Student Communication Forum (FKMY), which in 1989 claimed a membership of fifteen hundred students from some twenty campuses (*Tempo*, April 24, 1989, 30). Another organization which played a crucial role at this time was the Indonesian Front for the Defense of Human Rights (INFIGHT), a coalition of some of the smaller activist NGOs (notably Indro Tjahjono's SKEPHI) and many student groups, especially from Central Java. It became something akin to a national coordinating center for the new radical student movement.

These flexible, informal, and semiunderground modes of organizing student activism were a response to the tighter political controls on campuses. As a result, the student activism which emerged in this period was more resilient than its predecessors. It survived numerous incidents of repression. On the other hand, it was also splintered and marginalized. Small activist groups were often relatively isolated from the student body as a whole and faced difficulties in coordinating their activities on a national basis. As a result, demonstrations (at least of students alone) were rarely as large, nor the movement as nationally representative, as in the 1970s. Although broad sections of the student population apparently sympathized with the activists (on rare occasions many thousands could be mobilized), most students followed Daoed Joesoef's advice and got on with their studies.

These new activists had a far more uncompromising attitude toward the New Order than had their predecessors. They placed more emphasis on human rights (including examination of previously taboo issues like abuses in East Timor, Irian, and Aceh and the 1965–66 massacres), were more openly hostile to the military and its political role, and favored mass action. In the words of one Bandung student activist at his trial in 1990, "Going to the streets or demonstrating is the one and only potent tool for overthrowing an authoritarian regime" (Ammarsyah 1990, 226).

What above all characterized the new populist mood was exaltation of the common people, the *rakyat*. Student pamphlets, defense speeches, and essays stressed that they sought above all to empower the poor and defend them against exploitation and oppression. There was parallel hostility to the "elite," who were portrayed as beneficiaries of the exploitation of the masses. Mostly such discussions were made in classic populist terms of a broad dichotomy between *rakyat* and *elit* or *penguasa* (ruler). Some material reflected Marxist influence and more explicitly identified capitalism as the chief enemy (Aspinall 1993).

The general hostility to elite politics in part derived from a judgment that students in the 1970s had erred by intervening in national politics. They had consequently been *ditunggangi* (literally, ridden—used, taken advantage of) by elite interests (see, e.g., Akhmad 1989; Radjab 1991; Arief 1994). As if to symbolize the break, an early demonstration in Yogyakarta in August 1989 was directed against General (retired) Soemitro, the very man who fifteen years earlier, in the lead-up to Malari, had been considered a potential ally by some student leaders. Now, although Soemitro was long retired and had become an advocate of political reform, the radical activists condemned him. As a leaflet distributed on the day put it, "Who knows if he's again seeking our sympathy and support to use in the competition for the seat of power in 1993? . . . Whatever else, Soemitro is still a soldier whose ideology is to defend the status quo, who never sides with the people or defends the people's interests."

The new student activists also often castigated other critics of the government—intellectuals, NGO leaders, and the like—for their alleged conservatism and elitism. And yet many of the student activist groups which emerged in the late 1980s were closely connected to the elite opposition milieu. Major campaigns, on land disputes, for example, were generally organized jointly with NGOs like LBH (even if differences in approach frequently caused tensions). Moreover, whenever small student groups needed funds for a demonstration or other activity, they were usually obliged to seek donations from sympathetic "sponsors," often NGO leaders with access to unallocated campaign funds or dissident figures with business connections. The resulting financial dependence was often a conduit for influence, even if an irritating one.

The government response to the resurgent student activism from the late 1980s was the classic authoritarian mixture of inconsistently applied but sometimes severe repression, tempered by occasional toleration. From the start, some senior officials made belligerent statements. ABRI commander Try Sutrisno, for example, reminded students that a 1970 Kopkamtib decree banning demonstrations had not been rescinded. Between 1988 and 1994 over forty student activists were tried for various political offenses. Among the more celebrated early cases were the subversion trials in 1988–90 of three study group members in Yogyakarta who were accused of possessing and distributing banned "Marxist" books, including works by the famous novelist Pramoedya Ananta Toer. Seven ITB activists went on trial in Bandung in 1989–90 after they protested against a campus visit by interior minister Rudini. Security forces often violently broke up student demonstrations and closed down their publications. Activists were occasionally tortured. Most of all, they were harassed by constant low-level monitoring and intimidation. Student activists found it impossible to predict what kind of response their demonstrations would elicit. Intelligence officers would often "drop in" at meeting places "to chat" or for more straightforward interrogation. Security officers briefed university rectors and ordered them to enforce campus depoliticization (see, for example, *Suara Merdeka*, June 28, 1991). There was often confrontation, including violence, with the campus *menwa* (student regiments), which were directly supervised by local military commands.

But tolerance, co-optation, and concession also occurred. At the beginning, the response of certain officials, notably interior minister Rudini and several Fraksi-ABRI members, was welcoming; they described student activism as (*masih*—"so far") "normal," "honest," even "positive." In 1990, the government made a concession to demands for abolition of NKK/BKK by allowing campuswide student senates on state universities, although they remained subject to controls by campus administrators and had limited powers.

As *keterbukaan* progressed, student activism intensified. Activist groups emerged on many previously quiet campuses, in provincial towns in Java and beyond (e.g., Palu and Menado in Sulawesi). Although private campuses were still important, activism increased in big state universities like UI. Student publications flourished, and many (such as *Hayam Wuruk* at Diponegoro University in Semarang or *Arena* at IAIN Sunan Kalijaga in Yogyakarta) contained brazenly antigovernment material, condemning military abuses and sometimes even lampooning the president. Student protests voiced increasingly direct demands, including calls for repeal of the subversion law and the regime's five main political laws,[5] dissolution of the security agency Bakorstanas, abolition of *dwifungsi*, even for an extraordinary MPR session to remove Suharto from the presidency.

This escalation was accompanied by greater differentiation within student activism. In the depoliticized campus of the 1980s, students had been little exposed to open competition between differing political ideas. As a result, as well as being radical, the activists of 1988–90 put forward an often somewhat nebulous populist critique. Many student activists were unwilling to define their political outlook beyond a broad *visi kerakyatan* (populist vision) which entailed a general defense of the poor's political, economic, and social interests and denied that they were motivated by ideological considerations. As student activists gained experience and their ideas evolved, previously latent ideological divisions became apparent. In 1991, a bitter conflict divided INFIGHT, and splits soon followed in major citywide student bodies like FKMY. Although personal enmities, disputes over funding, and similar problems contributed, the splits also had a political dimension (partly reflected in some accusations of "communism" which were thrown around at their height).[6] Although a large degree of simplification is involved, and many groups did not fit easily into either category, by the mid-1990s it was possible to identify two distinct political poles among activist groups.

Liberal-Populist Students

One pole of the student movement may be described as liberal-populist because it combined the new populist tone with an essentially liberal political outlook, remaining close to the mainstream tradition of New Order student dissent. In the mid-1990s, many small groups could be included in this category, although they were neither ideologically nor organizationally cohesive. Most were loosely organized campus and city-based groups. Among the most significant were Yayasan Pijar (Pusat Informasi dan Jaringan Aksi untuk Reformasi, Information Center and Action Network for Reformation) in Jakarta, originally formed in 1989 by students centered around the Universitas Nasional (Unas) magazine *Politika* and Dewan Mahasiswa dan Pemuda Yogyakarta (the Yogyakarta Council of Youth and Students, or DMPY). Occasional attempts were made to group such organizations on a national basis. In 1994 students in Jakarta, Bandung, and some other cities established Aldera (Aliansi Demokrasi Rakyat, the Peoples' Democratic Alliance). This was an essentially underground organization with an ambitious political program, although it was centered on a few highly active individuals. Less formal networking between towns was vigorous, with frequent clandestine *lokakarya* (workshops) and *refleksi* (reflections) held to evaluate recent actions and discuss the way forward.

In the mid-1990s, these students increasingly raised what they sometimes referred to as "elite" issues concerning national-level corruption and political leadership. This was highlighted by a series of protests directed against Suharto in 1993 (see below). They tended to engage less than before in direct organization of farmers or workers; instead their typical modus operandi was relatively small demonstrations which involved considerable risk. Many liberal-populist students stressed the moral character of their struggle and the need for boldness (a sign at the doorway of the Yayasan Pijar office in 1993 read *"Ragu-ragu tidak usah masuk"* [If you're hesitant, you needn't come in]). Sometimes such students said their role was that of a pressure group able to put sensitive issues on the political agenda. Some felt students could do little more than *memanaskan situasi* (heat up the situation). Others argued that they were a "counterhegemonic" movement, aiming to roll back state intrusion in the societal realm. Many dreamed of Philippines-style "people power," but some also kept an attachment to the "moral force" traditions of the 1970s, though with a new populist veneer. It was common to describe the student movement as a moral rather than a political movement, or as a "social control." Frequent declarations of student "purity" (*kemurnian*) were similarly consistent with the 1966 traditions of hostility to partisan politics, as well as echoing the New Order regime's own obsession with subversive bodies infiltrating and manipulating social discontent.

The political outlook of these activists resists precise categorization, being an updated version of the liberal-populist mélange which had persistently arisen in middle-class dissidence under the New Order. It combined strong antiauthoritarianism (sometimes almost an anarchist spirit), antimilitarism, and antielitism, a populist emphasis on the *rakyat*, and liberal themes of regularization and accountability. The essential aim was democratic government. Semarang student Lukas Luwarso, in his defense speech at his 1993 trial (for participation in an election boycott or *golput* demonstration) used language which echoed that used in student trials fifteen years earlier:

> Lord Acton's dictum that power always tends to corrupt, and that absolute power corrupts absolutely, has been shown to be correct in reality. . . . The balance of powers in the state is the principal means by which it is possible to prevent the corruption of power. The best system of control [*pengawasan*] is the equal division of power between the Legislature, Executive and Judiciary, in addition to the existence of a free press and a free people who can give voice to their aspirations and engage in social control. All of this will result in a healthy political system and respect for the principle of the *negara hukum*. (Luwarso 1993, 42–3)

While some groups, especially in Central and East Java, remained skeptical of elite politics and continued to be involved in campaigns on land disputes and similar "populist issues," from the early 1990s others (especially those in Jakarta, like Yayasan Pijar) moved closer to middle-class opposition circles. Many groups invited prominent intellectuals, NGO leaders, and other critics to their meetings and sought their political advice. Some student activists from the 1980s joined NGOs, while others established their own, acting concurrently as the most confrontational wing of the NGO movement and as informal coordinating centers for student activists. Many former student activists likewise gravitated to particular opposition leaders and groups. For example, some student activists in Jakarta, like Rachland Nashidik of Yayasan Pijar, became very close to the secular intellectuals involved in Forum Demokrasi.

In part, this trend simply reflected the rapid generational turnover characteristic of student politics; in the same way that university prepares students for entry to the professions, student activism is an apprenticeship for middle-class political activism of all stripes. Student activists were integrated into wider oppositional circles once leaders of student groups established in the 1980s graduated and moved to NGOs and other organizations while maintaining links with their old campus networks. For some activists, however, a clear strategic shift was involved; given greater political openness from the early 1990s, they argued, it was time to *main elit* (play the elite game, as one Yayasan Pijar leader informed me in 1993) and to seek broader alliances in middle-class opposition (interview, Nuku Suleiman, September 7, 1993). Some suggested that this was because mobilizing farmers in land dispute protests in the 1980s had proved to be a dead end.

Popular-Radicalism: The PRD

From the late 1980s, there was a self-consciously radical element in the new student movement (see Aspinall 1993; Lane 1994, 1995). Some activists (especially in Central Java) were particularly influenced by the Marxist material they read in study groups and by leftist student movements in the Philippines and South Korea. They consciously strove to give the movement a more radical (*populis* was a frequent code word) tone and to break decisively from earlier traditions, arguing that students should eschew a moral or "corrective" role and instead mobilize "popular sectors" against the regime.

Such ideas appeared in the underground journal *Progres* in 1991. *Progres* circulated widely in activist circles and contained a wide range of material, including detailed reports on campaigns by workers, peasants, and students and critical analyses of opposition groups viewed as conservative. One edition of the magazine contained an interview with members of the "National Youth Front," revealing that some student activists now explicitly identified with the pre-1965 left: "The revolutionary movement was crushed by the forces of the fascist regime which is now in power, now we must rebuild the revolutionary movement in Indonesia" (*Progres* 3 [1], 1993, 20). Following the splits in 1991, a handful of activists, prominent among them Daniel Indrakusumah and Budiman Sudjatmiko, developed a clandestine network of small groups which grew especially rapidly at several Central Javanese campuses (especially in Yogyakarta, Solo, and Semarang), spreading to Surabaya and Jakarta and even outside Java. In 1994, this current came into the open nationally, with the public launch of the PRD (Persatuan Rakyat Demokratik, People's Democratic Union) in May and of Solidaritas Mahasiswa Indonesia untuk Demokrasi (Student Solidarity for Democracy in Indonesia, or SMID) in August. The PRD's two-page declaration called for democratization in the political, economic, and cultural fields and demanded the free formation of parties, abolition of the military's political role, full restitution of the rights of former political prisoners, and a peaceful and democratic resolution of the East Timor problem. This was an unprecedentedly blunt statement of opposition to the New Order.

Popular-radical students elaborated their views in more explicit programmatic form than did other groups. They also tended to be highly disciplined. Key organizers were divided between several "layers," with some assigned to "public" work while others remained underground, occupied full-time in coordinating tasks or working in industrial or rural areas. Their main political orientation was the organization and mobilization of subordinate classes, especially industrial workers. The PRD manifesto (released in 1996) suggested that workers had the potential to "be the vanguard in seizing and opening real democratic-liberal space" and in "dragging progressive allies" to join the struggle (PRD 1996, 45). An early manifestation of a "worker-student" alliance along Philippine or Korean lines occurred on May 1, 1995, with a demonstration by a thousand workers and 250 students in Semarang (the choice of International Workers' Day prompted a bellicose response from officials, who accused the students of following a "communist pattern" [*Gatra*, May 13, 1995, 32–3]). Subsequently, activists from SMID and the PRD's labor affiliate, Pusat Perjuangan Buruh Indonesia (Center for Indonesian Labor Struggle, or PPBI) organized numerous labor protests, including some strikes by over ten thousand workers.[7] Although their influence over workers remained limited, their capacity to organize large mass actions, plus their discipline and programmatic boldness, gave them a dramatic visibility in the developing democratic movement.

This wing of the student movement was clearly very radical. Although small, it was evolving in the direction of what I described in Chapter 1 as mobilizational opposition, openly aiming to replace the regime and using mobilization to pursue that goal. Indeed, in 1996, the organization relaunched itself as an open political party (see Chapter 7). However, this kind of militancy demanded great commitment and involved considerable risk. By mid-1996, the PRD and associated organizations could claim, at most, several hundred core activists (even if they were sometimes able to organize demonstrations involving many thousands). This group's heightened level of political activity and rhetoric ultimately marked it out for special repression.

Islamic Student Activism and the Impact of ICMI

In addition to secular forms of radicalism, an important Islamic element contributed to the student activist revival from 1987 to 1989. Many Islamic campuses (like IAIN Sunan Kalijaga and Universitas Islam Indonesia [UII] in Yogyakarta) became centers of energetic activism. Groups which campaigned on land disputes and similar issues attracted many members who saw their motivations partly in Islamic terms. Commitment to the poor was partly influenced by works by "leftist" Middle Eastern Islamic thinkers, like Ali Shariati, and the rediscovery of Muslim radicals from Indonesia's own past, such as the 1920s "red santri" Haji Misbach (this trend was especially evident among traditionalist Islamic students who were influenced by Abdurrahman Wahid's promotion of NGO-style social activism).

From the late 1980s, a distinct strand of specifically Islamic student activism was marked by some large demonstrations against restrictions on the wearing of the Islamic head scarf, *jilbab*, in schools, state lotteries, and *tempat maksiat* (places where gambling, drinking alcohol, and prostitution took place). In 1990, there were very large protests calling for the banning of the magazine *Monitor* and the imprisonment of its editor for his "insult" of the prophet Muhammad. These protests prompted criticism from secular radical students who saw the issue as one of press freedom and human rights. The mobilizing potential of Islamic students was further illustrated by two waves of demonstrations, some numbering in the tens of thousands, against a state lottery, the SDSB, in late 1991 and late 1993.

These campaigns drew much of their sustenance from a campus religious revival visible from the early 1980s, when students had begun to flock in growing numbers to campus mosques and Islamic study and prayer groups. This phenomenon reflected a nationwide process of middle-class Islamization, but it was also partly a product of the blocking of overtly political avenues for Islamic activism on campuses. The new activism of the 1990s thus partly drew on semiclandestine networks which were a legacy of the previously hostile environment toward Islamic politics. For example, in 1983–86 there had been heavy-handed government intervention in the large modernist student organization HMI. The aim of the intervention was to put a compliant leadership in place and force the organization to accept Pancasila as "sole basis" (Hassan 1987, 188–89). The intervention achieved its aims, but the organization split, giving rise to a wing (HMI-MPO) which kept Islam in its statutes as its philosophical base. Even in the early 1990s, the HMI-MPO remained dominant on many campuses. Campus mosques were also important organizing centers and focal points for intercampus networking. By the early 1990s, new networks of secretive *tarbiyah* (Arabic: education) groups which promoted a doctrinally purified form of Islam began to gain control of student senates on many state universities (Fealy 2001). These and similar networks in turn gave birth to informal coalitions like the Persatuan Mahasiswa Islam Bandung (Bandung Alliance of Muslim Students), which played a major role in organizing the protests against SDSB.

The formation of ICMI in 1990 and the subsequent rapprochement between modernist Islam and the government was an important turning point for the new Islamic student political activism. Many modernist students, including some who had previously been hostile to the government, accepted that ICMI represented a historic opportunity for Islam. Some HMI-MPO leaders, who had led a harried and underground existence through the 1980s, began to reconsider their position so that the division between HMI-MPO and the "official" HMI began to break down. Some leaders of the student protests of the late 1980s also moved close to ICMI. For example, Mohamad Jumhur Hidayat, an ITB student who in 1990 was jailed for protesting against interior minister Rudini, soon after his release became the right-hand man of ICMI secretary general Adi Sasono and executive director of his ICMI-linked research body CIDES. Eggi Sudjana, chairperson of HMI-MPO in the 1980s and a prominent figure in Jakarta student politics, as well as other modernist student leaders, were also recruited to CIDES. Operators like these sometimes acted as intermediaries, providing funding from ICMI sources for student protests and campaigns on issues which accorded with the goals of modernist activists (such as the release of Muslim political prisoners).

The rapprochement had a particularly noticeable impact on the official wing of HMI ("HMI Dipo," as it was often called, after the Jakarta street, Jalan Diponegoro, where its headquarters were located). HMI was the most important and largest of the officially recognized student organizations; one estimate in 1986 put its membership at 150,000 (*Tapol Bulletin 75*, May 1986, 23). Many former HMI members had since the 1960s made successful careers in business, bureaucracy, and government. In 1997, the magazine *Ummat* (August 4, 1997, 33) estimated that around two hundred of the five hundred members of the DPR had HMI backgrounds.[8] The HMI alumni association (KAHMI) was led by prominent figures like finance minister Mar'ie Muhammad. Such HMI "seniors" were intermediaries through whom leaders of HMI could access centers of politico-bureaucratic power. Rival leadership candidates at the 1997 HMI congress were backed by different government patrons: Fuad Bawazier, the director-general of taxation, who was close to the president's children, and minister for youth affairs and sport Akbar Tanjung (*Suara Independen*, September 1997, 9). From the early 1990s, a few HMI branches (such as the one in Surabaya) took part in the activism on land and other "populist" issues, but they were exceptional. As many other student groups became more openly critical of the government in the 1990s, HMI generally avoided following suit. Its members often had hostile relations with secular-oriented and radical students at the campus level. To the extent that HMI was prepared to mobilize its members, this tended to be in demonstrations like those against the state lottery (SDSB), which, while according with widely held Islamic social goals, involved less risk of confrontation with the security apparatus. HMI leaders were adamant that they did not wish to endanger their organization's infrastructure by engaging in premature, open antigovernment action. When political "momentum" arrived, they would "harvest the fruits" (*memetik buah*) of their patient cadre-building approach and mobilize their large following (interview with students at HMI national headquarters, Jakarta, December 23, 1993).

In contrast to HMI, other officially recognized *aliran*-based student *ormas* became increasingly critical of the government during the early 1990s. The nationalist (GMNI), Catholic (PMKRI), Protestant (GMKI), and traditionalist Islamic (PMII) student organizations, which alongside HMI were united in what was known as the "Cipayung group" (it was named after the place where its first meeting was held), had more or less succumbed to government pressures over the course of the 1970s. Through the 1980s these organizations had busied themselves with routine recruitment, training, religious and social activities, avoiding activities which might be construed as antigovernment. After *keterbukaan*, however, the new activist mood began to affect them also. The Cipayung group released some statements (some of which HMI avoided endorsing) criticizing government policies. This new assertiveness was partly an effect of the rise of activism pioneered by the smaller radical groups (many of whose members had taunted the Cipayung bodies for their alleged political cowardice). But it was also noteworthy that the groups which became more critical were from *aliran* more liable to be alienated than co-opted by the rapprochement between the government and modernist Islam. From the early 1990s, the Nahdlatul Ulama strongholds of Jember and Jombang became important centers of student activism, and the Pergerakan Mahasiswa Islam Indonesia (Indonesian Islamic Student Movement, or PMII) adopted an increasingly oppositional tone. Activists from the Sukarnoist Gerakan Mahasiswa Nasional Mahasiswa Indonesia (National Student Movement of Indonesia, or GMNI), and the Catholic Persatuan Mahasiswa Katolik Indonesia (Catholic Students' Association of Indonesia, or PMKRI) likewise took part in campaigning on land disputes and antigovernment protests; a group emerged in the former which, following the path set by the PDI, explicitly aimed to assert independence from government intervention (*Wawasan*, October 18, 1995).

Within this broad context, some of the Islamic student activism of the 1990s itself suggested a blurring of the divide between societal opposition and factional conflict within the state. Some of the anonymous leaflets distributed at the actions against *Monitor* in late 1990 claimed that the magazine's editor, Arswendo Atmowiloto, had not only deliberately intended to slur Islam but was also acting in a wider plot attempting to divide Suharto from the *umat* (because Arswendo had placed the president first in his readers' popularity poll, ten places above the Prophet Muhammad). This was in turn connected to "the support of Christians (Catholics) who at present are striving to get the presidential seat in their (L. B. Moerdani and co.'s) grasp. Part of ABRI supports that ambitious general in his attempt to overthrow President Suharto and take power unconstitutionally."[9] Demonstrating against the magazine was thus not only a way to defend the faith against insult but also a way to reject the machinations of Moerdani and his supporters.

In 1994, many students from HMI or who were otherwise linked to ICMI organized protests against a corruption scandal uncovered in Bapindo (Indonesian Development Bank). This allowed them to raise the theme of Chinese domination of the economy (a villain of the piece was a Chinese businessman, Edy Tansil) and accorded with factional goals, given that a subsidiary target was former finance minster Johannes Sumarlin, one of the triumvirate of Christian economic ministers castigated by ICMI activists. Another example of the ICMI influence on student politics was the Haryanto Dhanutirto affair of late 1995 and early 1996. Haryanto was transport minister, a key ICMI leader, and a close associate of Minister Habibie. In December 1995, bureaucratic opponents of ICMI leaked a confidential report which alleged corrupt activities by Haryanto, including a government-funded European shopping spree by his wife. The leak sparked intense press scrutiny. Numerous protests by liberal-populist student groups called for the minister's sacking. Activists linked to ICMI counterattacked by accusing officials unsympathetic to ICMI (especially the inspector general of development, Major General [retired] Kentot Harseno, who wrote the report, and minister of the state secretariat Moerdiono) of "treason" for "leaking state secrets" in order to harm Haryanto. Students from the HMI and other Islamic networks such as former HMI-MPO leader Eggi Sudjana organized lively demonstrations, again backed by a *Republika*-led press campaign, calling for those responsible to be punished. This was partly successful in diverting public attention away from Haryanto (*Suara Independen* 2 [7], January–February 1996, 31–32). The affair showed how ICMI's formation and the new political dispensation it represented polarized politics. The organization had the capacity to trigger snowballing mobilization and countermobilization by forces aligned with and against it (Porter 2002, 150–51).

The Impact of Tensions in ABRI

If student politics were influenced by the Suharto camp's rapprochement with modernist Islam, this raises the question of the relationship with the "other side" of elite friction: discontented ABRI officers. Some writers have argued that the rebirth of student activism from the late 1980s must be understood in this context, even that student protest was "encour-

aged" by military elements in order to put pressure on Suharto. Michael
Vatikiotis (1993, 162, 5), for instance, argues that "students were persuaded to demonstrate" and were "seemingly guided" by elements of the
military who were critical of President Suharto.[10]

Certainly, at the outset of *keterbukaan* in 1989, some military officers,
especially from the Fraksi-ABRI in the DPR, made extraordinary efforts
to appear sympathetic to student protest, visiting campuses and publicly
welcoming the reemergent student social consciousness (*Tempo*, October
28, 1989, 30; *Editor*, October 28, 1989, 27). From around the same
time, some officers also made more informal private approaches to student groups which had drawn attention to themselves by holding demonstrations. For example, students interviewed in Salatiga in March 1994
related that in early 1989 student activists in Central Java involved in
campaigning against the Kedung Ombo dam development were visited
by Brigadier General Ibrahim Saleh, who a year earlier had caused a stir
at the MPR session when he interrupted the election of Sudharmono as
vice president. Although he was initially disguised as a journalist, students soon recognized him. After questioning them, he told them to contact him if they needed funds or other support, and especially if they
wished to criticize President Suharto. He also offered to put them in contact with the Fraksi-ABRI and handed them an envelope containing
money. The students were somewhat perplexed by this approach; they rejected the money and did not pursue his offers.

Many activists recounted similar stories of being approached by military intelligence officers. For example, students interviewed in Jakarta in
November 1993 revealed that a regular pattern of contacts began in late
1989. The officers would typically initiate these contacts, often by taking
the students into custody and questioning them about their activities.
This would sometimes lead to more general and convivial discussions. In
turn, the students would seek information on elite conflicts. Although the
officers never openly criticized the president, they offered tidbits concerning conflicts or scandals involving senior officials. The students said
these officers appeared sympathetic to student aims and "encouraged"
(*mendorong*) them to continue protesting. On at least some occasions,
money was given. Many activists in East and Central Java informed me
of similar approaches, especially in 1993–94, although activists in those
provinces tended to be more militant and hence more suspicious of the
military. Intelligence officers often visited the boardinghouses which
served as student meeting places. Again they were mainly concerned to
discuss students' activities, but they also often professed sympathy with
their aims. According to one activist from Semarang, an intelligence officer told him, "We share the same vision; we've both been disappointed,

and we should work together to overthrow Suharto" (confidential interview, February 1994).

Many activists also carefully noted the military response to demonstrations, especially the particular leniency shown in early 1993 when, before and coinciding with the MPR session which saw ABRI elevate Try Sutrisno to the vice presidency, some students took the especially bold move of protesting against Suharto's reelection. At a January PDI leadership meeting in Bogor, Aldera students demanded that the PDI reject Suharto's renomination as president. Although the military used its usual brutality in dispersing the protest, it was a surprise to the protestors that none of those taken into custody were formally charged. Two months later, students who demonstrated right outside the MPR as it met on March 9 were allowed to proceed by the large contingent of troops present for a brief time in full view of the press. Only five were arrested (and were held for just over twenty-four hours); others were apparently ushered out of harm's way and onto passing buses by officers from the local territorial command.[11] According to several students detained at these protests, military interrogators sometimes concentrated on ascertaining whether they held antimilitary views or were merely opposed to the president. Students, not surprisingly, insisted on the latter, and this often seemed to ensure their rapid release.

In December 1993, security personnel allowed about a hundred students going under the banner of the Indonesian Students' Action Front (FAMI) to protest for several hours in the lobby of the DPR building. During this time the students attacked Suharto very forthrightly, holding a banner reading *"Seret Presiden ke Sidang Istimewa MPR"* (Drag the President to an Extraordinary Session of the MPR [extraordinary MPR sessions were the constitutional means to remove a president from office]) and shouting *"Gantung Suharto!"* (Hang Suharto!). However, the focus of the demonstration was the "security approach," especially the killing of four villagers at a recent land protest in Nipah, Madura. When the students began to abuse the military, they were attacked. Of those arrested, twenty-one were subsequently put on trial. According to student activists interviewed between December 1993 and March 1994, this led many in both student and elite opposition circles to criticize the protestors for injudiciously attacking two competing powers at the same time (see also Prasetyo 1994).

Such experiences, and more general perception of conflict in the ruling elite, made many students confident that there existed a political space to protest. To cite just one example, a contributor to a magazine produced by the Bandung group Student Movement Committee for the Indonesian People (KPMURI) in 1992 noted a new "permissive attitude" by authorities toward student demonstrations and urged students to "seize" the opportunity to develop a mass-based movement (*Realita* 1, April 1992, 28–32).

Such analyses, however, occurred in the context of considerable hostility toward the military, especially in the smaller radical groups. Unlike in the 1970s, when the 1966 student-military coalition was a comparatively recent memory, the historical backdrop of the student movement of the late 1980s and 1990s was the hostile military-student relations of the 1970s. Contemporary activists often believed that the 1966 students helped disguise ABRI's seizure of power and insisted that they would never repeat this error.

From the start, therefore, many student activists explicitly rejected being drawn into elite conflicts. Bandung student Ammarsyah, for example, argued at his 1990 trial that the national leadership crisis approaching 1992–93 was of no concern to student activists because "the issue of succession is not a requirement of the common people" (Ammarsyah 1990, 228–29). Many activists opposed contemplating collaboration with even anti-Suharto military elements or tailoring demands to focus only on Suharto. Students linked to the PRD were particularly antimilitary, frequently characterizing the political system as "fascist" and, from about 1993, including abolition of *dwifungsi* as a routine demand at their demonstrations. Although these students also believed it necessary to be cognizant of splits within the ruling elite, they argued that the appropriate strategy was simply to escalate mobilization. In the words of the PRD's 1996 manifesto, "The emergence of popular resistance can *encourage* splits in the Suharto regime itself" (PRD 1996, 33; italics in original).

Nevertheless, from at least early 1993, many student groups did increasingly target Suharto and his family in their demonstrations and publications.[12] This was partly a matter of students expressing long-standing antagonism toward the president in the increasingly open political context of the mid-1990s. It was, moreover, a time when his family's depredations were becoming increasingly obvious. However, it also reflected some students' assessment that it was advantageous to focus on the president, given that a certain space seemed to exist for doing so and because it was riskier to challenge the military directly. Some students, especially from various liberal-populist groups, also agreed with the argument made by Forum Demokrasi intellectuals that Suharto was the main obstacle to democratization. Among many activists there was a half-joking tendency to describe all social and political injustices as being "because of Suharto." There was even an acronym to describe this concept: UUS— *Ujung-ujungnya Suharto*, which, roughly translated, means "something which can be traced back to Suharto." And so, in the mid-1990s, one body of student activist opinion argued that criticism of any political problem should be directed back to Suharto; all criticism should be "*di-UUS-kan*" (brought back to Suharto). This approach was succinctly expressed by a Yayasan Pijar sticker: *Soeharto: Dalang Segala Bencana: SDSB, Nipah, Haur Koneng, Dili, Tanjung Priok* (Soeharto: Mastermind of all disasters: SDSB, Nipah, Haur Koneng, Dili, Tanjung Priok [the four place names referred to locations of various massacres of civilians over the previous ten years]).

For a time, this approach prompted lively debate among student activists. At several meetings I attended in late 1993 and early 1994, some radicals argued that anti-Suharto students were playing into the hands of the military, risking a repeat of 1966 and aiming only for change in "person" rather than "structure." The counterview was that personification of power meant that Suharto himself represented a "structural" obstacle to democratization.

However, the distinction became less relevant as Suharto loyalists took over key military commands in 1993–94. With the decline of Moerdani-era malcontents, student activists could see that prospects of a serious break with Suharto in ABRI were receding. Under the new breed of military leaders like Hartono and Feisal Tanjung there was less tolerance for student protest.[13] By 1995, students who had earlier expressed interest in the potential consequences of military disillusionment were suggesting that there was "no difference" between the military and the Suharto camp. One result was that militant students from a range of groupings began to unite on common platforms which combined both anti-Suharto (an "extraordinary session" of the MPR) and antimilitary (eliminate *dwifungsi*) slogans (*Suara Independen* 5, October–November 1995, 13–14).

Although military discontent clearly influenced the evolution of student activism from the late 1980s, it must be concluded that its role in triggering student protest was mostly minor and indirect. Certainly, none of the militant student activist groups which constitute the main focus of this chapter seriously considered an alliance with military elements. Instead, student protest in the 1990s was marked by the emergence of uncompromising antimilitarism.

The Turn to the Masses

Averse to "elite politics," the small radical groups which emerged from the late 1980s were mostly strongly attracted to the idea of the *"rakyat"* (the people), and many became directly involved in the political problems of the poor, especially land disputes and industrial conflict. In doing so, they took the populist orientation and structuralist ideas nurtured in the NGO movement in more frankly political directions and aimed to encourage mass mobilization and political organization among the poor. This closely resembled the development of student activism in South Korea and the Philippines, and some Indonesian students certainly strove to learn from and emulate those countries' experiences. But it was a novel development for New Order Indonesia.

Systematic attempts to make links with subordinate classes began in the mid-1980s, as some study group members turned to "structural" theories and sought alternatives to the "elitist" approaches of the 1970s. Early contacts with poor communities were achieved via existing NGOs, new organizations established especially for the purpose, or existing study groups. These activities were initially low profile, as when students entered local communities to gather data on land disputes for NGOs like LBH or to set up informal education groups of their own.

The first obvious sign of the shift in student politics came with a series of protest campaigns about "land cases" (*kasus tanah*) from late 1988. Disputes over land had been common throughout the New Order, but their pace accelerated through the 1980s as infrastructure development and industrialization encroached more into rural areas. Prominent early cases involving students included Kedung Ombo (a dam development) and Cilacap (a petrochemical plant) in Central Java, Badega (a tea plantation), Cimacan (a golf course), and Jatiwangi (a dispute over land owned by the air force) in West Java. In such cases, whether developers were state agencies or private developers, they frequently deprived residents of their land without meaningful consultation, compensation, or legal recourse. They were assisted by inadequacies in land registration and the general absence of legal protection for private citizens. Typically, local government and ABRI officials acted in concert with developers, using intimidatory and violent methods to enforce acquisition (see Lucas 1992, 1997; Hariadi and Masruchah 1995; Stanley 1994; Aspinall 2004).

Local people in such cases usually accepted whatever assistance students, or anybody else, could offer them. ("They viewed us as gods," student activists would often reply when interviewed about initial reactions by village people to their offers of assistance.) Often students would make initial contacts via NGOs or individual students with personal connections in the local area. Then, typically, a number of students would "live in" in the affected area in order to become trusted by the local people and to document and assess the "case." This initial period could last up to several months, depending on the level of repression and fear in the community and the proclivities of the students involved. As the campaign developed, student activists would provide local community members with training, which might range from basic organizational matters and analysis of the case in hand, to *penyadaran* (consciousness-raising) on legal and political rights, to even more complex analysis of the New Order state and political theory. They would also sometimes assist exploring legal avenues of appeal, in conjunction with relevant NGOs, like LBH or SKEPHI. Above all, students assisted planning and organizing protest campaigns, which usually demanded either cessation of land alienation or greater compensation. Such campaigns could involve demonstrations by students and local people in the area of the dispute, in regional capitals, or in Jakarta.

From an early stage, several student study groups had been especially interested in the working class as a potentially strategic political force. Interest grew rapidly during the post-1990 upsurge of industrial unrest. After about 1992, the organization of industrial workers became a major priority for some students and former student activists, especially from the popular-radical current (but not only those affiliated with the PRD). Student involvement in labor organizing followed a pattern similar to that in rural communities. Activists might visit or live in workers' quarters; sometimes they would leave their studies altogether and take jobs in factories known for poor working conditions or histories of labor unrest. Student activists again saw their main roles as providing consciousness-raising and facilitating organization. They singled out particularly militant workers for attention and through a slow and laborious process constructed informal networks within and between factories. Students would then "socialize" basic demands and concepts regarding the right to strike and other legal entitlements, the dignity of labor and its role in production, how to plan actions to maximize impact on company profitability, and so forth. Often the medium-term result was the organization of strikes. As well as winning particular economic demands, the aim was to increase the workers' militancy, organization, and self-reliance. This was often conceptualized as assisting the construction of a cohesive and class-conscious working class. Initially, owing to extensive military intervention in labor disputes, students went to great pains to hide their involvement in industrial activism, although from 1995 militant students openly supported striking workers.

Involvement in such work in rural villages or working-class districts often required significant personal transformation, given that many students came from privileged urban backgrounds. Becoming organizers of workers or farmers was often a great cultural challenge. Many did not adjust well; there were many tales of well-meaning students being unable

to communicate well with rural people because of the students' inability
to adapt their mode of speech, dress, and behavior. For some, working
among the poor was a temporary experience, after which they would return to campus. For others it involved considerable personal sacrifice, for
which the phrase *bunuh diri kelas* (class suicide) was sometimes used.
Living in conditions of often considerable privation, suspending or leaving university education, adopting the idiom of the common people,
wearing their clothing—all of this could be an exhilarating experience,
but it could also mean abandoning the dreams of material progress fostered in the nation's new middle-class society. There were also considerable risks involved because security forces used more unconstrained violence against subordinate classes, and the students who organized them,
than against purely campus protests. Some of the students involved in
this kind of work were tortured severely.

   This "turn to the masses" was an extension of the populist evolution
of thinking in critical intellectual circles over the previous decade. It took
the engagement with the poor pursued by many NGOs in a more openly
political direction. It also resulted from the radicalization of some students produced by marginalization under "normalization of campus
life." But activist groups' motivations for seeking political alliances with
subordinate classes varied greatly. Especially in the early years there were
distinctly romantic overtones. For some students, working to defend the
poor was primarily a moral calling; for others, it was a tactic to adopt
when repression made direct attacks on the government impossible (once
conditions opened up, these students reoriented to issues of "national"
importance, like the presidency). Many activists, especially those working with NGOs like the LBH, viewed such work as an opportunity to extend legal protection to disenfranchised groups, thus working toward the
establishment of a *negara hukum*. Some who organized industrial workers described themselves as social-democratic and were interested only in
establishing trade unions, arguing it was inappropriate to prematurely
engage workers in political activity. Others, especially from the PRD, argued that organizing subordinate classes politically was crucial for
achieving democratization and an egalitarian social order. Theirs was essentially a revolutionary outlook.

   What united the majority of such student activists was an insistence
that their aim was the eventual "empowerment" (*pemberdayaan*) of the
poor. In its widest sense, this meant fostering a sense of self-respect and
dignity. To this end, student activists (like many in smaller mobilizational
NGOs) organized theater groups and published journals in which workers and village people could express their views about their living conditions, problems of daily life, desires, and aspirations.[14] Empowerment

also implied facilitating the development of mass organizations for subordinate groups. After the early land dispute campaigns of the late 1980s, many student activists concluded that their own involvement had overshadowed the affected communities. Thereafter, students often focused on training peasant or worker organizers and building local networks in which their own role was not so prominent.

It is not easy to assess the degree to which student activists (and more broadly, other middle-class activists involved in NGOs and kindred organizations) were central to the increased labor and farmer activism from the late 1980s. Clearly, such activists played an important role in organizing particular campaigns and shaping and articulating the interests of subordinate classes in them. For example, land disputes first attracted national media attention when students assisted affected communities to hold demonstrations in 1989–90. It is not unusual, of course, for middle-class elements to play "midwife" roles during early stages of lower-class mobilization. But it is also important not to exaggerate the middle-class role. Signs of growing industrial and rural unrest were clear from at least the late 1970s. Even in the 1990s, students and other activists became involved in particular land disputes usually only after they were alerted to them by media coverage. Most industrial strikes seemed to occur spontaneously, without the influence of student or NGO activists, facilitated instead by the mobility and growing literacy of the labor force. Students and other middle-class activists were thus influenced by the popular upsurge as much as they influenced it. The deepening socioeconomic gap and other social and political problems linked to industrialization, early inchoate protests by lower-class groups—such factors conditioned the growing radical tendencies of student activism from the mid-1980s. Student and NGO campaigns on land disputes and other concerns of the poor in turn, via the national press, had a significant impact on the political sensibilities of broader middle-class layers, implanting a growing awareness of social inequality.

Toward 1998

During the mid-1990s, it was difficult to speak of a cohesive student movement in Indonesia, as student activism had merged with different social and political forces. Some students became involved in the emerging activism of subordinate classes; others looked to dissident elite circles. A distinctly Islamic student movement emerged, in part linked to networks which reached into the state via ICMI. This diversification of student activism reflected the emergence of a more diverse civil society and a wider spectrum of political forces. It also must be understood as a product of restrictions on campus-based student activism and the resulting search by the most motivated students for off-campus political strategies.

Despite increased heterogeneity, however, the *ideal* of a cohesive student movement did survive; hence, through the 1990s all manner of student groups frequently called for activists to go "back to campus," reemphasize basic campus recruitment work, colonize student representative institutions, and the like. Activists succeeded in these aims on certain campuses, like Universitas Nasional in Jakarta and Gadjah Mada in Yogyakarta, which became highly politicized. Overall, students remained the social group with the highest rate of antigovernment political organization and mobilization. By the mid-1990s, the new political activism was beginning to spread to hitherto largely inactive groups like the Cipayung organizations. There were also signs of invigoration of the previously compliant student senates and other representative organs; by 1995–96, many student senates were demanding the repeal of the ministerial decree which made these bodies subordinate to campus administrations (*Kompas*, October 10, 1996).

Even so, most students remained politically inactive during *keterbukaan*. Indeed, as the quotation at the start of this chapter illustrates, some of the activist student groups openly decried the "apolitical," "materialistic," and "consumption-oriented" attitudes of their classmates, as if to underline their own minority status and moral superiority. While economic prosperity lasted, most students were clearly inclined to concentrate on their studies and future careers.

Even if student activism in 1989–95 assumed new forms and was less cohesive than in the 1970s, it was not necessarily less important. Some students were abandoning the "moral force" and dissident-style politics of the 1970s and evolving toward a pattern of mobilizational opposition. They saw a need to found their own explicitly political organizations and engage in mass mobilization, and they aimed to bring down the regime. Students also pioneered new forms of political action and assisted the political activation of subordinate social groups. Overall, they had a major impact on the politics of *keterbukaan*, especially by testing and expanding the political space for new forms of protest. In the words of one activist, "We would demonstrate and see whether we were arrested. If we weren't, then we'd move on to a higher level" (interview, Nuku Suleiman, September 7, 1993). In this way, public protest became reestablished as a normal part of political life. More specifically, the activism of the early 1990s laid the ground for the explosion of the student protest which rocked Indonesian politics in 1998.

6

Megawati Soekarnoputri and the PDI

> The process of change in the PDI is like the process by which a caterpillar be-
> comes a butterfly. One is a worm, a caterpillar, and the butterfly is very beautiful,
> and yet they are the same creature.
>
> Megawati Soekarnoputri (interview, December 11,
> 1995)

Before late 1993, Megawati Soekarnoputri seemed an unlikely candidate
to lead an anti-Suharto opposition movement, let alone to become president. To be sure, she was the daughter of Indonesia's first president,
Sukarno, who was still very popular as a symbolic counterpoint to the
corruption of the New Order's leaders. But she was one of the most retiring and unassuming of the former president's children. When she was
prevailed on to reenter formal political life in 1987, she did so through
the vehicle of the Indonesian Democracy Party (PDI), a party which even
her younger sisters, Rachmawati and Sukmawati, denounced as an un-
worthy inheritor of the Sukarnoist tradition. Even after Megawati became a member of the national legislature for the party, she took little
part in public debates and was often absent from legislative sittings.

Yet a taste of Megawati's political future was provided in December
1993 when, at a PDI congress in Surabaya, she became the center of an
almost hysterical campaign to obtain the party leadership. Crowds lined
the streets when she arrived in town. Hundreds of enthusiastic supporters surrounded the conference site and demonstrated, prayed, ate, and

slept on the streets outside. Whenever Megawati entered the hall where the congress was being held, or rose to speak, she was mobbed; whenever her party opponents tried to obstruct proceedings, they were jeered. Throughout it all, Megawati presented a model of her future performance—aloof and barely forthcoming, but also apparently unflappable. By the end of the conference, despite the efforts of the government officials in attendance and their allies in the party, it was clear that Megawati had the overwhelming support of the PDI grass roots. Just over two weeks later, and amid signs of considerable army and government disunity, she was affirmed in her post as the new chairperson of the PDI.

Much of the Indonesian press sensed that a dramatic change had taken place. Over the following three years, Megawati's portrait was on the cover of more Indonesian current affairs magazines than that of any other political figure. During the same period, a newly invigorated and optimistic PDI represented the greatest test yet of the regime's capacity to manage dissent. Increasingly blatant government attempts to undermine Megawati transformed her into a symbol of resistance to the New Order.

Other analyses of the Megawati phenomenon have focused on her enigmatic political personality and on the revival of popular enthusiasm for Sukarno (McIntyre 1997; Brooks 1995). Both elements are undeniably important, yet Megawati's rise was remarkable in other respects also. First, it shows the disarray in the upper echelons of the ruling establishment in the later years of Suharto's rule. Regime policy toward Megawati and her party was confused by significant political misgivings among some military officers, by competition between Suharto's loyal lieutenants and by misunderstandings between "the old man" and his now far younger military subordinates.

Megawati's rise was also remarkable because of the political vehicle through which it took place. The PDI was an unlikely source for a political challenge to the New Order. The elite dissidents, NGO activists, and student radicals surveyed in preceding chapters operated more or less outside the official corporatist framework. They were exemplars of civil society and alegal and even illegal opposition. The PDI, in contrast, was a semiopposition in every sense. Created by the government in 1973, it had since that time participated in official political structures and procedures, including general elections and legislatures. By doing so, it subjected itself to numerous explicit and implicit limitations, neatly encapsulated by the Law on Political Parties and Golkar, which designated the government as the *pembina* (guide) of the parties. Government intervention in the party was constant and deep. Candidates for party leadership at all levels were "screened," military and Interior Ministry officials always attended important party functions, and the party largely depended on government funding. It did not make fundamental criticisms of the regime. It even barely possessed anything resembling a political program; unlike the groups discussed in the previous chapters, it was difficult to obtain written documents from the PDI which contained anything but vague statements of principle. In part this was because its formal "program" included documents like the "Broad Outline of State Policy" adopted every five years by the MPR.

Yet the party also had a mass base which far exceeded that of more informal opposition groups. This was partly because the PDI was more than the organizational shell which appeared in the formal arena. Party structures were grafted onto deeply rooted political forces, and its popular strength relied on informal and personalistic mechanisms and appeals. It was this combination of legality and popular support which made the PDI an ideal vehicle for the kind of populist mass political phenomenon embodied in Megawati's rise to prominence.

The Historical Legacy: The PDI as Semiopposition

There was another important difference between the PDI and the groups studied in preceding chapters. While these could mostly, directly or indirectly, trace their origin to the old "New Order coalition," the PDI was descended from one of the major victims of 1965–66. This was the PNI, the Indonesian Nationalist Party, which before the New Order had been the preeminent political vehicle of Sukarnoist populism and nationalism. The PNI had a big following and won the largest vote in the 1955 elections. Many of the party's leaders were local landlords and bureaucrats who, despite their vehement nationalism, had an essentially conservative social and political outlook. The party developed an image as a vehicle of bureaucratic and corrupt careerists, but in the later Sukarno years it faced considerable competition from the PKI for the same secular base. Overall, the party drifted to the left, and a strong radical faction, headed by Surachman, developed inside it (Rocamora 1975).

The PNI and its affiliated organizations were an important secondary target of repression after 1965. Beginning with the party congress of April 1966 (McIntyre 1972, 206–10), the army intervened openly in party affairs, ensuring that right-wing leaders amenable to army dominance attained the leadership. Although the pattern of coercion varied from province to province, some party leaders were killed, and many were imprisoned or harassed. Others lost their jobs, while many student supporters in the Sukarnoist student organization (GMNI) were driven from universities. The PNI left wing was eliminated by repression, and the large center was mostly cowed. Some nationalist newspapers were banned. Eventually, virtually the entire party base in the civil service was uprooted by "monoloyalty" provisions, by which civil servants had to re-nounce party ties and were absorbed into Golkar. Decades later, former PNI members talked of those years as a period of deep fear, paralysis, and "vacuum" in the party's grass roots.

The PNI was poorly equipped for the new hostile environment. Hav-ing being wedded to government since independence, its members had lit-tle experience of independent politics. Cut off from former sources of state protection, they became bewildered and paralyzed. Moreover, the PNI had from the late 1950s endorsed Sukarno's shift to authoritarian rule, and all the ideological packaging which went with it. When the New Order government extended Sukarno's ideological formulas—Pancasila, the "family principle" (*kekeluargaan*, by which society was likened to a harmonious family), and so on—to justify further restrictions on political contestation, the party was unable to respond effectively. After all, Sukarnoists themselves rejected concepts like "opposition" as part of alien liberal culture.

So, unlike the major organs of political Islam, which had not faced comparable repression in 1965–68 and which had a coherent coun-terideology, Sukarnoists became largely passive and ineffective from the early 1970s. After gaining a paltry 6.9 percent of the vote in the 1971 election, in 1973 the PNI was forced into an undignified merger with four small secular and Christian parties to form the PDI. This new party was in turn consumed by internal conflict for the first two years of its exis-tence, after which the government selected two former PNI leaders, Sanusi Harjadinata and Usep Ranawidjaja, to head it. However, these two leaders eventually tried to pursue a moderately critical line. By 1980, they fell prey to a combination of intense internal factional disputes and blatant government intervention.

Over its first fifteen years the PDI became a "docile partner" of gov-ernment (McDonald 1980, 249). It was led by a layer of accommoda-tionist figures who were dependent on the patronage and *restu* (blessing) of government officials for their positions. Even during election cam-paigns these leaders stressed their loyalty to key tenets of the New Order system and denied that the party represented an opposition. They rarely criticized government legislation in the DPR and always endorsed Suharto's reelection. The most critical party leaders could do little more than plaintively call for the proper implementation of the ideals of the "family principle" and "Pancasila democracy." The party did not aim to replace the government and take power for itself, but instead requested that it be allowed to take part in the business of government, for example, by actively participating in the "formulation, implementation, and evaluation" of the government's five-year plans. Underlying this docility was the repressive tenor of Indonesian politics during the New Order's first two decades and continued fear in the party's grass roots. On the surface, however, the immediate cause of the PDI's problems was debilitating factional conflict. During the 1970s and early 1980s, no party congress took place without uproar. There were bitter splits in every central leadership board, public expulsions and counterexpulsions of leading members, occupations and sit-ins in party buildings, and fierce public battles for control of regional branches.

Internal disputes flowed partly from the enforced cohabitation within the PDI of five very different political organisms. The struggle for fair representation for leaders of the old prefusion parties was a recurring theme in internal strife. However, because of their superior numbers, PNI members dominated the new party, and most key protagonists in internal conflicts were from the old Sukarnoist party. Although leadership "outs" invariably accused the "ins" of harboring dangerously antimilitary or leftist tendencies, in fact there were very few ideological or policy differences in the conflicts. Instead, competition for leadership positions and patronage resources was the driving force, and here the ferocity of the conflict was largely a result of the sadly reduced circumstances in which the party found itself. In the past, the PNI had been oiled by funds secured by leaders entrenched in the bureaucracy. "Monoloyalty" stripped the PNI and its successor of these resources and made competition for remaining patronage sources more desperate. The closure of career paths in the bureaucracy intensified competition among ambitious party members for regional and national leadership positions. These were stepping stones for the greater prizes of seats in regional and national legislatures, which in turn meant access to various unofficial financial benefits and business opportunities. With these, PDI leaders could then build their own client bases for mobilization in internal disputes and move further up the party hierarchy.

Factional disputes facilitated and were encouraged by government intervention. In conditions where "screening" (whereby candidates for party leadership posts and DPR seats had to obtain from intelligence bodies certificates of "noninvolvement" in the "September 30 Movement") was routine, aspirants to party leadership had to find patrons in the ruling elite. In the regions, such patrons might be local military commanders, Interior Ministry officials, or the local governor. At the center they were generals, ministers, and other players in national politics. This system resulted in the PDI's domination by a layer of thoroughly domesticated party bureaucrats and a spiral of internal conflict and government intervention. Through the 1970s and 1980s, government and military leaders repeatedly supported one group of PDI leaders, only to shortly afterward provide their factional opponents with funds, official recognition, and media access. Next, officials would cite "internal conflict" to justify directly interfering in leadership selection (an example was in 1979, when Kopkamtib commander Admiral Sudomo assumed direct control of party affairs; van Dijk 1979, 117–43; 1981, 101–24). In this way, the government sidelined even moderately independent leaders and cultivated a constant state of disorder in the party.

Prelude to Rebirth: The Soerjadi Period, 1986–1993

The PDI reached its nadir when the colorless party bureaucrat Sunawar Sukowati became leader (1981–86). This low point in the party's fortunes was encapsulated by its adoption in 1981 of "four political attitudes," including a proposition that the "PDI unites itself with the national leadership of President Suharto." The most independent leaders were forced out of the party or left it in disgust. As part of the wider withdrawal into civil society then taking place, some of them established ostensibly cultural and educational bodies to maintain their informal networks. Even Sukarno's children made a "family consensus" not to support any party.

Even so, the party remained torn by intense factional warfare. In April 1986, the party's third congress ended in chaotic deadlock and, in a move unprecedented even in the New Order, delegates called on Interior Minister Soepardjo Roestam to appoint a new leadership board. The man he chose as the new party chairperson was Soerjadi. He was in many ways a prototypical New Order party politician. He had risen to prominence entirely within the New Order period by attaching himself to powerful military patrons. In the late 1960s, Soerjadi had been a leader of the tiny promilitary wing of the Sukarnoist student group, GMNI, which had joined with the anti-Sukarno Indonesian Student Action Front (KAMI) in endorsing the "New Order." From this time, Soerjadi had been closely associated with Lieutenant General Ali Moertopo and his OPSUS (Special Operations) group. In the 1970s, he had participated in Moertopo projects like the Indonesian National Youth Committee (KNPI). He also maintained an association with the Wanandi brothers, the Sino-Catholic former 1966 student activists associated with the Moertopo-aligned Centre for Strategic and International Studies (CSIS).[1] From the late 1970s, CSIS had moved closer to General Moerdani. The new secretary-general, Nico Daryanto, while less politically experienced, had a Catholic Party background and long-standing CSIS ties.

During their years in control of the party, Soerjadi and Nico were in many ways unremarkable New Order party leaders. They were committed to the existing political system and frequently made traditional pledges of loyalty to the New Order and denials that the PDI was an opposition. However, they were unhappy that the PDI had become a target of almost universal derision and wanted to invigorate it, if only to make it a more active participant in "Pancasila democracy." In pursuing this goal, they were assisted by two wider political phenomena.

First was the mounting tension in the governing elite in the late 1980s. Moerdani's influence was a crucial factor in Soerjadi and Nico Daryanto's appointment to the party leadership.[2] In following years, a more critical PDI evidently became a means for the Moerdani camp to pressure their rivals, especially Golkar chairperson Sudharmono and later the palace camp more generally. Not only were there rumors that circles associated with Moerdani or the Wanandi brothers were providing the PDI with funds, but Moerdani himself went out of his way to state publicly that the *rakyat kecil* (small people) placed new hopes in the PDI. In 1987, he also publicly contradicted Sudharmono by arguing that an "extraordinarily large" electoral victory for Golkar would have negative consequences for Pancasila democracy.[3] During the election campaign that year, most observers believed that ABRI took a relatively neutral stance, or at least backed Golkar less vigorously than in the past.

The second factor was less tangible but at least as important. This was the slowly rising pressure from below in favor of political change. Many supporters of the PDI had arguably never viewed the New Order government as legitimate, but had instead been mostly too fearful to challenge it. By the mid to late 1980s the memories of the intense repression of the 1960s were fading and frustrations with the New Order's corrupt and bureaucratic rule were growing. This was brought home in dramatic style during the 1987 elections. The official PDI campaign was not markedly more critical than previously, but Soerjadi invited several prominent individuals including Sukarno's children Megawati and Guruh, to participate. Surprising most observers, wherever they went these two attracted massive crowds, many of whom carried portraits of Sukarno. The PDI's national vote increased by almost 3.5 million, up from 8 to 11 percent. It was not so much the figures which caused concern to the government, but rather the style and content of the campaigning, especially the ubiquity of portraits of Sukarno. The coordinating minister for people's welfare, Alamsyah, wrote a letter to President Suharto, which was later leaked, noting the "extraordinary and surprising courage in [PDI] campaigning," including the use of Sukarno's portraits and slogans of "Golkar is corrupt."[4]

In the years following the 1987 election, Soerjadi and Nico embarked on a systematic attempt to revitalize the party. Fighting incessant internal conflict, the two constantly toured the regions and established a structure of party village "commissioners," thereby circumventing "floating mass" restrictions. They tried to recruit a new breed of party activist, especially among intellectuals and other professionals via an advertising campaign and a renewed party *balitbang* (research and development body). They persuaded well-known national figures to join the party, including movie stars and artists like Sophan Sophiaan and Mangara Siahaan, the prominent economic commentator Kwik Kian Gie, and later the banker Laksamana Sukardi (number two in Lippobank and a former vice president of Citibank in Indonesia). Such individuals had not experienced the long process of grooming by government normally required to emerge from party ranks. Owing no particular loyalty to Soerjadi or other party leaders and having independent incomes, they were also less susceptible to influence by the disbursement of party posts or patronage (Laksamana Sukardi, for example, turned down an offer of a DPR seat in 1992).

Party leaders also openly appealed to the mood for change in society. Almost reluctantly, and asking for the government's "understanding" (Daryanto 1992, 97), Soerjadi and Nico adopted increasingly critical positions on a range of issues, going beyond the vague populist pronouncements of the past. The research and development body under Kwik Kian Gie began to develop reasoned alternative policies, including a 1991 antimonopoly bill, and Kwik proposed that the party form a shadow cabinet (a novel move, given that in Pancasila democracy minority parties were not supposed to aspire to alternative government status).

The contradiction between Soerjadi's conservative instincts and his attempt to harness the new mood for change was played out during and after the 1992 general election. Despite new restrictions on campaigning (like a ban on the display of portraits, aimed at Sukarno's supporters), the elections were again conducted in conditions of relative openness. Local PDI campaigners were not harassed as much as in the past, and Soerjadi praised ABRI for its "neutrality." The turnout at PDI election rallies was even greater than in 1987. Hundreds of thousands flocked to hear party speakers, especially Megawati and Guruh, even in relatively small provincial towns. Some press reports estimated that up to 3 million people turned out in Jakarta (*Reuters*, May 31, 1992). The youthful composition of these crowds was obvious, and the party tried hard to project an image as the "party of youth."

Outspoken campaigners, like Guruh and Sophan Sophiaan, repeatedly condemned the lack of openness, the "social gap," "*korupsi*," "*kolusi*," and even "*nepotisme*," campaigning particularly hard on such themes in areas badly affected by clove and citrus monopolies owned by Suharto's

children. Kwik Kian Gie (1992, 99–100) condemned those who treated
the state like a "monarchy" or a "plutocracy," while Guruh told one
crowd, "Our democracy is sick. . . . We, especially small people do not
feel freedom. We feel frightened" (*Reuters*, June 3, 1992). Moreover,
amid heightened elite tension concerning succession, for the first time the
party touched on the presidency. Its formal position was that future oc-
cupants of the post should serve only two consecutive terms. Soerjadi
stuck to this, although Suharto himself said it was an emasculation of
the constitution (*Tempo*, May 23, 1992, 14–20). According to several
PDI members, Soerjadi also promised that the party would present its
own presidential nominee at the 1993 MPR session. Certainly, at rallies
he spoke in terms of "change in the national leadership." Others went
further. Sophan Sophiaan publicly nominated Guruh Soekarnoputra as
presidential candidate to a rapturous reception by twenty thousand supporters in Banjarmasin. Nico Daryanto made the PDI the first political
force to nominate ABRI commander General Try Sutrisno for the vice
presidency.

Largely as a result of such campaigning, the PDI vote again sharply increased, this time from 11 to 15 percent. After the election, Soerjadi was
under pressure to deliver on the party's new reformist image. However, it
was widely known that Suharto had been angered by the party's campaign. The party leadership would be up for reelection at a congress
scheduled to be held after the MPR session in March 1993; given the
standard pattern of government intervention at such events, further
provocation would clearly endanger Soerjadi's chances. Soerjadi thus relented, first formally accepting the election results, despite thousands of
reports of harassment and irregularities received by party headquarters.
Next, he resisted pressure to support an alternative presidential candidate. A group of nineteen PDI MPs signed a letter calling for just this,
and for a time it seemed that the MPR might be obliged to hold its first
ever vote on the presidency. Eventually, a party leadership meeting was
held near Jakarta in January to resolve the issue. With troops dispersing
student demonstrators outside, and despite bitter debate inside, eventually Soerjadi forced through his position, and the meeting endorsed
Suharto's reelection. Around the same time, Soerjadi made many attempts to reassure the government and Suharto of his benign intentions.
As he put it, "The PDI will not be a Sukarnoist force and will not be a
'people power' confronting the government. It will continue to be a Pancasila force, a partner of the government" (Halawa 1993, 52).

All this came too late to save Soerjadi. He had displeased the president
and was too closely tied to the Moerdani camp, whose star was on the
wane. In mid-1993 many Moerdani appointees retained military posts,

but the purge was beginning and those officers who remained were not inclined to take risks for the PDI's sake. Immediately after the MPR session, it soon became clear that Soerjadi had lost government "blessing." He was implicated in a court case concerning the abduction of two supporters of his factional opponents, following which the new ABRI commander Feisal Tanjung emerged from a meeting with Suharto to state that the PDI should not elect a leader who was "legally flawed." Soerjadi's PDI opponents gained greater freedom of movement and were even allowed to occupy party headquarters unhindered for three days. Finally, as branches selected congress delegates, Interior Ministry and military officials indicated in their customary "directions" (*pengarahan*) to intending delegates that they should abandon Soerjadi. His past military backing now counted for little. In the face of clear signals from the palace, officers from the Moerdani camp took little action to defend him.

The anti-Soerjadi campaign climaxed during the party congress in Medan in July 1993. On the very first day, immediately after speeches by the president and other senior officials, some four hundred supporters of Soerjadi's factional enemies crashed a jeep into the conference site and commandeered the site for six hours. To preempt utter collapse, Soerjadi's supporters reendorsed him as chairperson by acclamation in the first session the next day. On hearing this, the mob again forced their way in, after which the congress did not resume.

The guiding hand of the authorities in the debacle was plainly visible. Soerjadi's opponents were allowed to come in large numbers to Medan, where they openly proclaimed their intentions. The local military command was responsible for security, yet few guards were present during the attacks. As one leader of the attack remarked, "this is a sign that they [the government] blessed our actions" (*Jawa Pos*, July 24, 1993).[5] Senior officials soon announced that the government did not recognize any congress decisions and considered the Soerjadi leadership a "failure." Interior minister Yogie S. M. declared the PDI leadership "decommissioned" and announced an "extraordinary congress" for later in the year. A caretaker board charged with organizing this congress was formed at a meeting of provincial party leaders closely supervised by Minister Yogie. Not surprisingly, this caretaker board contained no Soerjadi supporters.

The Rise of Megawati

It was widely expected that the "extraordinary congress" would produce a pliant leadership. Among those touted as new leaders, Budi Hardjono, a contemporary of Soerjadi's from the military-backed wing of the

GMNI in the 1960s, appeared to have considerable support at ABRI headquarters. Soerjadi's attackers at Medan, who had now renamed themselves the Persatuan dan Kesatuan (Unity and Oneness) group, also looked to be rewarded. Ironically, however, the crisis allowed Megawati Soekarnoputri to step forward as the leading candidate for party leadership, although she was a person much less favored by the president than Soerjadi had ever been.

Megawati had joined the PDI as a DPR candidate in 1987. She had subsequently been one of Soerjadi's main election crowd pullers. Afterward, she had maintained a low profile, reportedly rarely attending DPR sessions. Nevertheless, she had quietly identified with the emerging party reform group (for example, she was one of the nineteen PDI members of the national legislature who in January 1993 had called on the party to nominate its own presidential candidate). But initially, of course, it was Megawati's family name which ensured that she would be an immensely popular candidate.

Megawati's leadership bid was announced on September 11, 1993, when one hundred PDI functionaries from seventy branches visited her home and asked her to stand. Her campaign quickly gathered momentum. It became clear that she had the overwhelming support of party members and much of the broader political public (as indicated by numerous readers' polls in the press.) In response, a government-organized campaign against her candidacy gathered pace at the local level. Intending congress delegates were brought before officials, usually the local *kaditsospol* (heads of directorates of Social-Political Affairs in the Interior Ministry), but sometimes more senior officials, and instructed to support one of Megawati's competitors. Many delegates were reportedly refused funding or permission to attend the conference before they signed statements to this effect.[6] Such local-level intervention had long been the New Order's primary means of exercising control over the parties; if a party could be controlled from the grass roots up, there was little chance that "problematic" leaders would emerge in it at the national level.

Megawati's campaign was organized by a tightly knit group of supporters in what became known as her "Success Team." They included outspoken PDI legislators and campaigners like Mangara Siahaan, Djathi Koesoemo, and Sophan Sophiaan (all Soerjadi-era recruits) and, significantly, senior journalists like Eros Djarot of *DëTik* and Panda Nababan of *Forum Keadilan*. Team members discussed tactics, organized lobbying, communicated with branches, and coordinated a vigorous press campaign. They devoted much energy to combating government pressures, often by instructing PDI members to give the appearance of concurrence. In the words of Mangara Siahaan, their advice was to "take the money, take the facilities, go to Surabaya, and vote for Megawati" (interview, December 1, 1995).

The Success Team, itself partly composed of experienced journalists, was well aware of the power of the press in the relatively open climate of the time and assiduously cultivated sympathetic coverage. The results were remarkable. Megawati's face adorned the front pages of major newspapers and magazines for weeks, and her grassroots momentum was portrayed as virtually unstoppable. There was also unprecedented coverage of government obstruction tactics. In order to defend the facade of constitutional propriety, senior officials were prompted to issue increasingly strong denials that such intervention was officially sanctioned.[7] In turn, Megawati's success team copied reports of these assurances and distributed them in bulk to party branches.

Megawati and her followers also strove to avoid triggering more decisive intervention. During her campaign, Megawati launched a booklet entitled *I Have Unfurled the Flag!* (Soekarnoputri 1993), which outlined her political vision. This booklet did not fall far outside mainstream PDI/New Order discourse, comprising mostly broad reaffirmations of the importance of national unity, Pancasila, the 1945 constitution, and the like. Its central preoccupations were derived from the populist traditions of Sukarnoism, including a commitment to the *wong cilik* (small people) and overcoming the "social gap." It also included a section on democracy and human rights. The vagueness of the language and its susceptibility to multiple interpretation allowed Megawati's supporters to read into the document, as with her other statements, a subtext of advocacy of far-reaching reform.

In her frequent press interviews before the Surabaya congress, Megawati avoided directly accusing the government of trying to sabotage her candidacy. Instead, she simply stressed that she would be willing to become party chairperson only if elected by the majority, that the congress should be conducted fairly, and that she would not *minta restu* (seek a blessing, i.e., government endorsement). This was in contrast to her chief competitor, Budi Hardjono, who claimed to be a good candidate because "in addition to having support from above, I also have support from below" (*Jakarta Jakarta*, November 27–December 3, 1993, 17). In effect, Megawati's sole platform became the assertion of her party's independence.

Megawati's campaign coincided with continuing tensions within the ruling elite. During 1993, the president was restoring his personal control over ABRI. Some of the new breed of loyalists, prominently the *santri* commander in chief Feisal Tanjung, were already in command positions. There was also considerable tension centered on the October 20–25

Golkar conference, during which defense and security minister Edi Sudradjat and ABRI chief of staff for social and political affairs Hariyoto
P. S. failed to secure a military chairperson, resulting in displays of ABRI
dissatisfaction.

There was much public speculation that these tensions provided crucial leeway for Megawati. Prominent PDI member Laksamana Sukardi
argued in terms which might have been borrowed from political science
literature on democratization: "If there are splits in the power center,
there is usually an opportunity for democracy. The coming PDI extraordinary conference is a reflection of such splits in the political elite, which
has already divided into different power centers, in anticipation of succession" (*DëTik*, November 24–30, 1993, 11).

The palace camp had clear interests in Megawati's failure. There were
indications that a revived PDI under Megawati would nominate her as its
presidential candidate during the next MPR session in 1998, yet it was
widely believed that Suharto was strongly opposed to facing any competitor in an MPR vote. All those in the bureaucracy committed to another sweeping Golkar victory were also concerned. Already press reports were speculating that the PDI vote might double, especially in East
and Central Java.

It was logical for interior minister Yogie S. M. to oversee the campaign
against Megawati, given his ministry's role as the organizational main-
stay of Golkar. Local ministry officials frequently doubled as Golkar
functionaries, and their career success depended on Golkar electoral
"*sukses.*" Staff of the ministry's Social-Political Affairs section conducted
much of the most energetic obstruction before the Surabaya congress. But
ABRI involvement was also extensive. There were reports (which ABRI
denied) that Feisal Tanjung issued an order to territorial commands to
prevent Megawati's election. Certainly, many territorial commanders intervened openly, especially Suharto loyalists like commander of the Central Java Diponegoro Military Command (Kodam) Soeyono.

In contrast, military elements who were uneasy about Suharto and
frustrated with their progress in Golkar were less determined to ensure an
overwhelming Golkar electoral victory (Fraksi-ABRI member Major
General Sembiring Meliala said as much in his famous *DëTik* interview
quoted in Chapter 2). The press often implied that these military elements
were using the possibility of a Megawati victory as a bargaining chip for
the Golkar conference and, later, to express dissatisfaction with the outcome there.

Megawati's circle was well aware of the opportunities afforded them
by friction in the military. Around the time her candidacy became public,
there was contact between the Megawati group and at least some senior

officers.[8] Some Megawati supporters also suggested that officers in some regions largely abstained from the anti-Megawati campaign (interview, Sophan Sophiaan, December 3, 1995; see also Cornelis Lay in *DëTik*, November 24–30, 1993, 12; *Editor*, December 2, 1993, 28–9). Megawati from the outset was careful not to attack *dwifungsi* or ABRI as an institution. Instead, she used language reminiscent of that of discontented officers themselves: "As long as ABRI continues to side with and struggle for the interests of the people, why should *dwifungsi* be questioned? Perhaps the intellectuals could question it if in the future ABRI becomes only a tool of power. . . . But personally, I am among those who do not like talking about an ABRI-civilian dichotomy. You see, rejecting ABRI's dual function is the same as rejecting historical reality. It's ahistoric" (*DëTik*, November 24–30, 1993, 6).

Overall, the evidence is far from conclusive. Some supporters of Megawati felt that the military mostly acted in concert with Interior Ministry staff. It appears that at least initially Budi Hardjono was the preferred ABRI candidate, including for officers dissatisfied with Suharto. Budi himself boasted of his military ties and was reported to be close to "antipalace" officers including Harsudiono Hartas, Sembiring Meliala, and Hariyoto P. S. (*Kompas*, November 10, 1993; *Editor*, November 25, 1993, 32; *Jakarta Jakarta*, November 27–December 3, 1993, 17; *Forum Keadilan*, December 9, 1993, 89). In this view, discontented military elements were seeking a candidate who, like Soerjadi, would owe primary loyalty to ABRI.

It was in this context that the extraordinary party congress opened in Surabaya on December 2. It was obvious from the start that a large majority of congress delegates backed Megawati. On the second day, representatives of 256 of 303 branches in attendance declared their support for her, many with fiery oration, others with voices cracking with emotion. Even so, it appeared almost certain that the congress would again end in deadlock. Caretaker board members, who chaired congress sessions, and the Persatuan dan Kesatuan group appeared determined to block Megawati's election. Initially they attempted to do this by forcing through the *formatur* system for electing the new party chairperson. Under this system (which was also endorsed by Minister Yogie S. M. in his opening speech), a caucus of delegates would meet privately, draft a list of new party leaders, and present it to delegates for approval. Megawati's supporters knew that this would allow for government intervention behind closed doors and argued instead for a free vote on the conference floor. Frustrated on this ground, Megawati's opponents then tried to prevent the congress from reaching any decision. Deadlock would allow the government to step in as "mediator" and, as in 1986, appoint a new leadership.

As a result, the congress became increasingly farcical. Organizers abandoned all pretense at impartiality, sometimes suspending sessions without warning and leaving the congress site altogether. Lights were turned off in the middle of sessions; mass brawls often seemed imminent. On the final day, organizers suspended proceedings, vacated the hall, and did not reappear even after frantic participants sent out search parties.

These tactics were pursued on the basis of close coordination with government officials, especially Interior Ministry officials. *Kaditsospol* from all provinces had accompanied delegates to Surabaya in order to ensure they honored earlier promises (their presence was so noticeable that Megawati supporters put up a banner outside the conference hall reading "This is a PDI conference, not a Congress of *kaditsospol*"). The activities of these officials were coordinated by senior ministry officials, notably "director of social guidance" Mulyono Gendon, who was also a member of the "Election Victory Department" of the Golkar Central Board, a fact made much of by journalists.

According to participants, some military officers did attempt to intervene against Megawati. However, the most senior officer present was the close associate of Edi Sudradjat, chief of staff for social and political affairs Hariyoto P. S. (who, it will be remembered, later supported the YKPK). He monitored proceedings closely but took little action to intervene. Megawati and some of her supporters suggest that either at or immediately prior to the congress, he and other senior officers made an assessment that Megawati's bid could only be stopped by massive and transparent intervention and, on this basis, decided to abstain.[9]

Since the early New Order, intervention like that attempted at Surabaya had featured in gatherings of all kinds of state-recognized political organizations. It was not even particularly unusual for different elements of the security apparatus to have conflicting agendas. What was new was, first, the extensive press coverage which the intervention attracted. The conference occurred at the height of *keterbukaan*, and the media reported the efforts to frustrate Megawati, and their incompetence, with much relish. This was the first detailed exposure of the contradiction between claims to respect the parties' formal independence and the methods used to "engineer" dominance by progovernment elements within them. Second, unlike in the past, most conference delegates did not succumb to the pressure. Instead, they openly defied the wishes of officials who could be expected to apply considerable retribution once they returned home. The failure of normal methods of intimidation added a new desperation to the efforts of officials and made their efforts appear crude. As Ariel Heryanto (1996, 258) notes, it also gave birth to a new term in the Indonesian political vocabulary—*arus bawah* (undercurrent)—used to signify the increasingly common *keterbukaan* phenomenon of a movement for change emanating from below.

By conference end, Megawati had clearly demonstrated her overwhelming support. At five minutes to midnight on the final day she entered the conference hall and declared herself "de facto" PDI chairperson. In the following fortnight there was a distinct change in mood. On December 13, Megawati met Minister Yogie S. M., after which he stated that there was a "large possibility" that she would be the next PDI chairperson. She next held several highly publicized meetings with military and other regime figures, including, surprisingly, Suharto's daughter Siti Hardiyanti Rukmana. It was announced that leaders of the party's provincial boards would assemble for a "National Consultation" to finally elect a new leadership.\|There was now little serious question that Megawati would be the new chairperson; the chief concern was now the composition of her central leadership board.\|

Caretaker board and Persatuan dan Kesatuan leaders, still backed by Interior Ministry officials, maneuvered to stack the National Consultation with supporters. As deadlock again loomed, and in a climate of intense press criticism of Minister Yogie, several army officers dramatically assumed management of the meeting. The main actors were Jakarta commander Major General Hendropriyono and special forces commander and director A (Internal Affairs) of the Strategic Intelligence Agency (BAIS) Brigadier General Agum Gumelar. When the meeting convened on December 22, these officers quickly halted further attempts at obstruction, and Megawati was almost immediately elected unanimously as chairperson. For two days there was intense bargaining on the composition of the new central leadership board. It appears that a pliable board was the central condition for government acceptance of Megawati's appointment. She was strongly pressured by the army officers and Interior Ministry officials on this point and was eventually forced to exclude several core supporters (such as Sophan Sophiaan and Aberson Marle Sihaloho, who were accused of being "anti-*dwifungsi*") and accept many of her party opponents. In subsequent years, the compromised character of this board would be central to the government's attempt to undermine and eventually remove Megawati from her position.

Much of the Jakarta press strongly praised Hendropriyono and Agum Gumelar, and there was much open speculation about military "backing" for Megawati.[10] Some scholarly accounts also take this line. Damien Kingsbury (1998, 137, 122), for example, suggests that parts of ABRI saw in Megawati "an opportunity to embarrass Suharto," even that as a leader she was "in part a creation of a faction of ABRI." Angus McIntyre (1997, 12–14) suggests that military officers contemplated a "limited alliance" with a Megawati-PDI in order to forestall a Habibie presidential candidacy and suggests that Megawati may have agreed to support an ABRI presidential candidate.[11]

However, although Megawati's rise was clearly a publicity coup for ABRI, it is difficult to untangle the motives of the officers involved. At first sight, it appears that Suharto himself had finally recognized the inevitability of Megawati's rise. He certainly made many public signals which seemed to suggest that he would accept Megawati as party leader. For example, during the Surabaya congress, Minister Yogie said after meeting with Suharto that the government had no objection to Megawati becoming leader. Megawati's later highly publicized meeting with Suharto's daughter seemed an even clearer sign of presidential approval. Megawati herself said that she was unsure whether Suharto had finally given his "blessing" to her appointment (interview, December 11, 1995). A plausible interpretation is thus that Agum Gumelar and Hendropriyono simply misread such public signals, as well as general orders to "resolve" the PDI conflict. One source who spoke to Agum on the matter suggested that the special forces commander was assured by Feisal Tanjung that Megawati was permitted to become leader and that he even received confirmation from Suharto's son Bambang Trihatmodjo that the president had no objections to this outcome (confidential communication, February 2000).

Even so, it appears that before long, palace circles including the president himself, came to view Hendropriyono's and Agum's actions as part of a wider conspiracy involving supporters of Moerdani, Catholics, and Nationalists, which aimed to promote Megawati in the attempt to undermine ICMI, Habibie, and Suharto himself.[12] Later in 1994, Agum and Hendropriyono were transferred to other positions, an action which was widely interpreted as a sign of Suharto's displeasure.

Despite the complexity, a simplified myth of "military backing" became part of standard accounts of Megawati's rise. Even many of Megawati's supporters believed that support from a section of ABRI played a significant role in her win. Partly as a result, in the early years of Megawati's leadership, there was far more good will for military elements among PDI reformers than in, say, the student movement or other parts of alegal opposition. In particular, Hendropriyono and Agum were widely admired for having "saved" Megawati. Some of Megawati's key supporters claimed that there was wider sympathy for Megawati among younger "red and white" officers because she was ideologically close to them and shared their concerns about resurgent Islam. Some even expressed confidence that in a crisis, such as mass protests sparked by Megawati's nomination as president, the PDI would receive military backing (the model of Philippines style "people power" was clearly in their minds). In return, they stressed that while the PDI remained remote from power, it would not attack *dwifungsi* but merely advocate military neutrality with respect to the political parties.

Care must nevertheless be taken not to exaggerate the military's role. Megawati did not take the leadership of the PDI primarily, or even substantially, as a result of military backing. Megawati herself strongly denied she owed any debt to Hendropriyono and Agum Gumelar. She said they did not provide her with an easy road to the leadership, being among those who intensely pressured her on the composition of the leadership board. She argued that ABRI accepted her becoming leader only because they "could see no other path" which would not have adverse security implications (interview, Megawati Soekarnoputri, December 11, 1995). After two failed congresses, great and obvious manipulation would have been required to frustrate Megawati's leadership aspirations. In the words of Major General Sembiring Meliala, who had recently been moved out of the Fraksi-ABRI in the DPR (and much later, after Suharto's resignation, joined Megawati's party), this would have been "too vulgar" (interview, November 16, 1996). Blatantly blocking Megawati's leadership would have run counter to the then prevailing atmosphere of *keterbukaan*. The officers involved were unwilling to attempt this, at least in the absence of very clear instructions from Suharto. In the final analysis, what ensured that Megawati became PDI leader was her grassroots support and her supporters' refusal to succumb to customary forms of intimidation. The military role was primarily a reaction to these phenomena.

Megawati as Leader, 1994–1996

The disarray and confusion in military ranks which accompanied Megawati's rise was also a product of a transitional phase in the military. As noted in Chapter 2, discontent and competition in the military were at a high point in late 1993, in part precisely because Suharto was then intervening intensively in transfers and appointments. Some associated with Megawati's rise (such as Hariyoto P. S.) were among the last members of the old Moerdani circles to hold senior posts. As Suharto loyalists consolidated control, Megawati's prospects became bleaker.

Though her tenure as PDI leader began with a triumphal tour of regional towns, Megawati's momentum was checked from the start by a continuation of the kind of tactics used at Surabaya. For the next two and a half years debilitating internal conflict paralyzed the PDI. In addition to the aggressive Persatuan dan Kesatuan group, other conservative forces were active in the party. Most local (especially province-level) leaders had obtained their positions with the sponsorship of local bureaucratic and military patrons. Many now feared being displaced by Megawati supporters or losing bureaucratic approval if the PDI became more oppositional. These people could be used by the government to prevent Megawati from consolidating her hold on party structures.

Problems began with provincial party board elections through 1994. Time and again, the kind of tactics used at Surabaya were redeployed, except they were now generally subject to less media scrutiny, especially after the banning of *Tempo*, *Editor*, and *DëTik* in June. Only in a few provinces, like the former PNI stronghold of Bali, did Megawati supporters secure unambiguous victories. Most provincial boards (some seventeen of twenty-seven by late 1994 according to one count; *Forum Keadilan*, November 24, 1994, 105) remained in the hands of Soerjadi-era appointees. Even where Megawati supporters won, provincial governors sometimes refused to recognize them.

Conflict was especially bitter in East Java. Here, the election of a Megawati supporter, Soetjipto, as provincial chief was challenged by Latief Pudjosakti, who proudly admitted to being a "lackey" (*antek*) of the government and military (*Forum Keadilan*, November 10, 1994, 36). He established a rival board and was openly backed by Governor Basoefi Soedirman. Local authorities repeatedly withheld permits for meetings of Megawati supporters; such meetings were broken up by thugs. Megawati herself was repeatedly denied permission to speak in the province (Tim ISAI 1996, 36–51). At the same time, senior military officers, including Feisal Tanjung himself, began to deploy old-style antileftist rhetoric, warning against a revival of "Marhaenist" (a reference to Sukarno's old radical nationalist ideology), "Old Order," and communist forces in the PDI.

The first open attempt to topple Megawati occurred in December 1994 when members of the Persatuan dan Kesatuan group, headed by old-time party conservative Yusuf Merukh, formed a "Reshuffle" central leadership board. This group was given considerable room to maneuver, presumably to see whether it had the capacity to dislodge Megawati.[13] Although it was too narrowly based to represent a plausible alternative leadership and never obtained open government endorsement, it played an important disruptive role via the usual pattern of rival boards, demonstrations, and invasions of party meetings. All this, in another continuation of old techniques of control, added to the impression of disorder in the party, continually reinforced by pronouncements by government officials that Megawati was "too weak" to overcome the party's internal problems and that "reconciliation" was necessary.

The ambitions of regional military and government officials played an important role in the campaign against Megawati, but there was also central direction. Several ABRI leaders, especially Feisal Tanjung and other key "green" palace loyalists, did not attempt to conceal their sympathy for anti-Megawati elements. Army chief of staff Hartono was especially active. He was apparently the chief sponsor of the "Reshuffle" group (at the same time he supported a similar group in NU aimed against Abdurrahman Wahid).

For the first two and a half years, the campaign against Megawati continued to be undermined by poor coordination, in the context of growing competition between Feisal Tanjung and Hartono. Those officers competed in the moves against Megawati in order to prove their loyalty to Suharto. Other officers, like Edi Sudradjat, Bakin chief Lieutenant General Soedibyo, and commander of the ABRI Staff College Major General Theo Syafei (another officer who joined Megawati's party after the downfall of Suharto), were widely seen as opposed to overreaching intervention.[14]

In this climate, caution remained Megawati's overriding principle. She avoided overtly challenging the government on most key issues and did not spell out a comprehensive reform program or say her party was in opposition to the government. The aims of Megawati's PDI thus remained obscure. This partly reflected the aversion to conflict and division embedded in the Sukarnoist tradition and Megawati's personal convictions acquired, as she often stressed, at the feet of her father. Megawati repeatedly stressed that the party had to avoid sparking a political crisis, which might lead to bloodshed and endanger national unity:

Just to be patient in this Republic is a difficult challenge. In my view, I'm quite happy to be called *nrimo* [acquiescent to fate]. Because in my assessment the Indonesian people have a culture which must be faced with patience and with clear feelings and thoughts. . . . We are an archipelagic nation. Our history has shown that several times we have experienced splits. Now we give thanks that we have united as a nation with the philosophy of Pancasila as a glue. If not, you can imagine what would happen. How easy it would be for us to split ourselves or to be split. (*Kompas*, January 14, 1996)

Caution also related to the party's precarious political position and was viewed as imperative to avoid furnishing an excuse for intervention. Party treasurer Laksamana Sukardi, when asked why the party did not produce platforms outlining labor, youth, or similar policies, explained:

We are still very busy consolidating the party. There is so much government interference everywhere that it takes up a great deal of time and money to do this, just in traveling around to all the regions, for example. We are a poor party and we have to choose our priorities. And we believe that we already have the people's trust. We do have this trust already, so why should we have platforms? And why do we have the people's trust? Because it is a public secret that there is so much corruption in the present government. And it is a public secret that we are antiestablishment. (interview, Laksamana Sukardi, December 5, 1995)

Although the PDI under Megawati thus did not put forward a sophisticated critique of the political system, its message was powerful. In part this was because of its simplicity. Above all, Megawati stood for independence from state interference. When she addressed gatherings in the regions, she repeatedly stressed that party members had full rights to participate in politics and that they should not succumb to intimidation or bribery. She called on party members to reject the "culture of fear," have pride in their party, and resist pressures to disrupt it. Indeed, she argued that after joining the party in the 1980s, she had always viewed her main task as "breaking down the old trauma" [the legacy of 1965] in the party's mass support base (interview, December 11, 1995).[15] Attempts to undermine her only reinforced this central message. "It's not easy being the first party leader who was elected from below" was her refrain when questioned by the press about the PDI's problems.

Megawati's broader political message centered on promotion of respect for constitutional propriety. She and her supporters stressed that they did not stand for a radical overhaul of "Pancasila Democracy," but rather for its proper implementation. They called for the observance of existing laws which provided for equal status of the parties, free and fair elections, party control of party affairs, and so on. Megawati thus was able to use the stress on constitutionalism which had been part of regime discourse since 1966. Of course, there was nothing new about this; many dissidents and semiopponents down the years had made similar calls.

Even so, the nature of Megawati's message enabled her to avoid overt confrontation with the authorities, while minimizing the need to yield to pressure. Megawati's appeal seemed unremarkable, but it resonated powerfully with the populist Sukarnoist heritage—the stress on egalitarianism, appeals for social justice, and so on—which still underpinned official Pancasila discourse. It was certainly interpreted in this way by her followers. During many conversations in the mid-1990s, ordinary PDI members told me that noting the similarity between Megawati's language and that of the New Order entirely missed its deeper significance. They "knew" that Megawati's statements were an attempt to reclaim the ideals of Indonesian nationalism, including its commitment to social justice and equality. The New Order government had perverted the ideals of Pancasila; Megawati was simply restoring them.

Megawati built a formidable public persona, a charismatic appeal which was the cornerstone of the PDI challenge. She was widely viewed by her supporters as a person of honesty, simplicity, and patience, yet also of directness, moral and emotional conviction, courage, and determination. Her speeches were peppered with calls for party members to stand steadfastly for the ideals of the nation's founders and the values enshrined in Pancasila. They were usually delivered in a distinctive style which combined firm statements of principle with a tone of fond maternal condescension toward her audience, whether when admonishing them for being unruly or when telling them to diligently carry out their party duties. Stickers and other paraphernalia bearing her image often included messages like *"Aku tidak takut!"* (I am not afraid!) and *"Maju terus, pantang mundur!"* (Keep going forward, no turning back!). Her supporters viewed her as the personification of the popular will for change, as the bearer of various specifically "female" qualities (softness, "motherliness," etc.) and as the inheritor of her father's aura of national greatness and almost mystical identification with the masses. Many respected her precisely because she refused to mobilize her supporters in a head-on confrontation with the regime. As party leader Laksamana Sukardi later put it, "Mega wants nonviolence. . . . She has the power to command and can mobilize the masses wherever she pleases. However, she prefers that no victims fall for her political interests. If she was the type of leader who didn't care, she would ask her masses to take to the streets. If she asked them, well, all of them would definitely come" (interview, Laksamana Sukardi, July 17, 1998). In short, Megawati was the kind of leader who proved her mass support precisely by *not* mobilizing them politically.[16]

Megawati's leadership resulted in a visible energization of party ranks. She attracted large crowds whenever she visited regional towns. The party gained many new recruits and volunteers for minor posts, like village and subdistrict level coordinators, in places where previously people had been too scared to step forward. While government intervention remained relatively effective in the province-level boards, the sheer weight of numbers meant that Megawati loyalists dominated lower party organs.

Although Megawati was guarded when speaking publicly, many of her supporters were less so. Instead, they increasingly portrayed the PDI as the party of democratization and made the elimination of monopolies, corruption, and collusion the party's central economic demand. Some advocated changes in the electoral and party laws and DPR procedures in order to permit more decisive legislative control. The PDI was the only *fraksi* in the DPR roundly to condemn the 1994 press bannings. Outspoken PDI legislators sometimes mercilessly grilled, or even boycotted, government ministers during DPR commission hearings. In 1996, they rejected the government's proposed 1997–98 budget, calling for stronger anticorruption measures and legislative scrutiny. Legislator Aberson Marle Sihaloho, admittedly a party maverick, openly condemned *dwifungsi* and called for ABRI's "return to the barracks" (*Tiras*, May 9, 1996, 53).

Megawati also attracted growing support from beyond the PDI. First, a few old PNI-linked *ormas* which had largely been domesticated under the New Order, such as the nationalist student organization GMNI, became vigorous supporters. There were also several groups which had been set up in the early 1980s as vehicles for former PNI members who felt alienated from the PDI. Such organizations included Yayasan Pendidikan Sukarno (Sukarno Education Foundation), led by Megawati's sister Rachmawati, and the more militant Gerakan Rakyat Marhaen (Marhaen People's Movement, or GRM), with which Megawati's most radical sister, Sukmawati, was associated. During the early *keterbukaan* years, the leaders of these groups had frequently condemned the PDI. After Megawati became party leader, they mostly offered their support.

The Megawati camp also developed closer ties with groups beyond the PDI's old *aliran* base. Potentially most significant was a tacit alliance with Abdurrahman Wahid's Nahdlatul Ulama (NU). Megawati and Abdurrahman had known each other since childhood, and she greatly respected his political judgment. Megawati attended the 1994 NU congress in which Abdurrahman was narrowly reelected in the face of considerable government pressure for his ouster; in following months, the two often appeared together publicly. How far this alliance penetrated to the organizations' grass roots was questionable, although closer cooperation was welcomed particularly enthusiastically by the new generation of activist and prodemocratic NU youth. There was both historical precedent for this cooperation (the NU and the PNI were pillars of Sukarno's Guided Democracy regime) and a sense of shared fate, given that Abdurrahman and his allies were also being undermined in the NU and had in 1994 been roundly defeated in the PPP.

Several PDI leaders, such as Laksamana Sukardi and Sabam Sirait, also deliberately sought support from other prodemocracy forces, addressing meetings and seminars organized by NGOs and student groups. Some even developed ties with more unofficial opposition, including dissident groups (like the Petition of Fifty), critical NGOs, radical student groups (like the PRD), and labor organizations. Although some activists from such groups remained cynical about the political parties and criticized Megawati for being too hesitant, others began to look to the PDI as, if not their parliamentary voice, at least a potentially strategic asset given opposition forces' historic isolation from the electoral arena. Some radical students, such as those in the PRD, decided to abandon their old *golput*, or election boycott, strategy and throw their weight behind the PDI.

The PDI's moves to support Megawati as its presidential candidate highlighted its potential to challenge the government. In January 1996, several PDI legislators, including Aberson Marle Sihaloho, caused a media sensation when they circulated a petition promoting Megawati's candidacy, a majority vote on the president in the MPR, and for presidential candidates to campaign in favor of explicit platforms during the 1997 general election. While Megawati avoided comment on the proposal, Aberson was characteristically forthright: "If the people now want Megawati, Suharto will fall" (*Suara Independen* 7, January–February 1996, 26–27).

This presidential campaign could not, of course, open the way for change in government by constitutional process. Outright victory in the DPR poll, let alone in the MPR vote on the presidency, was unimaginable given the structure of the political system (for one thing, a majority of MPR members were, effectively, appointed by the president). But it did dramatize the threat which the PDI posed the government. For reasons which are discussed in the next chapter, it also spelled Megawati's doom. President Suharto was determined not to face a challenger in the MPR. Before turning to the crisis of 1996, however, it is appropriate to consider in greater depth the sources of Megawati's support.

Megawati Assessed

There were several reasons why the first major challenge to the government after *keterbukaan* should take the form of revivified semiopposition, originating from one of the hitherto mostly listless components of the official corporatist political system. The state's coercive power made it difficult to establish an independent political movement outside of and in direct challenge to the official system. The political parties, though subject to numerous constraints, had an organizational infrastructure and freedom of movement which alegal opposition lacked. Moreover, their pre–New Order origins meant that they "floated" on top of potentially restive mass constituencies. Throughout the New Order, constant management by the state apparatus had been required to contain the parties. Compliant leaderships were maintained only by the continual application of a mixture of coercion and inducements (succinctly expressed by the

Indonesian term rekayasa [engineering]). But this required a relatively unified state apparatus and relative passivity in society. As *keterbukaan* took hold, PDI members became more inclined to resist, and this management task consequently became more difficult. Lack of coordination among political managers exacerbated the problem.

The PDI revival must thus first and foremost be understood as a product of the generalized decline of fear in society in the *keterbukaan* years. More particularly, the paralysis of the old Sukarnoist populist support base was beginning to lose effect. A new generation had grown up who had not experienced the repression which ended the Sukarno era. The energization of the PDI was thus closely tied to growing frustration among youth and their search for an avenue for protest, reflected in the youthful composition of the large PDI election rallies in 1987 and 1992.

It was also not surprising that a major challenge to the government would assume a personalist form. Many opponents of the New Order had long believed that they needed a single unifying figure with strong mass appeal. Restrictions on political activity limited their ability to build institutionalized links to the masses. A new charismatic leader was sometimes viewed as a means to bypass this problem (hence, some Forum Demokrasi members' earlier hopes for Abdurrahman Wahid). In other struggles against authoritarian rule in Asia, such leaders were often female relatives of prominent male political leaders who were seen as having served and died for their countries. Burma's Aung Sang Suu Kyi was the daughter of the father of Burmese nationalism, Aung San, who was assassinated in 1947 on the eve of national independence. In the Philippines, Corazon Aquino was the widow of President Marcos's murdered nemesis, Benigno Aquino. Megawati was often compared by Indonesian commentators to these two women, and she was viewed by many as inheriting many of her father's attributes, especially his dedication to the nation.

Long before Megawati took the helm of the PDI, there were many signs of increased public enthusiasm for Sukarno as a symbolic focal point of protest against the New Order. This first became apparent in the late 1970s but was brought home on a mass scale by the sea of portraits of the first president at PDI rallies in the 1987 election campaign. Increasingly large crowds visited Sukarno's grave in Blitar on the anniversary of his death, birth, and other significant dates; some fifty thousand people turned out there on the twenty-first anniversary of his death in 1991 (*Tempo*, June 29, 1991, 15). Sketchy poll data also pointed to Sukarno's great popularity among youth (in a 1988 survey of Diponegoro University students in Semarang 72 percent of those questioned indicated that Sukarno was the "number one national figure" whom they admired; *Editor*, October 10, 1988, 22). Enthusiasm for Sukarno was a symbolic threat to the government, partly because it directly challenged the foundation myths of the New Order, also because the popular image of Sukarno—that he loved and was close to the *wong cilik*, that he did not use his office to benefit his family, that he died poor—drew much of its power as a form of protest against the perceived remoteness and corruption of New Order leaders (Labrousse 1993).

At least initially, much of the support for Megawati derived its intensity from her family background. In the words of a PDI member I met in Yogyakarta in December 1996, "We don't think about the details of the changes or the democracy we want. We only see Mega. Mega is Bung Karno, and Bung Karno struggled for the people. And we know that Mega also struggles for the unity, justice, prosperity, and greatness of the people."[17] Many of the stickers, posters, and other Megawati paraphernalia that proliferated after 1993 incorporated background pictures of Sukarno hovering behind his daughter, as if a guardian spirit.[18] Megawati herself assiduously cultivated this connection in the public mind, often mentioning this or that piece of advice that her father had given her. Her supporters all knew, as well, the story of Sukarno's house arrest in the early years of the New Order, his illness and death with only his immediate family caring for him (McIntyre 1997, 6). It was widely understood that Megawati and her siblings had nursed a grievance toward Suharto from this time, and this added to public respect for her.

In addition, Megawati soon began to build her own powerful public persona. Her supporters saw her as possessing many of her father's purported attributes (honesty, love for the people, commitment to national unity) as well as developing her own (notably gendered) qualities of simplicity, serenity, patience, "motherliness," and so forth. From the start, Megawati was a perplexing character for journalists and other observers to analyze, not least because she often seemed reluctant to speak publicly, at least at length. This reticence, it seemed, was a trait which went back to childhood; her sister Rachmawati noted that Megawati had always been quiet: "*Mbak* [Javanese for older sister] Ega has never talked too much, she is not an open person" (*Editor*, October 3, 1987, 10). When Megawati did speak, she often did so in generalizations. Yet even these were conveyed with great conviction. An account of one of her early campaign speeches in Jakarta in 1987 reports her talking in what might be thought of as banalities ("I do not wish to see the young generation in the 21st century be full of darkness and emptiness. Youth! Become eagles and fly as high as the sky, spreading your wings wide"), yet weeping as she spoke, and greatly moving her audience (*Editor*, October 3, 1987, 10).

Although there was little doubting the strength of Megawati's convictions or her effectiveness as a communicator, she was not widely believed to be a great strategic thinker. Certainly, there is little evidence from this period to suggest that Megawati herself had a clear long-term strategy or goal in mind. In her own private interviews with me, as in her many press interviews, Megawati generally displayed an unnerving tendency to answer specific questions about events or tactics with broad generalizations about principle. Some party leaders suggested that she did not speak very differently in internal party meetings. And while Megawati's advisers and supporters plotted and speculated about how the party should respond when the government finally decided it would tolerate her no longer, or about how a Megawati presidency might one day come into being, she herself seemed quite untroubled by such matters. She only insisted that the PDI respect the law.

There are two explanations for this aspect of her character. First, there appears to be little doubt that Megawati believed herself to be *destined* for greatness. Many of the things she told the press about what her father had told her seemed to imply that she believed he had thought her marked for political leadership. The implication was that she was finally putting into practice the task she had been bequeathed at his deathbed.[19] In fact, it is rather unlikely that Megawati felt any such sense before she became in involved in politics in 1987.[20] But it is not difficult to understand how a sense of destiny might have quickly grown in her when, as a political neophyte, she was mobbed by often highly emotional supporters in the 1987 and 1992 election campaigns. Although Megawati never said it quite so clearly, she sometimes implied that public adoration combined with her family heritage meant that greatness would one day come to her, without need for strategizing or action on her part. As she put it in 1996 (albeit in a rather more specific context), "I do not intend to mobilize the masses. But, I am convinced, there will be spontaneous support for me" (*Forum Keadilan*, July 1, 1996, 95).

Second, despite her sense of personal destiny and moral conviction, Megawati's political vision was in fact rather limited, even conservative. There are few indications, for instance, that she read widely or studied the political systems of other countries. Instead, her vision did not seem to go far beyond the general statements about honesty, Pancasila, national unity, and the like that she made publicly. In part, this was because she had inherited from her father (who was, in Herbert Feith's [1962] famous phrase, the exemplary "solidarity-maker" of postindependence Indonesia) diffuse nationalism and populism, rather than an interest in political systems or tactics. But it also resulted from the Suharto regime's success in controlling opposition. As I have argued throughout this book, one key to the New Order's longevity was not merely that it repressed opposition, but also that it rendered it ineffective by providing some civilian groups with avenues for circumscribed political action. Megawati was a perfect product of this system.[21] The PDI, the body in which she gained all her practical political experience, was controlled in such a way that most forthright opponents of the New Order were weeded out long before they became national leaders. Megawati's stress on strict legality thus mirrored the New Order's own rhetoric of constitutionality and legal order and also typified the mood of anxiety which pervaded political life when tolerated critics could rapidly make the transition to illegality.

Other Sources of Support

In addition to the personalized nature of Megawati's appeal, other factors accounted for the upwelling of support for her. These factors included the pervasiveness of informal modes of political organization, as well as broader social factors related to cultural identity and class.

One riddle of the Megawati phenomenon was how such a mass-based phenomenon could arise and be organized by a party which, though stronger than alegal opposition, was still institutionally weak. The PDI lacked a solid organizational infrastructure and high-quality cadres. It relied on paltry subsidies from the government to fund its operations. Since the late 1960s, its leadership had been systematically weakened by government intervention. To account for the strength of Megawati's challenge, therefore, it is necessary to look beyond formal politics, toward an array of more humble informal networks and patterns of organization which assisted to maintain the tenacity of the old Sukarnoist mass base. For example, many members of the old PNI and its affiliates, right through to the 1990s, remained organized in *arisan* groups (a kind of communal money-saving). Former PNI members used *arisan* meetings to maintain group cohesion and facilitate political discussion and communication. In former PNI base areas, like Central and East Java, supporters of the old party similarly regularly gathered for *slametan* (thanksgiving feasts) on auspicious dates, such as the anniversaries of the birth and death of Sukarno. Such practices remained widespread; according to one participant in 1993, there were as many as fifty PNI-oriented *arisan* groups operating in the Jakarta area alone (interview, Soeroto Padmodihardjo, November 30, 1993). Networks mediated by informal community leaders—owners of small businesses, Javanese mystics, martial arts teachers, artists, and the like—similarly assisted in maintaining the party's coherence at the local level. Nationalist or PDI-aligned *preman*, hoodlums or semicriminal elements, played a role in mobilizing young people for PDI rallies in the cities. Many former civil servants retained emotional attachments to old PNI symbols and networks. From the late 1980s there were numerous reports of retired village heads, ABRI officers, and other officials returning to the PDI fold.

The subterranean nature of such ties makes them resistant to analysis, at least in the absence of detailed local case studies. Such links maintained the old Sukarnoist *aliran* only imperfectly (it was still difficult to recruit new cadres and maintain ideological continuity). But they did serve other functions. They were an effective means of communication, enabling former PNI leaders in Jakarta to keep in close contact with party supporters throughout the archipelago. Such informal links also had considerable efficacy for mobilizational purposes (as indicated by the massive annual pilgrimages to Sukarno's grave). Overall, they served to maintain group cohesion, solidarity, and identity among former PNI supporters and enabled some Megawati supporters to bypass the intervention and paralysis experienced within formal PDI structures.

Oppositional politics are frequently uninstitutionalized and informal in repressive conditions. The point is that it was possible to make a serious misreading of Indonesian politics, especially the effectiveness of mass depoliticization, merely by observing formal institutions and the apparent acquiescence which occurred in the official arena. Below this level was a world of hidden political linkages and loyalties, where the old political *aliran* lived on. The Megawati phenomenon indicated that once political controls were loosened, old political forces could reemerge, albeit in modified form.

One glue that kept the old *aliran* base of the party alive was a distinct sense of cultural identity. The PDI promoted a secular nationalist appeal which stressed integrative symbols like Pancasila. Two of the parties which joined the PDI in 1973 were Christian. The PNI itself had received strong support in communities like the largely Protestant Bataks of North Sumatra and Balinese Hindus; in Java it was strongly identified with the nonorthodox Muslim *abangan* cultural variant. Cultural identification as non-*santri* remained an important binding force in PDI ranks. For example, many PDI members still held to Javanese mystical beliefs, and stories circulated widely in party ranks about rival *dukun* or "paranormals" striving to exert supernatural influences over party events like the 1993 Surabaya congress. There were obvious messianic and millenarian overtones in the attitudes of many Megawati supporters. Mystics linked to the party often spoke of portents signifying the end of the Suharto era (volcanic eruptions, earthquakes, and the like), while some PDI members believed that Megawati had received the *wahyu*, the mystical essence which endowed rulers with power and authority. During 1996, when the government finally moved against Megawati, tabloid newspapers aimed at the party's supporters like *Inti Jaya* carried reports that a ghostly lion's head was visible on Sukarno's gravestone, signifying the former president's anger at how the government was treating his daughter.

In the 1970s, the military establishment had played on fears of political Islam held by religious minorities and nominal Muslims. Secular nationalism had been bound tightly to the regime in pursuit of its anti-Islamist goals (and so, for example, it was no coincidence that Lieutenant General Ali Moertopo organized a restoration of Sukarno's grave at the height of the engineered panic about the Islamic "extreme right" in the late 1970s). In the early 1990s, the political climate was virtually reversed; Islamic political aims were being asserted energetically and, via ICMI, appeared to be securing government endorsement. It was not surprising that this should trigger an invigoration of non-*santri* cultural groups and so affect the PDI. Certainly, leaders of the PDI and allied groups frequently spoke about the dangers of "sectarianism" and "national disintegration" in terms similar to that espoused by ICMI critics like Forum Demokrasi and the YKPK. Some (but not all) pro-Megawati PDI leaders openly admitted they were concerned by what ICMI signified. Of course, PDI leaders had long been excluded from power and did not stand to lose as much in factional terms as ICMI's opponents in the governing elite. We should therefore not exaggerate the degree to which the rise of ICMI motivated the PDI resurgence. It is more accurate to say that the rise of ICMI, and the regime's new use of Islamic appeals, freed the old secular and nationalist ideologies to play a more oppositional role (by contrast, the Islamic-based PPP was *not* reinvigorated as an oppositional force during the 1990s).

The new Sukarnoism espoused by the PDI and Megawati was not merely a means to assert non-*santri* cultural identity. It derived its power from being the chief *antiestablishment* secular ideology. Its main appeal was egalitarian and populist and explicitly directed to the "common folk," the *wong cilik*, or *rakyat kecil*. Finally, therefore, we should also note the economic and class appeals which underpinned the PDI and Megawati's popularity.

In conditions where politically dependent crony business groups still dominated the economy, the PDI lacked significant backing from large capital. However, from the mid-1980s the party attracted increasing support from the growing independent middle classes—big city professionals (lawyers, intellectuals, journalists, and others) and some medium entrepreneurs. Under Soerjadi, the party made a deliberate effort to recruit from these sectors, especially intellectuals. Even more were attracted after Megawati became leader. Although some key Megawati supporters were long-serving professional politicians, many others had previously been artists, lawyers, managers, academics, and the like. Such individuals did not join the PDI for personal gain; doing so often harmed their careers. Many were children of the Sukarno-era national political elite, owed their middle-class status to this, and maintained emotional ties with the old Sukarnoist *aliran* (Sophan Sophiaan, for example, was the son of 1960s PNI leader Manai Sophiaan). Many joined the PDI because they saw it as a vehicle to pursue reform "constitutionally" and avoid the dangers associated with challenging the system from outside.

However, the PDI drew its primary social sustenance from much lower down the social hierarchy. Its functions, even those held in Jakarta, typically had a small-town provincial feel. The party grass roots, especially at the district level and below, tended to be organized by petit bourgeois figures: operators of medium-sized businesses, small shopkeepers, retailers, restaurant or food-stall owners, owners of small fleets of taxis or other kinds of public transport. Often such individuals resented being squeezed out by better-connected business groups. They disliked losing the most lucrative contracts awarded by local government agencies to businesses with Golkar links. After the rise of Megawati, many of the battles for control of regional branches were between relatively independent but marginal small entrepreneurs of this kind and local party bosses whose businesses were more dependent on government support.

The mass support base of the party, which supplied the crowds at the party's 1987 and 1992 election rallies, were from even more humble origins. These were the petty traders, owners of small "kiosks," un- or underemployed youth and the myriad others who constituted the urban informal sector. Many were not particularly attached to the PDI but were simply looking for an avenue to protest. *students?*

In short, the PDI retained much of the heterogeneous populist constituency of Sukarnoism. Its appeal exhibited many attributes typical of populist movements, including idealization of the "small people" and programmatic nebulousness. The Sukarno myth and, by extension, Megawati's popularity likewise retained their force primarily among poorer social layers attracted to the evocation of a golden past when the small people were elevated to the center of national life.

The core of the PDI economic appeal from the early 1990s was directed at *both* the old populist constituency and the new middle class. Opposition to "collusion," "nepotism," and "monopolies" exploited widespread resentment at the privileges granted to Suharto family members and other crony capitalists. It appealed to the regularizing instincts of middle-class professionals and to the many small and medium entrepreneurs who resented losing out to the well-connected giants. For example, a 1995 central leadership board statement argued that social inequality was caused not by the "number of large-scale or giant companies, but by the methods they use to carry out their business activities." What was needed was "the right to obtain equal business opportunities. The right to obtain equal access to, and facilities from, the government. Also genuine, fair and just competition" (*Kompas*, September 8, 1995). Criticism of "corruption" and "collusion" also attracted popular sectors which resented the "social gap" (another recurrent theme in campaign speeches) and the informal charges they were obliged to pay when dealing with the state apparatus.

From Semiopposition to Principled Opposition?

One theme of this chapter has been the apparent contradiction between the breadth of Megawati's mass support and the vagueness of her appeal. In part, this vagueness reflected the populism and cross-class base of the PDI, as well as its leaders' aversion to promoting political disorder. Above all, it resulted from the threat of state sanction. And so, Megawati suggested, it was crucial to stick to the "constitutional road" when dealing with the party crisis in 1994–95 in East Java. This meant, for example, always applying for the appropriate permits when holding political meetings and not holding them without permission: "We are different from those who want to make a rebellion. . . . If we did not always seek permission, we'd be caught in their [the government's] trap" (interview, December 11, 1995). Megawati's determination to maintain her party's semioppositional position in the formal system meant that she and her supporters were required to keep their public utterances and behavior within the confines of New Order Pancasila orthodoxy.

Despite Megawati's denials, however, it became clear that sections of the PDI were slowly moving the party beyond the semioppositional model toward an opposition of a more fundamental type. Many members were starting to see the party as an alternative government, hence alternative policies and an alternative presidential candidate. Such aspirations were incompatible with the role allotted for parties in the New Order political structure. Here was the making of a new conflict.

Prelude to the Fall

THE 1996 CRISIS AND ITS AFTERMATH

We're not the ones who know these things. Ask the government. They're the ones who know.

> Soerjadi, commenting on why he was reappointed as
> PDI leader (*Forum Keadilan*, August 26, 1996, 97)

On June 20, 1996, another PDI congress was held, this time in Medan, the capital of North Sumatra. It was the third in three years. In sharp contrast to the preceding two, this congress convened in an atmosphere of almost eerie calm. With a large contingent of soldiers guarding surrounding streets, party delegates heard addresses from interior minister Yogie S. M. and ABRI commander Feisal Tanjung, who told them that the congress was designed merely to overcome the party's "internal problems." There was none of the carnivalesque flavor that had marked the Surabaya congress of December 1993, when Megawati became leader. Certainly, no jeep crashed through the fence surrounding the conference venue, as happened in July 1993, the last time the party held its congress in Medan. Indeed, unlike every previous PDI congress since the party's foundation, the meeting proceeded smoothly and without disruption. It reached its final agenda item two days earlier than scheduled. This was a decision on the party leadership, which swiftly produced a unanimous vote to remove Megawati as chairperson. She was replaced by Soerjadi, who seemed as surprised by his rapid reversal of fate as most observers.

As the congress convened in Medan, the atmosphere in many other parts of the country was far less serene. In Jakarta, Megawati gave a speech before a large crowd, warning them not to be overcome by emotion, but also telling them, "Today, let us show the people of Jakarta, the nation, that we should uphold democracy" (*Media Indonesia*, June 21, 1996). Some twenty thousand people then marched through Jakarta's central business district, cheered on by construction workers and at least some of the office workers gathered on the streets. Eventually the demonstrators made their way to Merdeka Square, where troops assaulted them in front of a contingent of reporters. Over one hundred were injured, and more than fifty detained. In following weeks, a wave of protests gathered pace around the country, culminating on July 27 with the most destructive and widespread rioting Jakarta had seen, at least since the Malari affair, twenty-two years earlier.

These events were the culmination of a government attempt to ouster Megawati that had been predicted almost from the moment she became the PDI leader. Nevertheless, they involved a considerable escalation of coercion on the government's part and embroiled, in one way or another, all the opposition groups discussed in previous chapters. Each group was confronted with new dilemmas and opportunities, and there were signs that a broad opposition coalition was forming. This was a coalition of a sort which had never previously confronted the regime. It had a high-profile leader, albeit a very reluctant one, in Megawati. It also had a reasonably clear platform of democratic reform and the capacity to mobilize a large mass following. It did not involve the entire spectrum of societal forces, it is true, in large part because of the government's success in cultivating modernist Islamic support. Nevertheless, the pro-Megawati coalition was precisely the kind of opposition that the New Order's political structures were designed to prevent. Its emergence signaled that the usual techniques of political control were beginning to falter. In order to suppress the coalition, the regime had to resort to crude and open action. This more overt reliance on coercion significantly undermined regime legitimacy, such that 1996 has been described by one observer as marking the beginning of the "long fall" of Suharto (Eklöf 1999).

Suharto Back in Control

By early 1996, Suharto had largely overcome the disunity in the ruling elite which had earlier contributed to the commencement of *keterbukaan*. Although Edi Sudradjat kept his post as defense and security minister, most of Moerdani's old military associates could now make only occasional splutterings of discontent from retirement or positions in the bureaucracy or national legislature. Where it counted most, in the dozen or so crucial ABRI command positions, control was now firmly in the hands of loyalists.

There were still frictions within the regime nonetheless. The death of Suharto's wife in April 1996 focused attention on the president's own declining health, as did a poorly explained medical checkup in Europe in July. Although it was by now obvious that Suharto intended to stand again in 1998, maneuverings for the vice presidency began to intensify. They occurred in a context in which even loyalists increasingly thought in terms of positioning themselves for the post-Suharto future.

It was now even less possible to speak of coherent factions in ABRI. However, observers increasingly identified three groups of especially influential officers. The first two groups were both actively cultivating support in modernist Islamic circles. The ascendant duo of Feisal Tanjung (still commander in chief) and Syarwan Hamid (chief of staff for social and political affairs from February 1996) had for several years been building links with Habibie and some of his ICMI associates (Syarwan Hamid was especially close to the intellectuals in Adi Sasono's think tank, CIDES). Building a relationship with Suharto's protégé and possible successor, and with his civilian supporters, put these officers in a strong position as Indonesian politics entered its transitional phase.

These two officers' most obvious rivals by early 1996 were the loosely allied pair army chief of staff Hartono and Kopassus commander and presidential son-in-law Prabowo Subianto. These two best personified the sultanistic element in the army, Prabowo by his family ties and fearsome reputation, Hartono by the particularly reckless lengths he went to show his loyalty to the president. He became something of a figure of fun even within the political elite when it was rumored that he was having an illicit relationship with the president's daughter Siti Hardiyanti Rukmana ("Tutut"). In March 1996, Hartono caused embarrassment in ABRI when he donned a yellow jacket and appeared next to Tutut at a Golkar rally, proclaiming ABRI's support for the organization and thus contravening the usually maintained fiction that ABRI was "above all groups." Whereas Feisal Tanjung and Syarwan Hamid were targeting the modernist mainstream via ICMI, these other two officers were building links to more militant Islamist groups that were especially hostile to what they saw as Chinese dominance and Christianization. These groups included Anwar Haryono's Dewan Dakwah and the Indonesian Committee for Solidarity with the Islamic World (KISDI; see, e.g., Schwarz 1999, 336–37).

A layer of up-and-coming army officers constituted a third group. Men like the commander of Kostrad (the army's strategic command) and former presidential adjutant Wiranto and the chief of staff of the Jakarta

Military Command, Susilo Bambang Yudhoyono, were seen by many observers as being comparatively professional and as part of the broadly defined "red and white" secular nationalist group. Although they had similar attitudes on the place of Islam in the sociopolitical map to those held by Moerdani and his supporters, these officers had been little involved in the factional disputes earlier in the decade. They also lacked the antipalace pretensions of the old Moerdani group.

The new military factionalism thus differed from that of several years earlier as all the important officers no longer doubted that to position themselves best for the post-Suharto period they had to secure Suharto's favor, or at least avoid antagonizing him. Officers still had their own personal ambitions, enmities, and clients, but there would now be no open defiance of the president, such as had occurred with the launch of *keterbukaan* in 1989 or the elevation of Try Sutrisno as vice president in 1993. Factionalism had become a competition among loyal lieutenants for the president's ear. Some officers conceded publicly that some measure of "democratization" was necessary, but they privately believed that reform must wait until after Suharto left the scene (even then, of course, the reforms they envisaged were minimal). Accordingly, they tended to extreme vagueness when speaking about reform, referring only to "future" or "long-term" processes. They certainly had little interest in making common cause with anti-Suharto opposition.

The Escalation of Opposition

The reimposition of unity in ABRI meant that Suharto could more confidently rely on coercion in handling political challenges. The return to repressive policies had begun with the press bannings of mid-1994. However, in a pattern common to many authoritarian regimes which pull back after limited liberalization, the return to coercion failed to end opposition, but instead galvanized it. As we have seen, previously highly cautious NGOs focused on "democratization," the PDI was preparing a presidential challenge, and student protestors were increasingly emboldened to attack the president directly. At the same time, Indonesia's fractured and dispersed opposition began to seek ways of cooperating against the regime.

One development that encapsulated this trend was the formation of the Komite Independen Pengawas Pemilu (Independent Election-Monitoring Committee, or KIPP) on March 15, 1996. This organization was modeled on bodies like PollWatch in Thailand and the National Citizens' Movement for Free Elections (NAMFREL) in the Philippines and aimed to mobilize thousands of volunteers to monitor the forthcoming 1997 elections and ensure they were conducted in a free and fair manner. Although many of KIPP's leaders insisted that the organization was politically neutral and morally based, its presidium and advisory council read like a virtual who's who of the country's extrasystem opposition.[1] The various groups involved played complementary roles. NGOs, especially the LBH (in the clearest example yet of its *lokomotif demokrasi* guise) played a crucial facilitating function, providing a network of regional offices and links to international donors. Student groups furnished a large pool of activists. Prominent intellectuals gave the group moral stature and media profile.

Despite its apolitical clothing, KIPP signaled a radically new approach to general elections, and one which suggested that critics of the regime were now searching for ways to directly challenge it on core issues of political power. Since 1971, Indonesia's most outspoken opposition elements had usually advocated election boycotts, or *golput*. This had been an important symbolic and moral statement of defiance, but one that underlined its advocates' lack of an effective political strategy. When activists first canvased the poll-monitoring option in late 1995, many of them discussed it as a more effective method to use the electoral moment to undermine the regime (this was especially the position of the PRD). The goal was to expose the massive electoral abuses that activists believed typified New Order elections. The more radical hoped it might trigger a major crisis along the lines of Marcos's disastrous 1986 election, especially if it coincided with a presidential bid by Megawati. It was this factor, of course, which made poll monitoring a meaningful choice. Previously, *golput* had been logical for middle-class critics alienated by the compliance of the two nongovernment parties. Now, there was the beginning of an effective electoral challenge in Megawati's PDI. Some of the regime's opponents were beginning to imagine an end to the regime in the not-so-distant future.

Government and military leaders recognized the significance of KIPP and responded to it in a very hostile manner. Its members, especially in regional towns, were harassed, meetings were broken up, and its activities were declared illegal in some provinces. Even activists in organizations like the LBH, which had previously been relatively safe from repression, were targeted. In the most spectacular case, a group of thugs surrounded and stoned the Medan LBH office while a meeting was under way inside to establish a local election-monitoring body; twelve hours later the building was burned to the ground.

The Unseating of Megawati

If KIPP was harassed, it was logical that the underlying threat of a Megawati presidential bid should also be dealt with. This was despite the impossibility of Megawati becoming president within the existing political system. The highly controlled character of the electoral system, the pressures brought to bear on voters (especially rural ones), the potential for widespread manipulation of results, and the preponderance of appointed members in the MPR prevented Megawati from making a successful bid for the presidency.

Even so, elements in government had strong motives to move against Megawati. Under her leadership, the party's vote would rise dramatically, to Golkar's detriment. Electoral fraud and intimidation could be used against this, but given new electoral monitoring initiatives like KIPP, and the growing restiveness of society which they articulated, this was likely to be a dangerous strategy. Militant sections of the extrasystem opposition, as well as many of her own supporters, would likely rally to a Megawati presidential bid, increasing the potential for mass unrest. This was the "Aquino scenario," although only the most radical of the regime's opponents dared hope that it would lead to Suharto's fall. But even if a PDI presidential campaign fell short of this aim, it would still have represented a fundamental departure from previous New Order general elections. In previous polls, all parties were obliged to portray themselves as loyal supporters of the government and its programs. Megawati's presidential bid would have introduced a new element of contestation over both program and candidate. Without repression this would necessarily have forced a response from Golkar and the government, dramatically widening the scope of public debate at a time when Suharto and his supporters were attempting to narrow it. In short, Megawati's challenge had the potential to force a dramatic opening of the political system, despite the fact that Megawati herself articulated no clear platform of democratic change.

It was also widely believed that Suharto was strongly opposed to facing a competitor in the MPR, for essentially personal reasons. He had always been elected unopposed, and observers believed that he viewed this as a crucial measure of his own legitimacy, even as confirmation of his personification of the national interest (Crouch 1996a). According to General (retired) Soemitro, as early as 1978, Suharto indicated that he would rather not stand for reelection if he were not the sole candidate (*Forum Keadilan*, August [special edition], 101). That the possible challenger was the daughter of the man he had deposed only doubled the insult.[2]

It is clear that the order for Megawati's removal came directly from Suharto, or at least that his officials knew that this was what he wanted. Even if some senior military officers feared that such a step would unnecessarily antagonize public opinion, they pushed such doubts aside. The interests of the ruler and that of the regime had fused into one. Suharto's dominance foreclosed the route to gradual regime opening offered by the PDI's revival and a loosening of the electoral system.

Signs that the coup de grâce was coming appeared in April 1996 when PDI leaders began to receive reports that Interior Ministry officials and ABRI officers were pressuring regional party officials to sign statements calling for another "extraordinary party congress." On June 3, the plan came into the open when a delegation claiming support from 215 of the party's 305 branches visited the Interior Ministry and asked permission to hold such a congress. The next day, longtime Soerjadi associate and head of the party's group in the DPR, Fatimah Achmad formed a congress-organizing committee, supported by another fifteen of the twenty-seven central leadership board members. These were mostly old Soerjadi camp followers and others who had been forced on Megawati by Hendropriyono and the other officers in December 1993 in exchange for government endorsement. Following classic New Order practice, interior minister Yogie S. M. and ABRI commander Feisal Tanjung immediately endorsed the congress as a means to overcome the party's "internal crisis."

Ironically, it immediately became apparent that Soerjadi was the government's favored candidate to replace Megawati. Because he retained residual support among some PDI functionaries whom he had appointed, he was the only PDI leader with even minimal credibility as a rival to Megawati. His return to favor showed how much ground the government had lost during *keterbukaan*.

From the start, it was clear to the public that Suharto had instigated this operation. Core palace loyalists were in charge, including Yogie S. M. and the ABRI leadership, with Syarwan Hamid acting as the chief operator.[3] At a time when only a few pockets of discontented Moerdani-era officers survived, this campaign against Megawati was far more decisive and better coordinated than previous ones, and there was next to no abstention from it at the local level. This is not to say that the campaign was especially sophisticated. On the contrary, because of Megawati's popularity it had to be conducted in a very crude manner. For instance, Megawati's supporters found that most requests for the congress from party "branches" had in fact been signed by only one or two individual branch officials, without being endorsed by conferences as required by party statutes. Some requests were outright forgeries, and others had been signed under duress. PDI leaders in the regions interviewed in late 1996 spoke of troops escorting district leaders to military offices where they were "invited" to decide who would attend the Medan congress. There were stories of branch leaders meeting in offices surrounded by troops and other threats of violence. Even when a branch leadership council met and formally rejected participation, it often transpired that by the time the Medan congress occurred one or two functionaries had relented to the pressures and decided to attend.

There was also a return to crude pressure on the media, in an attempt to preempt sympathetic coverage like that which assisted Megawati in 1993. Senior military officers, including Syarwan Hamid, instructed chief editors to report the conflict in a manner sympathetic to Megawati's opponents. Notoriously, journalists were even ordered to refer to the PDI leader not as "Megawati Soekarnoputri," but as "Megawati Taufik Kiemas," using her husband's name presumably in a futile attempt to counteract the benefit conferred on Megawati by her parentage. Some major media outlets (such as *Kompas*) hinted at what was really occurring, while a few publications aimed at the lower end of the socioeconomic market (notably the tabloid *Inti Jaya* and dailies *Merdeka* and *Harian Terbit*) remained relentlessly pro-Megawati, and their circulation figures soared. Others, especially the ICMI-linked daily *Republika* and the weekly magazine *Gatra*, dutifully portrayed the conflict as an internal party dispute.

The Pro-Megawati Coalition

In the 1970s, owing to the prevailing climate of repression, New Order political operators had been able to manipulate internal conflict in the PDI and remove independently inclined leaders from it with relative ease. The accumulated experiences of autonomous politics during *keterbukaan* now prompted more active resistance to government manipulation.

From the start, Megawati and her supporters rejected the call for a congress as unconstitutional. At a meeting with the foreign press, PDI leaders claimed that the party could bring millions of people onto the streets.[4] By the time the congress finally convened, even Megawati adopted an explicitly critical tone. She described the government as the chief culprit in the machinations and her own struggle as one for democracy. At no point, however, did she claim the mantle of leader of a broad prodemocratic coalition. Instead, her public demeanor and statements stressed her continued adherence to New Order legality, building up her image of stoic victimhood. As its main strategy, the party initiated hundreds of legal challenges against the Medan congress in every district from which delegates had attended. The aim, Megawati explained to her followers, was to stress the PDI's own "obedience to the law." Privately, PDI leaders said that another aim, given that it was almost universally believed that the challenges would ultimately fail, was to further expose the government's own manipulation of the judicial system and constitution and its disrespect for due process.

Following the announcement of the congress plans, the party splintered ferociously at the grass roots. A large number of local leaders caved in to government pressure and supported the congress. At the provincial level, party boards split about fifty-fifty, while district-level boards remained more solidly behind Megawati. The vast bulk of the *arus bawah* (subdistrict or village coordinators, party security guards, and ordinary party members) were fanatically loyal. Statements of support for Megawati flooded in to party headquarters, even from many branches which had supposedly backed the congress. Many PDI members pledged in their own blood that they were "ready to die for Megawati." Some seized control of party offices and formed local "caretaker boards" to replace defectors to the Fatimah-Soerjadi camp. After the congress, the split became irrevocable. Pro-Megawati branches often maintained control over party buildings (although in some towns these were surrendered to the authorities) but lacked official recognition. The government, meanwhile, put procongress leaders into electoral and other official bodies.

From early June, a wave of mass protest began, arguably the most widespread hitherto under the New Order. Large demonstrations took place in almost all of the large and medium-sized towns of Java, Bali, and Sumatra, as well as in Kalimantan, Sulawesi, Maluku, Nusa Tenggara, and Irian Jaya. The focus of most of these demonstrations was condemnation of the Medan congress, of government intervention, and of PDI "traitors." Some also conveyed wide-ranging demands for reform. Most were peaceful, but in some places (especially cities with large student populations, like Bandung, Yogyakarta, and Surabaya) stone throwing and other clashes with troops occurred. On June 20, when the congress convened in Medan, and during the following week, protests peaked in almost all Indonesia's major urban centers.

The protests took place without direction from Megawati or national PDI headquarters. Instead, they were mostly organized by ad hoc informal action committees, typically involving local PDI leaders (who often remained highly cautious), party members (often more spirited but inexperienced), and crucially, non-PDI student-based groups and NGOs, which were more accustomed to oppositional street politics. For PDI leaders, such committees were a means to protest without implicating local party organs.

Activists from the PRD and its student affiliate, SMID, were especially active in these campaigns. As noted in Chapter 5, this current represented the first clearly mobilizational opposition to emerge in the late Suharto years. They openly stated that they wanted to bring down the government. However, the PRD was also very small, and although its members were very militant (often romantically so), they harbored few illusions about their own capacity to put in place a revolutionary regime. From an early date, therefore, they were especially interested in building coalitions with other opposition groups, including moderate ones like the PDI. The aim in the short term was to radicalize and broaden the scope of opposition to the regime; the longer-term aim was to pave the way for the kind of "popular democratic coalition" government they envisaged one day replacing the New Order.

Popular-radical activists had been among the first to recognize the possibilities afforded by Megawati Soekarnoputri's 1993 election as PDI leader. Sensing impending political crisis, they began to believe that it might be possible to overthrow the regime in the medium term. From at least 1994, PRD and SMID leaders had begun discussing abandoning the previous *golput* strategy of election boycotts and actively explored possibilities for cooperating with the PDI (e.g., by meeting with PDI legislators and other leaders; see, e.g., Gunawan 1999, 73). This was accompanied by a readjustment in their analysis of Indonesia's class structure, with the "urban poor," whom they viewed as constituting the PDI support base, now conceptualized as a strategic class force which could play an important "triggering" role in political change (Akhmad 1994; Mahardika 1997).[5] During the 1996 crisis, PRD cadres liaised with "informal leaders" of the PDI, often bypassing provincial and district leaderships, contributing their knowledge of mass mobilization techniques—how to maintain discipline, identify provocateurs, and so forth—and trying to radicalize the PDI's mass following. In the words of one Yogyakarta SMID activist interviewed in late 1996,

The PDI activists and masses had no experience of organizing actions. If students were not involved, their actions tended to be smaller and also less political. [Those present would] just abuse Soerjadi, Fatimah, and PDI functionaries who defected, and there wouldn't be any political slogans, like abolish *dwifungsi* or repeal the five political laws. When we introduced these elements, the PDI masses greeted them very enthusiastically. Our strategy was for a radicalization of the PDI masses in order to push Megawati forward, so that she wouldn't be left behind by the masses. We fully understood that many opportunists surrounded Megawati, but we saw her masses as a great potential, although we knew that they would not move forward without their leaders. (confidential interview, December 4, 1996)

The PRD was not the only student-based group to participate in such coalitions. Virtually the full range of liberal-populist and popular-radical groups discussed in Chapter 5 did so. For example, members of the militant group Aldera led by Pius Lustrilanang held demonstrations in Bandung, where they threw stones at security forces. In Jakarta, Pijar activists marched in demonstrations chanting the slogan "Megawati! *Reformasi!*" In the words of one of the organization's leaders, because "the key problem at present is the narrowing of power so that it is held personally in the hands of the president," promoting Megawati as an alternative president was a "good start for delegitimation" of the government (*Kabar dari Pijar* 3, 1996, Internet edition). The campaign also involved the greatest yet protest action by the nationalist NU-aligned Protestant and Catholic Cipayung student groups (GMNI, PMII, GMKI, and PMKRI). In Bali, the Gerakan Rakyat Bali (Bali People's Movement, or GRB), which organized some very large protests, was essentially a coalition between GMNI activists and PDI members. Similar coalitions were important in Bandung, Jakarta, and elsewhere.

Beyond students, the pro-Megawati coalition included a wide range of alegal, semi-, and proto-opposition groups. In a press release, KIPP called for the elections to be postponed until democracy in the PDI was restored. Abdurrahman Wahid publicly defended Megawati, and younger NU followers supported protests in many towns. Retired military officers like Soemitro and Rudini expressed their dismay at the government "engineering" against Megawati. In a repeat of the dissident pattern of the past, on July 1 twenty-four prominent figures signed a "statement of concern" decrying the spread of violence in political life and practices which threatened to "kill Pancasila democracy." Most of those who signed the statement were involved in the YKPK, with the addition of Abdurrahman Wahid, leaders of the Cipayung student organizations (except HMI), and several other individuals. A few days earlier, a coalition of some thirty student groups, women's organizations, NGOs, and other bodies, including Pijar, GMNI, PMKRI, the PRD, SMID, and LBH, proclaimed the formation of an Indonesian People's Council, MARI, at a meeting in the LBH offices. As well as defending Megawati, the MARI platform included demands for increased minimum wages, lower prices, repeal of the five political laws, and an end to "corruption, manipulation, collusion, monopolies and bribery" (Human Rights Watch Asia / Robert F. Kennedy Memorial Center for Human Rights 1996, appendix 5). Moreover, in a departure from the dissident pattern of petitioning the power holders, the leaders of this group were quite open that they intended to mobilize against the government. In short, the attack on Megawati was triggering the coalescence of the kind of principled and mobilizational opposition that had always been anathema to the regime.

Those who supported Megawati had varying motivations. There was a large element of simple sympathy in response to the machinations against her. Many of her new supporters from liberal middle-class opposition circles still doubted her personal abilities and the PDI's capacity to become a vehicle for democratization, given its continuing ideological commitment to "Pancasila democracy." Some groups, however, believed that by attacking Megawati the regime was giving them the kind of unifying issue and symbol that they had long lacked. The scope of MARI demands, for example, reflected a deliberate attempt to widen the aims of the movement and build a broad antiregime alliance. By mid-July, some of the younger radical activists associated with groups like the PRD, Aldera, and Pijar began to believe that they might be seeing the long-awaited "momentum," the moment for a decisive struggle against the regime.

In Jakarta, immediately after the June 20 protest, the focus shifted to PDI headquarters on Jalan Diponegoro. Megawati had received permission from the regional commander, Major General Sutiyoso, for her supporters to maintain control over the building, so long as they did not mobilize on the streets. By mid-July daily "democracy forums" (*mimbar demokrasi*) there were attracting large crowds. The mood became increasingly militant, with some speakers (like those from the PRD and other activist groups, or more outspoken PDI leaders like Aberson Sihaloho) condemning not only intervention in the PDI but also Suharto, *dwifungsi*, and other pillars of the political system. In the regions, divisions began to emerge (e.g., over whether to surrender branch offices to local authorities) between cautious pro-Megawati branch officials and the smaller radical groups and PDI members who supported a more confrontational approach. Action committees continued to organize demonstrations, which were in many places becoming larger and more vociferous. Local party leaders typically focused more on legal challenges and shoring up support in regional party organs. Megawati's own caution was the major factor ensuring that the movement did not escalate more rapidly and acquire sharper antiregime focus; in the words of one PDI member in Yogyakarta whom I interviewed later in the year, "We were all waiting for an order from *Mbak* Mega."

One signal of the hardening mood was the behavior of the PRD, which believed most strongly that the PDI crisis presented an opportunity for potentially decisive antiregime mobilization. Budiman Sudjatmiko, the PRD's chairperson, was a prominent speaker at the *mimbar demokrasi* at PDI headquarters. The group also increased the tempo of protest actions by workers; on July 8, Dita Sari, the leader of the group's labor organ, and over twenty other PRD members were arrested at a protest by some twenty thousand workers in Surabaya. Finally, on July 22, the PRD publicly launched itself as a party, in defiance of the Law on Political Parties and Golkar, in a fiery ceremony at the Jakarta LBH office (it had quietly changed itself from an "alliance" to a "party" at a congress in April). At the launch it released a ninety-five-page manifesto that set out a class-based analysis of the New Order regime, a strategy for its overthrow, and a program for a "multi-party popular democracy" led by a "popular democratic coalition" (PRD 1996, 37).[6]

The Failure of Elite Divisions

Throughout this period, many PDI supporters hoped for a break in elite ranks that might assist Megawati. As might be expected, there were indications of concern in both the old "red and white" military camp and among some senior officials who were unsympathetic to ICMI, such as the head of Bakin (the State Intelligence Coordinating Agency), Moetojib, the minister of the State Secretariat Moerdiono, and Ministers Sarwono Kusumaatmadja and Siswono Yudohusodo.

Such officials held that Megawati did not represent a sufficient threat to justify moving against her. Doing so in such a "vulgar" manner was only harming the government's and ABRI's legitimacy and increasing the risk of instability. As Greg Fealy (1997, 36) suggests, there was a feeling among such elements that "allowing [Megawati] to remain as party leader . . . would have signaled a growing political openness and maturity," crucial for the inevitable political transition.

Many PDI supporters especially placed hopes in Edi Sudradjat. Wild rumors circulated that he was providing troops to guard Megawati, that he had offered his resignation, and the like. Edi did express his reservations in public, telling a group of pro-Megawati DPR members that he could "truly understand" their disappointment. At a time when most officials were simply reiterating endorsement of Soerjadi's leadership, he also called for reconciliation between Megawati and Soerjadi (*Media Indonesia*, June 27, 1996). Megawati's supporters also sent delegations to DPR Speaker Wahono stating that he was still "objective" concerning the PDI (*Media Indonesia*, June 26, 1996). On July 19, Wahono made a well-publicized speech in which, without directly referring to the PDI, he commented on the spread of "hypocrisy," including in "the leadership layer, where words are often not the same as their deeds." He also cautioned against undemocratic methods and "engineering," which could endanger the nation as it approached leadership transition (*Jawa Pos*, July 20, 1996; *Tiras*, August 1, 1996, 10–11). After the July 27 violence, he was particularly clear, calling on ABRI to reduce reliance on "repressive reactions" (*Kompas*, August 1, 1996).

However, beyond a few vaguely couched expressions of unease, and some leaked information, Megawati and her supporters received little concrete support from within the ruling elite. Officials simply did not see Megawati and the PDI as important enough to warrant risking their positions when it was clear that Suharto wanted her removed. The choice of Megawati's replacement was also significant; many in the old Moerdani camp believed that if Megawati had to go it was better for her to be replaced by Soerjadi, who had historic links with these circles and might still be an agent of influence for them. Moreover, discontented elite elements now lacked the kind of institutional resources, especially territorial ABRI command positions, which they might have used for Megawati's benefit. The fact that some PDI leaders placed their hopes in Edi Sudradjat (who was not part of the ABRI command structure and had limited influence in the serving officer corps) underlined the paucity of support where it really counted.

The new ABRI leaders (and, we may assume, Suharto even more so) knew that opposition groups hoped for a split within the ruling bloc. As chief of the general staff Lieutenant General Soeyono said,

That is what the people who shout outside the PDI headquarters, those people on the streets, hope for. A split in ABRI would be the key to their success. That's what they hope for. It's like when the PKI formed a fifth column in the old days. They could do that because they succeeded in splitting ABRI. But how could that be possible these days? Could they really get people in ABRI to revolt? No way. You can see for yourself, nowadays ABRI is solid. How could they possibly split us? (*Forum Keadilan*, August 12, 1996, 17)

With ABRI and the ruling elite relatively united, by mid-July the campaign against Megawati escalated. Rumors circulated that the military was preparing to take the Jakarta PDI office by force, prompting hundreds of Megawati supporters to guard it around the clock. On July 22, Feisal Tanjung warned that protests at the office were becoming subversive. Syarwan Hamid appealed for Soerjadi to take it over and warned that the movement developing around the country was "the old song of the PKI." Finally, on July 25, President Suharto received Soerjadi and told him that "bald devils" (*setan gundul*) were using the PDI for their own purposes.

The July 27 Affair

The attack on the PDI office and subsequent rioting on July 27 have been described in detail elsewhere, so brevity is possible here (see, e.g., Luwarso et al. 1997, 22–35, 43–6; YLBHI 1997, 3–26; Eklöf 1999, 41–48).[7] In the early hours of that morning, several thousand uniformed police and soldiers cordoned off the area around the PDI headquarters and trucks disgorged perhaps two hundred men dressed in red T-shirts; it was subsequently revealed that many of them were especially hired manual laborers and street toughs (Randall 1998; Eklöf 1999, 46). Over the following hours, they rained stones and projectiles at the office, observed by uniformed police, who blocked the road and occasionally passed them stones. After some negotiations with those inside, at around 8:30 A.M., a large body of police spearheaded a final assault, and they and the red-shirts forced their way in. Although military sources denied that anything untoward happened, the defenders claimed blood was shed.

Meanwhile, a large crowd had gathered beyond the military cordon. As rumors spread that many in the office had been killed, stone throwing began. Although PDI leaders appealed for calm, sporadic clashes continued, with sections of the crowd at one point chanting "ABRI are killers" and burning a nearby police post. The crowd grew for some hours, swelled by residents of nearby slum areas, high school students, and other passers-by. Around 2:00 P.M. troops made a concerted attack, using tear gas, water cannons, and batons but not firing. The crowds scattered, and from this point running battles and widespread rioting took place throughout a large part of Eastern Jakarta. Many thousands of poor *kampung* residents joined in. The activists from opposition groups among them were able to exercise little control.[8] Eventually, some fifty-six buildings were destroyed, more than two hundred people were arrested, and four (according to official figures) were killed.

The Aftermath: Repression and the Failure of Regime Propaganda

The July 27 riot was the signal for a comprehensive crackdown on dissent. Regime leaders from Suharto down immediately launched a fevered propaganda offensive, reviving the communist specter in a way not seen since the 1970s. They accused those responsible of being communists who had aimed to overthrow the government (there was even a television drama entitled *Terjebak* [Trapped] which portrayed the story of a student activist ensnared by a sinister left-wing group). Senior ABRI officers, especially Syarwan Hamid and Feisal Tanjung, singled out the PRD, denouncing it as a reincarnation of the PKI. In following weeks, it became the target of a near-hysterical propaganda campaign, and many PRD members were hunted down. Ultimately fourteen of them were tried for subversion, with allegations focusing on the content of their party's manifesto. They eventually received prison terms of between eighteen months and thirteen years.

A wide range of alegal, semi-, and proto-opposition groups were caught by the crackdown, including the groups involved in MARI and many PDI members. There were raids on NGO offices in the regions, many activists were temporarily detained, and some were abducted and tortured.[9] Muchtar Pakpakhan of the labor union SBSI was arrested, as was PDI legislator Aberson Sihaloho and 124 hapless people who had been in the PDI headquarters when it was attacked. Senior officials also targeted NGOs, with coordinating minister for political and security affairs Soesilo Soedarman saying that there were thirty-two "problematic" NGOs, including LBH and WALHI, against which unspecified action might be taken (*Republika*, November 4, 1996). In such conditions, an atmosphere of fear blanketed unofficial opposition, and many groups scaled back activities. This retreat was summed up in the word *tiarap* (literally, to lie face down with one's face hidden), which was how many groups described their attitude in late 1996.

Nevertheless, the regime made little headway in imposing its version of the July 27 affair. In a post–Cold War world, and with Indonesia's own conflicts of 1965 a distant memory, warnings of communist infiltration had lost their power to convince. They even seemed anachronistic to the more sophisticated urban population. Even immediately after the riots, newspapers printed readers' letters that openly questioned the official account. PRD leaders who remained at large gave press interviews, contemptuously dismissing government accusations. The National Human Rights Commission released findings on the affair which contradicted the official version, stating that twenty-three persons remained missing and that security forces were involved in the takeover of the PDI building. In one opinion poll of five hundred urban dwellers, only 13 percent of respondents agreed that the PRD was behind the riots, a large majority blaming the security forces, Soerjadi, or the government (Luwarso et al. 1997, 269–92). The government's campaign was also hampered by considerable incompetence of execution, as when the family of PRD leader Budiman Sudjatmiko was accused of PKI links, it subsequently emerged that they were pious Muslims affiliated to Muhammadiyah.

Despite the repressive atmosphere, various opposition elements continued to seek ways to challenge the regime. Megawati's PDI focused on its series of legal challenges.[10] The groups that had borne the brunt of the post-July repression, meanwhile, began to reorganize. Even the PRD, which had decisively made the transition to illegal opposition, began to rebuild underground. Before the end of the year it was organizing demonstrations on several campuses using various "front" organizations. During a visit to Indonesia in late 1996, I was struck by the new optimism of many in NGO, student, and other activist circles, even those in hiding. There was a growing feeling that the regime was turning in on itself and approaching terminal crisis; *pembusukan* (decay) was a term widely used to describe this process.

Islam and the 1996 Crisis

From the early 1990s, as we have seen in previous chapters, the changing tenor of relations between government and the Islamic community accentuated divisions in the potential support base of opposition. After modernist Islamic leaders joined ICMI, many began to feel that they had a stake in the political system and, with few exceptions, largely avoided opposition initiatives outside the system.

This factor had a big impact during the 1996 PDI crisis. Elements within NU, under the leadership of Abdurrahman Wahid, took Megawati's side. But the *aliran* complexion of the pro-Megawati forces was similar to the secular-oriented "rainbow coalition" which had supported YKPK (with the addition of more radical student-based groups and NGOs). Few significant modernist Muslim organizations gave support.[11] Instead, the PDI crisis provided an opportunity for "green" military leaders (most prominently Syarwan Hamid) to attempt to consolidate a reactionary army-Islamic alliance directed against secular opposition (see Honna 1999, 102–3).

The new military leaders had for some time been attempting to integrate Islamic appeals into their "latent danger of communism" discourse (Honna 1999, 95). Some Islamic groups had supported the military-led campaign against communist "organizations without form" in 1995; even Amien Rais had given credence to the threat of "night communists" (*Republika*, October 24, 1995). Before July 27, some actively participated in the campaign against Megawati (PPP leaders furnished part of the excuse for the attack on the PDI headquarters by complaining that the democracy forums disrupted their own nearby office and that speakers were insulting the party).

Mobilization of Islamic opinion was especially central to the propaganda campaign after July 27. In a parody of the 1960s anticommunist military-Islamic coalition, Islamic organizations issued a series of public statements and held rallies to condemn the PRD and "the PKI revival." Many such organizations, like the Council of Islamic Scholars (MUI), were corporatist bodies linked to the government, but leaders of almost all the major modernist groups, including Muhammadiyah, took part. The HMI leadership endorsed a statement which called for the authorities to "investigate thoroughly and process [the PRD] in accordance with the law" for "hitching a ride [*membonceng*] on the riot action" (*Tiras*, August 15, 1996, 84). It appears that intellectuals in CIDES, the ICMI think tank headed by Adi Sasono, gave Syarwan Hamid an assessment of the PRD which he used in designing the campaign against the group.[12] In part, the motivation was fear of losing their new positions of influence. One young CIDES staffer in late 1996 told me that his main concern was that "whatever happens, we mustn't let ICMI be like the PDI or PRD." He feared that if ICMI activists were too "vulgar," the organization might rapidly lose official favor and proreform elements be excised from it.

While such strategic calculations undoubtedly played a part, the vehemence of the attacks was also due to long-held feelings among ICMI sympathizers that the "rainbow coalition" opposition was motivated by resentment toward modernist Islam's new place in the political sun. Many Islamic leaders said this after July 27. Adi Sasono evoked the bloody image of the 1984 Tanjung Priok massacre in one press interview:

The funny thing is that those who are abusing the government now are the people who just kept quiet when the Tanjung Priok incident occurred. In fact, among those who are abusing the government now, there are even some who helped those who committed those killings at Tanjung Priok. So, it is as though the atmosphere then in the past was really ideal. Then [it was as if] there was no need for a Forum Demokrasi, no need for a KIPP, and no need for a 1 July [Statement of] Concern. Now, this makes me ask, why weren't they concerned when the Tanjung Priok incident occurred? That there are several community leaders who express their concerns, well, we have to consider that on its own merits. We don't need to be suspicious. We have to pay proper attention to that statement. But, it raises the question, doesn't it . . . that there are people there who were involved in massacres, people who were involved in very wicked political engineering? And now they are suddenly concerned. Where does all that come from? (*Forum Keadilan*, September 23, 1996, 98)

The barely veiled implication was that Moerdani and his supporters were behind opposition to the government. Certainly, it was a widely held view among activists sympathetic to ICMI that Megawati owed her place to a conspiratorial alliance of Christian and Nationalist military officers and officials who were desperate to frustrate Habibie and the rise of Islam: "They are the reactionaries; we are the revolutionaries," was how one young CIDES intellectual put it to me.

In a sign of the evolution of "civilianization" and "demilitarization" arguments previously used to justify involvement in ICMI, Adi Sasono publicly downplayed the significance of the PDI affair, arguing strongly that the "main current" in ABRI was still committed to "a process of renewal oriented to openness and democratization." He argued that political reform had been progressing steadily in preceding years but was endangered by the impatience of the "radical idealist group" (*Paron*, August 10, 1996, 21).

The 1996 crisis brought to a head the tensions that had been building in the Petition of Fifty group since 1993, when prominent Muslim members like Anwar Haryono and A. M. Fatwa had declared their sympathy for ICMI. In 1996, the first open break came in response to General Hartono's March declaration of ABRI support for Golkar. ABRI-Golkar enmeshment had been a core concern of the Petition of Fifty since its formation, so it was not surprising that the group released a letter condemning Hartono and calling for his dismissal. Yet Hartono was one of the senior officers who had been most active building links to modernist groups, including Anwar Haryono's own Dewan Dakwah. Fatwa and Haryono objected strongly to the working group's letter and issued a "minority note" suggesting that advocating Hartono's removal was interfering too far into the president's prerogative. They later also condemned the group's denunciation of the attempted ouster of Megawati, alleging that the group was "taking sides" and needed to note the left-wing radicalization which contributed to the July 27 affair. In several press interviews Fatwa suggested that he and Haryono (who was sick and rarely attended working group meetings) felt like a "minority" in the group and that its hard-line approach had been appropriate in the early 1980s but not now that the "security approach" was lessened. Eventually, Haryono resigned and Fatwa was expelled, effectively bringing to an end the coalition between modernist Islam and secular dissidence that had been embodied in the Petition of Fifty since the 1980s.[13]

The split in the Petition of Fifty revealed in microcosm how Suharto's initiative of co-opting part of the Islamic community through ICMI was succeeding in dividing potential opposition. Because the putative leader of the coalescing opposition coalition, Megawati, lacked significant (modernist) Muslim support, it was difficult for her to appear as the embodiment of the whole of society against the regime like, say, Corazon Aquino had in the more homogeneous culture of the Philippines. So long as this fissure continued to divide opposition, prospects for society-initiated democratic transition would remain bleak.

However, the 1996 crisis also underlined the ambiguous nature of co-optation. Those Islamic groups that the government called on for support had their own agendas. For example, a meeting of *ulama* in East Java in late July, attended by the governor and regional military commander, departed from the script when participants made additions to a prepared statement condemning the PRD and communism. They called for investigations of various past massacres of Muslims, including in Tanjung Priok and Aceh (*Tiras*, August 15, 1996, 84–5). In the following weeks, there were many public calls (alongside a Human Rights Commission investigation into the July 27 incident) for an investigation into the 1984 Tanjung Priok massacre. This was obviously targeted at Moerdani and his supporters and was doubtlessly partly intended to detract from the current crisis. But it also suggested a far-reaching investigation of military methods of control that far exceeded anything desired by palace loyalists, and General Feisal Tanjung quickly ruled it out (*Straits Times*, September 17, 1997).

As noted in Chapter 3, by the mid-1990s there was growing concern among some ICMI supporters that there were risks in identifying too closely with the government (especially the president) when it was becoming both manifestly less popular and more resistant to reform. Such doubts grew after July 27. As Nurcholish Madjid put it in one interview, by giving Islamic legitimacy to the "[power] structure," ICMI ran the risk that "Islam itself will lose its legitimacy" (*Ummat*, December 23, 1996, 20). Many Muslims who participated in the post–July 27 condemnation of communism thus did so in a qualified manner. For example, a September mass rally in Surabaya organized by Angkatan Muda Muhammadiyah (Muhammadiyah Young Generation) to condemn communism also called for "concrete and drastic steps to punish those who practice corruption and collusion" (*Forum Keadilan*, September 23, 1996, 25). Muhammadiyah leader Amien Rais told the crowd that the organization's support for the government was not without reserve: "Muhammadiyah members will support the government so long as the New Order is still straight (*masih lurus*), as long as the New Order can prove that it is able to eliminate corruption and prevent collusion" (*Tiras*, September 12, 1996, 86).

Another important sign of equivocation was ICMI's official statement on the riots, eventually released on August 8. Although this restated support for the New Order and condemned the PRD, it was guarded in assigning blame, emphasizing the need to respect "the presumption of innocence" (*Republika*, August 9, 1996). ICMI sources indicated that this statement was largely owing to the intervention of Adi Sasono, who also carefully avoided publicly condemning the PRD. Likewise, the tone of

Republika reporting shifted noticeably after July 27, with the paper running prominent, sympathetic reports on the PRD and interviews with its leaders.[14]

Prominent reformist ICMI figures like Adi and Amien used press interviews on the PDI/PRD affair to argue that economic and political reform was needed to prevent unrest and radicalization. Amien reemphasized arguments he had made since late 1993 about the urgency of presidential succession, telling one magazine that recent political events had merely been an "external symptom" of the "real disease," which was that there was "an important organ in the body which is sick." To make it absolutely clear that he was referring to the presidency, he stressed that "the main problem in the political field is indeed the question of succession in the national leadership" and called for leadership rotation in 1998 in a way which would be "smooth, elegant, constitutional and legal, and which need not give rise to a heated atmosphere, let alone lead to unrest in the *arus bawah*" (*Tiras*, August 1, 1996, 85–6). In an interview two years later, Amien suggested that the July 27 affair was one of several incidents which had led him to believe that substantive reform was impossible while Suharto remained in power (personal interview, July 15, 1998). Amien was now on his way to becoming the country's leading opposition figure.

Abdurrahman Wahid's Rapprochement with Suharto

In contrast to Amien Rais, after July 27 Abdurrahman Wahid made a sudden political reversal and began reconciliation with Suharto and his camp. He advised Megawati to drop her lawsuit against the ABRI leaders and give up confrontation. Next, he held a series of highly publicized meetings with General Hartono, the very officer who had tried to have him unseated in 1994. Responding to Abdurrahman's new stance, in November 1996, President Suharto himself attended a Nahdlatul Ulama congress in Probolinggo, East Java, and publicly shook Abdurrahman's hand, as if to symbolize the healing of the rift between them. Abdurrahman immediately declared that NU would "not object" to supporting Suharto's reelection, if that were the will of the MPR (*Kompas*, November 4, 1996).

In the months leading to the 1997 election, Abdurrahman went even further. Stunning political observers and many of his own supporters, he "opened his constituency for Golkar's campaign," escorting the president's daughter Tutut around NU *pesantren* (Mietzner 1998, 181). Important NU figures became Golkar candidates, and according to Abdurrahman ally Matori Abdul Djalil, by early 1997 "almost all" *pesantren* were oriented to Golkar (*Tempo Interaktif*, February 2, 1997). Abdurrahman also effectively backed Tutut's vice presidential aspirations, repeatedly suggesting that she was a "future leader" (*tokoh masa depan*) with whom it was important for the NU to develop links.

These moves were greeted with relief by many *ulama* who had long been worried by deteriorating NU relations with the government. However, they provoked confusion among Abdurrahman's sympathizers in the PDI, Forum Demokrasi, and other secular opposition groups. There was even criticism from younger NU followers who had been active in antigovernment campaigns in preceding years.

Abdurrahman offered several explanations for his tactical reversal. For example, he said it was necessary to support Golkar in order to prevent PPP from getting too many votes because such an outcome "would have been interpreted internationally as a victory for political Islam."[15] It seems most likely, however, that the shift was driven mostly by the conclusions he drew from Megawati's removal and the changing configuration of the ruling elite. His own position was increasingly vulnerable. In late 1996, there were anti-Christian and anti-Chinese riots in Situbondo and Tasikmalaya, towns in East and West Java where NU support was strong. Abdurrahman publicly claimed that these riots had been "engineered" to undermine NU and his own position, and he blamed elements in ICMI for them. As his previous allies in Moerdani circles in ABRI grew weaker, it appears Abdurrahman felt he had to make an adjustment toward the ascendant palace camp.

By doing so, Abdurrahman also hoped to prevent his modernist/ICMI foes from monopolizing access to Suharto. Abdurrahman sometimes hinted at this, such as at one seminar in January 1997 when he suggested it would be dangerous if the "green" group in ABRI were able to ally with "Muslim sectarians" and influence succession (*Tempo Interaktif*, February 1, 1997). He attributed Suharto's new receptiveness to NU to the president's recognition that ICMI had been "captured" by "militant Muslim activists." Suharto, Abdurrahman insisted, now realized that his previous support for ICMI had come at the cost of political support from NU and non-Muslims (*Detektif dan Romantika*, November 23, 1996, 57; *Ummat*, November 25, 1996, 33). Abdurrahman thus combined his rapprochement with Suharto with intensified attacks on Habibie and other ICMI leaders, reiterating that Habibie was "not suitable" to be vice president because he was "emotional" and "liked to get his own way" (*Detektif dan Romantika*, November 23, 1996, 56–61).

Observers sympathetic to Abdurrahman Wahid have portrayed his volte-face after the July 27 affair as an unavoidable response to coercion or the threat of it. For Greg Barton (2002, 221), Abdurrahman "realised he had no choice but to negotiate a truce with Soeharto," while Robert Hefner (2000, 198) suggests that Abdurrahman was "beaten into silence." Such depictions of Abdurrahman having no choice are unconvincing. Other choices clearly were available; Megawati refused to submit to far greater pressure, while Amien Rais opted for a more critical stance toward the president when he could have gained short-term benefit from following the opposite course. In a more general sense, however, Abdurrahman's reversal does illustrate the dilemmas of semiopposition in an authoritarian system like Suharto's when political space suddenly narrows. The NU leader had never had a clear strategy for democratization beyond a vaguely defined commitment to NGO-style "empowerment of civil society" and hope for a negotiated transition to a more democratic system. Such a strategy offered some hope when the regime was experiencing substantial internal factionalism and overseeing a political opening in the early 1990s. When Suharto clamped down, semiopponents were forced to choose either a more open break with the regime or accommodation. Abdurrahman opted for the latter course, putting the interests of his own constituency before a broader struggle for democratization. As when he had taken a similar course in the mid-1980s, NU reaped considerable immediate benefits, including a renewed flow of development funds for *pesantren* (Mietzner 1998, 181–2).

This time, however, Abdurrahman showed a failure of political imagination. He remained focused on the short-term interests of his organization and on the perennial struggle between traditional and modernist Muslims for access to state resources. Abdurrahman evidently did not sense how imminent the succession crisis was, nor that this meant politics in Indonesia was not going to easily return to its conventional New Order pattern. It was Amien Rais, with his talk of sickness at the heart of the body politic and of the urgent need for presidential succession, who more accurately gauged the political dynamics at play.

The 1997 General Elections: Defeat in Victory

Although Abdurrahman's shift helped the government, regime legitimacy continued to slide. Many of the government's actions seemed to reflect inchoate awareness of this problem. During the first months of 1997, there were numerous incidents of seemingly disproportionate repression against urban middle-class opposition. Preparations for the May election took place in an extraordinarily tense security climate.

In the past, elections had played an important legitimizing function for the regime, not so much because the Golkar victories were seen as genuine popular endorsements, but because they showed the government's ability to assert its will over the population. The mobilization of overwhelming financial and administrative resources, the humiliation wreaked on the parties, the ritualistic flavor, even the openness of the pressures brought to bear on voters all seemed designed to communicate that even when the population was handed an opportunity to challenge it, the regime could remain impervious. Elections had also played an important role in maintaining the corporatist political system by ensuring that tolerated semioppositional but mass-based political forces could maintain a stake, no matter how tenuous, within it. Because of the government's rigidity in dealing with discontent over the preceding months, the 1997 election simply dramatized the exclusion of opposition, rather than its co-optation. The result was that the elections also failed to demonstrate New Order political control.

In the months before the election, Megawati at first pretended that her PDI, rather than Soerjadi's, remained within the formal system. Branches followed each stage of the election process—submitting lists of candidates, registering objections to the candidature of Soerjadi followers, and so on. Unheeded at every turn, Megawati at the outset of the campaign appealed to her followers to take no part in campaigning organized by Soerjadi. In stark contrast to what occurred in 1992, official PDI campaign functions were virtually deserted. In many cases they degenerated into farce when Megawati supporters disrupted them, as when they threw venomous snakes onto a platform in Kediri, where Soerjadi was speaking (*Antara*, May 21, 1997). In many towns, Soerjadi-PDI candidates took to campaigning from trucks in case speedy exit was called for; elsewhere they canceled campaigning altogether.

It was not until a week before the poll that Megawati announced she would not vote and appealed to her supporters to follow their own consciences. Although the message was clear enough, she stopped short of explicitly encouraging others not to vote, an illegal act. Given Megawati's reticence, as in previous elections the boycott campaign failed to develop momentum. Instead, the PPP campaign became the chief outlet for popular frustrations and attracted large crowds. Despite their broadly progovernment sympathies, the PPP leadership ran a relatively spirited campaign, condemning (as the PDI did in 1992) *korupsi* and *nepotisme*, even if only in general terms. A striking phenomenon was the transformation of many PPP rallies by what became known as the *Mega-Bintang* (Mega-Star) phenomenon, whereby many participants carried Megawati's portrait or waved banners mixing the PPP's green star symbol with the PDI's red. This phenomenon was partly instigated by maverick PPP branch leaders, especially Moedrick Sangidoe in Solo. A range of other illegal and alegal opposition groups, including the now underground PRD, also encouraged it (according to PRD members interviewed a year later, the organization distributed five hundred thousand "Mega-Star-People-Alliance" leaflets in Jakarta alone). Above all, it was promoted by PDI members who, without clear direction from Megawati, were seeking some form of involvement in the campaign. In any event, the phenomenon became such a cause for concern that the government declared it illegal.

Another striking feature of the campaign was its violence. Approximately four hundred were killed, most in motor vehicle accidents, but others during violent incidents. The worst of these was a large riot in Banjarmasin, South Kalimantan, where officials said some 123 looters perished in a shopping center fire. During the final week of campaigning in Jakarta, several poor districts became sites of virtual *intifada* as local youths threw stones at security forces and pro-Golkar toughs. Highlighting the government's failure to maintain "politics as normal," the final day of campaigning was canceled in the capital.

As if to confirm the growing disjuncture between the popular mood and official politics, the election produced a record Golkar victory of 74.5 percent. This result was simply not credible to much of the public. Rather than enhancing the government's legitimacy, the election result in fact undermined it.

A Deepening Crisis of Hegemony

Signs of the unraveling of the co-optation of modernist Islam were one sign of the growing hegemony crisis. Another was the regime's obvious inability to convince the population of its version of the July 27 affair. Sporadic urban unrest signaled a deterioration of the regime's much-vaunted ability to maintain stability. The political base of the regime was also narrowing (despite Abdurrahman Wahid's late conversion), with the exclusion of important semioppositional groups like Megawati's PDI. Increased reliance on repression and the closure of channels for formal participation within the official political system made it increasingly likely that the eventual political transition would have to begin from outside it. As LIPI researcher Mochtar Pabottingi (1996, 93) argued in a magazine article in August 1996, "closing the door to a healthy transition in power produces a risk of a drastic change that will be very bad for our nation."

The Fall of Suharto

For ABRI there are only two choices now. Either stand in front of Suharto and assault the people who are demanding a reduction in prices and the overthrow of Suharto, or stand behind the people, who are growing ever stronger and greater, with the consequence of submitting to the control of the people. Because the people are everything. The Voice of the People is the Voice of God. Overthrowing a tyrannical and arrogant regime is an obligation for all devout people. The people united cannot be defeated!!!

> Leaflet distributed by Komite Perjuangan Rakyat untuk
> Perubahan (People's Struggle Committee for Change),
> Yogyakarta, early May 1998

In March 1998, Indonesia witnessed another familiar New Order political ritual. This was the general session of the People's Consultative Assembly, the MPR. An observer sitting in the auditorium of the building as the assembly met might have believed that Indonesian politics was following its usual pattern. In his accountability speech for his last five years in office, Suharto calmly listed the achievements and successes of the government's development programs. Just about the only sign that anything was amiss was the assembly's revival of an old law which authorized the president to enact virtually any emergency measure he saw fit. There were odd voices of dissent (such as that of PPP legislator Khofifah Indar Parawansa), but assembly members had been repeatedly warned not to interrupt proceedings. Overall, the mood was one of complacency. Finally, on March 10, the MPR Speaker, Harmoko, asked the one thousand assembly members the following question: "Do you agree to our electing Haji Muhammad Soeharto as president of the Republic of Indonesia for the period of service 1998–2003?" A moment later Harmoko brought down his gavel, signifying agreement. The newspaper *Media Indonesia* (March 11, 1998) described the response: "The applause reverberated. It thundered. And applause was not enough. The MPR members stood up to demonstrate their feelings of respect and happiness that one of the general session's agenda items (the election of the president) had been completed."

The smoothness of proceedings inside the assembly meeting was reminiscent of the PDI congress that had removed Megawati almost two years earlier. However, as with the PDI congress, the atmosphere inside the meeting contrasted dramatically with that in other parts of the country. In March 1998, Indonesia was six months into an economic collapse which had closed factories, ground construction sites to a halt, and made the middle class of Jakarta and other cities storm supermarkets in search of rice and other staples. Outside the national legislature building, a clamor for Suharto's resignation was beginning and would shortly take the form of the largest student movement in Indonesia's history. In a little over two months, following riots in Jakarta in which over one thousand people died, much of the ruling political elite abandoned Suharto. Even Harmoko, the very man who had prompted such scenes of joy in the MPR, gave Suharto a deadline to resign.

Despite this eventual outcome, there had been real grounds for optimism on Suharto's part. There were signs of political unrest in the first months of 1998, but opposition still lacked strong organization. As a result, in a pattern typical of regimes in which the hard-line element is strong, the initiative passed to the most militant and easily mobilized sectors: students and the urban poor. Their mobilizations and rioting eventually raised the cost of governing to such an extent that many in the ruling elite abandoned Suharto.

The Political Dynamics of Late Suhartoism

The disjuncture between the mood of calm inside the MPR in March 1998 and the gathering storm on the outside was very much a function of the kind of political regime that Suharto's had become after thirty-two years in power. It was a regime with growing sultanistic characteristics. According to H. E. Chehabi and Juan Linz (1998a, 7), sultanistic regimes are characterized above all by the "personal rulership" of a single leader.

In such regimes, loyalty to the ruler is based on "a mixture of fear and rewards to his collaborators," rather than ideology or charisma, and the ruler "exercises his power without restraint." As a result, "corruption reigns supreme at all levels of society," the leader makes repeated arbitrary decisions, and the ruling circle is chiefly made up of individuals who owe their positions to "their purely personal submission to the ruler." The ruler dominates the state apparatus by patronage mechanisms. As Richard Snyder (1998, 53) suggests, "The central role of patronage in these regimes creates an authority structure that is radial in nature, with the dictator occupying a central hub that is linked via patronage spokes to clients both within the state and in civil society."

Chehabi and Linz (1998a, 9) explain that no regime fits the ideal type perfectly, but that "the concept of 'sultanistic regime' is not a genetic but an evolutionary one, in the sense that most such regimes develop out of other forms of rule." A process of "sultanization" is especially likely toward the end of a ruler's term in office:

One of the biggest problems facing any nondemocratic regime is succession, since very few have any fixed and accepted rules to regulate the passing of power from one ruler to another. Authoritarian leaders thus often stay in office well beyond the point where they can effectively exercise power. Within the regime the lack of a widely accepted successor can then lead to an inertia where all involved agree to postpone the inevitable as long as possible. At this point those who enjoy the closest personal access to the aging ruler, often family members, can wield great influence behind the scenes, since they are in a position to manipulate him in ways that further their own interests. One might call this phenomenon *fin-de-règne* sultanism. (Chehabi and Linz 1998b, 35)

It is not the intention here to deny that there had been a personalist element in the New Order regime from early on. From the 1970s, Suharto's primacy in the regime had been widely acknowledged. His skills contributed substantially to the design of the New Order, as well as to its longevity. Early on, Suharto's family members had used their links to him to further their business activities, and various corruption scandals involving them were widely known from the late 1960s. Suharto had also from time to time lashed out harshly against people who criticized him personally or his family members.[1]

But these personalist elements in the early New Order were tempered by other factors. Initially, there was an element of pluralism in the regime's upper echelons, provided by the collective leadership of the senior army leadership and the input of senior technocrats and other civilian politicians. The regime was a collective enterprise, grounded in the military-civilian alliance of 1965–66, and it took Suharto the better part of the 1970s to establish his unquestioned dominance. Even on the corruption issue, Suharto himself was viewed early on as being a man of relatively modest appetites, and the most spectacular cases of corruption involved other regime players (like Ibnu Sutowo, the extravagant head of the Pertamina state oil company).

As time passed, the personalist and sultanistic features of the regime became more and more obvious. The above passage from Chehabi and Linz describes almost perfectly the final years of Suharto's rule. Suharto was aging, ailing (it was rumored that he sometimes fell asleep in cabinet sessions), increasingly remote from his subordinates, and beyond challenge. According to one former minister, Sarwono Kusumaatmadja (interview, October 19, 1998), Suharto "dropped his old habit of listening to people and just ranted at them."

The more sultanistic cast of the regime was also evident in the government's relations with societal forces. During the early years of the New Order, the military had been able to erect a corporatist system which co-opted major sociopolitical forces inside regime structures. In the final years of the regime, this pattern of incorporation began to fail. This was a complex process, but one important contributing factor was Suharto's own inflexibility. The attack on Megawati in 1996 bore the typical sultanistic hallmarks of pursuit of the ruler's personal power at the expense of the longer-term interests of the regime. There were other examples. Although Suharto had occasionally publicly attacked his critics since the 1970s, in the final years his outbursts became more frequent, personal, and emotional. He singled out for harassment relatively minor figures who caused offense without threatening him any way, sometimes alerting the public to people who would otherwise have remained obscure.[2]

The internal sultanistic element in the regime was most obvious in the role of the first family, whose business interests were promoted with increasing disregard for legal nicety or public sensitivity. Bizarre schemes were devised to increase the family fortune, and the president increasingly openly intervened on his children's behalf. Their greed was far outstripping that of other elite families. Suharto's children also acquired growing political influence. Tutut played a prominent role in the 1997 Golkar election campaign, while she and her brother Bambang Trihatmodjo had major influence on selecting candidates for the final Suharto-era DPR. From the mid-1990s, it was openly speculated that Tutut was being groomed for the vice presidency. An air of palace decadence accompanied such developments. There was open feuding between the children, as in a squabble over gold deposits in Busang in East Kalimantan, which turned out to be bogus. Increasingly grotesque rumors circulated about family greed in business affairs, illicit personal relationships, sexual excess, and involvement in the drug trade.

Suharto's decisions also appeared increasingly unpredictable, and he showed a new propensity to dismiss senior officials at will, without clear explanation.[3] The age gap between Suharto and his military and civilian subordinates was widening, and there were many communication problems between them. The upper levels of military and government increasingly resembled the "personal staff" typical of sultanism.

In the military, the purge of Moerdani-era officers was essentially complete by 1997 and some of the so-called green Suharto loyalists who had dominated the military for the preceding five years were shifted to executive and legislative positions. Syarwan Hamid became chief of the Fraksi-ABRI in the national legislature in 1997; Hartono was appointed minister of information. The president's son-in-law Prabowo Subianto was appointed Kostrad commander in February 1998 and became increasingly influential in the officer corps. Whatever secret ambitions he may have harbored, he was becoming the obvious leader of a palace guard in ABRI. By early 1998, Prabowo and his allies (men like Major General Zacky Anwar Makarim, head of the intelligence agency BIA from August 1997, and Sjafrie Sjamsoeddin, who took over the crucial Jakarta Military Command) controlled much of the internal security apparatus and the chief strategic commands in and around Jakarta (*Indonesia* 1998, 184). The group around Suharto's former adjutant General Wiranto, who became army chief of staff in June 1997 and then armed forces commander in February 1998, balanced Prabowo's clique. Wiranto was surrounded by his own coterie of officers, like Susilo Bambang Yudhoyono, who became chief of staff for social and political affairs in March 1998. As noted in the previous chapter, although these officers were loyal to Suharto, they were looked on with some hope by many secular intellectuals and were distinguished from their chief rivals by their continuing adherence to ABRI's mainstream secular traditions.

Since the early 1990s, Suharto had prevented the emergence of any coherent proreform element in the regime by purging Golkar, ABRI, and state institutions of groups which indicated doubts about his leadership. In 1997, the attempt to broaden the regime's support base via ICMI was also being seriously revised. Some ICMI reformers, especially Amien Rais, had become openly critical of aspects of government policy. The dissipation of the threat from the Moerdani group, plus Suharto's reconciliation with Abdurrahman Wahid, made the cultivation of modernist Islamic support through ICMI less important. ICMI reformers thus began to fare badly. The most dramatic incident was Amien's forced resignation from the ICMI Council of Experts after he criticized policy (i.e., the president and his family) on the massive Freeport mine in Irian Jaya and the Busang scandal. According to Amien Rais, Suharto directly told Habibie to ensure Amien's removal. Habibie came to Amien and discussed his dilemma; Amien agreed to step down in order "to save ICMI from an attack from Suharto" (interview, Amien Rais, July 15, 1998). Suffering the fate of Wahono's group five years before, in 1997 ICMI fared badly in the allocation of Golkar seats in the DPR and MPR. Among those who were removed as MPR candidates on Suharto's insistence were Adi Sasono and Dawam Rahardjo. Parni Hadi lost his job as the chief editor of *Republika*, apparently because Suharto disapproved of the ICMI newspaper's increasingly critical tone. There were also rumors that Adi Sasono would shortly be removed as ICMI general secretary.

It was not only that no significant reform group could emerge near the center of the regime. The inertia produced by Suharto's continuing dominance also percolated down to the lowest levels of the state apparatus through the same patrimonial mechanisms that had previously contributed to the regime's stability, unity, and effectiveness. The lowliest bureaucrats were dependent for personal advancement on displaying loyalty to their immediate superiors or patrons, who were in turn under the same pressure from above. As a result, there was tremendous inflexibility built in to the system. An editorial in the magazine *Detektif dan Romantika* (with a cover featuring a picture of Suharto rendered as the king of spades) thus argued during the March 1998 MPR general session that exaggerated vigilance against even minor political challenges in 1997–98 was caused by officials fearing to lose their economic privileges if they alienated the president:

Isn't that fear [that Golkar votes would decline in the 1997 election or that there would be an "interruption" during the MPR session] really fear of the highest leader of [Golkar], namely the Chairperson of the Board of Patrons [Suharto]. . . . They are afraid of losing the benefits which they have obtained up to now. . . . This reminds us of a saying which perhaps sounds like a classic, if not a cliché: in America people first become rich and then engage in politics, while in Indonesia people engage in politics in order to seek (and maintain) riches. (*Detektif dan Romantika*, March 7, 1998, 3–4)

Even so, many members of the ruling elite were not blind to the looming political crisis. On the contrary, even some senior officials privately believed that Suharto's increasingly erratic style was endangering not only a stable political transition but also rational policy formulation and the mundane business of government.[4] A few began to make concrete preparations for the post-Suharto era. A team of intellectuals around Habibie, for example, began to draft blueprints for political and economic reform (*Far Eastern Economic Review*, June 25, 1998, 24–25). According to Honna (1999, 113–20), some serving ABRI officers also had growing concerns about Suharto's increasingly capricious rule, clumsy political management by the senior military leadership, and the implications of both for the military's long-term institutional interests. Some officers, especially those associated with the Wiranto-Yudhoyono group, made speeches that raised the prospect of reform, albeit in extremely vague terms, once Suharto left office.

Some groups in the ruling elite were thus privately disillusioned with aspects of Suharto's rule and thinking about how they might take advantage of the eventual collapse of his presidency. However, so long as political conditions remained "normal" and Suharto's power was unchecked, they would not take independent initiatives aimed at removing him from power or significantly altering the political structures of the regime. Even as economic conditions worsened in early 1998, nobody in the government's inner circle had sufficient courage to urge the president to prepare for succession or initiate meaningful political reform. Factionalism in the upper levels of the regime revolved around trying to get presidential backing. Most officials were still mesmerized by Suharto's past ability to outwit challengers. Others believed that it was futile to spark conflict before he passed from the scene and that the key was to be positioned to take advantage of the eventual vacuum.

The increasingly sultanistic character of the regime affected how it fell. The palace's venality greatly undermined regime legitimacy and fueled the explosiveness of the transition. Most important, the regime's identification with, and domination by, Suharto's personal interests ruled out a negotiated solution to the final crisis. Snyder (1998, 53) asserts that in many sultanistic regimes, "when state institutions are thoroughly penetrated by the dictator's patronage network, the political space for the emergence of regime soft-liners is minimal, and the ruling clique and the state are essentially fused into a unitary, hard-line actor." The dictator is generally unable to separate his long-term interests from those of the state or regime and is thus unwilling to cede power. His dominance also prevents the emergence of soft-liners with sufficient authority to initiate political liberalization or negotiate with opposition forces. Even otherwise moderate opponents thus accept that their only realistic strategy is to try to overthrow the government. For this reason, most sultanistic regimes "end in a more or less chaotic way" (Chehabi and Linz 1998b, 37). Mark Thompson (1995, ix–x), for example, argues that in the Philippines

Marcos had to be brought down because he would never step down. Marcos clung to power because the personal character of his rule meant that he had no outside interests that could be retained if he relinquished authority. . . . Marcos had neither an institutional base nor extensive popular support. He, his family, and his friends *were* the regime. . . . His personalism ruled out an authoritarian-initiated transition, making his overthrow necessary if democratization was to take place.

Suharto's regime had initially not been as personalist as this. The New Order had possessed a strong institutional base in the army and bureaucracy and considerable civilian support. It had managed to incorporate and co-opt a wide array of social and political forces. Even in the late 1990s, therefore, opposition forces remained stamped by the previous decades of semiopposition. They resembled more the disunited, hesitant, and organizationally weak opposition which arises under authoritarian semipluralism rather than the determined, underground, and maximalist opposition typical of sultanistic regimes proper. Most moderate opposition leaders were reluctant to contemplate overthrowing Suharto and thus lacked a credible strategy for regime change.

However, as in the Philippines and other sultanistic regimes, the president's dominance of the state apparatus prevented a regime-initiated transition. The reimposition of Suharto's control in the ruling elite, especially the army, had blocked the evolution of a significant soft-line element. In the end, there was no alternative to society-initiated regime change, despite the fact that the legacy of semiopposition and semipluralism meant that most opposition groups were not prepared for it. Opposition groups were catapulted to the forefront of a turbulent political transition.

The Economic Crisis and Its Impact

By the mid-1990s the government was increasingly unpopular on political grounds, but it was still able to deliver steady improvements in living standards to much of the population. The cataclysmic economic collapse from late 1997, by removing this prop of performance legitimacy, propelled a range of social and political forces into action and was the proximate cause of Suharto's political downfall. However, the economic crisis led to Suharto's resignation largely by exposing in stark form the political problems that had accumulated over previous years. The particular pathway by which it matured into a political crisis was likewise shaped by the preceding evolution of the regime's internal features and its structuring of state-society relations.

There has been much debate concerning the causes of the financial crisis that swept through East Asia from mid-1997. Although it is impossible to address these perspectives in detail, an element of financial panic or contagion was clearly involved. In July 1997, the Thai currency collapsed, causing rapid reassessment of risk by lenders and investors throughout the region. Pressure on the Indonesian rupiah began almost immediately because it was widely recognized that Indonesia's economy resembled Thailand's in certain respects, including high corporate foreign debt and underregulation of the financial sector. It was also widely believed that there were greater distortions in the Indonesian economy owing to corruption than in other East Asian economies. Private banks, in particular, had become milch cows for their owners and politically well-connected borrowers, leading to a ballooning of bad loans. In this sense, the eventual severity of Indonesia's crisis was due to a conflict between its increasingly "rational," globalized, and liberal economy and its ossified political structure. In the end, the patrimonial framework for organizing the polity and domestic economy proved unable to withstand the market scrutiny and vulnerability to capital flows associated with integration into the world economy—the very thing that had been the key to economic success in the 1980s and 1990s.

Conflict between the market imperative and political structure was obvious after Indonesia asked for assistance from the International Monetary Fund (IMF) in October 1997. In the words of Richard Robison and Andrew Rosser (1998, 1600), "it soon became clear that the *quid pro quo* for IMF assistance would be a series of neo-liberal reforms which would strike at the heart of the politico-business and conglomerate power." Business interests associated with the first family were targeted in the first IMF rescue package announced on October 31. Finance minister Mar'ie Muhammad closed sixteen banks, including several owned by Suharto family members or associates.

Suharto's family members immediately mounted a counteroffensive, signaled first by an extraordinary outburst by Suharto's son Bambang Trihatmodjo, whose Bank Andromeda was among those closed. He said that the closures were a "political movement" aimed at ensuring "Father is not elected again as President." He threatened to "confront whoever is behind Pak Mar'ie" (*Detektif dan Romantika*, November 15, 1997, 16–18). In the final months of 1997, it became evident that Suharto's children were exercising growing influence on economic policy and appointments (for example, it was soon rumored that Mar'ie would not be reinstated as finance minister). As the months passed and IMF prescriptions became more exacting, decisions were made which went against the spirit, if not the letter, of the IMF agreements to dismantle monopolies such as that on cloves owned by Suharto's youngest son, Hutomo Mandala Putra ("Tommy").

Uncertainty about succession exacerbated the economic crisis. In democratic Thailand and South Korea, governments held responsible for financial collapse were replaced in late 1997, leading to partial recoveries in confidence. In contrast, increasingly fevered rumors circulated in Indonesia concerning Suharto's worsening physical and mental health. In early December, he took a ten-day rest, and canceled a scheduled visit to Iran. Several days later, rumors that the president had suffered a stroke or even died triggered an 11 percent plunge in the rupiah in a single day's trading (*South China Morning Post*, December 10, 1997). There were also rumors of a coup, which businessman Hasjim Djojohadikusumo (Prabowo's brother) and several officers publicly denied.

The final collapse of the economy occurred after Suharto announced an unrealistic budget on January 6. Within a week, the rupiah dropped through the ten thousand to the dollar mark and the government was again forced to call in the IMF. On January 15, Suharto signed a more stringent deal. Even so, amid reports that massive private loan defaults were imminent and that Habibie would become vice president, the rupiah plunged once more on January 22, touching seventeen thousand to the dollar, one-seventh of its precrisis value. The full effects of the crisis began to hit both the middle classes and the poor. Bankruptcies multiplied and prices of consumer goods soared. By the end of December 1997, a million workers had reportedly lost their jobs (*Kompas*, December 30, 1997). The most severely affected sectors were precisely the modern industrial and services sectors that had been the driving force of the export-led boom since the mid-1980s.

The initial societal response was muted. The urban working class was badly affected by the job losses but anyway lacked strong organization, so that through 1998 it played little role as an organized political force (Aspinall 1999). The initial middle-class reaction was panic, including an early January rush on supermarkets in Jakarta and other towns. In contrast, the urban poor seemed restive, and from early in the crisis Indonesia was swept by increasingly apocalyptic predictions of violence focusing on this group. In January and February there was a spate of riots targeting ethnic Chinese shopkeepers in several towns, mostly along Java's northern coast.

Suharto responded to the crisis with the tactical instincts of the military man, albeit an increasingly erratic one. Faced with an economy in free fall, he gave tactical concessions to the markets by agreeing to the demands of the IMF. At the political level he moved to shore up his base. In the second half of 1997 the president went through the familiar ritual of claiming that he would be willing to step down if "the people" no longer supported him. Golkar chairperson Harmoko insisted that the organization would renominate him. ABRI and the two minor parties followed suit. It was uncertain, however, whom Suharto would choose as vice president until he indicated a full two months before the MPR session that he preferred Habibie. Presumably he aimed to preempt a repeat of 1993, when ABRI nominated Try Sutrisno for the post before attaining his express approval. This time, ABRI, now led by Habibie ally Feisal Tanjung, fell in line.

From late 1997, a very repressive security atmosphere prevailed. Officials warned that "small," "certain," "radical," or "impatient" groups were trying to use the monetary crisis to bring down the government. In January and February, as the MPR session approached, security forces broke up virtually every antigovernment street demonstration, no matter how tiny, and arrested its participants. Security forces warned the press and raided antigovernment groups. Not even criticism by economists was tolerated, and several who had criticized the government's response to the crisis were called before military intelligence. From early February, Kopassus troops under Prabowo's command abducted activists, especially from the PRD and other small prodemocracy groups (see Eklöf 1999, 165–70).

Meanwhile, in continued pursuit of a military-Islamic alliance against opposition, Suharto and several ABRI officers sought to fan anti-Chinese sentiment, blaming price rises and scarcities on "speculators" and "hoarders" and talking of conspiracies to undermine the rupiah.[5] Prabowo, and the Islamic groups around him, played the most obvious role in this campaign (Schwarz 1999, 345–48; Mietzner 1999, 72–73; Sidel 1998, 180–85; Eklöf 1999, 134–47). Prabowo was widely rumored to be behind the anti-Chinese riots in January-February. There was even a clumsy attempt to implicate Catholic Chinese businessman Sofyan Wanandi of CSIS and, by implication, Benny Moerdani in a PRD bomb plot.[6]

At the same time, government and ABRI leaders continued to say that they supported "change," even sometimes "renewal" (*pembaruan*) or "reform" (*reformasi*); the crucial ideological ground that Pancasila democracy had assumed its "final" form had already been ceded during the *keterbukaan* years. However, because Suharto did not endorse them, official pronouncements on reform remained vague. Their main theme was instead that change had to be "gradual," "constitutional," and via the "existing system." Indeed, the insistence on "gradual reform" became a means to threaten those who wanted more rapid political change.[7]

The Stirring of Opposition: October 1997– January 1998

Despite its evolution in an increasingly sultanistic direction, the regime had by no means become a classic sultanistic regime with little or no public space for opposition. Instead, there was still a considerable element of pluralism, with a broad spectrum of semi- and alegal opposition scattered through various institutions. Unlike more clearly sultanistic regimes, like Somoza's Nicaragua or the Shah's Iran, revolutionary groups were thus unable to assert hegemonic influence over antigovernment activity (although it is possible that groups like the PRD would have become increasingly influential had the political stalemate continued). Instead, from late 1997 there was a rising tide of criticism from diverse sources.

Some of this criticism followed a familiar pattern. For example, in a petition in late December 1997 the leaders of YKPK called on the MPR, in elaborately polite terms, not to "sacrifice [Suharto] by again forcing him to shoulder" the presidency, because he "has struggled and served in a range of tasks continually for over fifty years, his age is advanced, he has various health impediments, and because he is longed for by his closest family" (*Inti Jaya*, January 9–13, 1998, 12). This was the final but by now rather pathetic culmination of the political logic which had underpinned the group's coalescence in 1995; Bambang Triantoro told the press that Suharto's most appropriate replacement was the vice president and former ABRI commander Try Sutrisno. If Suharto was reelected, he added, then Try should stay on as vice president (*Suara Merdeka*, January 15, 1998). Some officials, like Minister Siswono Yudohusodo, also made halfhearted attempts to promote Try's vice presidential candidacy. But the tightening of loyalist domination meant that this attempt could not replicate ABRI's success in 1993. After Suharto's choice of Habibie became clear, and with Harmoko and Syarwan Hamid in charge of Golkar and Fraksi-ABRI, opposition to Habibie dissipated, and Try himself announced that he was not prepared to be renominated.

There were also increasingly strident calls for change from the expected range of alegal and proto-opposition groups. The Petition of Fifty called for Suharto to be replaced, and Forum Demokrasi advocated rapid political reform. NGOs intruded ever more directly into the political arena. In January, LBH published a list of thirteen officials who it considered "oppose human rights"; then it and other NGOs advocated a special session of the MPR to hold Suharto accountable for the economic collapse and remove him from power. Academics also ridiculed government attempts to resolve the economic crisis and called for political reform. In January, nineteen political researchers from the Indonesian Institute of Sciences (LIPI) called for the election of a new president. An illustration of the initiatives taken by middle-class critics in early 1998 was Suara Ibu Peduli (Voice of the Concerned Mothers), a group formed by women academics and activists from major women's NGOs and feminist groups. In February, defying the ban on street protests, several of its members demonstrated in central Jakarta against price rises, especially for powdered milk. The heavy-handed response by the security forces, plus the nature of the issue involved (which members described as involving "relegitimation of motherhood"; interview, Gadis Arivia, July 20, 1998) gained extensive media coverage and greatly dramatized the repressive climate (see Budianta 2003).

Criticism also came from sources closer to the ruling elite: onetime trade minister (and Prabowo's father) Soemitro Djojohadikusumo condemned the "institutional disease" of "excessive protection, bribery, monopolies, collusion and corruption" in the economic system (*Detektif dan Romantika*, January 17, 1998, 28–29). Another retired technocrat minister, Mohammad Sadli, called for the replacement of the government (*Reuters*, January 9, 1998).

Student protests against the government's handling of the crisis began in several towns from around December 1997. Polls of opinion on several campuses found that most students opposed Suharto's reappointment. Established student-based groups like Yayasan Pijar and the Cipayung organizations held demonstrations or released statements calling for a new president. Although still underground, the PRD also sought ways to sharpen antiregime sentiment on campus and in some urban *kampung* in Jakarta to which PRD activists were relocated after the May 1997 general elections.

As the oppositional mood spread during early 1998, the question of opposition leadership remained central. Many small groups existed which were prepared to challenge the regime, but they lacked leaders with a national profile. Their continuing organizational fragmentation limited their capacity to coordinate mobilization. In these circumstances, many still believed it necessary to find a popular national leader who could become a symbolic rallying point for people who opposed Suharto. A charismatic leader, it was hoped, could allow opposition to bypass its institutional weaknesses.

In the early 1990s, some critics of the regime had hoped to transform Abdurrahman Wahid into such a figure via Forum Demokrasi. In late 1997, however, Abdurrahman counted himself out of this role by remaining publicly reconciled with Suharto. Despite the impact of the economic crisis, Abdurrahman publicly stated that Nahdlatul Ulama entrusted President Suharto alone to "process" succession. He warned those who wanted to take "unconstitutional" action in the lead-up to the MPR session that the NU would form part of a "people's movement" against them. He even reprimanded the West Java branch of the NU for supporting Edi Sudradjat for the vice presidency, stating that "if each person nominates their own candidate" there could be "candidates from the streets" (*calon jalanan*) (*Suara Pembaruan*, October 10, 1997; *Kompas*, November 9, 1997; *Jawa Pos*, November 17, 1997).

More so than Abdurrahman, Megawati was the obvious choice as the symbolic leader of opposition. The events of 1996 had already raised her status to that of chief victim of the Suharto regime. Throughout 1997, Megawati and her supporters had spent considerable energy and political resources to keep her wing of the PDI's organizational structure largely intact and its mass base almost entirely so. But, given her narrow political horizons, Megawati remained focused on internal party matters. She was especially preoccupied with the large number of legal suits demanding annulment of the formal recognition for Soerjadi's leadership.[8]

As the economic crisis deepened, Megawati almost reluctantly turned her attention to the broader canvas. In several speeches between late December 1997 and February 1998, she said she was breaking her "long silence." Still using her familiar Pancasila terminology, she blamed the government directly for the economic collapse. "Arrogance of power," "rampant greed in the life of the political and economic rulers," and "lack of transparency and the murder of democracy," she said, were all responsible. In January, for the first time, Megawati announced that she was willing to serve as president and began to criticize the president directly. She condemned the "cult of the individual," which meant that "all aspects of national and state life have become very unhealthy because they are very dependent on the person of President Suharto" (Soekarnoputri 1997). She suggested the nation should "give him time to rest" and evoked his role in deposing her father, arguing that Suharto should not become de facto president for life. "As an officer with a noble spirit, he will certainly not do something which he once opposed and made taboo." She also pointedly reminded her audience that people who had believed her father was indispensable were proved wrong and that he had "willingly and sincerely let go of all his positions and sacrificed all that he owned in order to fulfill the demands of the time" (Soekarnoputri 1998).

There were different views within the PDI about how to develop a presidential campaign, given that Megawati and her party were now excluded from the formal political system. Some, especially Megawati's husband, Taufik Kiemas, urged caution, while others like Haryanto Taslam favored greater mobilization. Party members established "*posko*

gotong-royong" (*"gotong-royong* coordination posts"), small shacks
draped with PDI regalia, in urban areas to dramatize the party's mass
support and act as grassroots coordinating centers. Pro-Megawati party
branches around the country held public meetings supporting her candidacy. Several alegal opposition groups with tenuous links to the party
also demonstrated in an attempt to stiffen Megawati's resolve.[9] Briefly, in
mid February it appeared that the chief challenge on the streets might
come from a repeat of the 1996 pattern of coalition building between
PDI and radical students, when several hundred people linked to the
party protested in the capital, calling for punishment of corrupt officials
and businesspeople responsible for the crisis.[10] Certainly, hard-line officers in ABRI around Prabowo viewed the PDI as a threat, reflected in the
March 2 abduction by Kopassus of Haryanto Taslam and his incommu-
nicado detention until April 17.

However, as in 1996, the PDI's oppositional capacity foundered on
Megawati's passivity. Beyond stating her readiness to take power, Megawati did little to promote her cause. Although she continued to criticize
the government in her regular addresses to supporters, she made no attempt to mobilize them. This was partly because she still wished to give
the impression that she would become president only as a spontaneous
expression of popular will. As party leader Kwik Kian Gie put it, as
Megawati had declared her willingness to stand for the presidency, it was
now up to society. "Mega herself will not take any action whatsoever"
(*Tiras*, January 26, 1998, 91).

Megawati's passivity partly reflected her continuing stress on constitutionalism. From the start, she had depended on her party's ability to
maintain its foothold within the electoral system. Now that it was excluded, all she was willing to contemplate was moral pressure on the government. By reiterating calls for the constitutionally mandated authorities
to resolve the crisis, Megawati had become something of a dissident,
making moral appeals to those in power. Her unwillingness to mobilize
her mass base and her reluctance to intervene in wider politics meant that
she largely isolated herself from political developments in the final
months of Suharto's reign.

Amien Rais, in contrast, from late 1997 suddenly became *the* chief opposition figure. Although forced from the ICMI leadership, he still enjoyed tremendous authority as Muhammadiyah chairperson. At a seminar at the LBH office in September he accepted a challenge by the
"paranormal" Permadi to accept "presidential nomination." He stated he
had no illusions he could become president, but he also suggested that his
"candidacy" had symbolic and educative importance (*Detektif dan Romantika*, October 4, 1997, 90; *Forum Keadilan*, October 20, 1997, 84).

In a series of press interviews and speeches before gatherings of students and Muhammadiyah members, Amien acknowledged Suharto's years of service to the nation. But he also called on Suharto, in light of the economic crisis, to stand aside, initiate a negotiated transition, and make way for "some form of collective leadership" (*Detektif dan Romantika*, November 29, 1997, 66). The core of Amien's message was not dissimilar to what he had advocated since his 1994 "Succession: A Must" speech, but its tone was now more urgent. In November, he accused Suharto of running a "one-man show" and suggested that his children should be considered economic criminals (*Detektif dan Romantika*, November 29, 1997, 65, 66). In a January interview with an underground magazine, he said Suharto's leadership had "produced social, political and economic diseases which now appear quite chronic, indeed have already become a terminal cancer." He called on the MPR to replace Suharto with a presidium that would include figures like himself and Megawati, as well as military, bureaucratic, business, and other figures (*Suara Independen* 4 [1], January 1998). As in the past, the centerpiece of Amien's appeal was for a negotiated transition. In particular, he insisted that ABRI would have to be a crucial player in any political settlement, calling for a "grand and clean coalition" between military officers, technocrats, technologists [by this he meant Habibie supporters who advocated a state-supported leap into advanced technology], businesspeople, intellectuals, religious leaders, politicians, bureaucrats, managers, and community and NGO activists (*Kompas*, February 16, 1998).

In an ironic twist for one of those ICMI activists who in early 1993 had advocated "same person, change of policy," Amien Rais now depicted Suharto's continued hold on the presidency as the root of Indonesia's problems. His language was virtually identical to that used by Forum Demokrasi intellectuals at the earlier date:

My thesis is simple: it is not possible for us to hope for a change in the style of leadership, state management, central or regional government administration, if there is no replacement of the president. So, it's not possible to change the system without changing the president. As I have repeatedly said, it's precisely the person [*sang figur*] who influences the system. And the person perpetuates the system to maintain the status quo for all time. It is an illusion if people hope that, with his advanced age, Pak Harto can carry out fundamental or drastic reform. (*Forum Keadilan*, January 12, 1999, 24)

Amien also sought a more inclusive nationalist image, appearing with prominent non-Muslims and downplaying earlier statements that might alienate non-Muslims (Mietzner 1999, 68; *Suara Pembaruan*, February 20, 1998). Most importantly, however, Amien's challenge drove a wedge into the nexus between the president and modernist Muslims.

Opposition at an Impasse: January–March 1998

Over the preceding decade, reformers had held different positions on the
"Suharto question." At the end of 1997, there was still variation. ICMI
activists remained linked to Suharto, at least because of their association
with Habibie. Some militant Islamist groups like Dewan Dakwah were
being brought even more firmly into the Prabowo-Suharto orbit. Abdurrahman Wahid had also aligned with the Suharto camp, even if many of
Abdurrahman's supporters believed that this was merely a temporary maneuver. More important, Amien's transformation into Suharto's leading
public critic indicated that the policy of co-optation via ICMI was running its course. By late 1997 sultanization of the regime, economic catas-
trophe, and the succession crisis were drawing opposition groups together in seeking Suharto's removal.

However, although political tensions were building and oppositional
sentiment was widespread, organized opposition remained weak. No vehicle could claim to be a viable alternative government, or even unite a
broad spectrum of opposition groups on an explicit democratic platform.
A wide range of semi-, alegal, and proto-opposition groups existed, but
as argued in previous chapters, their varying interests weighed more
heavily on them than the struggle for democratization per se. This dispersed and largely unorganized character had protected opposition from
repression in the past; now it greatly undermined its mobilizing and bargaining power. Dissident-style criticisms and appeals to those in power
continued to erode regime legitimacy but were unable to force major
concessions. In short, opposition was still marked by the structural weaknesses and ineffectiveness associated with New Order semipluralism and
semifreedom, even though the dynamics of sultanization and the economic crisis were pointing toward a dramatic and possibly violent end to
the regime. A new initiative was needed to break the political impasse.

ICMI secretary-general Adi Sasono made one attempt when in early
January he proposed a "national dialog" between government and military figures, ICMI-aligned modernist Muslims like Amien Rais, and "critical figures" like Abdurrahman Wahid and Megawati. Adi depicted this
as a means to open negotiation on the economic crisis, presidential succession, and a new political format, a way to "reduce the level of radicalization in society and prevent the possible occurrence of social upheaval" (*Kompas*, January 5, 1998).[11] He was trying to play an
intermediary role between government and opposition. However, he was
too marginal a figure in the ruling elite to be able to begin a negotiated
regime transition, and government and military leaders dismissed his initiative. Even so, his plan might have created greater unity in opposition

ranks. Amien Rais promoted it as a means to find a common platform to unite himself, Megawati, and Abdurrahman, the three leaders with the largest mass followings (*Kompas*, January 7, 1998). As Marcus Mietzner (1999, 71) notes, such an alliance between traditionalist and modernist Muslims, plus Sukarnoists, would have constituted a significant threat to Suharto.

However, even as a means of uniting opposition, the "national dialog" eventually proved abortive. In part, this was because of Suharto's unexpected designation of Habibie as his preferred running mate. This decision "split the Habibie group from the potential coalition," and Adi "called off his planned national dialogue on Habibie's instructions" (Mietzner 1999, 70). Even before this, Abdurrahman had effectively buried the proposal, saying that the government, especially President Suharto, saw no need for dialog, so there was no point. A mass-based political alliance between himself, Megawati, and Amien would be like "waking a sleeping tiger" (*Suara Pembaruan*, January 10, 1998). He warned that "ABRI and all social-political organizations which support the government will unite and confront such an alliance." It was best to be patient, avoid alliance building, and wait for the government to initiate dialog (*Media Indonesia*, January 8, 1998; *Kompas*, January 9, 1998;). Abdurrahman shortly afterward had a stroke, which put him out of action for much of the coming crisis. Overall, Mietzner (1998, 198) argues, in the months leading to Suharto's resignation, NU's role was "reactive, if not passive"; the organization wanted to avoid damaging its relations with the government.[12]

Former environment minister Emil Salim took Jakarta by surprise by on February 11 by launching a vice presidential "campaign" with a declaration signed by 128 academics, NGO activists, former technocrats, and retired civil servants, who called themselves "*Gema Madani*," or "Echo of Civil Society." This challenge came from the heartland of the technocratic-intellectual milieu that had been one early social foundation of the New Order and showed the hunger for alternative leadership in middle-class circles (within weeks, ten thousand signatures were collected on a petition). However, as a former bureaucrat, Emil was very cautious, and this caution ensured that his challenge became symbolic only. His supporters "saw with horror how in one public meeting after another, Emil was sidelined by his unwillingness to speak out" (Harrison 1999, 26). He refused to criticize the president directly and begged his supporters not to act "outside the system" (*Suara Merdeka*, February 22, 1998).

The failure of Adi's "national dialog" showed the elite opposition's limited capacity for united action. There were personal dimensions to the distrust between Amien, on the one hand, and Abdurrahman and Mega-

wati on the other, although it also reflected deep suspicions dividing modernist Islam from Islamic traditionalists and Sukarnoist nationalists. The
disunity also reflected the persistence of the semioppositional pattern, as
well as President Suharto's continued ability to split the coalition of interests against him by offering some measure of participation within the
system. The bait of a Habibie vice presidency (hence potential succession)
was still enough to tame most ICMI supporters. The earlier challenge
from NU under Abdurrahman had been neutralized by the promise of
lessened political pressures and greater government support for NU activities at the grass roots.

By February 1998, the criticisms made by Amien, Megawati, NGOs,
and others had helped to further undermine Suharto's legitimacy. However, they now faced a dead end. They lacked the means to bring about
change constitutionally but feared that a more confrontational approach
involving mobilization of their followers might trigger chaos that would
play into the hands of hard-liners. Suharto also still enjoyed a near-myth-
ical reputation as a political tactician, and some felt that they had written
him off too soon in the early 1990s. There was thus a problem of deeply
ingrained habit: figures like Emil Salim, Megawati, Abdurrahman Wahid,
and even Amien Rais were used to operating within regime parameters,
focusing on incremental gains, and speaking the language of euphemistic
criticism. The most obvious example of this in late 1997 and early 1998
was Abdurrahman's refusal to align himself with the emerging movement
against Suharto. But there was also an air of reluctance in many of
Amien's and Megawati's comments on presidential succession. Amien,
for example, said it was "unthinkable" that he could become president
and suggested that regime figures like ministers Habibie, Hartono, Gi-
nandjar Kartasasmita, and others were well qualified for the job (*Forum
Keadilan*, October 20, 1997, 84). Megawati likewise announced her willingness to be nominated with characteristic indirectness, stating that she
would do so only if several officials she named did not have the boldness
to nominate themselves (Soekarnoputri 1998).

As the MPR session neared and it looked as if the familiar political rit-
uals would be played out, a mood of despondency began to affect many
in elite opposition circles (Harrison 1999). Many sensed that the long-
awaited "momentum" might be arriving. But there was also acute awareness that opposition lacked the institutional levers or mass strength for a
successful challenge. Even Amien Rais, as Mietzner (1999, 73) notes,
seemed to lack confidence and considerably softened his stance. He called
on his followers not to join demonstrations and disassociated himself
from those who wanted to "disrupt" the MPR (*Republika*, February 8,
1998). He told supporters that he had met Habibie, who had explained

that the president was working "all-out" to resolve the economic crisis and called on them to give the president a last chance (*Jawa Pos*, February 11, 1998; *Jawa Pos*, February 19, 1999). If after six to twelve months the new cabinet did not overcome the economic crisis, he told the foreign press, he would lead a "people power" movement (*Australian Financial Review*, February 23, 1998). He was less explicit in talking to the domestic press, saying only that a "political explosion" might occur (*Suara Pembaruan*, February 27, 1998).

In this climate, the MPR reappointed Suharto unanimously in March and made Habibie his vice president. The new cabinet had the narrowest representation of elite opinion yet under the New Order. Suharto excluded those ministers from the preceding cabinet most respected in middle-class circles (like Mar'ie Muhammad and Sarwono Kusumaatmadja) and kept those most tainted by corruption scandals (such as Haryanto Dhanutirto and Abdul Latief). He made his daughter Tutut minister of social affairs and his longtime crony and timber tycoon Mohammad "Bob" Hassan minister of trade and industry. The cabinet encapsulated Suharto's rejection of political reform and deepened popular alienation. Economists and figures like Amien Rais publicly ridiculed its members' capacity to deal with the economic crisis. It also exacerbated divisions in the ruling elite. For example, the absence of ICMI reformers robbed Suharto of that organization's support (Mietzner 1999, 74).

The Student Revolt

Suharto's recalcitrance and his dominance over the ruling elite meant there could be no resolution of the political crisis from inside the regime. Instead, his supremacy was setting Indonesia on the path of society-initiated regime change. However, elite opposition remained weak and indecisive. In the end, it was student protest that finally broke the impasse. The 1998 student movement was detonated by several protests at the Depok and then Salemba campuses of the University of Indonesia between February 19 and 26, on the eve of the MPR session. Although these protests were not the first by students that year, given the university's decisive role in 1966, they attracted considerable press coverage and almost immediately triggered a rush of demonstrations around the country. Before the end of the MPR session on March 11, large protests had taken place on major campuses in Surabaya, Yogyakarta, Semarang, Bandung, Solo, Malang, Manado, Ujung Pandang, Denpasar, and Padang, even spreading to smaller regional centers like Kudus and Purwokerto. These often involved large numbers; as many as thirty thousand students mobilized at Yogyakarta's Gadjah Mada University (UGM) one day. The demonstrations called for reduction in prices of basic commodities and the rejection of *korupsi, kolusi,* and *nepotisme,* and *reformasi* in all spheres. Many also openly rejected Suharto's reappointment; he was even burned in effigy at UGM.

It is not difficult to explain why the political initiative passed to university students in early 1998. As noted in Chapter 5, university students in many societies are often susceptible to opposition politics because of their greater independence from obligations of employment and family life, their relative access to critical thinking, and similar factors. They are also able to mobilize with minimal organization owing to their concentration in large numbers on university campuses strategically located in major urban centers. Analysts of student activism suggest that students are especially liable to play an influential political role in societies undergoing rapid social change where politics are relatively uninstitutionalized (Emmerson 1968, 413–4; Altbach 1989, 13). The inability of political institutions to oversee a regime transition was the crux of the 1998 crisis.

Moreover, as we have seen, Indonesian student activism had developed a substantial organizational base and an ethos of activism earlier in the 1990s. Groups and modes of action that were born during this period had critical input into the upheaval of 1998. The older historical legacy was also important. Students were raised in a political environment where they were expected to be able to "save" the nation during crisis. From late 1997, commentators bemoaned the lack of student reaction to the economic and political crisis (see, e.g., *Kompas,* January 14, 1998). More radical student activists had previously viewed the legacy of 1966 as an obstacle because by instilling myths of students being a "moral force" it had depoliticized them and isolated them from other social groups. The 1966 legacy, however, was obviously important in 1998. Many student activists spoke about fulfilling their historic "duty," and many of their protests deliberately echoed the symbolism of the 1966 generation (for instance, there were many attempts to devise new versions of the *Tritura,* the famous "Three People's Demands" of January 1966).

A final important factor was the particular manner in which the economic crisis affected students. University education is crucial for the expansion and consolidation of the middle class. During the university boom of the 1980s and 1990s, the numerous smaller, less prestigious private institutions provided unprecedented access into the ranks of the elite for the children of ambitious lowly public servants, rich peasants, and small traders. Tertiary education had very important social meaning for this transitional layer; as Benedict Anderson (1977, 17) puts it with respect to Thailand in the 1960s and 1970s, it served as "a kind of symbolic confirmation that the boom was not fortune but progress, and that its blessings would be transmitted to the next generation within the family." For the more prosperous, quality tertiary education was transformed from a recognized privilege into something taken for granted, a natural accoutrement of the middle-class lifestyle. The economic collapse destroyed the foundations of this stability. Students' living expenses soared, as did the prices of books and paper. Many began to receive greatly reduced allowances from home, if not to lose them entirely. By September 1998, the government was reporting that between three hundred thousand and four hundred thousand students nationally were unable to pay their fees (*Republika*, September 1, 1998). This crisis particularly affected those who were the first in their families to receive university education and thus threatened the intergenerational expansion of the middle class. But it also rocked even more comfortable students' expectations. Following the pattern set since the late 1980s, the most radical activism in 1998 remained centered in smaller and provincial campuses that attracted more lower-status, upwardly mobile students. However, the 1998 movement mobilized students from the full spectrum, including the large elite campuses of Jakarta.

After the MPR session, the wave of demonstrations expanded, eventually reaching remote towns like Jayapura in Irian Jaya and Kupang in West Timor. By late March, the press was calling it the largest student movement in Indonesian history. In many places, students began to try to take their protests outside of campus grounds, often resulting in violent confrontations with security forces. Within weeks, students in Medan were throwing Molotov cocktails at troops. In all, between March 11 and May 2 there were violent clashes between students and security forces in at least fourteen different towns in Java, Sumatra, Bali, and Lombok (Human Rights Watch Asia 1998, 102–17).[13]

From the start, the government failed to present an effective united front in response. Some, particularly new ministers, tried to maintain a hard line. The education and culture minister told university rectors to enforce the ban on "practical politics" on campuses (*Kompas*, April 5, 1998). Although Kopassus operatives under Prabowo abducted some of the most radical activists, General Wiranto and most senior officers responded more gingerly, refraining from all-out repression. They rarely condemned the students outright, instead typically welcoming their protests as "positive contributions," warning them against "manipulation" by radical forces and suggesting more "constructive" means of conveying their views (e.g., *Jawa Pos*, April 10, 1998). At the same time, Wiranto insisted that protestors should not leave campuses. When they tried to do so, troops used all means at their disposal short of live ammunition—including tear gas, beatings, rubber bullets, even rocks—to prevent them.

As an alternative, Wiranto proposed dialog between students, ABRI, and government leaders. In the 1970s, such dialogs had broken down in acrimony when students read out their demands or walked out. In 1998 the proposals did not get even this far. Most students believed they were an attempt to sidetrack them and that the officers would be unable to offer significant reform while Suharto remained in office. The first attempt at dialog, in early April, failed altogether because the students who were invited refused to attend. The most radical simply rejected outright the idea of talking with what they considered to be an illegitimate government, while others insisted that they would meet only with Suharto. Leaders from the most important campuses boycotted the meeting that finally took place on April 18 (Stanley 1998; Eklöf 1999, 163–64).

The Student Activist Groups

The student movement of 1998 was not homogeneous. Its rapid growth necessarily gave it a high degree of fluidity and spontaneity. Students with widely differing political views and backgrounds often came together on the streets and in activist groups. Nevertheless, to a large extent, it showed traces of the divisions that had marked student activism through the preceding decade. It is possible to identify three main classes of organizations that played a significant role (although it is important to bear in mind that there was much overlap between these): militant activist coalitions, student senates and other representative bodies, and Islamic student groups.[14]

Militant Activist Coalitions

The activist groups that dominated student protest politics in the early 1990s were described in Chapter 5 as "liberal-populists" and "popular-radicals." By the mid-1990s they had established a new ethos of militant antiauthoritarianism, street protest, commitment to political democratization, and—at least in the case of popular-radical students—mobilization of the poor. In early 1998, many groups within these two traditions already existed on many campuses. Their members were experienced at producing and disseminating propaganda, organizing cross-campus networks, and holding demonstrations. As protest spread, such activists established ad hoc campus-based and citywide networks in most university towns. For example, the coalition responsible for many of the largest mobilizations in Jakarta and its surrounds was Komunitas Mahasiswa Se-Jabotabek (All-Jabotabek Student Community, with Jabotabek being the Jakarta-Bogor-Tangerang-Bekasi urban agglomeration), more commonly known as Forum Kota (City Forum, or Forkot). By May 2 Forkot claimed support on forty-six campuses. It was a heterogeneous, loosely organized body which drew students together from a wide range of backgrounds, including the militant radicals, activists from new campus action groups, and many with "Cipayung Group" backgrounds (especially from the Catholic PMKRI, the nationalist GMNI, the NU-aligned traditionalist Islamic PMII, and the Protestant GMKI, which, as explained in previous chapters, developed an increasingly antigovernment outlook over the 1990s). The most militant wing of the activist-based groups remained based around the PRD which, although small, had maintained intact underground networks, and was very influential in some cities.

Militant activist groups and networks started many of the first protests of 1998 and played a crucial role as pacesetters. They were the first to introduce openly anti-Suharto and antimilitary slogans in demonstrations and spearheaded the move to push protests outside campus grounds, directly contravening Wiranto's orders.

Student Senates and Other Representative Bodies

In contrast to preceding years, when only the most committed activists had engaged in public antiregime activities, once the student mobilizations of 1998 gained momentum, many students who held more moderate political views also participated. This included the student senates and other elected bodies which were formally recognized by campus authorities and which had been criticized for their passivity by more radical students through the preceding decade. Although they were not the first to become active, after March they organized protest seminars, delegations, and rallies on virtually all major campuses. According to University of Indonesia senate leader Rama Pratama, the senates tended to be "more bureaucratic and slower" than less formal groups, but once they moved into action they were "more legitimate" because they were based on clear representative mechanisms (interview, July 20, 1998). They were thus able to mobilize large numbers and assisted the student protest movement to spread nationally and acquire a mass character (Widjojo and Nurhasim 1999, 349).

Islamic Student Groups

In the 1990s, the mobilizing power of modernist Islamic groups on campuses, including HMI as well as less publicly visible networks of campus prayer and mosque groups, had occasionally been illustrated by protests such as those against the state lottery (SDSB) in 1991 and 1993. However, as described in Chapter 5, such groups had rarely engaged in explicitly antiregime activity, partly as a result of the ICMI-led modernist rapprochement with the government. In early 1998 there were signs that modernist Islamic groups remained cautious; for example, HMI did not endorse statements signed by other Cipayung group bodies which called on Suharto to resign.[15] However, after the larger campus protests began, a distinct modernist Islamic strand in student activism also became visible, although it remained generally marked by moderation and caution. This was partly due to mobilization by HMI, which mostly channeled its members' activities through the student senates and informal Islamic student fronts, such as the Liga Mahasiswa Muslim Yogyakarta (Yogyakarta League of Muslim Students, or LMMM). A significant development came in late March, about a month after the first round of mobilizations, when a new national organization, Kesatuan Aksi Mahasiswa Muslim Indonesia (Indonesian Muslim Students' Action Front, or KAMMI) was formed.[16] This organization was based on a network of campus mosque groups of the type that had underpinned the big anti-SDSB protests of 1993 and eventually organized some of the larger rallies and public meetings of April and May, although it was politically very cautious.[17]

Student Purity Versus People Power

The organizational heterogeneity of the student movement was mirrored by a wide spectrum in political views and strategies, although this was sometimes obscured by common agreement on general slogans like "reduce prices," "*reformasi*," and "stop violence." However, from the start it was clear that there were two wings in the student movement, which Muridan Widjojo and Moch. Nurhasim (1999) describe as a more militant "Anti–New Order Movement" (*Gerakan Anti Orde Baru*) and a more moderate "Correct-the-New-Order Movement" (*Gerakan Koreksi Orde Baru*). This division was essentially a continuation of the divide that had marked student activism since the 1980s. The first group consisted of the activist coalitions, which were generally linked to the older liberal-populist and popular-radical groups discussed in Chapter 5, although they also drew on many activists from the non–HMI Cipayung groups. From the start, the activist coalitions made more radical demands, openly calling not only for Suharto's removal (which many senates and Islamic groups initially shied away from) but also for fundamental restructuring of government.[18] The most radical groups, especially but not exclusively those associated with the PRD, also demanded elimination of *dwifungsi* from the outset. The second, more moderate group essentially consisted of the student senates and the modernist Islamic groups. They generally used more euphemistic language and advocated Suharto's removal by the constitutional path of a special session of the MPR. They also especially avoided attacking *dwifungsi*. By early May, however, the demands of almost all groups had converged on one overriding immediate goal: the removal of Suharto. As a pamphlet produced by Forkot on May 18 put it, "We have only one enemy: Suharto."[19]

Because more moderate groups were involved in the 1998 protests than had been the case in the early 1990s, there was a marked revival of 1970s-style "moral force" discourse. UI senate leader Rama Pratama, for example, described the student movement in April as a disinterested moral force concerned only to monitor and advise the government:

We don't want to fight over concepts, because the concepts have already been discussed by many experts before. After all, the government has many expert staff of its own, who are cleverer than us. The problem is how those concepts can be implemented. Students aren't arrogant. If the government already has its concepts, please put them into practice. We'll criticize them. That is what we mean by a moral and intellectual movement. Don't think students are Superman, who can do everything. (*Gatra*, April 11, 1998, 68)

The moral tone was also reflected in a widespread emphasis on "purity" (*kemurnian*). As Vedi Hadiz (1999, 111–12) notes, even for some militant students, the notion of student "purity" implied rejection of collaboration with all other political forces. This applied above all to elements from the ruling political elite, and there is certainly very little evidence for any significant contemplation by students of 1966-style collaboration with ABRI. Many students, however, also rejected cooperating with elite opposition and mobilizing alongside the urban poor or other groups.

Set against the emphasis on morality and purity, but sometimes coexisting uneasily with it, was a more radical vision of student activism which had grown out of the rejection of all things associated with the New Order in activist circles from the late 1980s. In 1998, the most militant students did not conceal that they aimed to build a "people power" movement uniting students with the lower classes. Contrast the above statement by Rama Pratama with the following extract from a flyer dis-

tributed in Yogyakarta by the PRD-linked student group Komite Perjuangan Rakyat untuk Perubahan (People's Struggle Committee for
Change, or KPRP) after running street battles in early May:

"Come on, advance and resist!!!" That's the cry of the people of Yogyakarta, who
didn't tremble when they confronted the attacks of the security forces who support the *koruptor* Suharto during the protest which went from the middle of the
day yesterday to the early hours of the morning. Amazing and awe-inspiring!!!
Because of the action, thousands of the people filled the streets to overflowing,
protesting against Suharto, spreading along the streets from Jalan Gejayan, Jalan
Solo, the Janti intersection, Jalan Colombo, right through to Kauman. The people barricaded the streets with trees and rocks to obstruct the trucks of the security forces that wanted to pass. The people have shown their real strength, although they understand the risk they face. But the people continue to resist
because in the end, there is little choice, this is the only way to achieve change.
. . . Our slogan is "OVERTHROW SUHARTO." That's what we'll cry when we
take to the streets.

The main expression of the tension between "purity" and "people
power" was thus in tactics. There were divisions even inside some of the
activist groups like Forkot over whether students should protest outside
campus and join with nonstudent masses. Sometimes the dispute over
this became very bitter; in Jakarta at one point Universitas Kristen Indonesia students rallied outside the Salemba campus of the Universitas
Indonesia taunting a crowd of student protestors inside and calling on
them to come out and join them (*Detektif dan Romantika*, April 25,
1998, 50; interviews, UI students, July 10, 1998).

Many senate leaders took great pains to stress the nonviolent and
gradualist nature of their movement, early on denying that students
would hold street protests. The large rallies organized by KAMMI and allied Islamic groups also tended to be confined within campuses or
mosques. Such students feared that if they took to the streets nonstudents
would join them and rioting might result. This was what military leaders
constantly warned them against (even if what students most feared was
that military provocateurs would infiltrate their ranks and incite clashes
in order to discredit them). By early May, previously cautious students
began to venture outside campus gates. Even so, they still tried to avoid
confrontation, distributing flowers to troops, emphasizing the slogan "*reformasi damai*" (peaceful reform), and deploying student marshals to
separate students from nonstudent onlookers.

For more radical students, it was crucial to leave campus grounds. In
most cities some groups distributed pamphlets in bulk to the general population explaining their demands and encouraging them to take action.
To combat the danger of military provocation, some of the pamphlets

exhorted the population not to attack Chinese-owned businesses but to instead damage military facilities. The most militant students believed that confrontation with security forces could be beneficial. Students in Solo, for example, prepared four "layers" of activists for demonstrations; first a group would attempt to push through army lines, and when force was used against them, three more groups would be ready with stones, catapults, and finally, Molotov cocktails. Such students argued that physical clashes between the army and students were a useful tactic to win popular sympathy; in Yogyakarta, for example, local residents sometimes joined demonstrations (as opposed to simply watching them) when they witnessed students being assaulted or were assaulted themselves by security forces pursuing students through *kampung*.

Such confrontational tactics arguably did not obtain majority support in the months leading to Suharto's fall. Islamic groups and student senates organized many (though not all) of the largest demonstrations inside campus grounds. However, the pacesetting role played by the student movement's militant wing was crucial. By late April, not only had student demands become increasingly blunt, but students were trying to venture beyond the gates of many campuses, dramatically increasing pressure on the security forces and eventually triggering the final crisis.

The Escalation of Opposition

The historical legitimacy of student activism in Indonesia, plus students' middle-class origins and responsible image largely explain the government's difficulties in dealing with student protest. Students were able to garner considerable support from other political actors so that in March and April they became the vociferous centerpiece of a broad middle-class coalition. This coalescence of support around the students was first evident in the role of intellectuals and alumni associations (themselves often led by participants in earlier waves of student activism) which supported protests on many campuses. Rectors, deans, and lecturers addressed many student demonstrations. Critics of the regime of every description—NGO activists, retired generals, pro-Megawati PDI leaders, Muslim figures—did the same. Artists organized a month-long "earth exorcism" festival, which used art as a "medium of liberation" and involved over 170 cultural performances in numerous towns between early April and May (Clark 1999, 38). Suara Ibu Peduli eventually adopted a logistical support role, coordinating the delivery of food and other supplies to the students who occupied the DPR building in mid-May. One particularly important initiative came in response to the disappearances of antigovernment activists (later revealed as being the work of Kopassus troops acting under Prabowo's orders). Several NGOs, led by the LBH, formed the Komisi untuk Orang Hilang dan Korban Tindak Kekerasan (the Commission for the Disappeared and Victims of Violence, or Kontras) to investigate and campaign on the issue. The publicity this group generated put intense pressure on ABRI, especially after several victims resurfaced and made dramatic public testimony. When ABRI was struggling to contain student protest, senior officers were forced to make embarrassing denials of responsibility.

The escalation of student protest fundamentally changed the environment in which other political actors operated. Elite critics of the regime like Amien Rais had previously been reluctant to risk their own organizations or mobilize their own followers against the regime. Amien had Muhammadiyah's vast network of education, health, and other institutions to consider. He also had to contend with pressures from local-level Muhammadiyah leaders who feared a deterioration of relations with authorities. Throughout early 1998, therefore, although Muhammadiyah branches and affiliates held some large rallies in sports stadiums and mosques, they did not endorse street protests. From late February, however, students began to act as proxies for the followers whom leaders like Amien were reluctant to mobilize. And it was Amien, among all the elite critics of the regime, who first and best recognized the implications of this. Almost immediately after the MPR session, he toured campuses where he addressed rallies and urged students to continue their struggle. By mid-April, he was beginning to talk openly of "people power," telling one student audience, "If democratic means to bring about change have reached a dead-end, there is no other way except a mass movement" (_Suara Merdeka_, April 12, 1998).

In contrast, although her PDI released a statement rejecting Suharto's accountability speech at the MPR, during the following weeks Megawati did not overcome her suspicion of mobilization. Her party became partially paralyzed, and reports of Megawati's activities virtually disappeared from the press. The abduction of party leader Haryanto Taslam by Kopassus caused considerable trauma in PDI leadership circles. Megawati did make some appearances (notably at a rally the day after the shootings at Trisakti University in mid-May, discussed below), and other PDI leaders addressed student protests. Overall, however, Megawati played a minimal role in the final anti-Suharto upsurge.[20]

Elite opposition leaders also carefully observed developments within the regime. As in the past, they knew that they would eventually have to deal with ABRI, which still had the capacity to use greater repression. Many elite opposition players continued to promote a negotiated transition as a solution to this conundrum and appealed for the military to support reform. Amien Rais remained a vigorous proponent of this; he kept links with several senior ABRI officers and arranged well-publicized meetings with, among others, army chief of staff General Subagyo Hadi-siswoyo and chief of staff for social and political affairs Lieutenant General Susilo Bambang Yudhoyono. These officers publicly praised the "mature" and "wise" character of his criticisms (see, e.g., *Kompas*, March 26, 1998). According to Mietzner (1999, 69–70), they also warned him "not to overstep the clear line between criticism of Soeharto and the mobilization of the masses against him."

Early on, after his meetings with officers, Amien acknowledged that restraint was called for and claimed such meetings marked the beginning of potentially fruitful dialog to resolve the political impasse (*Suara Pembaruan*, March 28, 1998; *Kompas*, March 28, 1998). However, as student protest spread, Amien realized the opposition's bargaining power had increased. He began to appeal openly to ABRI to distance itself from the president. By late April, he was publicly calling on it to choose between defending the Suharto family or the nation.

The Denouement: Trisakti, the Jakarta Riots, and Their Aftermath

After initially maintaining a hard line, by early May Suharto and his senior officials began to concede that some measure of political reform was necessary. ABRI in particular was showing increasing strain. It was under unprecedented public attack for the disappearance of activists, and its attempt to keep student protests corralled inside campuses was failing, with some local commanders allowing students to demonstrate on the streets. On May 4, conforming to IMF strictures, the government announced rises in electricity and fuel prices. This triggered larger and more violent demonstrations, frequently spreading to nonstudents. In Yogyakarta, for example, clashes between students and security forces escalated when thousands of residents from surrounding *kampung* joined in attacking the security forces. In Medan, clashes with students triggered destructive rioting which engulfed the city and surrounding areas for several days.

Once more, elite opposition intensified. Amien Rais called for the president to step down immediately, and his appeals to the military became even more direct. Signs of rupture close to the core of the governing elite also became visible. For example, on May 6 ICMI leader Achmad Tirtosudiro called for a special session of the MPR, implying he supported the replacement of the president (*Kompas Online*, May 7, 1998). Even the

tame legislature began to show unaccustomed vigor, with a DPR commission calling on the government to reverse the price rises (*Antara,* May
8, 1998).

The long-awaited climax finally occurred at Jakarta's Trisakti University, which was well known for the elite social origins of its students. It
had been a site of enthusiastic but not especially radical activism since
late February. On May 12, when troops prevented Trisakti students from
marching to the DPR, they sat in the road and distributed flowers to the
soldiers. As they were returning to campus, firing began, and four students were killed. Over the next two days, on May 13 and 14, the most
serious rioting yet in modern Indonesian history took place. Many of the
main commercial centers in Jakarta were destroyed; many citizens—
mostly of Chinese descent—were robbed, beaten, or raped. According to
the National Human Rights Commission, some 1,188 people lost their
lives, most of whom were looters trapped in burning shopping centers.
Serious rioting also occurred in Solo in Central Java.

The Trisakti killings and subsequent riots had a huge political impact.
Media representations of the Trisakti victims stressed their respectable
and devout middle-class backgrounds. Interviews with distraught parents, photographs of the victims surrounded by neatly clad family members, and reports of their youthful idiosyncrasies, hobbies, and aspirations filled the press. There was an unprecedented outpouring of national
grief and anger, and those killed were immediately transformed into
pahlawan reformasi, "heroes of reform." The day after the killings,
prominent opposition activists, including Amien Rais and Megawati,
came to the campus and addressed the crowds there, while government
officials scrambled to express their condolences.

The rioting in Jakarta had an even greater impact because it discredited the Suharto government's claim that only it could prevent political
disorder. From early in the decade figures like Amien Rais had argued
that political reform was essential to prevent chaos. It was now clear that
the continuation of the regime, or at least Suharto's presidency, was
bringing Indonesia to the precipice of serious violence. Pressure on
Suharto to step down increased greatly. As a statement signed by Abdurrahman Wahid (who was now slowly recovering from the effects of his
stroke) and other religious leaders put it, "For the sake of saving the Indonesian nation and state from chaos and division, the president should
consider taking the best step" (*Kompas,* May 17, 1998).

Elite opposition began to get more organized. On May 14, Amien Rais
announced the formation of Majelis Amanat Rakyat (the People's Mandate Council, or MAR), which combined a range of ICMI and other
Muslim figures like Adi Sasono and Dawam Rahardjo, former ministers

including Emil Salim and Siswono Yudohusodo, intellectuals and journalists like Goenawan Mohamad of *Tempo*, dissidents like Ali Sadikin,
and leaders of NGOs, including the LBH. Amien suggested that the
group could be the embryo of a "kind of collective leadership . . . a kind
of presidium consisting of all manner of components of the nation,"
which could take over from Suharto when he resigned (*Kompas*, May 15,
1998).

Even this move, however, dramatized the divisions within the elite opposition. The PDI and NU representation in MAR was minimal, while
some of those listed as members immediately denied involvement. When
Prabowo accused the group of being "unconstitutional," Amien chose to
deny that MAR was intended as a "competitor" of the government (*Republika*, May 16, 1998). On May 15, another organization, Forum Kerja
Indonesia (Indonesian Working Forum) was set up. It included NU and
PDI figures, as well as MAR members. Megawati and Abdurrahman
Wahid were listed as members of its advisory board.[21] Although Amien
continued to make halfhearted appeals for some form of collective leadership to replace Suharto, elite opposition continued to be deeply divided
and was far from being in a position to form an emergency government.

As opposition leaders struggled to react, on May 18 a delegation of
student senate leaders visited the DPR to demand that its leaders convene
an "extraordinary session" of the MPR. Seventy-five of them insisted that
they would stay overnight. They were allowed to do so with the support
of Fraksi-ABRI head and longtime Habibie ally Syarwan Hamid (*Forum
Keadilan*, June 15, 1998, 17). The next morning, busloads of students arrived, and the occupation of the DPR building began. Within twenty-four
hours, the image of thousands of students dressed in their university jack-
ets swarming over the building had already become an iconic image of *reformasi*.

As the ruling elite began to fracture, the wave of mobilization peaked
around the country. Immediately after the Trisakti killings, very large student demonstrations took place in many cities. In Surabaya, Semarang
and Padang students occupied Radio Republik Indonesia stations, forcing them to broadcast their demands. May 20 had long been planned as
a national day of action. In Jakarta, Amien Rais canceled a planned mil-
lion-person rally at the National Monument after being warned off by
the military, but in Yogyakarta over half a million students and others
converged on the town center, while a similar number rallied in Bandung.
Demonstrations started by students, but often involving many tens of
thousands of others, also took place in Semarang, Solo, Ujung Pandang,
and other towns and cities. Indonesia was undergoing its moment of
"popular upsurge" (O'Donnell and Schmitter 1986, 53).

The mood of disaffection spread to virtually all social sectors. Even stock exchange traders held a protest against Suharto (*Jawa Pos*, May 20, 1998). Journalists, too, became increasingly bold in reporting the political crisis, with a rapid breakdown of censorship after the Trisakti killings. The major Islamic organizations, including those which had hitherto been cautious (like the NU) and those which were close to Prabowo (like Dewan Dakwah) called for Suharto to step down.[22] Even leaders of Golkar affiliates like the National Indonesian Youth Committee (KNPI) and the corporatist labor federation FSPSI did the same.

The Final Fracturing of the Ruling Elite

The urban unrest and the student mobilizations performed a fundamental role of opposition: raising the costs of rule. Despite the intricate web of ties which bound the ruling elite to Suharto and the system he had established, its members eventually faced a stark choice between abandoning Suharto or confronting a spiral of unrest. The costs of governance were rising rapidly. After the rioting of May 13 and 14, fresh outbreaks of violence seemed imminent. With students singing for the "hanging" of Suharto, Harmoko, and other members of the ruling elite, and the houses of Harmoko and chief Suharto crony Liem Sioe Liong burned down by mobs, the choices could not be clearer. In the words of one anonymous figure who was requested to join the reform committee which President Suharto proposed on May 19 as part of his attempt to stay in power, "Are you crazy? The people will burn down my house" (*Far Eastern Economic Review*, June 4, 1998, 22).

The societal upsurge provided the context for the final abandonment of Suharto by the ruling elite. The most dramatic development came on May 18, when Golkar chairperson and DPR Speaker Harmoko called on the president to step down. In response, Suharto frantically attempted to reach a compromise and retain power. In a last attempt to use the appeal of Islam and deepen the divisions within potential opposition, on May 19, during a private meeting with prominent Muslim leaders including Nurcholish Madjid and Abdurrahman Wahid, he proposed to form a "reform committee," reshuffle the cabinet, hold general elections, and resign thereafter (a process which might have taken months, if not years). His speech was broadcast nationally, with the leaders looking on. Although they privately suggested to the president that he step down, the Islamic leaders publicly endorsed the proposal as a means to avert further bloodshed. Abdurrahman went so far as to appeal for an end to protests (*Jawa Pos*, May 20, 1998).[23]

However, students continued to occupy the DPR building, and elite support for Suharto continued to evaporate. Habibie himself approached Suharto and advised him to step aside; according to one aide, he gave the president a letter to this effect on the night of May 19 (interview, Z. A. Maulani, July 18, 1998). On May 20, heckled and harassed by students, Harmoko gave Suharto a deadline of three days, after which the DPR would begin impeachment proceedings. That evening, fourteen cabinet ministers informed the president that they would not be willing to serve in his reshuffled cabinet. It was at this point that Suharto finally recognized that his position was untenable and decided to resign.

It is ironic that the members of the ruling elite who moved decisively against Suharto in those last days included those viewed as loyalists: Harmoko, Syarwan Hamid, even, eventually, Habibie. The reason is obvious: because Habibie was vice president and these other figures were close to him, they presumably calculated that they were well positioned to secure power in a successor government, especially given the ill preparedness of opposition to take over (in the final event, this proved untrue only for Harmoko, who was too discredited by his reputation for slavish loyalty to Suharto to revive his political career).

The situation in the military, which had the capacity to keep Suharto in power by force, was more complex. In certain respects, the entire military leadership maintained a hard line until the last. On May 18, immediately after Harmoko called on the president to step down, General Wiranto shocked many when he dismissed Harmoko's views as merely those of an "individual," saying that Suharto remained Indonesia's constitutionally appointed president. This seemed to suggest that Wiranto and ABRI were prepared to defend Suharto to the last.

Nevertheless, there was clear division within ABRI. It had long been apparent that Prabowo and his supporters harbored political ambitions of their own and were moving to undermine the Wiranto group. In the months leading to Suharto's fall, they also took a particularly hard line against dissent. Kopassus operatives under Prabowo had been behind the abductions of political activists. They were also widely believed by the public to be responsible for the Trisakti shootings and for mobilizing provocateurs to foment the rioting of May 13 and 14 as part of a plan to discredit Wiranto and gain ascendancy in the armed forces. A series of investigations since 1998 has thus far failed to provide compelling evidence for such a plot, although many suspicious circumstances have still not been fully explained.[24]

The other main group, centered on Wiranto and Susilo Bambang Yudhoyono, also remained officially loyal to Suharto, as Wiranto's May 18 remarks indicated. However, they also tried to appear more sympathetic to the proreform mood. Not only had they promoted dialog with students, but Yudhoyono had cooperated with civilian intellectuals in designing reform plans (Richburg 1999, 77; Mietzner 1999, 82). As the crisis entered its final days, this group sent out some clear signals of support for change. For example, on May 16 Yudhoyono attended a political meeting with retired officers and other prominent figures in which he accepted a petition calling for Suharto's removal from office. As he did so, he told those attending that he hoped the petition would constitute "valuable input, not only to ABRI itself, but also to the nation and state" (*Jawa Pos*, May 17, 1998; *Kompas*, May 18, 1998). Similarly, it is remarkable that after many weeks of violent confrontations at university gates between student protestors and troops, students were allowed to occupy the DPR building on May 18. Over the following days, they were effectively protected by troops beyond the control of the Prabowo group.

By far the most important contribution made by the Wiranto leadership was refraining from, indeed rejecting, the path of extreme coercion. After all, this would have been possible; some officers informed Amien Rais that they were prepared for a "Tiananmen" solution (referring to the 1989 massacre of students and others in Beijing, *Jawa Pos*, May 21, 1998).[25] That Wiranto refused such an option was of crucial importance to the end of Suharto's presidency. Refraining from extreme force to keep Suharto in power effectively meant abandoning him, becoming a means to short-circuit the political crisis and prevent further damage to the state as a whole. For Wiranto and his group, it was also a way to preempt a move for power or other precipitate action by Prabowo (and immediately after Suharto resigned, Wiranto secured Prabowo's dismissal as Kostrad commander).

Signals of eroding military support for Suharto also formed a positive feedback loop with growing civilian opposition. Many students and other activists took heart from the rumors that the military was wavering. As a widely circulated, but probably apocryphal, story put it, a military officer told students that "if there is a thousand of you, we will repress you, if there are ten thousand we will watch you, but if there are a hundred thousand, we will join you." For more conservative organizations, the influence was even greater. Mietzner (1999, 84) notes that many key Muslim organizations and leaders were prepared to attack Suharto openly only when "they were sure that Soeharto had lost the backing of the armed forces." A similar process was also at work with the Golkar organizations and government politicians who eventually abandoned Suharto.

Despite all this, the senior ABRI leadership did not take open action against Suharto. They did not call for him to stand aside or give more explicit encouragement to civilian politicians. The earlier erosion of military autonomy—its transformation into Suharto's "fire brigade"—had deprived senior military officers of the independent political experience and initiative to follow such a course. In R. William Liddle's (1999a, 104) phrase, the military were "relatively weak actors" in the regime's endgame. Wiranto had served for three years as a presidential adjutant and was close to the president's family. He remained highly deferential toward Suharto until the last, even though he could see that his position was hopeless.[26] Equally important were the divisions in the officer corps. Wiranto and his allies' room to maneuver was greatly constrained by the constant possibility of being replaced by their factional enemies. Wiranto made his May 18 statement of support for Suharto after the president offered army chief of staff Subagyo emergency powers (Mietzner 1999, 82–3). In this way, Suharto's divide-and-rule policies largely succeeded in forestalling a military move against him.

The Opposition's Two-Pronged Attack

It is important not to lose sight of the basic societal impulse which underlay the military's vacillation. Senior officers were reacting to events beyond their control. They knew that they had the physical repressive capacity, at least in the short term, to bring the antigovernment movement to heel. They had not yet used unconstrained force against the students, nor even against rioters in Jakarta and Solo. However, they also knew that the movement's repression could be achieved only at great cost. After all, it was the use of lethal force at Trisakti University which triggered the rioting of May 13 and 14. They justifiably feared that more of the same might result in even greater turmoil.

In effect, opposition forces pursued an ultimately successful two-pronged attack. The spread of mass mobilization dramatically raised the costs of governing and presaged a head-on confrontation between state and society. But the tone of most middle-class opposition was still moderate. Prominent opposition leaders stressed they wanted a peaceful and negotiated transition: *reformasi damai*, or "peaceful reform," as one of the catchphrases of April and May put it. They were mostly careful to focus their opprobrium on Suharto and his coterie. Almost the entire spectrum of opposition forces (except for radical student groups) avoided attacking ABRI as an institution, even as they criticized particular acts of military brutality. As the political crisis peaked, Amien Rais and others kept lines of communication open with senior officers and other regime leaders, stressing they desired a negotiated transition. By focusing on Suharto's removal, the opposition also offered the political establishment, including ABRI, a path to extricate itself from the crisis. Amien Rais could hardly have put it more plainly when, speaking at the memorial service for the murdered Trisakti students on May 13, he told the assembled crowd that ABRI now had a choice between "choosing to defend the interests of the people or the interests of a certain family" (*Republika*, May 14, 1998). On May 20 he appealed desperately for the military not to take the path of repression, urging it instead to think of the "long-term," suggesting that "power based on armed force will not last long" (*Jawa Pos*, May 21, 1998).

Indonesia's democratic breakthrough thus differed from the four-player model identified in much transitions literature (e.g., Cheng 1989), in which moderate opposition and regime soft-liners negotiate a transition to democracy while fending off challenges from radical opposition and hard-liners in the regime. In the Indonesian case, it was possible to identify a radical wing of opposition, represented by elements of the student movement and the rioting urban poor, although it was not well organized. Elite figures like Amien Rais constituted the leaders of the moderate opposition. In the early *keterbukaan* years, it had seemed that a soft-liner/hard-liner division was emerging within the regime. But Suharto's dominance had prevented this division from maturing. As a result, in early 1998 the top leaders of the regime remained united behind Suharto. It was only the escalation of opposition in the first five months of the year which finally neutralized the military and prized the senior leadership of the regime away from Suharto. Guillermo O'Donnell and Philippe Schmitter (1986, 27) argue it is precisely at times of maximum disorder and opposition mobilization that "the soft-liners are forced . . . to reveal their predominant interest" against attempts by hard-liners to seize power or otherwise enforce a return to reactionary policies. In Indonesia in May 1998, opposition did more than this. Even if the cracks along which the final splits occurred had long been visible, it was opposition which forced a significant soft-line element into being for the first time.

Indonesia's Opposition and Democratic Transition in Comparative Perspective

MANY scholars of democratic transitions have argued that the structure of a nondemocratic regime greatly influences how a transition takes place and the subsequent prospects for democratic consolidation. As Juan Linz and Alfred Stepan (1996, 55) put it, "the characteristics of the previous nondemocratic regime have profound implications for the transition *paths* available and the *tasks* different countries face when they begin their struggles to develop consolidated democracies" (italics in original). They correlate different transition paths and outcomes with different types of nondemocratic regimes: authoritarian, totalitarian, post-totalitarian, or sultanistic.

The Indonesian experience adds at least two dimensions to this discussion. First, one element of regime type which requires particular attention is how the nondemocratic regime deals with opposition. Any regime will use a distinctive combination of repression, toleration, sanctions, and rewards to control and constrain opponents. This combination will fundamentally shape the organizational form, strategies, and ideological character of opposition, including the relative distribution of what I have termed mobilizational, alegal, proto-, and semiopposition. The resulting patterns of opposition will in turn significantly affect the possibilities for, and the pattern of, democratic transition and consolidation.

Second, there are implications for democratic transition when the nondemocratic regime is itself changing to another nondemocratic form. Indonesia's regime was moving from an authoritarian regime that allowed considerable pluralism toward a more sultanistic pattern, in which the personalist domination of the ruler narrowed representation within the regime. This transformation had important implications for the mode of collapse of the Suharto regime, and for what followed it.

The suddenness and violence of the transition was in large part a product of Suharto's personal dominance. As in many sultanistic regimes, the dominance of the ruler and his refusal to plan for succession meant that regime change could take place only as a consequence of opposition mobilization. No group in the ruling elite was autonomous enough to initiate democratization or negotiate meaningfully with opposition forces. As a result, Indonesia's transition involved rapid escalation of protest, considerable violence, and the abrupt collapse of the government.

However, although Suharto was a dominant player in the New Order regime from the start, for most of its life his regime was not a classic sultanistic regime in which the ruler's arbitrary dominance prevented even moderate opposition. Although the New Order was repressive, it also tolerated many forms of independent and semi-independent societal organization, and it controlled opposition by co-optation as well as by coercion. The legacy of this semipluralist structuring of opposition in 1998 meant that organized or principled opposition remained weak in certain crucial respects. The groups which were strongest organizationally were those which had flourished by working within or around the New Order's rules. They tended to be the most risk-averse, the most likely to accept compromise with the regime, and the least likely to have clear democratic goals and ideology. Groups that possessed clear democratic goals, and were prepared to mobilize their followers to realize them, were fragmented, suppressed, and marginalized. Overall, opposition was well suited to the tasks of eroding regime legitimacy and even to raising the costs of governance. However, it was unable to form a credible democratic alternative at the point of the regime's collapse.

Southeast Asian Comparisons

In order to explore these points more fully it is helpful to compare Indonesia with neighboring countries where there have been similar cases of dramatic mobilization against authoritarian or semiauthoritarian rule. Three cases are of especial interest: the fall of Marcos in the Philippines in 1986, Burma's democracy uprising of 1988, and the "*reformasi*" protests in Malaysia in 1998.

The temptation to compare is greatest with the Philippines. This is partly because of obvious similarities between the "people power" uprising of 1986 and Indonesia's *reformasi* movement. In both cases, long-serving authoritarian rulers were forced from office by large mobilizations involving a wide range of organizations. In both cases, there was a split in the ruling elite; Marcos's attempt to steal the results of the snap election of February 7, 1986, led to a revolt by a substantial part of the military. Hundreds of thousands of civilians then surrounded the rebels to prevent loyalist troops from attacking them, prompting the final collapse of Marcos's rule.

In both cases, the tumultuous nature of the transition also largely resulted from the sultanistic cast of the regime. As Mark Thompson (1995, 4–5) puts it, "Marcos pursued not ideological goals but personal gain; and his regime was organized around family and friends, not strong state institutions." One could not make an equally blunt assessment of Suharto, especially early on in his rule. But as I have argued in previous chapters, there was a pronounced process of "sultanization" in his later years. If "Marcos' 'politics of plunder' and arbitrary repression alienated so many segments of Philippine society that he could hardly expect to find a place in it if he stepped down" (Thompson 1995, 5), much the same could be said for Suharto. In both regimes, the intransigence of the ruler, his dominance over the upper echelons of government, plus his personal identification with the regime meant that his overthrow was necessary for the process of democratization to begin.

There were also similarities in the patterns of opposition and control in the two regimes. For instance, David Wurfel's (1988, 205) discussion of the "reformist opposition" is strikingly reminiscent of the situation of elite dissidents in Suharto's Indonesia: "They were tolerated by Marcos, especially after 1974, as long as they were ineffective in mobilizing a mass following and developed no viable plan for replacing him." Civil society organizations which did not directly challenge the regime also became important for opposition and proto-oppositional activity. For instance, the number of NGOs grew rapidly in the Marcos years, in part (as in Indonesia) owing to sources of overseas funding (Clarke 1998, 64), but also because they provided a way for people to pursue independent and even antiregime activity under the cover of developmentalist programs. There were even obvious parallels between the role of Catholic Church leaders like Cardinal Jaime Sin in opposing Marcos and that played by prominent leaders of Islamic organizations, like Amien Rais of Muhammadiyah, in Indonesia. In both countries, repression made religious institutions important refuges for oppositional impulses.

The comparison is also compelling because Indonesia's opposition activists themselves were influenced by the Philippine example. "People power" made a lasting impression on them, and it was a common phrase in the democratic movement. At an early date, dissidents in the Petition of Fifty told the government that the event was a "valuable lesson for Indonesia."[1] Student activists looked to the Philippines as an exciting example of what could be achieved by mass action.[2] Even during the final months of the regime in 1998, the Indonesian press was full of speculation that the country might go down the "people power" path, while some protestors consciously strove to mimic modes of action (such as offering flowers to troops) they borrowed from the Philippines protestors (Boudreau 1999, 14–15).

However, as Vincent Boudreau (1999) has argued in a brief but illuminating comparative essay (upon which the following discussion draws heavily), there were also important differences. The most important was that in the Philippines, opposition was far more organized, confident, and aggressive than in Indonesia. This book has documented that there was a steady accumulation of opposition activity, as well as occasional outbursts of mass unrest, in the decade leading to Suharto's resignation. However, this opposition was fragmented and ineffectual when compared to the Philippines, where there was a wide array of political parties, armed groups, mass organizations, clandestine movements, and others which openly stated that they desired to remove Marcos from power. These groups engaged in a range of violent, electoral, and mobilizational strategies to achieve that end. Following the August 1983 assassination of Marcos's leading opponent, Benigno Aquino, there was almost continual political upheaval, and it was obvious for a long time that the regime was facing a serious crisis. The fall of Suharto was comparatively sudden, and it took place amid opposition that was much less organized.

There are many explanations for this difference, one of which was that sustained economic growth in Suharto's Indonesia (until the slump of 1997) dampened opposition, while economic decline in the Philippines inflamed it. Poor economic conditions alienated both the working and middle classes from Marcos and even convinced many businesspeople to support the opposition. For present purposes, however, it is important to stress the different nature of the two regimes and their origins. In Indonesia, despite its sultanistic features, especially in its final years, the New Order regime had been established by the military as an institution in which Suharto was initially merely first among equals. The regime was formed amid severe political conflict and a great massacre, and it was able to build upon the already illiberal political structures and ideas inherited from the Sukarno era. This combination of conditions gave the military tremendous advantages when it restructured the political system in the late 1960s and early 1970s. By contrast, authoritarian rule in the

Philippines was not the result of a deep, society-wide political crisis. Instead, from the start it was a personal project of Marcos himself. In 1972, Marcos had already served two terms as elected president, the maximum allowed him by the constitution. His declaration of martial law that year was widely acknowledged as having as its chief purpose the extension of his term in office. There certainly was growing political tension and violence before the declaration, but much of this was staged by Marcos himself (including armed attacks on senior officials) in order to justify assuming emergency powers. Although Marcos used martial law to lock up his chief opponents, his government was never able to remake the political landscape with anything approaching the success of Indonesia's military.

In Indonesia, the military was able to entirely restructure the parties and other institutions of the civilian political elite. In the Philippines, many members of the former civilian ruling elite resisted Marcos and his regime. The traditional opposition, consisting of leaders of the political parties which had dominated Philippines politics since independence, were strong economically. Many were members of oligarchic families who possessed independent economic resources, unlike Indonesia's pre–New Order civilian elite who were mostly bureaucrats and therefore vulnerable to measures like "monoloyalty." Moreover, while many anticommunist civilians in Indonesia initially saw themselves as being in coalition with the army, in the Philippines many in the traditional elite knew that martial law was directed against themselves. For instance, Marcos's political rival since the 1950s, Benigno Aquino, was one of the first to be arrested after martial law. Aquino haunted Marcos throughout his presidency, first from prison and exile, then as martyr to the opposition cause. Although some traditional politicians were for a time co-opted by Marcos, others opposed him from the start.

The situation of the left was also very different from that of the left in Indonesia. Although Marcos used the communist threat to justify martial law, the radical left was actually small in the late 1960s and early 1970s. Thus, rather than being founded amid a cataclysmic counterrevolutionary purge, Marcos's regime actually assisted the growth of the left. As Wurfel (1988, 226) put it, by deepening popular alienation, "the declaration of martial law in 1972 rescued the NPA [the Maoist New People's Army] from oblivion." In fact, military repression was effective in the early years, but by the early 1980s, the NPA's rural insurgency was becoming a major threat to the regime, while a network of urban left-wing organizations contributed to the anti-Marcos opposition. As well as being an important political force in its own right, the left also motivated greater opposition to the regime from elite groups like business, the Catholic Church, and the traditional opposition, which feared that prolonged authoritarianism might eventually lead to a revolution.[3]

As a result of this better-organized opposition, from an early stage Marcos was compelled "periodically to toy with the idea of opening opportunities for opposition participation in politics" (Boudreau 1999, 4). In 1978, he even announced political "normalization," which he described as "a shift from authoritarianism to liberalism" (Wurfel 1988, 233). This would have been unimaginable coming from New Order leaders, who believed that theirs was the natural and final form of government for Indonesia. Moreover, in Indonesia, because the regime controlled the political parties from within, elections held few dangers for it. Facing greater opposition, Marcos badly needed elections to bolster his own legitimacy, but they also held greater risks for him. When his opponents decided to boycott them, they highlighted his political isolation. But when they decided to run, elections provided them with an important platform. In order to win, Marcos had to engage in massive and transparent electoral fraud (something that was hardly necessary in Indonesia, so tightly were the party system and populace controlled). After the assassination of Aquino, the traditional opposition was able to agree on a candidate in the 1986 presidential elections, the murdered senator's widow, Corazon Aquino. (In Indonesia, by contrast, the regime excluded potential opponents like Megawati from the electoral process.) The massive fraud used to deny Aquino victory eventually triggered the final crisis which brought Marcos down in February 1986.

In summary, if a key similarity between Indonesia and the Philippines was that in both places personalist rule set the scene for the tumultuous overthrow of the regime, the key difference was that in the Philippines the "regime alternative"—opposition forces that aimed to replace the regime (Thompson 1995, 9)—were much stronger. Of course, the Philippines opposition was also divided. There were vigorous debates about alliances, the role of violence, participation in elections and other things. However, almost from the start, there were leaders and groups who openly stated they aimed to remove Marcos from power and form a government of their own, in contrast to the mostly dissident and semioppositional styles of politics in Indonesia. When the final crisis came in the Philippines in early 1986, opposition had already staked a claim to national leadership. As a result, when Marcos fled the country, there was a direct transition to democratic government, and Corazon Aquino became president. The process was at a much earlier stage in Indonesia, where opposition was more fractured and opponents like Megawati were kept out of the electoral system.

Burma was not as appealing as the Philippines for Indonesian democracy activists. The Burma democracy uprising in 1988 was brutally put down by the army. Between March 1988, when the first demonstrations began, and September 18, when the military took over government, waves of massive protest swept through all the major towns in the country, bringing the regime to its knees. General Ne Win, who had been in power since 1962, relinquished formal control. Even so, the military eventually asserted its absolute authority and massacred thousands of civilians. The military later ignored the result of an election that its party lost in 1990 and has remained in power to this day.

If a major difference between the Philippines and Indonesia was that in the former country there was a much longer buildup of organized opposition, the case of Burma presents the opposite contrast. In Burma, the upheaval was even more sudden and violent than in Indonesia. Prior to 1988, organized opposition was weak. Not only was there nothing resembling a Philippine-style "regime alternative," there was little of the semiopposition or proto-opposition characteristic of Indonesia. The Burmese regime was even more repressive than Suharto's had been, and it was more effective at suppressing opposition.

The Burmese military regime was established in 1962 as the result of a coup against the elected government of Prime Minister U Nu. The country had been wracked by ethnic and communist insurgencies, and many in the public were so disillusioned with parliamentary government that they greeted the military takeover with apathy or cautious support. In contrast to Indonesia, however, where the military came to power in an already nondemocratic system and at the head of a broad anticommunist coalition, in Burma the military overthrew a democratic government and acted almost alone. From the start, the Burmese military was hostile to virtually all forms of civilian political activity outside its control. It quickly took action against all signs of dissent. The only political organizations allowed were the regime's own Burma Socialist Program Party (BSPP) and its affiliates (the equivalent of Golkar-affiliated *ormas*). A few social and religious groups (chambers of commerce, market associations, native-place societies, monks organizations, and the like) survived, but they were strictly prohibited from engaging in politics (Kyaw Yin Hlaing 2004). There were few avenues for even semioppositional participation in regime structures or euphemistic public criticism of the government.

Covert, clandestine, and informal forms of opposition were all that were possible. For instance, reminiscent of Indonesia during the most repressive phase of the New Order, one type of organization was study groups formed by students, lawyers, writers, and others in which participants would "read books and articles on politics, history, and social analysis" (Kyaw Yin Hlaing 2004, 395; Fink 2001, 183–86). Just like the study groups formed by critically minded students in Indonesia after NKK/BKK (the government's "Normalization of Campus Life" policy), these discussion groups became vehicles through which members could gain access to independent information, hone their critical skills, and make preparations for antigovernment activity. In contrast to Indonesia, underground illegal opposition was also important, with members of the Burmese Communist Party (BCP) playing an important role in such groups (of forty-two groups identified by Kyaw Yin Hlaing [2004], five were directly linked to the BCP and fifteen were sympathizers).

As in Indonesia, there were also dissident former army generals and politicians who occasionally wrote open letters criticizing this or that aspect of the regime and warning it to change its ways. But the political space was very limited for such individuals; in Burma, army officers who fell out with Ne Win were often locked up rather than being politically marginalized or cut out of business deals as they usually were under Suharto. As a result, elite politicians or ex-regime dissidents sometimes fled Burma altogether and made common cause with the ethnic and other armed insurgencies which ringed the Burmese heartland (as, for example, U Nu did in the late 1960s when he established a Patriotic Liberation Army along the Thai-Burma border [Lintner 1989, 72]).

The more repressive political climate in Burma, including the more brutal behavior of the armed forces and the lack of space for even semi-opposition activity, meant that Burma's 1988 democracy uprising was more sudden and violent than Indonesia's. One similarity, however, was that in both places students played a crucial role. I noted in the previous chapter that students are frequently prominent in democratic movements when institutional avenues for broader opposition are restricted; Burma was another striking example of this general phenomenon.[4] In Indonesia, however, the final bout of protest took place after many years of sustained and lower-level mobilization by students. In Burma, by contrast, a nonpolitical brawl between students and youths linked to the ruling party within days led to antiregime street protests and, within months, to a society-wide revolt. One reason for the rapid escalation was the sheer brutality of the military's response (it is believed that forty-one students were suffocated in a prison van which carted the wounded away from the first street demonstration); another was that simmering resentment against the regime had never been vented because there were no channels for even ineffective nongovernmental political activity.

Burma's democracy uprising was thus more reminiscent of the movements which sprang seemingly from nowhere in Eastern Europe in 1989. Beginning with a minimal level of formal organization in March 1988, it quickly became a mixture of peaceful mass movement and revolutionary insurrection. According to Bertil Lintner (1989, 156), by August there were strike centers in over 200 of Burma's 314 townships. There was also considerable violence, with protestors in many places capturing and beheading informants and security officers. At the height of the uprising, state institutions began to crumble, and there were defections by ordinary soldiers and police. Committees were established at the local level to carry out all kinds of ordinary government functions.

Despite the brutal and indiscriminate repression which ended the protests and accompanied the military coup in September, when the government later announced it would hold elections, its opponents rapidly cohered around the National League for Democracy (NLD). This party was led by several prominent dissidents, including Aung San Suu Kyi, the daughter of the nationalist leader Aung San. The NLD rejected the military regime in fundamental terms. Contrast, for instance, the uncompromising tone of Suu Kyi's campaigning with that of Megawati Soekarnoputri, who was in many respects her Indonesian equivalent: "As she traveled around the country, her speeches focused increasingly upon the behavior of the military, which she eventually described as fascist and an obstruction to peaceful change. By June 1989, she publicly accused Ne Win of being the real leader of the military government, the source of the people's hardships, and the man who destroyed everything her father stood for and tried to achieve" (Silverstein 1990, 1012). Although Suu Kyi was eventually detained and not allowed to stand for election, the NLD went on to win an overwhelming majority in the 1990 elections, apparently very much to the surprise of the military, which refused to transfer power to it.

A crucial difference from Indonesia is thus that when the political opening happened, an organized, fundamental, and united opposition which decisively rejected the regime and called for its replacement rapidly sprang into existence. From having minimal organization, opposition made a rapid leap toward becoming a highly effective regime alternative. This was a product of the Burmese regime's extreme repressiveness. Because there had been little space for semioppositional politics in the "gray area" between state and society, there was also relatively little of the ambivalence and hesitancy that was so characteristic of much Indonesian opposition. In Burma, the moment the regime appeared to tremble, would-be opponents were ready to absolutely reject its leaders, its political structures, and its ideology.

Burma's democratic opposition ultimately failed to topple the regime, but this had more to do with the internal cohesion of the Burmese military than any weakness of the opposition itself. The role of Ne Win, although much less known than that of Marcos and Suharto, appears to have been as central as in those other regimes. Like both other leaders, as he aged Ne Win also "seemed to become increasingly mercurial and isolated from reality" (Steinberg 1990, 11). The stories which circulated about his personal and family life were even more bizarre (Lintner 1989, 85–94). The temptation to describe the regime as sultanistic is thus strong (though I am aware of no Burma scholars who have done so), and it seems remarkable that even at the height of the 1988 uprising no senior military officers broke with the regime, even though many in the opposition hoped they would do so. Unlike in both the Philippines and Indonesia, where some officers tried to safeguard military institutional interests by distancing themselves from their respective presidents, the Burmese regime proved to be a collective enterprise of the entire officer corps. Especially after the suppression of 1988, many in the military apparently feared that a future civilian government would punish them. This was an important factor in their decision to reject democratization and the results of the 1990 election (Taylor 1991, 202).

In any case, the military regime which has been in place since 1988 has once again closed avenues for legal or tolerated opposition. The NLD has not been banned outright, but its members and followers are harassed, and its leaders, including Aung San Suu Kyi, have often been detained. Once again, the predominant modes of opposition are illegal, informal, and clandestine. Indeed, many of the regime's most vehement opponents were forced out of the country altogether after 1988; armed resistance along the border as well as various forms of transnational civil society organizing became common methods of opposing the regime. The difference from before the 1988 uprising, however, is that even though it is still harassed, opposition now has much greater clarity and unity of purpose than it did prior to 1988. In the form of the NLD and Aung San Suu Kyi, it is a kind of government-in-waiting.

Malaysia presents yet another contrasting pattern. In Malaysia in September 1998, it was Indonesia's anti-Suharto movement which was the model. Activists who aimed to end the seventeen-year rule of Prime Minister Mahathir Mohammad consciously mimicked Indonesia's anti-Suharto uprising of a few months before. In a wave of protests unprecedented in Malaysian history, tens of thousands of people took to the streets, calling for *reformasi* and deriding the *korupsi, kolusi,* and *nepotisme* of the government, terms which were obviously borrowed from Indonesia.

As in Indonesia, this upsurge came in the wake of the Asian financial crisis of 1997. Unlike in Indonesia, a split in the government did not follow the upsurge, but precipitated it. Again, the split was linked to the succession issue; Mahathir's deputy, Anwar Ibrahim, represented a challenge to Mahathir, in part because he had cultivated an image of himself as a future leader with reformist ideas. Anwar took advantage of the financial crisis to promote his leadership credentials; whereas Mahathir favored greater state intervention in the economy in order to ride out the storm, Anwar supported IMF-style austerity measures. He resisted bailouts to companies linked to the ruling party, saying publicly that the economic crisis was beneficial because it would allow "creative destruction" and undermine "perverse patronage" (Case 2002, 132). Mahathir took quick action, dismissing Anwar from his posts and allowing him to be charged for abuse of power and sodomy, for which he was eventually sentenced to long prison terms, though not before appearing in court with a black eye as the result of a beating by police.

This event prompted the coalescence of a broad opposition coalition with a high degree of coordination. NGOs, political parties, and other opponents of Mahathir formed umbrella organizations to campaign for greater democracy and coordinate the protests (Abbot 2001: 292–93). One such group, Adil (the Movement for Social Justice), was led by Anwar Ibrahim's wife, Wan Azizah Ismail, who spoke at many meetings in defense of her husband and in favor of reform. The protests, however, failed to bring down Mahathir's Barisan Nasional (National Front, or BN) government. In a November 1999 election, its share of the vote fell, but it still won more than the two-thirds of seats in parliament it needed to amend the constitution. Mahathir himself remained prime minister until he handed over to his new deputy, Abdullah Badawi, in 2003.

This outcome was partly due to the very different nature of the political regime in Malaysia, despite efforts by some Malaysian protestors to equate Mahathir with Suharto. Only a few observers have characterized the regime as outrightly authoritarian; most have instead used terms like "semidemocracy" (Case 1993, 2002), a "repressive-responsive regime" (Crouch 1996b), or "soft authoritarianism" (Means 1996). The Malaysian government did use repressive measures against its opponents, including a draconian Internal Security Act which allows detention without trial, restrictions on associations, stringent press controls, and curtailment of the independence of the judiciary. The use of authoritarian controls became especially pronounced under Mahathir during the 1980s and 1990s. Despite these authoritarian features, however, the regime retained the form of a parliamentary democracy. Unlike in Indonesia, there was little intervention inside opposition parties or restrictions on who could run, and unlike in the Philippines under Marcos, the polls were generally clean. To be sure, the government manipulated electoral boundaries (Lim Hong Hai 2003) and used repressive measures to its own advantage (for instance, it restricted the circulation of opposition newspapers). Although it had never come close to losing power through elections, "it was faced with strong opposition parties that regularly mobilized about 40 percent of the voters" (Crouch 1996b, 240). The government had lost power at the state level; at the time of the 1998 protests, the Parti Islam se-Malaysia (All Malaysia Islamic Party, or PAS) held power in Kelantan. The government was also disciplined by running in competitive elections and was more responsive to social pressures than in most purely authoritarian regimes. As a result, it possessed considerable legitimacy in the eyes of the population.

One reason why the Malaysian *reformasi* movement did not bring down the government was thus that elections were still seen by most Malaysians as the appropriate way to change the government. In truly authoritarian Indonesia, Burma, and the Philippines, mass protest was the only realistic choice. In Malaysia, by contrast, the protest movement peaked quickly, in part because "many activists shifted their attention from lobbying the BN for change to contesting elections" (Weiss 2001, 224). For instance, Wan Azizah's Adil transformed itself into a new multiethnic political party, Keadilan (National Justice Party). In short, opposition in Malaysia has a fundamentally electoralist and parliamentary dynamic, unlike in Indonesia under Suharto, where those who wanted to replace the government knew that participation in elections would at best have to be in conjunction with other tactics.

Most of the reasons why the Malaysian *reformasi* movement of 1998 did not result in an electoral defeat for the government need not detain us here. One important factor which has echoes with the Indonesian experience, however, is the way by which ethnic and religious cleavages divided opposition. In Indonesia, Suharto attempted to play on societal divisions, for instance, by favoring modernist Muslims when he believed he was losing support from traditionalist Muslims, secularists, and minority groups. In Malaysia, politics were even more communally divided. These divisions have been essential for keeping the same coalition in power since independence in 1957. The Malaysian population contains large "nonindigenous" minorities with, in the late 1990s, about 27 percent of the population Chinese and 8 percent Indian. The Barisan Nasional government is a coalition that unites the Malay-based United Malays National Organization (UMNO) with parties drawn from the main ethnic minorities. Since racial riots in 1969, the government has promoted policies aimed at ending Malay economic and social disadvantage while rigidly maintaining social peace. UMNO has thus been able to garner support from Malays who benefited from the government's positive discrimination and economic development policies, while the Chinese and Indian parties in the Barisan Nasional retained significant support from constituencies fearful of political disorder if the ethnic compromise should break down. Opposition to the ruling coalition has tended to take the form of "ethnic outbidding," in which disgruntled voters turn to parties which promise to defend the interests of their communities more vigorously than the Barisan Nasional. The two major opposition parties are communally defined; although the Democratic Action Party (DAP) is officially multiracial, it is effectively a voice for ethnic Chinese who feel disadvantaged by government policies favoring Malays, while PAS appeals to disenchanted Malay voters by emphasizing Islam. Although they may have been equally opposed to the government, these parties have had great difficulty in uniting because of their divergent interests and appeals.

One of the novel developments of the 1998 protest movement and the 1999 elections was the degree to which opposition groups were able to forge links across ethnic and religious divides (Weiss 2001, chaps. 5 and 6). The protest movement which arose in response to Anwar's dismissal and trial mobilized mostly Muslim Malays, but many of the NGOs which led it were headed by Chinese and Indian activists, and the protest movement also galvanized non-Malay protest around shared issues. In the 1999 election, the major opposition parties, including Keadilan, PAS, and the DAP formed an "alternative front" (Barisan Alternatif) which they consciously styled as nonracial. However, this show of unity did not end the ethnically and religiously divided structure of Malaysian politics. PAS made important gains, and the Malay vote for the Barisan Nasional declined, apparently to below 50 percent. However, the Barisan Nasional was able to achieve a good result overall in part because some Chinese voters turned away from the opposition, partly because they feared that Islamic forces would be a chief beneficiary of the Anwar affair. The specter of Islamist government by the PAS became a major election issue. The Barisan Alternatif was unable to survive far beyond the elections, with the DAP eventually pulling out because of concerns regarding PAS's Islamist agenda.

Regime Structuring of Opposition: Implications for Authoritarian Erosion and Democratic Construction

Despite their great differences, one common thread that unites the Malaysian, Burmese, and Philippines experiences is that in each of these countries opposition constituted a stronger regime alternative than in Indonesia. In the Philippines, opposition consisted of an amalgam of leftist and traditional opponents of Marcos who openly strove to remove him from power and form a government of their own. In Malaysia, although opposition was divided along communal lines, it was based on political parties which aimed to attain political power through elections. Burma was closest to the Indonesian case, in that opposition was weak under military rule and the crisis of 1988 happened suddenly. During the Burma democracy uprising, opposition was also disorganized and disunited. Even so, an opposition which aspired to replace the government rapidly formed around the NLD. In Indonesia, although oppositional politics and an oppositional mood grew during the 1990s, not only were opponents of the regime divided, but few of them believed they could remove Suharto from power and replace his government with one of their own. Even during the mass mobilizations of 1998, there was remarkably little planning or preparation for what kind of government would follow Suharto.

It is tempting to conclude, therefore, that it was not opposition forces at all which overthrew Suharto, but an economic crisis. There is something to be said for this view. The economic downturn from late 1997 contributed to the rapid escalation of unrest and was crucial in determining the timing of the regime's collapse. However, an exclusive focus on the external shock fails to provide a satisfactory explanation for the manner by which Suharto was driven from power (it is also worth remembering that mass mobilizations in the Philippines, Burma, and Malaysia were also preceded by economic decline or crisis). Nor does it explain why Suharto's resignation was followed by a democratic transition rather than by a reconstituted version of authoritarianism. Moreover, many of the processes which help to account for the dramatic manner of the regime's collapse were visible well before 1997. They included the general faltering of regime legitimacy and the blockage to gradual political reform represented by Suharto's increasingly sultanistic rule. Above all, an exclusive focus on the economic crisis fails to take into account the growth of opposition which preceded 1997.

Between the initiation of *keterbukaan* (openness) in 1989 and Suharto's resignation in 1998, an uneven but distinct escalation of oppositional political action took place. This was visible in a broad spectrum of groups and behaviors, ranging from the increasingly vigorous human rights advocacy of NGOs, the new mass mobilization strategies pursued by student activists, to attempts by semioppositional bodies like Megawati's PDI to assert greater independence from government control. The ideological break with the New Order was sharper than before, as some critics began to abandon their earlier euphemistic critiques and put forward clearer programs of political change.

However, this growth of opposition took place against a very particular historical backdrop, vastly different from that in the Philippines, Malaysia, or Burma. Indonesia's New Order regime came into being as the result of a society-wide convulsion in which the army led the extermination of the country's largest civilian political force, the PKI. The massacres of 1965–66 left a lasting legacy of fear which afterward greatly constrained opposition. Equally important, the military rose to power at the head of a broad anticommunist coalition. Unlike in the Philippines, where Marcos established authoritarian rule for more transparently personal reasons, or in Burma, where the military held a coup against civilian politics in general, in the early years of the New Order the Indonesian military retained the enthusiastic loyalty or grudging support of many civilian political groups which feared a left-wing resurgence. In dealing with surviving civilian groups, the military was well placed to use not only coercion and threats, but also cajolery, co-optation, and the promise of participation in regime structures. A growing economy furnished it with ample resources to reward those who cooperated. Former civilian allies of the military feared the violence they knew the military was capable of, but they were also complicit in the establishment of the regime, viewed it as essentially legitimate, and were reluctant to condemn it in blanket terms.

This combination of circumstances gave the military an unparalleled position of political dominance. It was able to realize its far-reaching ambitions for restructuring the political domain. Building on the antiliberal political structures and discourses inherited from the Sukarno era, it created a corporatist system in which the very idea of opposition became anathema. The state allowed many civilian organizations to survive, but its control reached even *inside* those organizations, especially those with overtly political goals like parties. In these circumstances, would-be-opponents had few options besides semioppositional compromise inside regime structures, retreat into ostensibly apolitical civil society activity, or dissident-style moral appeals for change. Although there were plenty of groups which criticized the government, the notion of actually aiming to overthrow or replace it was soon seen as hopeless romanticism or dangerous radicalism by all but a tiny fringe.

Over the life of the New Order, opposition continued to be fundamentally shaped by the regime's policies and techniques for handling dissent. Coercion was always an essential ingredient in these policies. There was considerable unpredictability in how repression was applied, so that it was often difficult for opposition actors to predict whether a particular act would be repressed. Even at the height of "openness," however, repression generally followed the underlying pattern established early in the New Order. Coercion was greater when opposition appeared among the poor than when it was a purely middle-class phenomenon. It was also greater when groups openly flouted regime ideology and when they encouraged mobilization rather than simply making moral appeals for change. The security forces' underlying logic was to prevent the emergence of principled and mobilizational opposition: groups which explicitly set out to replace the regime and to mobilize a mass constituency to achieve that end. When previously tolerated groups showed signs of moving toward this model, they rapidly became an illegal and persecuted opposition. The regime was particularly liable to suppress attempts to establish alliances between different sectors of potential opposition, such as that which arose in 1996 to defend Megawati.

However, coercion was only part of the regime's approach. The stick of repression was effective largely because it was complemented by the carrot of limited pluralism. In Burma, the absence of toleration for virtually all forms of civil society activity fostered a brooding resentment of military rule that erupted suddenly in 1988 and rapidly led to a principled and mobilizational opposition. In Indonesia, many potential opposition leaders were long-schooled in the politics of compromise, negotiation, and ambivalence. Because the Suharto regime tolerated limited forms of societal initiative and participation, most middle-class critics never saw clandestine and mobilizational opposition as their only option. Many continued to operate within institutions which were under state control, such as political parties. Those who did so could operate safely, provided they couched their criticism in regime terminology and did not overtly challenge the regime's core assumptions and interests. The state also tolerated a wide array of proto-opposition groups in the civil society arena, so long as such groups focused primarily on particularistic aims (even potentially regime-challenging ones such as strengthening the rule of law). Dissidents became habituated to couching their critique of the regime in abstract and moral terms, knowing that they would be suppressed if they called on their followers to mobilize. Overall, it was this combination of niches within the system with repression for those who stepped outside it which resulted in the many ambivalent forms of participation-opposition which have been discussed in this study.

Yet opposition *did* grow markedly during the New Order's final decade; it may not have been as organized or combative as it was in the Philippines under Marcos, but it was far stronger and more open than in Ne Win's Burma. Opposition grew in a manner, however, that was shaped fundamentally by the regime's combination of coercion and toleration. The growth of opposition was visible in three main areas.

The first was the resurrection of mobilization as a normal feature of political life. Strikes, demonstrations, and other forms of public protest became far more frequent in the 1990s. In 1988, a single street march by a hundred university students was so unusual that it received extensive press coverage; by 1996, mobilization had become a commonplace mode of public expression. Even the major crackdown from the middle of that year only brought it to a temporary halt. Protest was pioneered above all by students, peasants, and workers, although it was eventually practiced by a wide variety of groups. However, protests were still marked by important limitations. In contrast to the Philippines, where protests were often planned and coordinated as part of a deliberate strategy to bring down Marcos, in Indonesia, the spread of a mood of protest outstripped the growth of opposition organizations which could articulate and channel that mood (practically the only group that organized demonstrations as part of a deliberate strategy to bring down the regime was the PRD, but this was far smaller than the left in the Philippines). In particular, despite the spread of political unrest to urban lower classes during *keterbukaan*, attempts to organize lower-class groups remained vulnerable to repression and were mostly rudimentary and semiformal in character. Public protest actions tended to be associated with a distinct style of informal, ad hoc, even semiorganized political organization, with the student *komite aksi* as the prototypical model.

This is not to say that there was no growth of organization. On the contrary, a second major expression of the growth of opposition was a proliferation of more formal alegal and proto-opposition in civil society, that arena of associational life where groups pursued specific interests but did not themselves attempt to gain government office. Dissident groups were few in number, but NGOs were prolific and even flourished during the repressive conditions of the 1980s (as they did in many other authoritarian countries in Southeast Asia). Some of these groups existed on the margins of state tolerance, exploiting legal ambiguities like the *yayasan* (foundation) format. Others, such as community development NGOs, had less problematic relations with the state. By the early 1990s it was possible to discern the outlines of an increasingly vigorous associational life which was beginning to play important democratizing functions: contesting and constraining state power, harboring critics of the regime, and enabling counterhegemonic ideological production.

However, repression set outer limits on the growth of civil society, and the density of associational life never approached what it had been prior to the New Order. Its class representation was also much narrower. Most tolerated critics in civil society organizations were lawyers, intellectuals, students, journalists, and the like. Proto-opposition civil society organizations—religious bodies, NGOs, professional organizations, and the like—also thrived in large part because they were tolerated by the state.

They were tolerated because they articulated only particularistic interests and aims. In turn, these aims weighed more heavily on them than their interests in political democratization per se. This contributed to often profound internal conflicts of interest (such as that in the Legal Aid Institute described in Chapter 4). Many NGOs, in seeking to achieve their specific aims, were driven to seek cooperation with government agencies, even though they sometimes strongly believed in "popular empowerment" and "bottom-up" approaches. Moreover, once NGOs became established and acquired programs, staff, offices, and other institutional interests, their leaders frequently developed a survivalist mentality which limited their capacity to challenge the state directly. The same logic applied even more strongly in the mass Islamic organizations like Nahdlatul Ulama and Muhammadiyah, which each ran hundreds of *pesantren*, universities, schools, hospitals, and orphanages. The very institutional interests upon which the growth of civil society were founded tended to become a drag on civil society's capacity to oppose the regime.

The third major arena for oppositional activity was that ambiguous gray area between state and society, the zone of semiopposition where critics operated within institutions which were formally part of the state or connected to it via corporatist arrangements. In this study, we have touched on the emergence of groupings with critical views within core state institutions such as ABRI, and the mirror image of this process, attempts by societal elements to colonize parts of the state apparatus or affiliated institutions (ICMI). The PDI was a classically semioppositional organization which participated in the highly constrained electoral and legislative systems. Semioppositional participation within institutions affiliated with or dominated by the state could be a disillusioning and corrupting experience. The daily compromises required fostered acceptance of regime ideology and gave rise to a mentality of acquiescence to regime norms. As the PDI found, trying to assert the independence of such bodies could result in long and debilitating struggles for control. When the party made tentative steps toward becoming a more fundamental opposition, like the parties of the traditional elite in the Philippines, the government took steps to prevent it from happening. So all-consuming was the resulting conflict that Megawati and other PDI leaders never seriously addressed broader political issues and were certainly unable to devise a comprehensive ideological challenge to the regime.

Even so, an important conclusion implied by the Indonesian case is that in polities where repression limits open contestation in the societal domain, the gray area between state and society may be an important locus of resistance and reform. It was here that many of the most serious contests concerning Indonesia's political future were played out, often as battles for control *inside* organizations rather than as zero-sum contests between state and society. This is the case even though the characteristic political style within this zone was semiopposition; it involved apparent co-optation, compromise, and muted criticism and was associated with ideological obfuscation rather than ideological differentiation from the regime. Studies of opposition under nondemocratic regimes may miss much if they focus only on the search for a principled opposition possessing a clear counterideology and located in a societal domain outside of the state and resistant to its intervention, such as that which confronted Marcos in the Philippines. Many effective authoritarian regimes repress this kind of opposition. Its absence is not necessarily a sign of lack of resistance, nor of strong regime legitimacy.

In summary, by the end of the Suharto era, opposition was not "weak" in a general and undifferentiated sense. On the contrary, there was sustained and serious regime-challenging opposition through the regime's final decade. However, opposition remained overwhelmingly shaped by the experience of thirty years' semipluralism and routinized coercion. There was a widespread mood of political alienation, plus considerable willingness to protest. However, those groups which were more principled in their opposition to the regime were vulnerable to repression and shorn of institutionalized mass support. Organizations which possessed relatively strong institutions, such as the PDI, were more compromised and did not present a convincing ideological or programmatic alternative. A dissident mentality prevailed in which opposition groups framed their criticisms in moral terms and stressed their aversion to "practical politics" (this was evident in a wide variety of forms, ranging from the "moral force" outlook common among student activists to Amien Rais's notion that Muhammadiyah should be concerned only with the "high politics" of speaking out on ethics and morality). Overall, there was a proliferation of quasi- and semioppositional activity, combined with considerable organizational fragmentation, ideological ambivalence, and programmatic incoherence.

However, even a fragmented and ambivalent opposition may be well suited to performing some of the functions needed to promote democratization. In Indonesia, despite and perhaps partly because of its dispersed character, opposition contributed significantly to what Guillermo O'-Donnell and Philippe Schmitter (1986, 50) refer to as "corroding the normative and intellectual bases of the regime." During the 1990s, as civic and opposition organizations became more numerous and assertive, their impact on public consciousness increased. Protests, legal challenges, and other forms of advocacy campaigning, especially when publicized by the press, came to dominate public political discussion. Although many crit-

ics of the government dreamed of eventual regime transformation, even
overthrow, only the most radical were open about this; the aims of most
middle-class alegal and proto-opposition groups were instead summed up
in terms like *penyadaran masyarakat* (community consciousness raising,
a term popular among many NGOs) or *membangun opini publik* (building public opinion, a slogan of moderate student activists in the late
1980s).

Such counterhegemonic activities had an important impact, slowly but
perceptibly shifting the terrain of political legitimacy under the government's feet. The change in government discourse on human rights and democratization themes over the 1990s was one result. In the late 1980s,
these terms still had the taint of subversion about them. A decade later,
although government officials still warned against "irresponsible" elements who used them for destructive ends, blanket hostility was no
longer possible. Most officials made increasingly frequent symbolic and
rhetorical concessions to democratization, undermining their own claims
that Pancasila democracy was already "final." This was a complex
process, and many factors contributed to it, including the changing international context and the fading of the "trauma" of 1965–66. In part,
however, regime spokespeople were responding to a new political culture
which was propagated by opposition groups. In the long term, the ideological shift so generated meant that once Suharto's presidency collapsed,
the surviving ruling elite could not avoid substantial democratic reform.

However, undermining a regime's legitimacy will not by itself bring it
down. After all, as Adam Przeworski (1986, 53) notes, many illegitimate
regimes may be maintained in power for long periods by threat of force
alone. An obvious example is Burma, where military rule has persisted
despite the massive democracy uprising of 1988 and the 1990 election in
which the military's party lost. Crucially, therefore, Indonesia's dispersed
and fragmented opposition was also eventually effective at performing
another important function: encouraging a decline of fear among members of society and increasing their willingness to take political action.
Some opposition actors viewed this as a primary aim (it was one of
Megawati Soekarnoputri's constant themes). It is also important to note
the crucial role played by the more radical elements, especially students,
who pioneered street protest and other forms of mobilization despite
great personal risks and often with little hope of winning immediate
goals.[5] Their exemplary role encouraged a spread of protest, even if
broader layers of society were drawn into action incrementally, often via
initially nonconfrontational methods (such as by participating in state-
sanctioned bodies like the PDI).

Eventually there was a steady expansion of political organization and action contesting the regime on multiple fronts. These activities succeeded in performing a third crucial task of democratic opposition: raising the costs of rule. As O'Donnell and Schmitter (1986, 7) note, even the gradual spread of new forms of political action, although "not too immediately and threatening to the regime . . . tend to accumulate, become institutionalized, and thereby raise the effective and perceived costs of their eventual annulment." By the time Suharto moved decisively to rein in *keterbukaan* in 1994–96, he was obliged to use more open repression, exposing the coercive basis of his regime and the thinness of its hegemony. He thus set the scene for the dramatic societal upsurge of February–May 1998, when opposition finally succeeded in raising the costs of governance to such an extent that the regime split. In this perspective, the economic crisis was important primarily as a signal which dramatically shifted many opposition actors' and ordinary citizens' expectations of likely success if they took action.

However, in order to bring about a successful democratic transition, even raising the costs of authoritarian rule is not enough. Opposition must also engage in what Stepan calls the "creation of a viable democratic alternative." This, he argues, is central to the final democratic breakthrough. "A crucial task for the active opposition is to integrate as many antiauthoritarian movements as possible into the institutions of the emerging democratic majority. . . . If the opposition attends only to the task of erosion, as opposed to that of construction, then the odds are that any future change will merely be a shift from one authoritarian government to another, rather than a change from authoritarianism to democracy" (Stepan 1993, 67).

The opposition behaviors and structures which developed under the New Order were ill suited to the tasks of democratic construction. Despite rudimentary alliance-building attempts, no single political party, coalition, or other body could unify groups who favored democratization. There were often great hopes that the latest elite-level initiative, like Forum Demokrasi in 1991 or Amien Rais's "People's Mandate Council" (MAR) in 1998, would finally be a vehicle for uniting opposition, but such attempts always floundered. They failed partly because their leaders feared the regime's repression and partly because they wanted to preserve their existing organizational assets (hence, for example, Forum Demokrasi stagnated owing to Abdurrahman Wahid's fears for the NU). But they were also undermined by communal divisions. The deleterious impact on opposition of such divisions is another important lesson from the Indonesian case (even if such divisions were not as great an obstacle as they were in Malaysia).[6] Suharto and his lieutenants were adept at nurturing and manipulating divisions between groups which could potentially unite against them. Their use of Islamic appeals during the campaign against Megawati in 1996 was one illustration of this, as was Suharto's attempt a year later to draw closer to Abdurrahman Wahid while at the same time taking measures to rein in Amien Rais and other modernist Islamic activists in ICMI.

Not only did unity prove elusive, but Indonesia's opposition also had difficulties in presenting an unequivocal and elaborate ideological or programmatic alternative to the regime. The small groups which tried to do this, like the Petition of Fifty or the PRD, were kept small by repression. Semioppositional groups like the PDI, ICMI, or the NU, which were stronger organizationally, could not openly challenge regime ideology if they wanted to remain within official structures and keep receiving patronage or other benefits. Megawati Soekarnoputri, Amien Rais, Abdurrahman Wahid, and other leaders of such groups were experts at conveying double meanings within seemingly standard regime terminology and treading the line of tolerated criticism. Such people were skilled at blurring their critique, not sharpening or clarifying it. The result was that opposition was unable to cohere around a common platform, beyond vague slogans like *"demokratisasi"* or *"hak asasi manusia"* (human rights). Even in the final upsurge leading to May 1998, opposition groups' slogan was *"turunkan Suharto"* (bring down Suharto). Very few were clear about what form of government they wanted to put in place, nor who should lead that government. The consequences of this for what followed the fall of Suharto are considered in Chapter 10. First, however, it is necessary to consider underlying reasons why opposition grew in Suharto's final decade. Two common explanations for the growth of opposition to authoritarian rule were canvased in Chapter 1: economic growth leading to a more assertive middle class and disunity within the ruling elite.

Opposition and Social Structure

Over the last decade and a half, there has been great scholarly interest in the political consequences of economic growth and attendant social change in Southeast Asia. The rapid growth that most countries in the region experienced after the 1960s, coupled with obvious pressures for more democratic government, revived interest in structuralist and modernization approaches to political change, especially concerning the role that middle classes play in democratization. Overall, however, the picture in Southeast Asia has been mixed. In Thailand, political parties and NGOs supported by the Bangkok middle class have played a crucial role in rolling back military dominance. In Singapore, where economic

growth and social change have been greatest, the middle class has supported authoritarian rule, or at least acquiesced to it. In some countries
where democratic movements were strongest, such as the Philippines in
1986 and Burma in 1988, there had not been economic expansion and
growing middle classes, but rather economic stagnation and social crisis.

In their comparative study of democratization, Dietrich Rueschemeyer,
Evelyne Huber Stephens, and John Stephens (1992) argue that historical
context is crucial for determining whether middle and subaltern classes
join forces in a democratic coalition. Middle classes in particular are not
invariably democratic but are apt to ally with whatever force (including
the authoritarian state) appears most likely to advance their interests at a
given historical moment. In Indonesia, the immediate historical context
for the evolution of opposition to Suharto was the New Order coalition
of 1965–66. This was an authoritarian political alliance in the classic
sense, uniting the state, the beleaguered urban middle classes, and other
anticommunist political forces (notably, the major Islamic organizations)
against the threat of a rising left. The massacres created an organizational
vacuum on the left and in subaltern classes, which still continues. During
the 1970s, the regime consolidated, the military pushed aside its former
allies, and the threat from the left dissipated. As a result, the New Order
coalition itself began to deteriorate. However, it did not entirely dissolve.
Although many intellectuals, former student activists, and others were
disillusioned with aspects of the regime, economic growth continued to
deliver substantial material benefits to the urban middle classes as a
whole. Many former allies were kept within at least the semioppositional
embrace of the regime by the distribution of patronage. The regime itself
attempted to preserve its founding coalition by pursuing economic
growth and inculcating in the population widespread fear about the latent communist threat and the potential to return to the "trauma" of the
1960s. In the 1970s, even when erstwhile allies of the military—like university students—turned to opposition, their criticisms were marked by
nostalgia for the foundational ideals of the regime and hostility toward
disorderly politics from below.

This study suggests that the *keterbukaan* years marked the beginning
of the replacement of the old authoritarian New Order coalition by a
new cross-class democratic alliance. This was reflected both in the invigoration of middle-class political opposition, by signs of unrest in the
lower classes, and by attempts to establish new forms of cross-class political cooperation. The new political assertiveness of the middle class was
reflected in greater press boldness in response to the largely middle-class
readership, the growing range of voluntary associations, and the greater
vigor of liberal political ideas in intellectual circles. Indonesia seemed to

be undergoing the pattern propounded by classic modernization theory, with economic growth giving birth to a larger middle class with interests in democracy. This conclusion is reinforced by the experience of 1998, when the middle classes supplied the leaders as well as many of the foot soldiers for the *reformasi* movement, with students, intellectuals, NGO activists, artists, even professionals like doctors and stockbrokers all playing a part.

However, much of the impetus for the invigoration of opposition during the *keterbukaan* years came from below. This was not always evident on the surface, although many examples could be cited, starting with the student-farmer demonstrations of 1988–89, which heralded the return of protest as a normal part of political life. Similarly, the PDI became a more formidable force owing largely to the energization of its previously passive lower-class base. NGOs, the ideological engines of middle-class reform, were particularly concerned about the empowerment of the poor and were important in encouraging a middle-class sensibility which combined general sympathy for the disadvantaged with support for political and legal reform.

In this respect, Indonesia's experience would seem not to be unique. In Thailand, for example, some journalists labeled the large "Black May" protests against the military in 1992 a "mobile phone mob," but other observers noted that many of the participants were in fact from the urban poor and other groups (McCargo 1997, 271–72). In the Philippines, furious and energetic networking and alliance-building among middle- and lower-class groups characterized the final years of the anti-Marcos struggle. It is also noteworthy that in Singapore and Malaysia, where reform movements have had less success in reaching out beyond middle-class constituencies, democratization has made less progress.

However, the vicissitudes of political reform in Indonesia after 1998 suggest it is necessary to avoid overstating the solidity of the new democratic alliance. As noted above, cross-class alliance building was far less advanced than in the Philippines under Marcos, for example, where an anticommunist massacre of Indonesian proportions had never taken place. In Indonesia, repression kept political and other forms of organization relatively weak among the lower classes. As a result, their political and social frustrations were largely unmediated by unions, other civil society organizations, or the party system. During the 1990s, the spread of protest outgrew the capacity of semiunderground forms of organization, resulting in growing explosiveness in the lower classes. This was demonstrated by the series of riots after 1996. During the final societal upsurge of 1998, the sectors where middle-class activists had been most active (the organized working class and disenfranchised farmers) played little direct role. Instead, violent rioting and other forms of mobilization by the urban poor (among whom there had been comparatively little organizational effort) were pivotal. Despite some moments of genuine cross-class mobilization, the middle class and the urban masses were mostly uncoordinated, even often at cross-purposes, the former being partly driven by fear of the latter. Again, the comparison with the Philippines is instructive; the "people power" protests of 1986 were largely peaceful, a product of much greater levels of organization and the leadership that the church and opposition groups were able to exercise over the population.

That the precondition for the middle-class upsurge of 1998 was a severe economic collapse also suggests that caution is required. During the *keterbukaan* years of continued growth, most middle-class people were not inclined toward opposition. The most obvious product of the middle-class boom was a new consumer culture. Overall, the middle class remained a small minority of the population, and many of its members were directly or indirectly dependent on the state for their prosperity. The government continued a ceaseless propaganda barrage stressing that economic development would be endangered if authoritarian policies were relaxed. All this produced deep currents of conservatism and apathy. It provided the state, and organizations which promised gradual change in partnership with the state (like ICMI), significant middle-class support. It meant that antigovernment student activists remained a minority on campuses and that most critical groups, such as NGOs, had difficulty obtaining funds from domestic sources.

Put another way, the accumulation of much opposition along the blurred divide between state and society and the many hesitant forms of participation-opposition discussed in this book were not merely produced by the regime's combination of repression and co-optation. These forms of political behavior also reflected deeper middle-class ambivalence regarding authoritarianism and democracy. Indonesia's middle class would hardly be unique in this respect. In many successful development-oriented authoritarian regimes middle-class resentment of arbitrariness, predatory behavior, and bureaucratic dominance can generate support for political reform but be balanced by gratitude to the regime for economic growth, structural dependence on the state, and a general sense of insecurity.

In much middle-class opposition in Indonesia there was a barely concealed fear of social and political disorder. During discussions with leaders from a wide variety of groups in the mid-1990s, I was frequently struck by their great concern about the possibility that destructive mass unrest (*gejolak*) might accompany and endanger future political democratization. As a result, some saw the rise of the "undercurrent" (*arus bawah*) in politics as a potentially double-edged sword. From the mid-1990s, leaders of groups like the YKPK and the PDI spoke incessantly of the looming danger of "national disintegration," a phrase which gave vent to a gamut of fears of social breakdown.

Concern about unrest could have contradictory effects. Many members of Indonesia's middle class and political elite who advocated reform argued that government actions—corruption, repression, manipulation of religion, and so forth—were inflaming social tensions and increasing the potential for disorder. Disaster could be averted only by rectifying bad policies and "channeling" (*menyalurkan*) the people's aspirations through peaceful, institutional means, in other words, by political reform. In this view, coercion and "floating mass" policies, which may have been appropriate during the "emergency" conditions accompanying the birth of the New Order, were losing their effectiveness and would ultimately result in explosions. Elite advocates of limited reform, such as General (retired) Soemitro and Amien Rais, often said this. A spectacular demonstration of the adoption of such views on a mass scale occurred in 1998, when middle-class and elite opinion turned decisively against Suharto once it became obvious that his continued occupancy of the presidency was leading the country toward chaos.

However, while unrest from below remained a vague fear, it could greatly exacerbate caution in middle-class opposition. The starkest illustrations were those members of the political elite who were disheartened by the new honeymoon between the government and Islam (including some in groups like the YKPK). Often these people were nervous about broadening political conflict into society, because they were members of minority groups themselves (typically Christians) or were otherwise acutely aware of the dangers of sectarian violence. The extreme hesitance of members of minority groups was simply the clearest example of a more general phenomenon. Megawati's reluctance to mobilize her mass following against the government, for example, stemmed directly from her fear that once she unleashed them it would be impossible to restrain her followers from violent acts. This fear greatly contributed to Megawati's cautious response to the crisis of mid-1996 and to her virtual absence during the societal upsurge in 1998.

In 1998, the absence of a strongly organized threat from below made the ruling elite more likely to agree to demands for democratization in the short term. There were few prospects of a serious overturning of the social order. The longer-term implications of this situation were less propitious for democracy. The old New Order authoritarian coalition between the state and the middle classes had broken down, but it had not yet been decisively replaced by a new democratic coalition uniting middle- and lower-class groups. Tentative steps had been taken in this direction, but the lower classes remained largely unorganized. In the longer term, this lack of organization implied a pattern typical of third-wave democratizations, whereby lower-class groups would have to engage in many future struggles to develop independent organizational capacities, win social and economic gains, and deepen the democratization process. It also suggested, however, that in the wake of the collapse of the Suharto regime, many elements of the old governing elite would survive with their political resources largely intact and quickly attempt to reestablish themselves within the new democratic framework. This process became visible even after the first democratic elections in 1999 gave Golkar a greatly reduced share of the vote (see, e.g., Hadiz 2003; Mietzner 2003).

Opposition and Regime Disunity

As noted in Chapter 1, much democratization literature suggests that the appearance of division between regime hard-liners and soft-liners is crucial for explaining political liberalization, associated increases in opposition activity, and subsequent democratization. Many studies of Southeast Asian politics concur that increased democratic mobilization often coincides with tensions inside authoritarian regimes (e.g., Hedman 2001, 929, 947). An important conclusion suggested by the Indonesian case, however, is that merely noting the correlation between regime disunity, liberalization, and increased opposition in fact tells us little about processes of regime change. While the focus in much democratization literature is the emergence of division within the regime, the Indonesian experience suggests that it is equally important to observe how groups in society make readings of elite conflict, endeavor to identify the opportunities and spaces so afforded them, and use them for their own ends. Such processes are as important for democratization as the initial appearance of the divisions.

In Indonesia, the relationship between elite conflict and escalation of opposition was neither direct nor unidirectional. There was no *dalang* (the puppeteer of Javanese *wayang* shadow theater) manipulating and orchestrating opposition, even if Benny Moerdani played this role in the imagination of some modernist Muslims, and perhaps in the imagination of Suharto himself. There were certainly occasions when elite conflict impinged directly on opposition, as when military officers approached student activists or established contacts with Megawati and her supporters in the PDI. Such approaches gave opposition actors greater political confidence but did not mean that they had been transformed into agents of military influence (though there were, of course, plenty of military agents in opposition ranks).

The Indonesian experience suggests that societal groups which favor democratic reform will typically have a variety of responses to the appearance of divisions within an authoritarian regime, ranging from simple escalation of uncompromising antiregime mobilization to attempts to penetrate the state apparatus and strengthen the reform impulse from within. The relative weight of moderate versus confrontational approaches will depend on the regime's own history, structure, and internal cohesion. In regimes with a history of considerable semipluralism and semiopposition, as in Indonesia, it is likely that there will be greater willingness for compromise and negotiation by opposition actors.

In Indonesia, some more radical groups, especially those with origins in the student movement, plus some in NGO circles, took a strong line against any hint of conciliation, "conspiracy," or flirtation (*main mata*) with regime groups. Some student and other groups, however, selected the targets of their protests with one eye to elite conflict, hoping to minimize repression (like students who targeted Suharto in 1993, believing that discontented army officers would allow them to do so). Others, such as the PRD, believed that even this carried seeds of opportunism and that increased popular mobilization on all fronts was the appropriate method to split the ruling bloc.

Most middle-class and elite opposition actors, however, went much further. They scrutinized the contours of regime conflict in the search for sympathizers, negotiating partners, and allies. The Islamic activists who joined ICMI and looked to Habibie and Suharto for protection, and others who sought to forge links with discontented military elements (for example via the YKPK), are the most obvious examples. Even leaders of alegal dissident groups and NGOs often carefully monitored elite politics and tried to establish lines of communication with potentially sympathetic officials. They did this for many reasons, partly in order to attain protection, information, or access to financial resources, but also to influence potential reformers in the regime and convince them of the necessity of a gradual and negotiated path from authoritarian rule. As a result, middle-class opposition became entangled with factional competition within the regime. The reasons for this entanglement have been well canvased in this study; they mostly related to the historical origins of the New Order in the military-civilian coalition of 1965–66 and its subsequent semipluralist structuring of opposition. Prominent intellectuals and critics, the leaders of NGOs, political parties, and religious organizations, were already long-accustomed to having personal links with the power holders and compromising with them. In conditions where frontal opposition remained risky, most had no interest in departing from long-established patterns, especially when the regime seemed to be opening up.

The Indonesian case also suggests, however, that it is important not to lose sight of the societal context in which conflicts within a regime emerge and evolve. In the late 1980s, the initial impetus for division—resentment in ABRI toward Suharto—was shaped largely by an independent dynamic and had relatively little to do with wider societal forces. As the conflict within the regime developed, however, societal pressures came to have a crucial bearing on how it was played out, giving rise to a version of what Stepan (1988, 39) describes as the "complex dialectic between regime concession and societal conquest." Both discontented ABRI officers and the Suharto-Habibie camp tried to win over potential societal allies by (intermittently) presenting a reformist public face. Conflict inside the regime would not have resulted in political liberalization in this way without escalating societal demands, or at least a societal audience whose allegiance it was politically advantageous to win. Instead, it would have led merely to internecine competition for position within the bureaucracy. That the conflict within the regime occurred against the backdrop of an increasingly restive society completely changed its character. In the words of former Golkar legislator Marzuki Darusman (interview, November 29, 1995), "This is the key change during the last few years; public opinion is now an important ingredient in Indonesian politics."

By 1993–94, therefore, it seemed that Indonesia was evolving in the direction of a "four-player game" of democratization of the kind identified in O'Donnell and Schmitter's classic 1986 study. Moderate opposition was becoming increasingly organized and assertive, and for the first time a more radical opposition oriented toward mass mobilization was visible. Small but significant soft-line elements were emerging in the regime itself, both in ABRI and around ICMI, to complement the dominant hard-line bloc led by Suharto and his supporters. The political map was becoming increasingly complex, with growing diversification both inside and outside the regime and a cross-cutting web of connections between the two arenas. However, as in earlier periods of incipient tension in the military and rising oppositional activity in 1973–74 and 1977–78, Suharto's response was to reassert his authority. By 1994 Suharto had largely restored control over the senior ranks of the military. This allowed him to stifle the further development of elite conflict, end *keterbukaan*, and initiate harsher policies against opposition.

Because conflict in the ruling elite failed to mature into an open break between hard-liners and soft-liners, the *keterbukaan* period and its immediate aftermath were characterized for many opposition actors as much by waiting as by positive political action. There was a widespread belief that short-term caution was essential because regime leaders remained solidly united behind Suharto. Many groups believed they needed to identify the appropriate time for concerted action carefully and to avoid premature and potentially costly action; *menunggu momentum* (waiting for the momentum) was the term used to describe this attitude. Early in *keterbukaan*, some opposition initiatives, including the establishment of Forum Demokrasi and the LBH's assumption of the "locomotive of democracy" mantle, were partly based on an assessment that conflict in the ruling elite was intensifying.[7] When the conflict failed to develop further, many such initiatives floundered (one thinks particularly of Abdurrahman Wahid's volte-face in 1997). Although opposition actors clearly did face a genuine dilemma, it is difficult to avoid a conclusion that hoping for regime conflict trapped them in a kind of vicious circle; there was never a sufficiently deep split in the regime to constitute "momentum," yet by waiting and not escalating pressure on the regime, many groups contributed to the failure of existing fractures to deepen and made the hoped-for crisis more distant.

A second effect of the political closure from 1994–95, however, was encouragement of a more confrontational style of opposition. As he became more confident of his political base, Suharto ended even very moderate attempts to loosen the political system via the PDI and ICMI. In Malaysia in 1998, street protests were unable to gain momentum partly because other avenues remained open for people who wanted to challenge the government; Anwar Ibrahim's wife, Wan Azizah Ismail, whom many Malaysians viewed as a symbolic leader of resistance to the government similar to Megawati, was even allowed to form a political party and run for election. In contrast, the aura of victimhood which developed around Megawati after Suharto pushed her out of formal politics greatly undermined his regime's legitimacy. It is also possible that Amien Rais would not have emerged as the preeminent leader of *reformasi* had he not achieved the public profile conferred by his involvement in ICMI and subsequent demotion when he angered the president in 1997. By frustrating attempts to promote measured and gradual change from within the system, Suharto ultimately convinced many students, intellectuals, and others that mobilization from the outside was necessary to force him to step down, after which the process of reform could begin. Put differently, the decline of pluralism within official political structures and the closure of paths for semiopposition set the scene for the confrontation between state and society which eventually took place in 1998.

10

Legacies of Suharto and His Opposition

MORE than those in many countries, Indonesia's democratic transition has been marked by dramatic breakthroughs and moments of great optimism, rapidly followed by frustration and disillusionment. It has also been characterized by a high degree of continuity between the new democratic politics and those of the authoritarian past. The collapse of the Suharto regime occurred with the tumult and abruptness associated with processes of regime replacement, reminiscent of cases like the Philippines in 1986 or the abortive antiregime uprising in Burma in 1988. There was rapid escalation of mobilization, obvious and dramatic collapse of regime legitimacy, great violence, and a sudden fracturing of the ruling elite. However, when Suharto resigned, unlike in the Philippines, his government was replaced by a reconstituted version of itself. Suharto's handpicked vice president, B. J. Habibie, moved into the presidential palace and partly filled his cabinet with individuals who had held high office during the rule of his predecessor. Despite this development, Habibie's government initiated rapid political liberalization and reform, leading to Indonesia's first democratic general elections since 1955, which took place in June 1999 amid a renewed burst of optimism. In quick succession, former opponents of the Suharto regime became president: Abdurrahman Wahid in October 1999 and Megawati Soekarnoputri in July 2001. Both times, however, those with hopes for dramatic reform of the political system were quickly disillusioned. Progress was made in some fields, such as constitutional reform. However, Indonesian politics remained afflicted by many problems which had characterized the Suharto period, including pervasive corruption and money politics and a politically assertive military.

The suddenness and tumult associated with the collapse of Suharto's rule was dictated to a large degree by Suharto's personal dominance within the regime (although the suddenness of Indonesia's economic crisis also played a crucial role). There was a process of sultanization in the regime during its last decade or so, as well as a narrowing of space for tolerated opposition in the last three or four years. Suharto's growing personalist domination, and his inability to distinguish his own and his family's interests from those of the regime as a whole, made political reform from within the regime impossible. No group could emerge in the ruling elite to begin such a process. When such groups showed signs of emerging during the *keterbukaan* years of the early 1990s, Suharto removed them from power. The progressive splintering away from Suharto in the final months thus followed a sequence of disaffection typical of regimes in which the hard-line "standpatter" element is strong and political transition takes place by what Samuel Huntington (1991, 144–45) calls a process of "replacement." First, as we have seen, the most antiestablishment groups like students, intellectuals, and already alienated dissidents began to mobilize. Concurrently, more unfocused and explosive discontent mounted among the lower classes. Broader middle-class layers and more conservative establishment figures, such as former technocrats and entrepreneurs, next voiced their disquiet. Finally, after intense pressure from below, the ruling elite cracked open and deserted the president.

Despite the dramatic increase of pressure from below, organized opposition remained poorly institutionalized, divided, and predominantly cautious. Suharto's intransigence may have set Indonesia on the path of a society-led transition, but the middle-class and elite groups which dominated formal opposition remained stamped by the ambivalence and contradictions generated by decades under a regime which skillfully combined repression with toleration for constrained forms of political action. Opposition was poorly organized, and fractured opposition is more able to challenge authoritarian rule than prepare to replace it. Attempts to unite came very late in the day and were largely unsuccessful.

The organizational weakness and disunity in opposition allowed the bulk of the old governing elite to abandon Suharto, as a concession to the societal upsurge, yet retain power. To be sure, the hard-line elements most closely identified with the former president were excluded from Habibie's government. This was symbolized by the purge of Prabowo. But the military-bureaucratic base of the regime remained largely intact. Habibie broadened the base of the government only minimally, by including in cabinet representatives of ICMI and the two authorized political parties and by appointing some critical intellectuals to more junior advisory posts.

However, if Indonesia's dispersed and fragmented opposition had been unable to present a democratic alternative to authoritarian rule at the point of its collapse, it had been effective at inculcating an oppositional mood in society and in eroding the ideological bases of authoritarian rule. This meant that when Habibie took power, he could preside over a reconstituted version of Suharto's government, but not a reconstituted version of his authoritarian system. In the weeks and months following Suharto's resignation, the inchoate oppositional mood rapidly took concrete form. Typical of *ruptura* cases of democratization, which take place via a rapid breakdown of the authoritarian regime, the country experienced a societal upsurge which the Indonesian media labeled "political euphoria." Social forces and political demands which had been long repressed were suddenly expressed. A spirit of protest spread across the country. Farmers occupied land which had long ago been taken from them, protests in regional centers forced corrupt local administrators to resign, and political parties, labor unions, anticorruption groups, and other new organizations sprang into being. Much of the public saw Habibie as merely an illegitimate extension of the New Order, and he had to face down many protests calling for his removal as part of *reformasi total*. (As Habibie himself later put it, "During my 512 days in power I was continually rocked by no less than 3,200 demonstrations with one great theme: abusing Habibie"; *Kompas*, May 29, 2000). Habibie remained in office in the face of this outpouring only by hastily embarking on democratic reform. He released political prisoners, loosened restrictions on labor unions and political parties, and dismantled press controls. His most far-reaching step was to offer to hold free and fair elections as the way to resolve the political crisis. By making this promise, Habibie in effect reconstituted his administration as an interim government. The offer persuaded most sectors of elite opposition, as R. William Liddle (1999a, 111) put it, "to stop trying to overthrow Habibie through civil disturbance, as they had just overthrown Suharto, and to start planning for elections."

Even after the June 1999 election, however, Indonesia's transition remained dogged by the lasting impact of the Suharto era on opposition forces. Authoritarian rule may have suffered a collapse in legitimacy (indicated by Golkar's 22 percent share of the vote in the election), but the challenges of constructing a coherent ideological and institutional foundation for the new politics remained immense. The popular democratic upsurge of 1998–99 was so sudden that it largely repeated the New Order pattern of diffuse, uncoordinated, and ad hoc mobilization and organization. Certainly, it produced few wholly new organizations which were able to capture both the new democratic spirit and public attention on a mass scale. Instead, the groups which proved best equipped for the transition to electoral politics were those large organizations which had survived or even prospered as semiopposition through the New Order years. Megawati Soekarnoputri's PDI, Abdurrahman Wahid's NU, Amien Rais's Muhammadiyah, and the Islamic-based PPP each retained substantial popular support and an effective institutional infrastructure. These organizations either sponsored or refashioned themselves as political parties. The parties so formed dominated the new electoral landscape, together achieving some 64 percent of the popular vote (with Megawati's party winning half of that total). But these were the organizations which had been most deeply affected by the politics of compromise, survivalism, and deal making under the New Order. Their leaders were long accustomed to viewing the civilian and military leaders of the Suharto regime as legitimate political players. As a result, just as in the *keterbukaan* years, the line between democratic actors and their opponents became blurred.

During the October 1999 MPR session, Abdurrahman Wahid was elected president by successfully playing on the fears of Muslim politicians that a secular-oriented Megawati presidency would erode the political and cultural gains achieved by the Islamic community in the final decade of Suharto's rule. He also played on the fears of many in the military and Golkar that Megawati would initiate unpredictable and far-reaching political reform. A combination of personal ambition and communal suspicions once again ruled out a grand anti–New Order coalition. When Abdurrahman became president, he was thus obliged to retain Golkar, the military, and other New Order groups in the upper echelons of government. When Megawati replaced him twenty months later, she did the same. In consequence, Indonesia's post-breakthrough democratic transition became like Brazil's, which, as Guillermo O'Donnell (1992, 50) has observed, "appeared to be the work of a coalition of anyone and everyone."

The result was stonewalling and sabotaging of reform efforts from within and the inability of the new government to draw a clear line between the authoritarian New Order past and the democratic future. Limited progress, at best, was made in extricating the military from politics, punishing those responsible for past corruption and human rights abuses, and stemming the spread of communal conflict, separatist movements, and popular disillusionment with the legal system and political institutions. Indonesia's democratic opposition had made a great achievement by forcing Suharto out of office. But by the time of Indonesia's second post-transition election in April 2004, there was widespread public belief that reform was exhausted and that Indonesia was mired in problems from which it might not escape for many years. Such was the legacy of thirty-two years of coercion and semipluralism under Suharto's New Order.

Notes

PREFACE

1. Pancasila, the "five principles," is a brief statement of ideals incorporating belief in one God, humanitarianism, national unity, democracy through consultation and consensus, and social justice. Sukarno originally expounded it in 1945. Under Suharto, "Pancasila ideology" was fashioned into an all-encompassing justification for authoritarian rule (Morfit 1981; Ramage 1995; Bourchier 1997).

CHAPTER 1

1. Since the early twentieth century, the observant Islamic (or *santri*) community in Indonesia has been divided into two distinct streams. The traditionalists emphasize scholastic tradition and authority, mysticism, and adherence to one of the four Sunni law schools (usually that of Imam Syafi'i). The modernists, influenced by reformers in the Middle East, argued not only that Muslims should adapt to modern science and learning coming from the West, but also that Islam should be purified of centuries of accumulated local traditions and deviations by a return to the original sources of the religion, the Qur'an and *hadiths*. The leading figures in the traditionalist stream are the religious scholars (*ulama* or *kyai*) who run boarding schools (*pesantren*) in rural areas, while the modernists tend to be more urban.

2. Dissidence was a form of opposition which was particularly prevalent in Eastern Europe in the 1970s. The analysis of dissidence here is thus developed not only from Linz 1973 but also from Schapiro 1972 (which uses the term *dissent*), Rupnik 1979, and Bernhard 1993.

3. My thanks to Harold Crouch for suggesting this term.

4. In his influential 1959 article, Seymour Lipset argued that the correlation between economic development and greater democracy was largely due to the presence of a better-educated and more well-to-do middle class. Barrington Moore (even if his main focus was rural class relations) similarly famously wrote, "No bourgeois, no democracy" (1966, 418).

5. An example is South Korea, where middle-class groups supported the large

demonstrations against the Chun regime in 1987, only to withdraw that support after concessions were offered by Roh Tae Woo and when increased labor militancy and student radicalism seemed to portend a descent toward anarchy (Cheng 1990, 14, 16; Koo 1993, 159).

6. Richard Robison (1992, 341) has argued forcibly that it is necessary to dissect the notoriously vague category of the "middle class." The term applies to many varied subgroups, ranging through civil servants (of varied rank), medium (or sometimes even large, depending on one's viewpoint) capitalists, professionals, white-collar workers, and that spectrum of lowly clerks and petty entrepreneurs who fade imperceptibly down into the informal sector. The "middle class" is thus likely to be very heterogeneous in political outlook and behavior.

CHAPTER 2

1. As Crouch (1988a, 272) points out, however, the floating mass policy was never fully implemented.

2. For instance, on May 18, 1967, Ismid Hadad (of Harian Kami) wrote in *Nusantara* that "there are signs which suggest that Pak Harto is surrounded by a cordon consisting of elements whose integrity cannot be relied upon" (cited in Crouch 1975, 638).

3. For example, following a tightening of government control in the PDI, disillusioned politicians established a range of cultural and educational bodies for adherents of Sukarno's "Marhaenist" ideology (van Dijk 1981, 111).

4. Many have suggested that the Malari riots were fanned by provocateurs linked to Moertopo as a pretext to move against Soemitro and civilian critics; see Cahyono 1992, 143–70.

5. As one such businessman, Sofyan Wanandi, later put it at a time when military operators were accusing him of antigovernment activities, "We are cowards when it comes to politics. . . . We're afraid of making a wrong move" (*Gatra*, January 31, 1998, 33).

6. Reasons for middle-class conservatism in Indonesia have been well canvassed in the extensive literature on the topic, for example, Tanter and Young 1990; Robison 1990, 1996; Chalmers 1993; Bertrand 1996, 422–23.

7. According to then DPR Speaker Amirmachmud, "land problems" was the issue most often brought to the DPR by petitioners in the 1982–87 period (Radjab 1988, 65).

8. The "Current Data on the Indonesian Military Elite" series in the journal *Indonesia*, especially issues 36 (October 1983) and 56 (October 1993), provides useful information on the implications of generational change, and this paragraph draws on material presented in it.

9. According to former interior minister Rudini, the proportion of all regional heads from ABRI declined from 58 percent to 39 percent between 1988 and 1993 (interview, November 14, 1995).

10. The identities of those making the approach vary according to the sympathies of the storyteller. There were reports as early as 1988 that Moerdani personally warned Suharto about corruption in his family (*Indonesia Reports* 31,

June 1988, 35; Liddle 1996b, 629). Former ABRI commander Mohammad Jusuf was another person frequently named as having raised with Suharto his children's behavior.

11. Interviews, Roekmini, November 29, 1995; Sembiring Meliala, November 16, 1996. In interviews in the press at the time, they made similar comments: *Tempo*, July 8, 1989, 22, 30; *Editor*, July 22, 1989, 25–6; *Editor*, September 18, 1993, 41.

12. Roekmini said that both Moerdani and Harsudiono Hartas protected her against moves to have her called before BAIS, the Strategic Intelligence Agency (interview, November 29, 1995).

13. This group was quite conscious of what their collaboration with Ali Moertopo involved. As K. E. Ward (1974, 35) put it, "They have been primarily aroused since Gestapu [the September 30 Affair of 1965] by the fear of triumphant Islam, by anxiety lest the release of Muslim energies and the rehabilitation of Muslim organizations overthrow the balance between the secular forces and the Muslims." They thus believed that a period of military rule was necessary to put into effect economic modernization, to consolidate the supremacy of Pancasila, and to undercut the potential power of political Islam.

14. Hefner cautions against exaggerating the cultural enmity of the New Order establishment toward Islam. He notes, for instance, that in its first two years in power, the regime banned over one hundred mystical Javanist organizations linked to the left, and that "over the long term, then, the big losers under the New Order era were not *santri* Muslims but populist Javanists" (Hefner 2000, 84) .He concludes that "the logic of Soeharto's rule was not blind opposition to political Islam but a determination to centralize power and destroy all centers of civil autonomy and non-state authority" (Hefner 2000, 93).

15. Thus, Bertrand (1996) takes his argument too far by suggesting that openness was controlled from the start by Suharto to achieve a number of aims, including overcoming ABRI discontent. This analysis downplays the extent to which Suharto was reacting to actions taken by military opponents and, later, societal actors. It also understates how much politics passed beyond his control during *keterbukaan*, prompting clumsy and damaging repressive action to restore his authority.

16. Suharto personally instigated the ban when, on June 9, he accused elements in the media of trying to create "suspicion" inside the government. He was referring to recent coverage of a controversy surrounding Habibie's role in the navy's purchase of former East German ships, a role that had angered some in ABRI. The bans were thus intended not only to wind back press criticism but also to defend Habibie as part of the president's overriding aim of restoring unity inside the regime. Edi Sudradjat responded to the bannings by stating that officials needed to "adjust ourselves to the demands of the time" and that criticism of government corruption should not elicit a harsh response (*Kompas*, June 25, 1994).

17. My thanks to Ariel Heryanto for this observation.

CHAPTER 3

1. Soemitro makes this argument in virtually all the chapters in this volume. Rudini, who retired as interior minister in 1993, made many similar contributions in subsequent years (e.g., Rudini 1994, 1995).

2. He added that he was forced to do this publicly, by writing articles in the media, because Suharto had cut all contact with him since the 1988 MPR session, when he had told the press that the president would leave it to the MPR to select a vice president (interview, General Soemitro, December 6, 1995).

3. Special care should be taken here to stress that not all "red and white" officers were necessarily opposed to Suharto or interested in political reform. By the mid to late 1990s, a new generation of "red and white" officers were moving into senior command positions. Many of them were Suharto loyalists, the obvious example being General Wiranto, who was a former adjutant of the president. Wiranto clearly felt himself to be in competition with various "green" rivals, as the discussion in Chapter 8 reveals. But he was not opposed to Suharto.

4. These ideas were argued most strongly and in greatest detail not by serving officers but by retired ones. They included some, like Soemitro, who had retired long before *keterbukaan*, as well as those who were moved aside in the 1990s as part of Suharto's reassertion of control. The following analysis is based primarily on interviews with several then recently retired officers in 1994–96. A more complete account of military politics and ideology during the 1990s is found in Honna 2003.

5. This latter proposal was made by Harsudiono Hartas in 1991 (*Tempo*, August 17, 1991, 27).

6. The analysis of ICMI in this chapter relies greatly on Ramage's account.

7. For example, see the interview with the prominent modernist leader Anwar Haryono, "*Bekerjasma dengan ABRI, Kok Dianggap Aneh?*" [Cooperating with ABRI, Why Should That Be Considered Strange?] in *Republika*, September 8, 1996.

8. See, for example, Adi Sasono in *Paron*, August 10, 1996, 21, where he mentions changes including the adoption of human rights into the "official agenda," the creation of the National Human Rights Commission, and reduction of the role of security forces in labor conflicts.

9. Note that Amien had spoken in favor of succession, albeit cautiously, from as early as 1989 (Rais 1989).

10. He was sometimes willing to speak out publicly on such topics. For example, when former minister Frans Seda (a Catholic) alleged religious discrimination in appointments to bureaucratic posts (an obvious swipe at ICMI), Amien responded by complaining bitterly about the discrimination that Muslims had purportedly experienced at the hands of Christians in the past (*Republika*, October 10, 1996). Amien was also sometimes very outspoken about East Timor. Like some other Muslims, he viewed the East Timor dispute primarily through a religious lens and resented the international attention that human rights abuses there were attracting in the 1990s, believing that Western countries favored the East Timorese because they were Catholics. When Bishop Belo of Dili condemned mis-

treatment of the East Timorese to a German magazine, Amien attacked him viciously and criticized the government for "spoiling" Belo by not punishing him (*Merdeka*, November 11, 1996).

11. An article in *Media Indonesia*, February 26, 1996, for example, describes how Muhammadiyah members who were civil servants in East Java were being pressured by their superiors after Amien gave a speech indicating that at the last election he had voted for PPP.

12. As one rival, Din Syamsuddin (who was head of the research and development body of Golkar and close to General Hartono), put it, Amien had taken the organization too far into politics. "As a charitable movement, government support [for Muhammadiyah] is very important" (*Forum Keadilan*, July 3, 1995, 24; see also *Gatra*, July 1, 1995, 36).

13. A more detailed account of the origins of the Petition of Fifty, and the background, is found in Jenkins 1984.

14. The group was also adept at criticizing Suharto by using quotations from speeches he had himself made early in the New Order. They especially used an extract from a 1967 speech when Suharto had criticized Sukarno for perverting the *negara hukum* (law-based state) into a form of "absolutism" where power was concentrated in the hands of the president (see, e.g., Kelompok Kerja Petisi 50, 1987, 52, 61).

15. These were terms used in a statement made by a forerunner to the Petition of Fifty, the *Lembaga Kesadaran Berkonstitusi '45* (LKB, Institute for Awareness of the 1945 Constitution) for a meeting with ABRI legislators on October 17, 1979 (LKB 1980, 53).

16. This comment was made at a meeting between LKB representatives and Golkar legislators. References to "clobbering" are in LKB 1980, 42, 55.

17. Petition of Fifty leader Ali Sadikin argued very strongly in an interview with the author (November 16, 1995) that Moertopo bore primary responsibility for the New Order's abrogation of democracy.

18. In his defense speech at his subversion trial, for example, Dharsono (1986, 83–87) argued that *dwifungsi* should eventually "disappear."

19. On the Tanjung Priok killings, the Petition of Fifty "white paper," and the ensuing crackdown, see van de Kok 1986; Bourchier 1987; Tapol 1987; Burns 1989.

20. The main document containing these proposals is a letter dated January 3, 1990, to the DPR and MPR. According to Chris Siner Key Timu, this document was discussed among senior acting and retired ABRI officers, a discussion that was halted following a personal reprimand from Suharto.

21. In fact, this meeting had been precipitated in mid-1991 when, following a public debate about the ban on overseas travel by dissidents, group members met Admiral Sudomo, the coordinating minister for political and security affairs. Sudomo, a Suharto loyalist, insisted that the group still threatened stability and would be allowed to travel only if they publicly apologized to the president for "slandering" him (*Tempo*, June 1 1991, 22–3).

22. Mahasin was the only member of the group to have modernist Islamic as-

sociations. He was prominent in the HMI in Yogyakarta in the 1960s. He had joined ICMI but rapidly became critical of it.

23. Indeed, Abdurrahman suggested that some ABRI officers thought that Forum Demokrasi did not go far enough and that "Benny Moerdani's people" wanted them to "intensify the quarrel; they wanted us to be more political, more critical of Suharto" (interview, November 6, 1995). Some Forum Demokrasi members doubted this interpretation.

24. Some members of KINO ("basic organizational units" affiliated with Golkar) also felt threatened by the rise of ICMI, although they were even more politically conservative. KINO were secular organizations which had been important components of Golkar since its formation and which had long enjoyed generous apportionment of legislative seats, bureaucratic posts, and other privileges; see *Forum Keadilan*, October 7, 1996, 103.

25. Siswono had been a member of the Sukarnoist student organization GMNI in Bandung in the 1960s (he had temporarily been suspended from his enrollment as an ITB student during the purge of Sukarnoists which occurred after 1965). He later enjoyed considerable success in business and became a chairperson of HIPMI, the Golkar-linked Young Indonesian Businesspeople's Association.

26. In a three-part article entitled "*Wawasan Kebangsaan di Tengah Kebhinekaan*" [The National Vision in the Midst of Diversity], Siswono Yudohusodo criticized organizations formed on the basis of a "horizontal matrix," an obvious attack on ICMI (*Media Indonesia*, May 1994, 23–26).

27. Sarwono Kusumaatmadja later said that Suharto did not give any indication that he was preparing to abandon ICMI, but he did criticize ICMI "radicals" (interview, October 19, 1998).

28. Other groups included PCPP (Association of Intellectuals for Pancasila Development), the descendant of the earlier ICKI initiative. It drew many of its members from FKA-GMNI and Golkar KINO and was a rather conservative organization.

CHAPTER 4

1. See articles in *Prisma: The Indonesian Indicator*, no. 28, 1983, for this position.

2. For an excellent example of a comprehensive neopopulist alternative development program, see Sumawinata 1985.

3. LBH, for example, secured overseas funding, much of it from the Dutch social-democratic aid organization NOVIB, precisely as the financial support it received from the Jakarta city administration declined.

4. Some survey data seemed to confirm this. According to one survey of two hundred students from private and state universities in 1988, 4.8 percent of those questioned stated they intended to work for nonprofit organizations after graduating (*Tempo*, April 22, 1989, 33).

5. This was symbolized by the 1993 appointment of the University of Gadjah Mada's Professor Mubyarto, the doyen of neopopulist economists and longtime

advocate of a noncapitalist "Pancasila economy," as director of a special development program for backward villages in Bappenas, the National Planning Board.

6. INFID 1993b, 6, describes a meeting between INFID leaders and Sarwono in April 1993 in which the minister promised to "make public his support for NGOs."

7. For example, Walhi became increasingly prepared to confront the government, suing it in 1989 over the Inti Indorayon project and damaging relations with Emil Salim in the process. In 1994, it ventured further into politically sensitive territory when it took court action to have declared invalid a presidential decree which diverted reforestation funds to Habibie's airplane manufacturer, IPTN.

8. During the early 1990s there was intense and lengthy reflection, including among some of the bigger and better-established NGOs, about how to break free from old approaches and become a truly "counterhegemonic" movement aimed at "strengthening civil society" and pursuing "social transformation." For example, in 1992 an NGO meeting was held in Cisarua on the topic of "integrated rural development," where much criticism of the weaknesses of NGOs in ideological and paradigmatic terms was put forward (Fakih 1993, 2; see also Indeco De Unie 1993).

9. For an informative recent discussion of the role of NGOs in the labor field, see Ford 2003.

10. For contemporary evidence of LBH's concern for labor, see Mahnida 1981; Lubis 1981b.

11. Figures reported in 1996 were twelve branch offices and fourteen project bases in twenty-six provinces and approximately 160 lawyers (*Jakarta Post*, February 28, 1996).

12. On the early history of LBH, see LBH 1973; Lev 1987; Radjab 1995. Although LBH became organizationally independent in 1980, it still maintained close relations with the Bar Association and cooperated in forming defense teams in important political trials.

13. For instance, the advocate Yap Thiam Hien (who was prominent as the lawyer for many leading PKI prisoners in their trials in the late 1960s) had been detained at the end of 1967 and accused of communist links after he accused senior officials of involvement in extortion. This arrest greatly shocked many of the military's liberal allies.

14. Adnan Buyung Nasution's "Tiga Hambatan: Kultur, Konsepsi Politik dan Keadaan Ekonomi" [Three Obstacles: Culture, Political Conceptions, and the Economic Situation] (which appears to have been written in about 1976) in Nasution 1981, 23–48, provides a good example of such views.

15. In 1992, for example, the Jakarta office dealt with 613 political and civil cases, 382 labor cases, 343 land cases, 69 environmental cases, and 1152 "others" (marital, consumer, etc.) (YLBHI 1993, 5).

16. This decision was partly motivated by the earlier fate of Persahi (the Indonesian Law Graduate Association), the leadership of which was lost by liberal lawyers like Buyung and Harjono Tjitrosoebono after a military-organized stack at its 1969 congress.

17. Key documents outlining the concept include LBH 1981; Nusantara 1981; Lubis 1986; Nasution 1981, 1984, 1985.

18. This was the meeting where the concept was first officially formulated (Laporan Komisi Bantuan Hukum Struktural, 2, in LBH 1981).

19. The volume on "structural poverty" edited by Selo Soemardjan was widely quoted by LBH leaders, as were works by dependency theorists (see, e.g., Lubis 1981b).

20. In interviews in March 1994, Surabaya LBH activists said that the Surabaya branch, for example, had extensive networks of labor activists in industrial areas around the city and organized regular training sessions for workers at its headquarters.

21. According to Buyung, his criticism of "integralism" at a seminar at Yogyakarta's Universitas Gadjah Mada in September 1993 was discussed in a meeting of political and security ministers later that year, and he was thereafter prevented from addressing meetings at several campuses (interview, February 8, 1994).

22. Buyung was not the only LBH leader to advocate greater support for democratization. Most of the younger LBH activists were even more forthright on this topic (see, e.g., Hendardi 1993).

23. For an example of an LBH document suffused with the new civil society terminology and which positions the state as the chief adversary, see Radjab, Bastaman, and Hendardi 1991.

24. The May 1994 issue of LBH's *Jurnal Demokrasi*, for example, included articles on themes associated with the Indonesian left, such as the validity of May 1 as international workers' day, the importance of the term *buruh* (associated by the regime with the communist movement) to describe workers, and the fundamental incompatibility of interests between workers and employers. An editor of this edition was Wilson, later an important leader of the radical student-based PRD (People's Democratic Party) and its labor union.

25. This was so much the case that during my visits to Jakarta it was always possible to locate virtually any individual from any student or dissident group simply by waiting in the lobby of the LBH office; either the person I was looking for or someone associated with his or her organization would invariably soon appear through the doorway.

26. The director of the branch in Semarang, for instance, Puspoadji, was very hostile to those who wished to take LBH in a "political" direction (interview, February 17, 1994).

27. He added that he wished to learn about Habibie and Hartono's views about the political situation and how they viewed democratization. He said they told him they wished to pursue democratization, but "from within." He said he learned their views on democratization were "naive."

28. Much later, in November 1999, Buyung became the center of further controversy when he headed the team of lawyers defending military officers and other officials accused of human rights abuses in East Timor.

29. After the period covered in this study, renewed internal conflict and management problems contributed to the organization's international donors ceasing

their financial contributions, propelling LBH into an even deeper crisis. By mid-2003, most staff had not been paid for months and the organization was on the brink of bankruptcy (*Kompas*, June 25, 2003).

30. Though the fact that most NGOs relied on foreign funding should temper this conclusion.

CHAPTER 5

1. The language used was thus sometimes superficially similar to the pre-1965 left (Lane 1982, 126). Some student activists also began to initiate links with members of poor rural communities around 1977 (interview, Indro Tjahjono, November 29, 1993).

2. This quotation is from an article Joesoef wrote after ceasing to be minister (Joesoef 1984, 70).

3. A chief advocate of this view was Denny J. A. of the Kelompok Studi Proklamasi (Proklamasi Study Group; see Denny 1990). This attitude sparked much debate in the late 1980s, when activists involved in the *parlemen jalanan* (parliament of the streets, as the protestors sometimes called themselves) accused Denny and other study group proponents of elitism, labeling them "NATO" ("No Action, Talk Only"; Akhmad 1989, 92).

4. See, for example, Harsono 1990 on an early campaign by Yayasan Geni students to cooperate with *becak* (bicycle taxi) drivers against anti-*becak* traffic regulations.

5. The packet of five political laws consisted of laws on general elections, the legislature, political parties, referenda, and societal organizations (*ormas*).

6. Participants in the internal conflicts of the early 1990s typically described them as being between a "moral" or "ethical" wing of the movement and a "populist" or "political" one (Brotoseno 1992; Hakim 1992).

7. Former UI student activist and PPBI secretary general Wilson (1995, 13–24) lists twenty-nine student-worker solidarity demonstrations in 1990–95.

8. I am thankful to Lyndal Meehan for this reference. In the same year, Suharto addressed a fiftieth anniversary celebration of the HMI, praising the organization for its defense of Pancasila and for its "Islamic spirit" (*Kompas*, March 21, 1997).

9. The quotation is from a leaflet entitled *Seruan Pada Seluruh Kaum Muslimin: Arswendo Menghina Nabi Muhammad SAW dan Islam* (Call to All Muslims: Arswendo insults the Prophet Muhammad and Islam) distributed at Jakarta demonstrations.

10. Benedict Anderson (1989, 66) refers more cautiously to "rumors" that student activism "has been quietly encouraged by senior military personnel." The issues raised in this section are also discussed in Aspinall 1995.

11. At this time, the officer with overall responsibility for security at the MPR was the Jakarta commander, Major General Kentot Harseno, the man who was later accused of leaking the material which discredited ICMI-aligned Minister Haryanto Dhanutirto.

12. For example, the first 1993 edition of the Yogyakarta IAIN student mag-

azine *Arena* detailed the business interests of the Suharto family and was banned.

13. See, for example, statements by Hartono suggesting that student protest was becoming "destructive" and opposed to ABRI (*Dëtik*, March 9–22, 1994, 17).

14. For example, *Cerita Kami* (Our Story), a publication of the Yayasan Maju Bersama (Advance Together Foundation—a group based around a nucleus of University of Indonesia students) incorporated stories written by workers about their experiences of daily life, working conditions, and industrial campaigns. Compare this with similar working-class literature in South Korea (Koo 1993, 151–55).

CHAPTER 6

1. From the early 1980s, Soerjadi had been appointed to the directorship of a company owned by the Wanandi brothers (*Dëtik*, August 11–17, 1993, 11; Halawa 1993, 27).

2. Nico Daryanto claimed that the first inkling that he would become secretary-general came when Moerdani approached him and asked him to take the post (interview, October 24, 1995).

3. *Tempo*, September 13, 1986, 20; *Indonesia Reports* 21, June 1987, 32; *Indonesia Reports* 22, September 1987, 5. Thanks to Marcus Mietzner for drawing my attention to these articles.

4. A translation of this letter is in the politics supplement in *Indonesia Reports* 24, November 1987, 1–6.

5. In November 1996, I interviewed several PDI members and branch leaders in West Java who had participated in this attack. They explained that Social and Political Affairs staff in the Siliwangi Military Command had summoned them and instructed them to participate.

6. Sometimes the pressure was somewhat indirect, as when North Sumatra governor Raja Inal Siregar advised departing delegates to "carefully read the signs of the times." In less uncertain terms, the Diponegoro commander in Central Java, Major General Soeyono, told delegates not to support candidates who "were hitching a ride" on the names of their famous parents (*Tempo*, December 4, 1993, 30; *Jawa Pos*, November 18, 1993).

7. See, for example, the denial by Brigadier General Syarwan Hamid, the chief of the ABRI Information Center, that Feisal Tanjung had released an order that Megawati should not be supported (*Dëtik*, November 10–16, 1993, 20).

8. Various core supporters of Megawati indicated this to me. However, all those interviewed stressed that such meetings were "routine" and that there was no conspirational element. Megawati herself strongly denied that there was any contact before the announcement of her bid (interview, December 11, 1995).

9. Megawati suggested that ABRI officers had been instructed to ensure Budi Hardjono's victory but were reluctant to take action at the congress because "they saw the reality, if this was to be halted, the consequences could be fatal" (interview, December 11, 1995).

10. For example, *Forum Keadilan* (December 23, 1993) speculated (rather coyly) that Megawati was backed by "a very strong group" and that a "former ABRI official" (the implication, surely, was Moerdani) played an important role in organizing her strategy. In this connection, it is worth noting that Moerdani's chief rival, Sudharmono, said publicly that Megawati's election had been "engineered" (*Jakarta Post*, January 6, 1994).

11. The editors of Cornell University's journal *Indonesia* likewise argued that Agum Gumelar used Directorate A of BAIS "flagrantly in arranging the election of Megawati" (*Indonesia* 1994, 85).

12. According to one anonymous military source quoted by Jun Honna (1999, 94), it was Prabowo who suggested to the president that Agum had "failed" in the PDI affair.

13. Merukh claimed to have received 3 billion rupiah from the government (*Jakarta Post*, January 16, 1995).

14. Edi publicly condemned the Reshuffle group (*Merdeka*, February 16, 1995). Megawati was invited to speak to the Staff College to address classes during Syafei's tenure and received a warm response there from officers.

15. This was the message of a number of speeches made by Megawati to party members that I observed in 1994 and 1995.

16. See Angus McIntyre's (1997, 15) similar comments on Megawati's enigmatic silences: "Megawati became a mute symbol; or rather, a symbol because she was mute, a sign for decency amid the abuse of power of the Soeharto regime."

17. It is worth noting that even while admitting their "fanatical" loyalty to Megawati, many PDI members I spoke to remarked that they had always hoped that it would be Sukarno's oldest son, Guntur, who would step forward into national political life, as he had done—to no avail—in the 1970s.

18. My thanks to Rochayah Machali for bringing this to my attention.

19. For instance, before becoming party leader she told one journalist that she remembered her father telling her, "My struggle was perhaps easier because it was to banish the colonialists, but your struggle will be harder because you will confront [people of] your own nation" (*DëTik*, June 23–29, 1993, 8).

20. McIntyre (1997, 8) suggests that she became involved in the PDI almost casually, as a result of "post-parental freedom."

21. Indeed, it is worth noting that Megawati, along with her brother Guruh, had been beneficiaries of New Order patronage when they were given licenses to run four petrol stations by then Jakarta governor Tjokropranolo (*DëTik*, June 23–29, 1993, 8).

CHAPTER 7

1. It included representatives from large NGOs like LBH and WALHI, smaller mobilizational NGOS, radical student-based groups like the PRD and Pijar, dissidents like the Petition of Fifty, and prominent intellectuals like Nurcholish Madjid and Arief Budiman. Abdurrahman Wahid declined an invitation to be involved (*Surabaya Post*, March 8, 1996).

2. Another analysis which emphasizes the role of palace interests in Megawati's downfall was later given by the chief of the general staff of the army at the time, Lieutenant General Soeyono. He argued in his memoirs that the chief motive for removing Megawati was to eliminate her as a potential challenger to Suharto's daughter Tutut, who was at that time being groomed for a greater political future: "it was impossible that two roses should bloom at the same time" (Butarbutar 2003, 156).

3. Some reports in semiunderground bulletins at the time suggested that the operation was planned at an ABRI leadership meeting on March 24–28 and later confirmed at a meeting of Politics and Security Ministers ("Kudeta Megawati Dirancang Rapim ABRI," PIPA, May 3, 1996, KITLV Internet library, July 8, 1996). In an interview later published in *Tempo* (August 1, 1999, 44–45), Alex Widya Siregar, a Bakin informer and deputy treasurer in the PDI leadership later formed by Soerjadi, details the role played by Syarwan Hamid, BIA chief Syamsir Siregar, and director A of BIA Zacky Anwar Makarim in meetings where the "extraordinary congress" plan was first discussed with PDI leaders.

4. They also claimed that if elections were held in free conditions the PDI would gain 80 to 85 percent of the vote (*The Australian*, June 13, 1996). That this was in an English-language press release detracted from its significance; formal statements directed to party followers and the Indonesian press were more restrained.

5. The booklet in which Akhmad's piece appears, *Merebut Demokrasi dengan Kekuatan Rakyat* (Seizing Democracy with People Power) was circulated widely in PRD circles around the time the organization was formed in mid-1994.

6. As a further gesture of defiance, the party gave awards to such political pariahs as jailed East Timorese leader Xanana Gusmao and leftist novelist Pramoedya Ananta Toer. Another party, the Partai Uni Demokrasi Indonesia (Indonesian United Democracy Party, or PUDI), had been launched some weeks earlier by former PPP legislator and fierce critic of Suharto Sri Bintang Pamungkas. PUDI leaders included several figures associated with various NGOs and student groups, as well as some former PSI and PNI politicians.

7. Numerous "chronologies" and eyewitness accounts also circulated on the Internet; the above description partly draws on some of them and broadly follows the chronology I presented in *Inside Indonesia* 48, 1996, 6–7. According to a later investigation by *Tempo* magazine (August 1, 1999, 40–43), Suharto gave a verbal command to Feisal, Yogie, and coordinating minister for political and security affairs Soesilo Soedarman to take over the office. The director general for social and political affairs of the Interior Ministry, Sutoyo N. K., and Syarwan Hamid were the chief planners of the operation, while the chief of the Greater Jakarta military command, Major General Sutiyoso, held primary responsibility for coordinating operations in the field. Over the following years, press reports and other investigations continued to reveal details of high-level military and intelligence involvement in the attack. For instance, when he was interrogated by military police, Sutiyoso said that the order to take the office came from Suharto himself (*Kompas*, September 12, 2000). However, by the time she became presi-

dent in mid-2001, Megawati had apparently lost interest in the case. In August 2002 she endorsed Sutiyoso's reelection as Jakarta governor. A poorly organized court case in December 2003 acquitted two junior military officers who had been charged with responsibility for the attack.

8. Although there was none of the anti-Chinese violence that characterized the 1998 riots, contrary to some accounts (e.g., Eklöf 1999, 48), many eyewitnesses interviewed in late 1996 suggested that much antagonism was directed at security forces, especially the police, and that all police posts in the vicinity of the rioting were burned to the ground.

9. For the experiences of student activist Hendrik Sirait of Yayasan Pijar, see Luwarso et al. 1997, 165–77.

10. It should be noted that Megawati refused to defend the PRD publicly and claimed that she had never met its leaders like Budiman Sudjatmiko. PRD members in hiding I interviewed in late 1996 (and since confirmed) stated unequivocally that this was not so. They were bitter about Megawati's attitude.

11. The modernist Muslim leaders who participated actively in the campaign to defend Megawati were relatively marginal players. Ridwan Saidi's new and small organization, Masyumi-baru, joined MARI, but Saidi was a marginal figure (Fealy 1997, 28). Sri Bintang Pamungkas, the leader of the new (secular) party PUDI, was already excluded from the Islamic mainstream, having been "recalled" as a PPP legislator.

12. There were reports that documents about the PRD, which Syarwan Hamid distributed to journalists, included the fax address of CIDES, and Syarwan had to hastily recall these when it was pointed out to him. Adi Sasono strongly denied that CIDES had anything to do with the campaign against the PRD (*Forum Keadilan*, September 23, 1996, 95). Student activists recruited to CPDS, the think tank run by the ICMI intellectuals linked to Prabowo and Hartono, apparently did operate as agents in the pro-Megawati movement, informing on and facilitating the arrest of several activists (confidential interviews, December 1996).

13. A few modernist politicians, like Radjab Ranggasoli, remained active in the group, but they had never been as prominent as Haryono or Fatwa. The most prominent Masyumi leaders involved, notably Mohammad Natsir and Sjafruddin Prawarinegara, had died some years earlier.

14. This occurred after it emerged that Budiman was from a pious *santri* family (*Republika*, December 3, 1996). Robert Hefner (1997) provides an interpretation of this coverage and the condemnation it aroused in Dewan Dakwah circles.

15. This, according to Marcus Mietzner (1998, 186), was Abdurrahman's explanation at the conference of NU branches and *kiai* held in Mataram in November 1997. Adam Schwarz (1999, 332) quotes Abdurrahman suggesting that a large vote for the PPP (in the absence of a Megawati-led PDI) would mean that his opponents would say, "NU doesn't really support me," given the well-known enmity between him and the PPP leadership.

CHAPTER 8

1. In January 1972, for example, he threatened to use the armed forces to "smash" people who were using the *Taman Mini* entertainment park to attack him and his wife (the text of the speech is in Smith 1974, 235–40).

2. One example was Soebadio Sastrosatomo, an aging critic of the president and former leader of the long-disbanded Socialist Party, PSI. In mid-1997 Soebadio published a pamphlet (Sastrosatomo 1997) which included some harsh criticism of Suharto. However, he was a marginal figure, and his pamphlet was accessible to only a limited circle of activists. Nevertheless, it came to the attention of the president and prompted his ire, resulting in highly public persecution of the former PSI leader.

3. Examples include the removal of Satrio Budiardjo ("Billy") Joedono in December 1995 as trade minister (the first time a minister had been removed by Suharto without completing his full term), the removal of Wismoyo Arismunandar as army chief of staff in 1995, and the removal of Soeyono as chief of the general staff in 1996.

4. Former environment minister Sarwono Kusumaatmadja said that he finally lost faith in Suharto when amid the calamitous forest fires of 1997 he approached the president for assistance, only to find Suharto entirely uninterested in the subject (interview, October 19, 1998).

5. Wiranto, in contrast, warned against those who sought to manipulate interethnic and religious tensions (*Jawa Pos*, February 10, 1998).

6. On January 18, a bomb exploded in an apartment in Central Jakarta. The apartment was allegedly rented by PRD activists. Military investigators claimed to find documents there outlining a bombing campaign against shopping malls and similar targets and indicating that Wanandi and Moerdani were planning to topple the government (Eklöf 1999, 134–35; Mietzner 1999, 72). While the very different political outlooks of the PRD and the Wanandi brothers made any direct political alliance between them highly unlikely, it is possible that there were indirect connections between them, through such bodies as the Catholic student organization, PMKRI. In any case, the conspiracy had an attractive logic for those who sought to construct an authoritarian military-Islamic alliance. It enabled democratic opposition to be simultaneously equated with the bogeymen of leftism, the Chinese, Catholicism, and Moerdani.

7. In *Kompas* (January 27, 1998), chief of staff for social and political affairs Lieutenant General Yunus Yosfiah made comments to this effect.

8. By the end of 1997, however, the party was beginning to reach the end of the litigation road. The courts had refused to hear fifty-eight of sixty-two suits (*Inti Jaya*, January 7–8, 1998, 11).

9. One group was Solidaritas Indonesia untuk Amien—Mega (Indonesian Solidarity for Amien-Mega, or SIAGA), which was led by playwright Ratna Sarumpaet and student activist Pius Lustrilanang of Aldera. This group urged Megawati and Amien to form a united front of all prodemocracy groups. According to media reports, Megawati was very curt when receiving a delegation at her home (*Kompas*, January 24, 1998).

10. This action was held by a group called the Ranks of the Red and White (*Barisan Merah—Putih*), led primarily by local Jakarta PDI leaders. One hundred forty-six were arrested (*Inti Jaya*, February 13–17, 1998, 1).

11. In an interview in *Forum Keadilan* (January 26, 1998, 19) Adi also called (though using less direct language than Amien) for presidential succession.

12. Mietzner (1998, 189–91) explains that with Abdurrahman incapacitated several groups strove for influence in the NU. A group around Secretary General Ahmad Bagja and the NU youth organizations attempted to play an anti-Suharto role. Overall the accommodationist position was dominant.

13. Dave McRae (2001, 63–79) lists violent incidents at seventy-three protests between March 11 and May 13.

14. McRae (2001) presents an informative discussion, including cases studies of groups in various towns.

15. See the three-page typescript petition entitled "Seruan Suksesi Damai dan Terbuka untuk Keselamatan dan Masa Depan Rakyat dan Bangsa Indonesia" [An Appeal for Peaceful and Open Succession, for the Safety and Future of the Indonesian People and Nation], dated January 9, 1998.

16. Robin Madrid (1999) and Richard Kraince (2000) provide sympathetic accounts of this organization. Mietzner (1999, 79, 88), however, suggests that KAMMI had links with Prabowo, although it later abandoned him. Madrid (1999, 23) likewise notes that some KAMMI leaders made a "serious error" (although no further explanation is given as to motives) when they invited Prabowo to their founding conference.

17. According to Madrid (1999, 24), KAMMI demands were similar to most other groups, except that they avoided mentioning *dwifungsi*, believing "it was not time to challenge the military head on." National KAMMI documents also did not call for Suharto to stand down until May 20, although regional branches did so earlier.

18. And so, for example, in early May students at the philosophy faculty at Yogyakarta's Gadjah Mada University, long a base of radicalism, called for the MPR to be dismantled and replaced by a body freely elected by the people (*Detektif dan Romantika*, March 14, 1998, 27).

19. See McRae 2001, 20–24, for a more detailed discussion of student demands and how they converged on the call for Suharto's resignation. Even most of the pamphlets produced by more radical groups which I have in my possession focused on demanding Suharto's removal and did not explain what kind of government he should be replaced with, nor who would lead that government. Calls for the replacement of the government by a "presidium" or some form of coalition government became much more common after Suharto resigned (McRae 2001, 31).

20. For example, Megawati did not appear during the student occupation of the DPR (although her brother Guruh and other PDI leaders did) mainly because the party had received "credible information" from military sources that Prabowo intended to "frame her" by triggering further rioting (interview, Laksamana Sukardi, July 17, 1998).

21. Forum Kerja Indonesia appealed for the population to protest peacefully at local legislatures, endorsed Suharto's reported comments from Cairo (which he had ill advisedly visited) that he was willing to stand aside (a statement which the president later "corrected"), and appealed to ABRI not to obstruct the people from expressing their aspirations (*Kompas*, May 16, 1998; *Media Indonesia*, May 17, 1998).

22. Note, however, that according to Muhammad Najib and Kuat Sukardiyono (1998, 59), on May 18 Anwar Haryono of Dewan Dakwah, and formerly of the Petition of Fifty, suggested to Amien Rais and other Islamic leaders that it might be best to support Suharto's proposal to stay in power in order to "carry out reform," remembering his many policy concessions to the Islamic *umat* during the 1990s.

23. In one of the ironies of 1998, Amien Rais, who in the past had been accused of sectarianism by Abdurrahman Wahid, attacked Suharto for using Islam in this way, accusing him of attempting to "play off" religious groups and endangering pluralism (*Jawa Pos*, May 20, 1998). Abdurrahman in the past had frequently accused Amien of falling for exactly this ploy.

24. Prabowo's rebuttal of the accusations against him is found in *Asiaweek*, March 3, 2000.

25. Wiranto also blocked the president from declaring martial law (Vatikiotis 1998, 160; Mietzner 1999, 81; interview, Z. A. Maulani, July 18, 1998).

26. According to some sources, Wiranto finally brought himself, on the evening of May 20, to suggest privately to Suharto that the time had come to step down (Walters 1999, 81; interview, Z. A. Maulani, July 18, 1998).

CHAPTER 9

1. The quotation is from a letter from the Petition of Fifty working group, addressed to the MPR, the president, and other state institutions, dated February 25, 1986, and reproduced in Kelompok Kerja Petisi 50 1987, 98.

2. And so, for example, as early as 1994 Yayasan Pijar produced a flyer for distribution at one of the big demonstrations against the press bannings of that time which was headlined "Today People Power Begins" (Hari Ini People Power Dimulai).

3. As Benedict Anderson (1998, 216) notes, by the regime's final years, even the middle class and parts of the church hierarchy had adopted a "nationalist-Marxist vocabulary" propagated by the left.

4. There are striking similarities, too, in the way that in both countries students inherited an ethos of political struggle from the days of the movement against colonialism.

5. I am thankful to Daniel Lev, who in a contribution to the "Indonesia discussion" e-mail list in April 2002 suggested this formulation.

6. Another qualification deserves note. Although communal divisions did undermine opposition's capacity to act in concert against the regime, an element of communal competition also sometimes acted as a spur; some ICMI sympathizers, like Amien Rais, adopted a more critical attitude toward Suharto from 1996

partly because they sensed that secular nationalists and their allies were better positioning themselves for the post-Suharto order by being in the forefront of opposition.

7. For Adnan Buyung Nasution's thoughts on the need for NGOs and other opponents to carefully pick the time to challenge the regime, see Nasution 1995, 29.

Glossary

ABRI	Angkatan Bersenjata Republik Indonesia (Armed Forces of the Republic of Indonesia)
Adil	Movement for Social Justice (Malaysia)
Aldera	Aliansi Demokrasi Rakyat (People's Democracy Alliance), a student-based group founded in 1994
aliran	a political-cultural "stream"
BAIS	Badan Intelijen Strategis (Strategic Intelligence Agency)
Bakin	Badan Koordinasi Intelijen Negara (State Intelligence Coordinating Agency)
Bakorstanas	Badan Koordinasi Pemantapan Stabilitas Nasional (Coordinating Agency for the Maintenance of National Stability)
BIA	Badan Intelijen ABRI (ABRI Intelligence Agency)
BSPP	Burma Socialist Program Party
CIDES	Center for Information and Development Studies, think tank linked to ICMI
Cipayung Group	The alliance of five major national student organizations (GMNI, GMKI, HMI, PMII, and PMKRI) formed in 1972
CSIS	Centre for Strategic and International Studies
Dewan Dakwah	Dewan Dakwah Islamiyah Indonesia (Islamic Proselytizing Council of Indonesia)
DMPY	Dewan Mahasiswa dan Pemuda Yogyakarta (Yogyakarta Student and Youth Council)
DPR	People's Representative Council (the national legislature)
dwifungsi	ABRI's "dual" sociopolitical and defense function
FKMY	Forum Komunikasi Mahasiswa Yogyakarta (Yo-

gyakarta Student Communication Forum), an important student group at the end of the 1980s

Forkot   Forum Kota (City Forum), an important student group
formed in 1998, also called Komunitas Mahasiswa Se-
Jabotabek (All-Jabotabek Student Community), Jabotabek being the Jakarta-Bogor-Tangerang-Bekasi urban area

GMKI   Gerakan Mahasiswa Kristen Indonesia (Christian
[Protestant] Student Movement of Indonesia)

GMNI   Gerakan Mahasiswa Nasional Indonesia (National Student Movement of Indonesia), historically associated
with the Sukarnoist *aliran*

Golkar   Golongan Karya (Functional Groups), the state-backed
political party

golput   *golongan putih* (white group), the term used to describe an election boycott or, more accurately, casting
an invalid vote by piercing the blank ("white") part of
the ballot paper

gotong royong   mutual cooperation

HMI   Himpunan Mahasiswa Islam (Islamic Students Association)

HMI-MPO   HMI-Majelis Penyelemat Organisasi (HMI-Council to
Save the Organization), a splinter of HMI which rejected acceptance of Pancasila as "sole basis" in the
1980s

IAIN   Institut Agama Islam Negeri (State Institute for Islamic
Studies)

ICMI   Ikatan Cendekiawan Muslim se-Indonesia (Association
of Muslim Intellectuals of Indonesia)

IGGI   Intergovernmental Group on Indonesia

INFID   International NGO Forum on Indonesian Development

INFIGHT   Indonesian Front for the Defense of Human Rights, activist coalition in the late 1980s and early 1990s

INGI   International NGO Forum on Indonesia

ITB   Institut Teknologi Bandung (Bandung Institute of Technology)

kabupaten   regency, the regional administrative unit below the
level of a province

kaditsospol   *Kepala direktorat sosial-politik* (head of the Social and
Political Affairs Directorate of the Department of the
Interior)

KAHMI   Korps Alumni HMI (HMI Alumni Corps), the chief or-

	ganization for former members of the Islamic Students Association
kampung	backstreet urban residential area
Keadilan	National Justice Party (Malaysia)
keterbukaan	openness
KINO	Kesatuan Organisasi Induk (Basic Organizational Units), organizations affiliated with Golkar
KIPP	Komite Independen Pengawas Pemilu (Independent Election-Monitoring Committee)
Kopassus	Komando Pasukan Khusus (Special Forces Command)
Kopkamtib	Komando Operasi Pemulihan Keamanan dan Ketertiban (Operational Command for the Restoration of Security and Order)
Kostrad	Komando Operasi Pemulihan Keamanan dan Ketertiban (Army Strategic Command)
LBH	Lembaga Bantuan Hukum (Legal Aid Institute)
LIPI	Lembaga Ilmu Pengetahuan Indonesia (Indonesian Institute of Sciences)
LKB	Lembaga Kesadaran Berkonstitusi (Institute for Constitutional Awareness)
LP3ES	Lembaga Penelitian, Pendidikan dan Penerangan Ekonomi dan Sosial (Institute for Social and Economic Research, Education, and Information)
LSM	Lembaga Swadaya Masyarakat (self-reliant community institution)
Malari	Malapetaka 15 Januari (the Fifteenth of January Calamity), Jakarta riots which coincided with the visit by Japanese prime minister Tanaka in 1974
MAR	Majelis Amanat Rakyat (People's Mandate Council), established by Amien Rais in May 1998
MARI	Majelis Rakyat Indonesia (Indonesian People's Council), a coalition established during the 1996 PDI crisis
Masyumi	The major modernist Islamic party in the "Old Order" period
MPR	People's Consultative Assembly (Indonesia's supreme legislative body)
negara hukum	a law-based state
NLD	National League for Democracy (Burma)
NU	Nahdlatul Ulama (Islamic Scholars Association)
ormas	*organisasi kemasyarakatan* (societal organization), or sometimes *organisasi massa* (mass organization)

PAS	Parti Islam se-Malaysia (the All-Malaysia Islamic Party)
PDI	Partai Demokrasi Indonesia (Indonesian Democracy Party)
pesantren	Islamic boarding school
PKI	Partai Komunis Indonesia (Indonesian Communist Party)
PMII	Pergerakan Mahasiswa Islam Indonesia (Indonesian Islamic Student Movement), aligned with the NU
PMKRI	Persatuan Mahasiswa Katolik Indonesia (Catholic Students' Association of Indonesia)
PNI	Partai Nasional Indonesia (Indonesian National Party)
PPBI	Pusat Perjuangan Buruh Indonesia (Center for Indonesian Labor Struggle), workers' group linked to the PRD
PPP	Partai Persatuan Pembangunan (United Development Party)
PRD	Partai Rakyat Demokratik (People's Democratic Party), before 1996 the Persatuan Rakyat Demokratik (People's Democratic Union)
PSI	Partai Sosialis Indonesia (Indonesian Socialist Party)
Pijar	Pusat Informasi dan Jaringan Aksi untuk Reformasi (Information Center and Action Network for Reformation), a Jakarta student-based group
PUDI	Partai Uni Demokrasi Indonesia (Indonesian United Democracy Party), established in 1996 by former PPP legislator Sri Bintang Pamungkas
rechtsstaat	a law-based state
santri	pious Muslim
SARA	Suku, Agama, Ras dan Antar-Golongan (ethnic, religious, racial, and group identities)
SBSI	Serikat Buruh Sejahtera Indonesia (Indonesian Prosperous Labor Union)
SDSB	Sumbangan Dermawan Sosial Berhadiah (Social Philanthropists' Donations with Prize), a state-run lottery
SKEPHI	Jaringan Kerjasama Pelestarian Hutan Indonesia (Indonesian Network for Forest Conservation), before 1987 the Sekretariat Kerjasama Pelestarian Hutan Indonesia (Indonesian Joint Secretariat for Forest Conservation)
SMID	Solidaritas Mahasiswa Indonesia untuk Demokrasi (Indonesian Student Solidarity for Democracy), affiliated with the PRD

UI	Universitas Indonesia (University of Indonesia)
wong cilik	(Javanese) the "little people"
WALHI	Wahana Lingkungan Hidup Indonesia (Indonesia Environment Network)
YKPK	Yayasan Kerukunan Persaudaraan Kebangsaan (Foundation for National Harmony and Brotherhood)
YLBHI	Yayasan Lembaga Bantuan Hukum Indonesia (Indonesian Legal Aid Foundation)
YLKI	Yayasan Lembaga Konsumen Indonesia (Indonesian Consumers Foundation)

Bibliography

Abbot, Jason. 2001. Vanquishing Banquo's Ghost: The Anwar Ibrahim Affair and Its Impact on Malaysian Politics. *Asian Studies Review* 25 (1): 285–308.

Aditjondro, George Junus. 1990. Dampak Sistemik dan Kritik Kultural yang Terlupakan: Suatu Refleksi Terhadap Kampanye Kedung Ombo yang Lalu. *Kritis* 4 (3) (January): 54–59.

Adler, Glenn, and Eddie Webster. 1995. Challenging Transition Theory: The Labor Movement, Radical Reform, and the Transition to Democracy in South Africa. *Politics and Society* 23 (1) (March): 75–106.

Akhmad. 1994. Kaum Miskin Kota: Orang-orang tersingkir dari Kota. In *Merebut Demokrasi dengan Kekuatan Rakyat*, 30–34. Jakarta: Cahaya Indonesia Baru.

Akhmad, Fazlur. 1989. The Indonesian Student Movement, 1920–89: A Force for Radical Social Change? *Prisma: The Indonesian Indicator* 47: 83–95.

Akhmadi, Heri. 1981. *Breaking the Chains of Oppression of the Indonesian People*. Ithaca, NY: Cornell Modern Indonesia Project.

Alfian, Mely G. Tan, Selo Soemardjan, eds. 1980. *Kemiskinan Struktural: Suatu Bunga Rampai*. Jakarta: Yayasan Ilmu-Ilmu Sosial and HIPIS.

Altbach, Philip G. 1989. Perspectives on Student Political Activism. In *Student Political Activism: An International Reference Handbook*, ed. Philip G. Altbach, 1–17. New York: Greenwood Press.

Ammarsyah. 1990. Indonesia: Kisah Tentang Sangkur dan Topi Baja-Merebut Kembali Hak Hak Rakyat. Photocopied defense speech.

Anderson, Benedict R. O'G. 1977. Withdrawal Symptoms: Social and Cultural Aspects of the October 6 Coup. *Bulletin of Concerned Asian Scholars* (July–September): 13–30.

———. 1978. Last Days of Indonesia's Suharto? *Southeast Asia Chronicle* 63: 2–17.

———. 1989. Current Data on the Indonesian Military Elite. *Indonesia* 48 (October): 65–105.

———. 1998. Cacique Democracy in the Philippines. In *The Spectre of Comparisons: Nationalism, Southeast Asia and the World*, 192–226. London: Verso.

———, ed. 2001. *Violence and the State in Suharto's Indonesia*. Ithaca, NY: Southeast Asia Program Publications, Cornell University.

Anwar, M. Syafi'i. 1993. *Islam, Negara dan Formasi Sosial Dalam Orde Baru: Menguak Dimensi Sosio-Historis Kelahiran dan Perkembangan ICMI*. Supplement to *Ulumul Qur'an* 3 (3).

———. 1995. ICMI dan Politik: Optimisme dan Kekhawatiran. *Ulumul Qur'an* 6 (1): 4–7.

Arief, Andi. 1994. Memperjelas Arah Pemihakan Gerakan Mahasiswa. *Jawa Pos*, January 24.

Arief, Sritua, and Adi Sasono. 1981. *Indonesia: ketergantungan dan keterbelakangan*. Jakarta: Lembaga Studi Pembangunan.

Aspinall, Edward. 1993. *Student Dissent in Indonesia in the 1980s*. Working Paper No. 79. Clayton, Victoria: Centre of Southeast Asian Studies, Monash University.

———. 1995. Students and the Military: Regime Friction and Civilian Dissent in the Late Suharto Period. *Indonesia* 59 (April): 21–44.

———. 1999. Democratisation, the Working Class, and the Indonesian Crisis. *Review of Indonesian and Malaysian Affairs* 33 (2): 1–32.

———. 2004. Indonesia: Civil Society and Democratic Breakthrough. In *Civil Society and Political Change in Asia: Expanding and Contracting Democratic Space*, ed. Muthiah Alagappa, 61–96. Stanford, CA: Stanford University Press.

Barton, Greg. 2002. *Gus Dur: The Authorized Biography of Abdurrahman Wahid*. Jakarta: Equinox Publishing.

Bernhard, Michael. 1993. Civil Society and Democratic Transition in East Central Europe. *Political Science Quarterly* 108 (2): 307–26.

Bertrand, Jacques. 1996. False Starts, Succession Crises, and Regime Transition: Flirting with Openness in Indonesia. *Pacific Affairs* 69 (3): 319–40.

———. 1997. "Business as Usual" in Suharto's Indonesia. *Asian Survey* 37 (5): 441–52.

Billah, M. M. 1994. *Peta Ornop di Indonesia*. Seri Monografi 02/94. Jakarta: Circle for Participatory Social Management (CPSM).

Billah, M. M., Mufid A. Busyairi, and Helmy Aly. 1993. *Laporan Kunjungan Dialog Tentang Visi, Masalah Posisi dan Paradigma Ornop di Indonesia Serta Upaya Untuk Mengatasinya*. Jakarta: Pokker CPSM (Centre for Participatory Social Management). Sixty-four-page typescript.

Bina Swadaya. 1995. *Bina Swadaya: Badan Pengembangan Swadaya Masyarakat*. Jakarta. Thirty-two-page pamphlet.

Boudreau, Vincent. 1999. Diffusing Democracy? People Power in Indonesia and the Philippines. *Bulletin of Concerned Asian Scholars* 31 (4): 3–18.

Bourchier, David. 1987. The "Petition of 50": Who and what are they. *Inside Indonesia* 10: 7–10.

———. 1997. Totalitarianism and the "National Personality": Recent Controversy About the Philosophical Basis of the Indonesian State. In *Imagining Indonesia: Cultural Politics and Political Culture*, ed. Jim Schiller and Barbara

Martin-Schiller, 157–85. Athens: Ohio University Center for International Studies.

Bratton, Michael. 1994. Civil Society and Political Transitions in Africa. In *Civil Society and the State in Africa*, ed. John W. Harbeson, Donald Rothchild, and Naomi Chazan, 51–81. Boulder, CO: Lynne Rienner.

Brooks, Karen. 1995. The Rustle of Ghosts: Bung Karno in the New Order. *Indonesia* 60 (October): 61–99.

Brotoseno. 1992. Refleksi terhadap Format Gerakan Mahasiswa. *Bernas*, November 18.

Budianta, Melani. 2003. The Blessed Tragedy: The Making of Women's Activism During the *Reformasi* Years. In *Challenging Authoritarianism in Southeast Asia: Comparing Indonesia and Malaysia*, ed. Ariel Heryanto and Sumit K. Mandal, 145–77. London: RoutledgeCurzon.

Budiman, Arief. 1969. Ali Sadikin: One-Man Revolt. *Quadrant* 13 (5): 75–77.

———. 1973. Portrait of a Young Indonesian Looking at His Surroundings. *Internationales Asienforum* 4 (January): 76–88.

———. 1992. Indonesian Politics in the 1990s. In *Indonesia Assessment 1992: Political Perspectives on the 1990s*, ed. Harold Crouch and Hal Hill, 130–39. Canberra: Australian National University.

Burns, Peter. 1989. The Post Priok Trials: Religious Principles and Legal Issues. *Indonesia* 47 (April): 61–88.

Butarbutar, Benny S. 2003. *Soeyono Bukan Puntung Rokok*. Jakarta: Ridma Foundation.

Cahyono, Heru. 1992. *Peranan Ulama Dalam Golkar 1971–1980: Dari Pemilu Sampai Malari*. Jakarta: Sinar Harapan.

Case, William. 1993. Semi-democracy in Malaysia: Withstanding the Pressures for Regime Change. *Pacific Affairs* 66 (2): 183–205.

———. 2002. *Politics in Southeast Asia: Democracy or Less*. Richmond, UK: Curzon.

Chalmers, Ian. 1993. Democracy Constrained: The Emerging Political Culture of the Indonesian Middle Class. *Asian Studies Review* 17 (1): 51–60.

———. 1997. Rolling Back Democracy in the Late Soeharto Era: Some implications for Indonesia's Political Culture. *Asian Studies Review* 21 (2–3) (November): 53–66.

Chehabi, H. E., and Juan J. Linz. 1998a. A Theory of Sultanism 1: A Type of Nondemocratic Rule. In *Sultanistic Regimes*, ed. H. E. Chehabi and Juan J. Linz, 3–25. Baltimore: Johns Hopkins University Press.

———. 1998b. A Theory of Sultanism 2: Genesis and Demise of Sultanistic Regimes. In *Sultanistic Regimes*, ed. H. E. Chehabi and Juan J. Linz, 26–48. Baltimore: Johns Hopkins University Press.

Cheng, Tun-jen. 1989. Democratizing the Quasi-Leninist Regime in Taiwan. *World Politics* 41: 461–99.

———. 1990. Is the Dog Barking? The Middle Class and Democratic Movements in the East Asian NICs. *International Study Notes* 15 (1) (Winter): 10–40.

Clark, Marshall. 1999. Cleansing the Earth. In *The Last Days of President*

Suharto, ed. Edward Aspinall, Gerry van Klinken, and Herb Feith, 37–40. Clayton, Victoria: Monash Asia Institute.

Clarke, Gerard. 1998. *The Politics of NGOs in South-East Asia.* London: Routledge.

Collier, Ruth Berins. 1999. *Paths Toward Democracy: The Working Class and Elites in Western Europe and South America.* New York: Cambridge University Press.

Crouch, Harold. 1975. The Indonesian Army in Politics: 1960–1971. Ph.D. thesis, Monash University.

——. 1986. Islam and Politics in Indonesia. In *Politics, Diplomacy and Islam: Four Case Studies,* ed. Coral Bell, 15–29. Canberra: Department of International Relations, Australian National University.

——. 1988a. *The Army and Politics in Indonesia,* rev. ed. Ithaca, NY: Cornell University Press.

——. 1988b. Indonesia: The Rise or Fall of Suharto's Generals. *Third World Quarterly* 10 (1) (January): 160–75.

——. 1994. Democratic Prospects in Indonesia. In *Democracy in Indonesia: 1950s and 1990s,* ed. David Bourchier and John Legge, 115–27. Clayton, Victoria: Centre of Southeast Asian Studies, Monash University.

——. 1996a. All to Placate a Proud Sultan. *Australian Financial Review,* July 30.

——. 1996b. *Government and Politics in Malaysia.* Ithaca, NY: Cornell University Press.

CSIS (Centre for Strategic and International Studies). 1980. *NKK: Reaksi dan Tanggapan.* Jakarta: CSIS.

Daryanto, Nico. 1992. Nasionalisme dan Keadilan Sosial adalah Perjuangan PDI. In *Pemilu 1992: Harapan dan Janji,* ed. Tim Spes, 93–98. Jakarta: Grasindo.

Denny J. A. 1990. *Gerakan Mahasiswa dan Politik Kaum Muda Era 80-an.* Jakarta: CV Miswar.

Dharsono, H. R. 1986. *Soeharto on Trial: Gen. H. R. Dharsono's Plea,* Amsterdam: Lembaga Merah Putih.

Diamond, Larry. 1994. Rethinking Civil Society: Toward Democratic Consolidation. *Journal of Democracy* 5 (3) (July): 4–17.

Ding, X. L. 1994a. *The Decline of Communism in China: Legitimacy Crisis, 1977–1989.* Cambridge: Cambridge University Press.

——. 1994b. Institutional Amphibiousness and the Transition from Communism: The Case of China. *British Journal of Political Science* 24: 293–318.

Dwipayana, G., and K. H. Ramadhan. 1989. *Soeharto, Pikiran, Ucapan dan Tindakan Saya.* Jakarta: PT. Citra Lamtoro Gung Persada.

Effendi, M. Tohir. 1989. *Oposisi di Indonesia: Studi Kasus Kelompok Petisi 50.* Skripsi, Jurusan Ilmu Politik, Fakultas Ilmu Sosial dan Ilmu Politik, Universitas Indonesia.

Eklöf, Stefan. 1999. *Indonesian Politics in Crisis: The Long Fall of Suharto, 1996–1998.* Copenhagen: Nordic Institute of Asian Studies.

Eldridge, Philip. 1995. *Non-Government Organisations and Democratic Partici-*

pation in Indonesia. South-East Asian Social Science Monographs. Kuala Lumpur: Oxford University Press.

Emmerson, Donald K. 1968. Conclusion. In *Students and Politics in Developing Nations*, ed. Donald K. Emmerson, 390–426. London: Pall Mall Press.

Fakih, Mansour. 1993. *Studi Lapangan LSM di Indonesia.* Indeco De Unie, Bandung. Forty-six-page typescript.

Fealy, Greg. 1994. "Rowing in a Typhoon," Nahdlatul Ulama and the Decline of Parliamentary Democracy. In *Democracy in Indonesia: 1950s and 1990s*, ed. David Bourchier and John Legge, 88–98. Clayton, Victoria: Centre of Southeast Asian Studies, Monash University.

———. 1996. The 1994 NU Congress and Aftermath: Abdurrahman Wahid, Suksesi and the Battle for Control of NU. In *Nahdlatul Ulama, Traditional Islam and Modernity in Indonesia*, ed. Greg Barton and Greg Fealy, 94–109. Clayton, Victoria: Monash Asia Institute.

———. 1997. Indonesian Politics, 1995–96: The Making of a Crisis. In *Indonesia Assessment: Population and Human Resources*, ed. Gavin W. Jones and Terence H. Hull, 19–38. Canberra: Research School of Pacific and Asian Studies, Australian National University; Singapore: Institute of Southeast Asian Studies.

———. 2001. Creating "Total Muslims": The Tarbiyah Movement and Islamic Neo-revivalism in Indonesia. Paper presented to Indonesia Council Open Conference, July 10–11, Melbourne University.

Feith, Herbert. 1962. *The Decline of Constitutional Democracy in Indonesia.* Ithaca, NY: Cornell University Press.

Fink, Christina. 2001. *Living Silence: Burma Under Military Rule.* London: Zed Books.

Ford, Michele. 2003. NGO as Outside Intellectual: A History of Non-Governmental Organisations' Role in the Indonesian Labour Movement. Ph.D. thesis, University of Wollongong.

Forum Demokrasi. 1991a. *Mufakat Cibereum.* Four-page typescript dated March 17.

———. 1991b. *Sekali Lagi Tentang Forum Demokrasi.* Seven-page typescript dated May 13.

———. 1992. *Tumbuhkan Kembali Daya Kritis Masyarakat.* Five-page typescript dated April 19.

Foulcher, Keith. 2000. *Sumpah Pemuda*: The Making and Meaning of a Symbol of Indonesian Nationhood. *Asian Studies Review* 24 (3): 378–410.

Frantz, Telmo Rudi. 1987. The Role of NGOs in the Strengthening of Civil Society. *World Development* 15: 121–27.

Gunawan, F. X. Rudy. 1999. *Budiman Sudjatmiko: Menolak Tunduk, Catatan Seorang Muda Menentang Tirani.* Jakarta: Grasindo.

Hadad, Ismid. 1983. Development and Community Self-Help in Indonesia. *Prisma* 28: 3–20.

Hadiwinata, Bob S. 2003. *The Politics of NGOs in Indonesia: Developing Democracy and Managing a Movement.* London: RoutledgeCurzon.

Hadiz, Vedi R. 1997. *Workers and the State in New Order Indonesia*. London: Routledge.

———. 1999. Contesting Political Change After Suharto. In *Reformasi: Crisis and Change in Indonesia*, ed. Arief Budiman, Barbara Hatley, and Damien Kingsbury, 105–26. Clayton, Victoria: Monash Asia Institute.

———. 2003. Power and Politics in North Sumatra: The Uncompleted Reformasi. In *Local Power and Politics in Indonesia: Decentralisation and Democratisation*, ed. Edward Aspinall and Greg Fealy, 119–31. Singapore: Institute of Southeast Asian Studies.

Hakim, M. Arief. 1992. Faksi-faksi dalam Tubuh Gerakan Kaum Muda. *Bernas*, November 25.

Halawa, Ohiao. 1993. *Membangun Citra Partai: Profil Drs. Soerjadi, Ketua Umum DPP PDI 1986–1993*, Nyiur Indah Alam Sejati, Jakarta.

Harbeson, John W. 1994. Civil Society and Political Renaissance in Africa. In *Civil Society and the State in Africa*, ed. John W. Harbeson, Donald Rothchild, and Naomi Chazan, 1–29. Boulder, CO: Lynne Rienner.

Hariadi, Untoro, and Masruchah. 1995. *Tanah, Rakyat dan Demokrasi*. Yogyakarta: Forum LSM-LPSM DIY.

Harman, Benny K., Mulyana W. Kusumah, Hendardi, Paskah Irianto, Sigit Pranawa, and Tedjabayu, eds. 1995. *LBH: Memberdayakan Rakyat, Membangun Demokrasi*. Jakarta: YLBHI.

Harrison, Anita. 1999. Update from Jakarta. In *The Last Days of President Suharto*, ed. Edward Aspinall, Herb Feith, and Gerry van Klinken, 24–28. Clayton, Victoria: Monash Asia Institute.

Harsono, Andreas. 1990. Gerakan Menentang Jalur Bebas Becak di Salatiga. In *Kesaksian Kaum Muda*, ed. J. A. Denny, Jonminofri, and Rahardjo, 121–27. Jakarta: Yayasan Studi Indonesia.

Hassan, Muhammad Kamal. 1980. *Muslim Intellectual Responses to "New Order" Modernization in Indonesia*. Kuala Lumpur: Dewan Bahasa dan Pustaka Kementerian Pelajaran Malaysia.

———. 1987. The Response of Muslim Youth Organizations to Political Change: HMI in Indonesia and ABIM in Malaysia. In *Islam and the Political Economy of Meaning*, ed. William R. Roff, 180–96. London: Croom Helm.

Hedman, Eva-Lotta E. 2001. Contesting State and Civil Society: Southeast Asian Trajectories. *Modern Asian Studies* 35(4): 921–51.

Hefner, Robert W. 1993. Islam, State, and Civil Society: ICMI and the Struggle for the Indonesian Middle Class. *Indonesia* 56: 1–35.

———. 1997. Print Islam: Mass Media and Ideological Rivalries Among Indonesian Muslims. *Indonesia* 64: 77–103.

———. 2000. *Civil Islam: Muslims and Democratization in Indonesia*. Princeton, NJ, and Oxford: Princeton University Press.

Hendardi. 1993. Reformasi Politik Elemen Demokrasi. *Kompas*, April 28.

Heryanto, Ariel. 1993. Discourse and State Terrorism: A Case Study of Political Trials in New Order Indonesia, 1989–90. Ph.D. thesis, Department of Anthropology, Monash University.

———. 1996. Indonesian Middle-Class Opposition in the 1990s. In *Political Oppositions in Industrialising Asia*, ed. Garry Rodan, 241–71. London and New York: Routledge.

Hill, Hal. 1994. The Economy. In *Indonesia's New Order: The Dynamics of Socio-Economic Transformation*, ed. Hal Hill, 54–122. Sydney: Allen and Unwin.

———. 1996. *The Indonesian Economy Since 1966: Southeast Asia's Emerging Giant*. Cambridge: Cambridge University Press.

Honna, Jun. 1999. Military Ideology in Response to Democratic Pressure During the Late Suharto Era: Political and Institutional Contexts. *Indonesia* 67 (April): 77–126.

———. 2003. *Military Politics and Democratization in Indonesia*. London, New York: Routledge.

Human Rights Watch Asia. 1998. Chronology of Clashes Between Student Protesters and Government Security Forces, March 11, 1998–May 2, 1998. Appendix D in *Academic Freedom in Indonesia: Dismantling Soeharto-Era Barriers* (August).

Human Rights Watch Asia / Robert F. Kennedy Memorial Center for Human Rights. 1996. Indonesia: Tough International Response Needed to Widening Crackdown. 8 (8) (C) (August).

Huntington, Samuel P. 1991. *The Third Wave: Democratization in the Late Twentieth Century*. Norman and London: University of Oklahoma Press.

Ibrahim, Rustam, ed. 1995. *Agenda LSM Menyongsong Tahun 2000*. Jakarta: Center for the Study of Democracy (CESDA), LP3ES.

Indeco De Unie. 1993. Laporan Studi Tentang LSM. Transcript of NGO seminars held in March–May in Salatiga, Bandung, Boyolali, and Jakarta.

Indonesia (editors). 1994. Current Data on the Indonesian Military Elite, September 1, 1993–August 31, 1994. *Indonesia* 58 (October): 83–101.

———. 1998. Current Data on the Indonesian Military Elite, October 1, 1995–December 31, 1997. *Indonesia* 65 (April): 179–94.

INFID (International NGO Forum on Indonesian Development). 1993a. *Democratisation Through People's Participation: INGI AIDE MEMOIRES 1985–1992*. Working Paper No. 1.

———. 1993b. "Review of Advocacy, January-August 1993." Typescript.

Jenkins, David. 1984. *Suharto and His Generals: Indonesian Military Politics, 1975–1983*. Cornell Modern Indonesia Project Monograph Series no. 64. Ithaca, NY: Cornell Modern Indonesia Project.

Joesoef, Daoed. 1984. Mahasiswa dan Politik. In *Mahasiswa Dalam Sorotan*, 65–72. Jakarta: Kelompok Studi Proklamasi.

Kammen, Douglas Anton. 1997. A Time to Strike: Industrial Strikes and Changing Class Relations in New Order Indonesia. Ph.D. thesis, Cornell University.

Kelompok Kerja Petisi 50. 1987. *Meluruskan Perjalanan Orde Baru: pertanggung jawaban kepada rakyat Indonesia*. Jakarta: Kelompok Kerja Petisi 50.

Kingsbury, Damien. 1998. *The Politics of Indonesia*. Melbourne: Oxford University Press.

Koo, Hagen. 1993. The State, *Minjung*, and the Working Class in South Korea. In *State and Society in Contemporary Korea*, ed. Hagen Koo, 131–62. Ithaca, NY: Cornell University Press.

Kraince, Richard G. 2000. The Role of Islamic Students in the *Reformasi* Struggle: Kammi (Kesatuan Aksi Mahasiswa Muslim Indonesia)—The Indonesian Muslim Student Action Union. *Studia Islamika* 7 (1): 1–50.

Kuntjoro-Jakti, Dorodjatun. 1972. Multinational Corporation Dan Kemungkinan2 Pengaruhnja Atas Proses Industrialisasi di Indonesia. *Prisma* 5: 45–57.

Kwik Kian Gie. 1992. PDI Akan Memelopori Keterbukaan Perusahaan-perusahaan Besar Walaupun Milik Swasta. In *Pemilu 1992: Harapan dan Janji*, ed. Tim Spes, 99–105. Jakarta: Grasindo.

Kyaw Yin Hlaing. 2004. Burma: Civil Society Skirting Regime Rules. In *Civil Society and Political Change in Asia: Expanding and Contracting Democratic Space*, ed. Muthiah Alagappa, 389–418. Stanford, CA: Stanford University Press.

Labrousse, Pierre. 1993. The Second Life of Bung Karno: Analysis of the Myth (1978–81). *Indonesia* 57: 175–96.

Lane, Max. 1982. Voices of Dissent in Indonesia. *Arena* 61: 110–28.

———. 1989. Students on the Move. *Inside Indonesia* 19: 10–13.

———. 1991. *"Openness," Political Discontent, and Succession in Indonesia: Political Developments in Indonesia, 1989–91*. Australia-Asia Paper No. 56. Nathan, Queensland: Centre for the Study of Australia-Asia Relations, Griffith University.

———. 1994. Winning Democracy in Indonesia: New Stage for the Progressive Movement. *Links: International Journal of Socialist Renewal* 2: 19–36.

———. 1995. The Progressive Movement in Indonesia: An Update. *Links: International Journal of Socialist Renewal* 4: 101–6.

LBH (Legal Aid Institute). 1973. *Dua Tahun Lembaga Bantuan Hukum*. Jakarta: LBH.

———. 1981. *Hasil-Hasil Lokakarya Bantuan Hukum Se-Indonesia, Prapat, 20 s/d 23 November 1980*, Jakarta: LBH.

Lev, Daniel S. 1978. Judicial Authority and the Struggle for an Indonesian Rechtsstaat. *Law and Society Review* 13 (1): 37–71.

———. 1987. *Legal Aid in Indonesia*. Working Paper No. 44. Clayton, Victoria: Centre of Southeast Asian Studies, Monash University.

Liddle, R. William. 1973. Modernizing Indonesian Politics. In *Political Participation in Modern Indonesia*, ed. R. William Liddle, 177–206. Yale University Southeast Asia Studies Monograph Series No. 19. New Haven, CT: Yale University Press.

———. 1985. Soeharto's Indonesia: Personal Rule and Political Institutions. *Pacific Affairs* 58 (1) (Spring): 68–90.

———. 1988. Indonesia in 1987: The New Order at the Height of Its Power. *Asian Survey* 28 (2) (February): 180–91.

———. 1991. The Relative Autonomy of the Third World Politician: Soeharto and Indonesian Economic Development in Comparative Perspective. *International Studies Quarterly* 35: 403–27.

———. 1992. Indonesia's Threefold Crisis. *Journal of Democracy* 3 (4) (October): 60–74.

———. 1994. Can All Good Things Go Together? Democracy, Growth, and Unity in Post-Suharto Indonesia. In *Democracy in Indonesia: 1950s and 1990s*, ed. David Bourchier and John Legge, 286–301. Clayton, Victoria: Centre of Southeast Asian Studies, Monash University.

———. 1996a. Indonesia: Suharto's Tightening Grip. *Journal of Democracy* 7 (4) (October): 58–72.

———. 1996b. The Islamic Turn in Indonesia: A Political Explanation. *Journal of Asian Studies* 55 (3) (August): 613–34.

———. 1996c. *Media Dakwah* Scripturalism: One Form of Political Thought and Action in Indonesia. In *Leadership and Culture in Indonesian Politics*, 266–89. St. Leonards, New South Wales: Allen and Unwin.

———. 1999a. Indonesia's Democratic Opening. *Government and Opposition* 34 (1) (Winter): 94–116.

———. 1999b. Regime: The New Order. In *Indonesia Beyond Suharto: Polity, Economy, Society, Transition*, ed. Donald K. Emmerson, 39–70. Armonk, NY, and London: M. E. Sharpe.

Lim Hong Hai. 2003. The Delineation of Peninsular Electoral Constituencies: Amplifying Malay and UMNO Power. In *New Politics in Malaysia*, ed. Francis Loh Kok Wah and Johan Saravanamuttu, 25–52. Singapore: Institute of Southeast Asian Studies.

Lintner, Bertil. 1989. *Outrage: Burma's Struggle for Democracy*. Hong Kong: Review Publishing Company.

Linz, Juan J. 1970. An Authoritarian Regime: Spain. In *Mass Politics*, ed. Erik Allardt and Stein Rokkan, 251–83. New York: The Free Press.

———. 1973. Opposition in and Under an Authoritarian Regime: The Case of Spain. In *Regimes and Oppositions*, ed. Robert A. Dahl, 171–259. New Haven, CT, and London: Yale University Press.

Linz, Juan J., and Alfred Stepan. 1996. *Problems of Democratic Transition and Consolidation: Southern Europe, South America, and Post-Communist Europe*. Baltimore and London: Johns Hopkins University Press.

Lipset, Seymour Martin. 1959. Some Social Requisites of Democracy: Economic Development and Political Legitimacy. *American Political Science Review* 53 (1): 69–105.

Lipset, Seymour Martin, and Phillip G. Altbach, eds. 1970. *Students in Revolt*. Boston: Beacon Press.

LKB (Institute for Constitutional Awareness). 1980. *Publikasi III*. Jakarta: Yayasan LKB.

Lubis, Todung Mulya. 1981a. Bantuan Hukum Struktural: Redistribusi Kekuasaan dan Partisipasi dari Bawah. *Prisma* 5: 51–61.

———. 1981b. Keadaan Buruh kita Dewasa ini: Sebuah Tinjauan Hak Asasi Manusia. *Prisma* 1: 48–55.

———. 1986. *Bantuan Hukum dan Kemiskinan Struktural*. Jakarta: LP3ES.

———. 1991. Sektarianisme. *Tempo*, May 11.

———. 1993. Deregulasi, Sekuriti, Suksesi. *Forum Keadilan*, December 9.

————. 1995. Hanoch Hebe Ohee, dan Globalisasi. *Forum Keadilan*, May 11.

Lucas, Anton. 1992. Land Disputes in Indonesia: Some Current Perspectives. *Indonesia* 53: 79–92.

————. 1997. Land Disputes, the Bureaucracy, and Local Resistance in Indonesia. In *Imagining Indonesia: Cultural Politics and Political Culture*, ed. Jim Schiller and Barbara Martin-Schiller, 229–60. Athens: Ohio University Center for International Studies.

Luwarso, Lukas. 1993. *Bangkitlah Imajinasimu Indonesiaku, Pembelaan di Hadapan Pengadilan Negeri Semarang, Oktober 1993*. Seventy-four-page typescript.

Luwarso, Lukas, Santoso, Gibran Ajidarma, and Irawan Saptono. 1997. *Jakarta Crackdown*. Jakarta: AJI (Alliance of Independent Journalists), FORUM-ASIA (Asian Forum for Human Rights and Development) and ISAI (Institute for the Study of the Free Flow of Information).

Madjid, Abdul. 1991. Apa Fodem Punya Strategi? *Progres* 1 (4): 14.

Madjid, Nurcholish. 1994. Demokrasi, Demokratisasi dan Oposisi. Paper presented at LIPI seminar, February 7, Jakarta.

Madrid, Robin. 1999. Islamic Students in the Indonesian Student Movement, 1998–99: Forces for Moderation. *Bulletin of Concerned Asian Scholars* 31 (3): 17–32.

Mahardika, Mirah. 1997. Semi-proletar dan momentum Pemilu. *Pembebasan* 4 (February): 22–25.

Mahasin, Aswab. 1989. On the Outskirts of the Periphery: Popular Movements in the New Order. *Prisma* 11: 23–33.

————. 1995. Membangun Civil Society dari Kancah yang Rentan: Sebuah Pengantar. In *Agenda LSM Menyongsong Tahun 2000*, ed. Rustam Ibrahim, 1–10. Jakarta: Center for the Study of Democracy (CESDA), LP3ES.

Mahnida, Syahniar. 1981. Bobot Undang-undang Perburuhan. *Prisma* 5: 20–23.

Mainwaring, Scott. 1989. Grassroots Popular Movements and the Struggle for Democracy: Nora Iguacu. In *Democratizing Brazil: Problems of Transition and Consolidation*, ed. Alfred Stepan, 168–204. Oxford: Oxford University Press.

McCargo, Duncan. 1997. *Chamlong Srimuang and the New Thai Politics*. New York: St. Martin's Press.

McDonald, Hamish. 1980. *Suharto's Indonesia*. Blackburn, Australia: Fontana/Collins.

McIntyre, Angus. 1972. Divisions and Power in the Indonesian National Party, 1965–66. *Indonesia* 13 (April): 183–210.

————. 1997. *In Search of Megawati Sukarnoputri*. Working Paper No. 103. Clayton, Victoria: Centre of Southeast Asian Studies, Monash University.

McRae, Dave. 2001. *The 1998 Indonesian student movement*. Working Paper No. 110. Clayton, Victoria: Centre of Southeast Asian Studies, Monash University.

McVey, Ruth T. 1983. Faith as the Outsider: Islam in Indonesian Politics. In *Islam in the Political Process*, ed. James P. Piscatori, 199–225. Cambridge: Cambridge University Press.

Means, Gordon. 1996. Soft Authoritarianism in Malaysia and Singapore. *Journal of Democracy* 7 (4): 103–17.

Mietzner, Marcus. 1998. Between Pesantren and Palace: Nahdlatul Ulama and Its Role in the Transition. In *The Fall of Soeharto*, ed. Geoff Forrester and R. J. May, 179–99. Bathurst, New South Wales: Crawford House.

———. 1999. From Soeharto to Habibie: The Indonesian Armed Forces and Political Islam During the Transition. In *Post-Soeharto Indonesia: Renewal or Chaos? Indonesia Assessment 1998*, ed. Geoff Forrester, 65–102. Bathurst, New South Wales: Crawford House.

———. 2003. Business as Usual? The Indonesian Armed Forces and Local Poetics in the Post-Soeharto Era. In *Local Power and Politics in Indonesia: Decentralisation and Democratisation*, ed. Edward Aspinall and Greg Fealy, 119–31. Singapore: Institute of Southeast Asian Studies.

Moore, Barrington. 1966. *Social Origins of Dictatorship and Democracy: Lord and Peasant in the Making of the Modern World*. Harmondsworth, UK: Penguin.

Morfit, Michael. 1981. Pancasila: The Indonesian State Ideology According to the New Order Government. *Asian Survey* 21 (8): 838–51.

Najib, Muhammad, and Kuat Sukardiyono, eds. 1998. *Amien Rais, Sang Demokrat*. Jakarta: Gema Insani.

Nasution, Adnan Buyung. 1981. *Bantuan Hukum di Indonesia*. Jakarta: LP3ES.

———. 1984. Lembaga Bantuan Hukum, Konsep Bantuan Hukum Struktural dan Kritik. Paper read by Abdul Hakim G. Nusantara at Rapat Kerja Nasional II of Yayasan LBH Indonesia, 25 October, in Jakarta.

———. 1985. The Legal Aid Movement in Indonesia: Towards the Implementation of the Structural Legal Aid Concept. In *Access to Justice, Human Rights Struggles in South East Asia*, ed. Harry M. Scoble and Laurie S. Wiseberg, 31–39. London: Zed Books.

———. 1995. LBH dan Lokomotif Demokrasi. In *LBH: Memberdayakan Rakyat, Membangun Demokrasi*, ed. Benny K. Harman et al., 20–30. Jakarta: Yayasan Lembaga Bantuan Hukum Indonesia.

Nusantara, Abdul Hakim Garuda. 1981. Bantuan Hukum dan Kemiskinan Struktural. *Prisma* 1: 35–46.

O'Donnell, Guillermo. 1992. Transitions, Continuities, and Paradoxes. In *Issues in Democratic Consolidation: The New South American Democracies in Comparative Perspective*, ed. S. Mainwaring, G. O'Donnell, and J. S. Valenzuela, 17–56. Notre Dame, IN: University of Notre Dame Press.

O'Donnell, Guillermo, and Philippe C. Schmitter. 1986. *Transitions from Authoritarian Rule: Tentative Conclusions About Uncertain Democracies*. Baltimore: Johns Hopkins University Press.

Pabottingi, Mochtar. 1995. Foreword to *Menelaah Kembali Format Politik Orde Baru*, by Syamsuddin Haris and Riza Sihbudi, ed. Jakarta: PPW-LIPI, Yayasan Insan Politika, PT Gramedia Pustaka Utama.

———. 1996. Kegetiran 27 Juli. *Forum Keadilan*, August 26.

Peukert, Detlev J. K. 1991. Working-Class Resistance: Problems and Options. In

Contending with Hitler: Varieties of German Resistance in the Third Reich, ed. David Clay Large, 35–48. Cambridge: Cambridge University Press.

Porter, Donald. 2002. *Managing Politics and Islam in Indonesia*. London: RoutledgeCurzon.

Prasetyo, Yosep Adi. 1994. Penyidangan 21 Aktivis Mahasiswa: Pergelaran Teater Kebangsaan. *Bina Darma* 12 (45): 101–19.

PRD (People's Democratic Party). 1996. *Manifesto PRD: Menuju Demokrasi Multipartai-kerakyatan*. Ninety-four-page booklet.

Przeworski, Adam. 1986. Some Problems in the Study of the Transition to Democracy. In *Transitions from Authoritarian Rule: Comparative Perspectives*, ed. Guillermo O'Donnell, Philippe C. Schmitter, and Laurence Whitehead, 47–63. Baltimore: Johns Hopkins University Press.

Radjab, Suryadi A. 1988. Hak Rakyat Dalam Kapitalisme Bekas Jajahan. In *Kesaksian Kaum Muda*, ed. Denny J. A. and Jonminofri, 58–67. Jakarta: Yayasan Studi Indonesia.

———. 1991. Panggung-panggung Mitologi dalam Hegemoni Negara, Gerakan Mahasiswa di Bawah Orde Baru. *Prisma* 20 (10) (October): 67–79.

———. 1995. Orde Baru, Ideologi dan LBH. In *LBH: Memberdayakan Rakyat, Membangun Demokrasi*, ed. Benny K. Harman et al., 126–47. Jakarta: Yayasan Lembaga Bantuan Hukum Indonesia.

Radjab, Suryadi A., Syarif Bastaman, and Hendardi. 1991. Negara dan Hak-Hak Rakyat Atas Sumberdaya Politik. In *Demokrasi Masih Terbenam: Catatan Keadaan Hak-Hak Asasi Manusia di Indonesia 1991*, ed. Mulyana W. Kusumah, Hendardi, and Ruswandi, 1–71. Jakarta: Divisi Khusus YLBHI.

Raillon, François. 1985. *Politik dan Ideologi Mahasiswa Indonesia*. Jakarta: LP3ES.

Rais, Amien M. 1989. Keterbukaan dan Suksesi. *Editor*, July 15.

———. 1994. Suksesi 1998: Satu Keharusan. *Sintesis* 2 (9) (July): 5–21.

———. 1995. *Moralitas Politik Muhammadiyah*. Yogyakarta: Dinamika.

Ramage, Douglas. 1995. *Politics in Indonesia: Democracy, Islam, and the Ideology of Tolerance*. London: Routledge.

Randall, Jesse. 1998. Political Gangsters. *Inside Indonesia* 53 (January–March): 4–5.

Richburg, Keith B. 1999. Seven Days in May That Toppled a Titan: Back-Room Intrigue Led to Suharto's Fall. In *The Last Days of President Suharto*, ed. Edward Aspinall, Gerry van Klinken, and Herb Feith, 75–81. Clayton, Victoria: Monash Asia Institute.

Robison, Richard. 1986. *Indonesia: The Rise of Capital*. Sydney: Allen and Unwin.

———. 1990. Problems of Analysing the Middle Class as a Political Force in Indonesia. In *The Politics of Middle Class Indonesia*, ed. Richard Tanter and Ken Young, 127–37. Clayton, Victoria: Centre for Southeast Asian Studies, Monash University.

———. 1992. Indonesia: An Autonomous Domain of Social Power. *Pacific Review* 5 (4): 338–49.

———. 1993. Indonesia: Tensions in State and Regime. In *Southeast Asia in the 1990s: Authoritarianism, Democracy, and Capitalism*, ed. Kevin Hewison, Richard Robison, and Garry Rodan, 39–74. Sydney: Allen and Unwin.

———. 1996. The Middle Class and the Bourgeoisie in Indonesia. In *The New Rich in Asia: Mobile Phones, McDonalds and Middle-class Revolution*, ed. Richard Robison and David S. G. Goodman, 79–104. London: Routledge.

Robison, Richard, and Andrew Rosser. 1998. Contesting Reform: Indonesia's New Order and the IMF. *World Development* 26 (8): 1593–609.

Rocamora, J. Eliseo. 1975. *Nationalism in Search of Ideology: The Indonesian Nationalist Party, 1946–1965*. Quezon City: Philippine Center for Advanced Studies, University of the Philippines.

Rudini. 1994. *Atas Nama Demokrasi Indonesia*. Yogyakarta: BIGRAF Publishing and Lembaga Pengkajian Strategis Indonesia (LPSI).

———. 1995. Perubahan dalam Sistem yang Sama. Supplement to *Gatra*, March 11: xii–xiii.

Rueschemeyer, Dietrich, Evelyne Huber Stephens, and John D. Stephens. 1992. *Capitalist Development and Democracy*. Cambridge: Polity Press.

Rupnik, Jacques. 1979. Dissent in Poland, 1968–78: The End of Revisionism and the Rebirth of the Civil Society. In *Opposition in Eastern Europe*, ed. Rudolf L. Tokes, 60–112. Baltimore: Johns Hopkins University Press.

Sadikin, Ali. 1986. *Melaksanakan Cita-Cita Orde Baru Dalam Rangka Mewujudkan Negara Proklamasi 17 Agustus 1945*. Jakarta: Kelompok Kerja Petisi Limapuluh.

Saleh, Abdul Rachman. 1980. *Tanya Jawab Hukum Perburuhan*. Jakarta: Lembaga Bantuan Hukum. Eight-three-page booklet.

Sanit, Arbi. 1992. *Golput: aneka pandangan fenomena politik*. Jakarta: Pustaka Sinar Harapan.

Sasono, Adi. 1980. Tesis Ketergantungan dan Kasus Indonesia. *Prisma* 12: 73–86.

———. 1982. Indonesia dari Ekonomi Terpimpin ke Kapitalisme Terpimpin. *Prisma* 1: 35–50.

———. 1995. Apresiasi Kehadiran ICMI Terhadap Politik dan Kekuasaan di Indonesia. In *ICMI: Beberapa Catatan Kritis*, ed. Tamsil Linrung, Idham Hayat, and Hidayat Tri Sutardjo, 39–48. Jakarta: Amanah Putra Nusantara.

Sastrosatomo, Soebadio. 1997. *Era Baru Pemimpin Baru, Badio Menolak Rekayasa Rezim Orde Baru*. Jakarta: Pusat Dokumentasi Politik "Guntur 49."

Schapiro, Leonard. 1972. Introduction to *Political Opposition in One-Party States*, ed. Leonard Schapiro. London: Macmillan.

Schwarz, Adam. 1994. *A Nation in Waiting: Indonesia in the 1990s*. St. Leonards, New South Wales: Allen and Unwin.

———. 1999. *A Nation in Waiting: Indonesia's Search for Stability*, rev. ed. St. Leonards, New South Wales: Allen and Unwin.

Sidel, John T. 1998. *Macet Total*: Logics of Circulation and Accumulation in the Demise of Indonesia's New Order. *Indonesia* 66 (October): 159–94.

Silalahi, Harry Tjan. 1990. *Konsensus Politik Nasional Orde Baru: Ortodoksi dan Aktualisasinya.* Jakarta: CSIS.

——. 1991. Kemampuan UUD 1945 Untuk Melaksanakan Demokrasi Pancasila. In *Untuk Kelangsungan Hidup Bangsa,* ed. Hadi Soesastro, 224–39. Jakarta: CSIS.

Silverstein, Josef. 1990. Aung San Suu Kyi: Is She Burma's Woman of Destiny? *Asian Survey* 30 (10): 1007–19.

Simanjuntak, Marsillam. 1991. The Obstacles to Freedom to Organize. *Indonesian Human Rights Forum* 1: 9–12.

——. 1994. Democratisation in the 1990s: Coming to Terms with Gradualism? In *Democracy in Indonesia, 1950s and 1990s,* ed. David Bourchier and John Legge, 302–12. Clayton, Victoria: Centre of Southeast Asian Studies, Monash University.

Sinaga, Kastorius. 1993. Number of Local NGOs Mushrooming. *Jakarta Post,* November 2.

Smith, Roger M. 1974. *Southeast Asia: Documents of Political Development and Change.* Ithaca, NY, and London: Cornell University Press.

Snyder, Richard. 1998. Paths Out of Sultanistic Regimes: Combining Structural and Voluntarist Perspectives. In *Sultanistic Regimes,* ed. H. E. Chehabi and Juan J. Linz, 49–81. Baltimore: John Hopkins University Press.

Soedjarwo, Anton. 1978. Dicari orang2 yang mau berkotor tangan. *Prisma* 3: 58–60.

Soekarnoputri, Megawati. 1993. *Bendera Sudah Saya Kibarkan! Pokok-pokok Pikiran Megawati Soekarnoputri.* Jakarta: Pustaka Sinar Harapan.

——. 1997. Pesan Akhir Tahun Megawati. E-mail version distributed by *Siar,* January 7, 1998.

——. 1998. Pidato Ketua Umum DPP-PDI, Megawati Soekarnoputri menyambut HUT ke-XXV PDI, January 10, 1998. E-mail version distributed by *Kabar dari Pijar.*

Soemitro. 1992a. *Mengungkap Masalah Menatap Masa Depan,* Jakarta: Pustaka Sinar Harapan.

——. 1992b. *Tantangan dan Peluang 1993.* Jakarta: Pustaka Sinar Harapan.

Stanley. 1994. *Seputar Kedung Ombo.* Jakarta: ELSAM.

——. 1998. Behind the Student Demands. *Inside Indonesia* (July-September): 12–13.

Steinberg, David I. 1990. *Future of Burma: Crisis and Choice in Myanmar.* Lanham, New York: University Press of America and the Asia Society.

Stepan, Alfred. 1988. *Rethinking Military Politics: Brazil and the Southern Cone.* Princeton, NJ: Princeton University Press.

——. 1993. On the Tasks of a Democratic Opposition. In *The Global Resurgence of Democracy,* ed. Larry Diamond and Marc F. Platter, 61–69. Baltimore: Johns Hopkins University Press.

Sumawinata, Sarbini. 1972. Perspektif Pembangunan Djangka Pandjang: Beberapa Gagasan Strategi Sampai Tahun 2000. *Prisma* 5: 3–21.

——. 1985. Ekonomi Kerakyatan. *Prisma* 8: 96–123.

Sundhaussen, Ulf. 1981. Regime Crisis in Indonesia: Facts, Fiction, and Predictions. *Asian Survey* 21 (8) (August): 815–37.

Tanter, Richard, and Kenneth Young. 1990. *The Politics of Middle Class Indonesia.* Clayton, Victoria: Centre for Southeast Asian Studies, Monash University.

Tapol. 1987. *Indonesia: Muslims on Trial.* London: Tapol.

Taylor, R. H. 1991. Myanmar 1990: New Era or Old? *Southeast Asian Affairs,* 199–219.

Thompson, Edmund. 1993. Practising What You Preach. *Inside Indonesia* 36: 7–9.

Thompson, Mark Richard. 1995. *The Anti-Marcos Struggle: Personalistic Rule and Democratic Transition in the Philippines.* New Haven, CT, and London: Yale University Press.

Tim ISAI. 1996. *Megawati Soekarnoputri: Pantang Surut Langkah.* Jakarta: Institut Studi Arus Informasi (ISAI).

Tirtosudarmo, Riwanto. 1991. Mampukah LSM menjadi "Counter Hegemonic Movement"? *Kritis* 5 (3): 105–8.

Tjahjono, Indro. 1979. Indonesia di bawah sepatu lars: pembelaaan di muka Pengadilan Mahasiswa Bandung. Bandung: Komite Pembelaan Mahasiswa Institut Teknologi Bandung.

Uhlin, Anders. 1993. Transnational Democratic Diffusion and Indonesian Democracy Discourses. *Third World Quarterly* 14 (3): 513–40.

———. 1995. *Democracy and Diffusion: Transnational Lesson-Drawing Among Indonesian Pro-Democracy Actors.* Lund Political Studies 87. Lund, Sweden: Lund University.

———. 1997. *Indonesia and the "Third Wave of Democratization": The Indonesian Pro-Democracy Movement in a Changing World.* Richmond, UK: Curzon.

UN Industrial Development Organisation / Economist Intelligence Unit. 1993. *Indonesia: Industrial Development Review.* Vienna and London: UN Industrial Development Organisation.

van Bruinessen, Martin. 1991. The 28th Congress of the Nahdlatul Ulama: Power Struggle and Social Concerns. *Archipel* 41: 185–200.

van de Kok, Jean. 1986. Summary of Press Reports on the Trials of H. R. Dharsono and A. M. Fatwa. *Review of Indonesian and Malaysian Affairs* 20 (2) (Summer): 216–32.

van Dijk, Cees. 1979. Survey of Major Political Developments in Indonesia in the Second Half of 1978: (1) The Partai Demokrasi Indonesia (2) Golkar's Second National Congress. *Review of Indonesian and Malayan Affairs* 13 (1) (June): 116–50.

———. 1981. Survey of Major Political Developments in Indonesia in the Second Half of 1980: Crime Prevention, Anti-Chinese Riots, and the PDI Party Congress. *Review of Indonesian and Malayan Affairs* 15 (1): 93–125.

Vatikiotis, Michael R. J. 1993. *Indonesian Politics Under Suharto.* London: Routledge.

———. 1994. Party and Parliamentary Politics 1987–93. In *Democracy in In-*

donesia: 1950s and 1990s, ed. David Bourchier and John Legge, 236–42. Clayton, Victoria: Centre of Southeast Asian Studies, Monash University.

———. 1998. Romancing the Dual Function: Indonesia's Armed Forces and the Fall of Soeharto. In *The Fall of Soeharto*, ed. Geoff Forrester and R. J. May, 154–66. Bathurst, New South Wales: Crawford House.

Wahid, Abdurrahman. 1992. Demokrasi Seolah-olah. *Jurnal Demokrasi* 2: 19–21.

Walters, Patrick. 1999. The Week of Living Dangerously. In *The Last Days of President Suharto*, ed. Edward Aspinall, Gerry van Klinken, and Herb Feith, 81–4. Clayton, Victoria: Monash Asia Institute.

Ward, K. E. 1973. Indonesia's Modernisation: Ideology and Practice. In *Showcase State: The Illusion of Indonesia's Accelerated Modernisation*, ed. Rex Mortimer, 67–82. Sydney: Angus and Robertson.

———. 1974. *The 1971 Election in Indonesia: An East Java Case Study*. Clayton, Victoria: Centre for Southeast Asian Studies.

Weiss, Meredith. 2001. The Politics of Protest: Civil Society, Coalition-Building, and Political Change in Malaysia. Ph.D. thesis, Yale University.

White Book of the 1978 Students' Struggle. 1978. *Indonesia* 25 (April): 151–82.

Widjojo, Muridan S., and Moch. Nurhasim. 1999. Organisasi Gerakan Mahasiswa 98: Upaya Rekontsruksi. In *Penakluk Rezim Orde Baru: Gerakan Mahasiswa '98*, by Muridan S. Widjojo, Abdul Mun'im DZ, Arbi Sanit, Hermawan Sulistyo, Irine H. Gayatri, Moch. Nurhasim, and Soewarsono, 290–376. Jakarta: Sinar Harapan.

Wilson. 1995. Buruh dan Mahasiswa Bersatulah. Thirty-nine-page pamphlet.

Wurfel, David. 1988. *Filipino Politics: Development and Decay*. Ithaca, NY: Cornell University Press.

Yap Thiam Hien. 1973. Masalah Hukum dan Penyalah Gunaan Kekuasaan. *Prisma* 6: 21–29.

YLBHI (Indonesian Legal Aid). 1993. What Price Freedom? A Profile of the Indonesian Legal Aid Foundation, 1993. Thirty-five-page booklet.

———. 1994. Taking Part in Democratization: YLBHI's Four Years Plan 1994–98. Sixty-two-page booklet.

———. 1997. *1996: Tahun Kekerasan. Potret Pelanggaran HAM di Indonesia*. Jakarta: YLBHI.

Zhang, Baohui. 1994. Corporatism, Totalitarianism, and Transitions to Democracy. *Comparative Political Studies* 27 (1) (April): 108–36.

Index

Index